SAP PRESS e-books

Print or e-book, Kindle or iPad, workplace or airplane: Choose where and how to read your SAP PRESS books! You can now get all our titles as e-books, too:

- By download and online access
- For all popular devices
- And, of course, DRM-free

Convinced? Then go to www.sap-press.com and get your e-book today.

PP-DS with SAP S/4HANA®

SAP PRESS

SAP PRESS is a joint initiative of SAP and Rheinwerk Publishing. The know-how offered by SAP specialists combined with the expertise of Rheinwerk Publishing offers the reader expert books in the field. SAP PRESS features first-hand information and expert advice, and provides useful skills for professional decision-making.

SAP PRESS offers a variety of books on technical and business-related topics for the SAP user. For further information, please visit our website: *www.sap-press.com*.

Jawad Akhtar
Production Planning with SAP S/4HANA
2019, 1,010 pages, hardcover and e-book
www.sap-press.com/4821

Jawad Akhtar
Quality Management with SAP S/4HANA
2020, 950 pages, hardcover and e-book
www.sap-press.com/4924

Jawad Akhtar, Martin Murray
Materials Management with SAP S/4HANA: Business Processes and Configuration
2019, 946 pages, hardcover and e-book
www.sap-press.com/4711

Bernd Roedel, Johannes Esser
Inventory Management with SAP S/4HANA
2019, 494 pages, hardcover and e-book
www.sap-press.com/4892

Mahesh Babu MG

PP-DS with SAP S/4HANA®

Editor Megan Fuerst
Acquisitions Editor Emily Nicholls
Copyeditor Julie McNamee
Cover Design Graham Geary
Photo Credit iStockphoto.com/677623004/© ihsanyildizli
Layout Design Vera Brauner
Production Graham Geary
Typesetting SatzPro, Krefeld (Germany)
Printed and bound in the United States of America, on paper from sustainable sources

ISBN 978-1-4932-1872-1
© 2020 by Rheinwerk Publishing, Inc., Boston (MA)
1st edition 2020

Library of Congress Cataloging-in-Publication Data
Names: MG, Mahesh, author.
Title: PP-DS with SAP S/4HANA / Mahesh MG.
Description: First edition. | Bonn ; Boston : Rheinwerk Publishing, 2020. |
  Includes index.
Identifiers: LCCN 2019051871 (print) | LCCN 2019051872 (ebook) | ISBN
  9781493218721 (hardback) | ISBN 9781493218738 (ebook)
Subjects: LCSH: Production planning--Data processing. | Manufacturing
  processes--Data processing. | SAP HANA (Electronic resource)
Classification: LCC TS176 .M498 2020 (print) | LCC TS176 (ebook) | DDC
  670.285--dc23
LC record available at https://lccn.loc.gov/2019051871
LC ebook record available at https://lccn.loc.gov/2019051872

Contents at a Glance

Dear Reader,

If any vacation falls under the category of "advanced planning," a family Disney trip with five nieces and nephews under the age of seven is it.

As the official planner, you diligently schedule your days, arrange your ride times, and pencil in naps in order to keep everyone happy. But when you arrive at Magic Kingdom and find your arm pulled in five different directions—Space Mountain, Mickey ice cream bars, Elsa's autograph, the list goes on—then your best laid plans could become a casualty of the excited chaos. You'll need to regroup if you want to optimize those hard-earned fast passes!

When it comes to your organization's production planning and detailed scheduling, the process is, thankfully, a more exact science. Embedded PP-DS in SAP S/4HANA provides the advanced features and heuristics you need to perform complex planning. With this book, a product of author Mahesh Babu MG's expert guidance, you'll learn how to execute PP-DS smoothly and efficiently—two words that have never applied to my family vacations.

What did you think about *PP-DS with SAP S/4HANA*? Your comments and suggestions are the most useful tools to help us make our books the best they can be. Please feel free to contact me and share any praise or criticism you may have.

Thank you for purchasing a book from SAP PRESS!

Megan Fuerst
Editor, SAP PRESS

meganf@rheinwerk-publishing.com
www.sap-press.com
Rheinwerk Publishing · Boston, MA

Contents

5   Production Planning 169

6   Detailed Scheduling

7 The Alert Monitor

8 Advanced PP-DS Features

9   Administering PP-DS with SAP S/4HANA   413

10   Migration to Embedded PP-DS   447

Appendices

Preface

Welcome to *PP-DS with SAP S/4HANA*, a comprehensive review of the SAP S/4HANA production planning and detailed scheduling (PP-DS) functionalities and in-depth coverage of planning and scheduling processes and heuristics. This book is based on the SAP S/4HANA 1909 PP-DS features. Features of PP-DS in SAP Supply Chain Management (SAP SCM) and SAP Advanced Planning and Optimization (SAP APO) that are simplified and/or not available in SAP S/4HANA aren't covered in this book.

Who This Book Is For

This book is not only for those who work directly in PP-DS but also for those who work in related supply chain planning and manufacturing areas, such as SAP Integrated Business Planning for Supply Chain (SAP IBP) and SAP S/4HANA production planning, to enhance their understanding of the advanced planning features and integration offered by PP-DS in SAP S/4HANA (embedded PP-DS).

For those who've already worked with the PP-DS component in SAP APO, this book will be of great use in understanding the changes in embedded PP-DS and the integration requirements, as some of the functionalities available in the PP-DS component of SAP APO are no longer available in embedded PP-DS. In addition, core interface (CIF) integration architecture has drastically changed for most of the master data objects and some of the transaction data objects. For those who work in SAP ERP or SAP S/4HANA production planning and want to expand their knowledge of embedded PP-DS, this book provides in-depth knowledge in setting up PP-DS, master data and transaction data integration, planning and scheduling processes, heuristics, tools, some advanced embedded PP-DS features, and administering embedded PP-DS.

If you're a planner or scheduler, and you already work with PP-DS or have just started to work with PP-DS, this book is helpful in providing the various options available for users in terms of controlling and executing embedded PP-DS systems.

How This Book Is Organized

This book is arranged in 10 chapters; the following list provides an overview of the topics covered in each chapter:

- **Chapter 1: Introduction to PP-DS with SAP S/4HANA**
  This chapter introduces the planning and scheduling processes in general and PP-DS in SAP solutions. A comparison is provided of the PP-DS component in SAP APO and the PP-DS in SAP S/4HANA solution (embedded PP-DS). We then cover the key simplification items in embedded PP-DS compared to the PP-DS component in SAP APO, followed by the various deployment options for PP-DS and an introduction to the embedded PP-DS architecture.

- **Chapter 2: Master Data**
  This chapter covers the master data that is required in embedded PP-DS, which is commonly required for all PP-DS processes. Any scenario-specific master data objects are covered in their respective chapters. In this chapter, you'll learn about the integration requirements for various master data objects, such as the location and product/material master data, resources and work centers, external procurement and in-house production sources of supply, and classes and characteristics.

- **Chapter 3: Configuration**
  This chapter provides you with the basic configuration required to set up embedded PP-DS, including the activation of PP-DS. Management of the planning versions and supply chain model, integration settings required for CIF communication, and setup of the PP-DS global parameters are covered here. This chapter also describes the PP-DS configuration for managing heuristics and planning procedures, and the settings for controlling the PP-DS transactions (e.g., the order views and the detailed scheduling (DS) planning board). The basic settings required for the PP-DS optimizer are also covered in this chapter.

- **Chapter 4: Data Transfer for Transaction Data**
  This chapter covers how to activate the transfer of transaction data between the ERP and PP-DS sides of the SAP S/4HANA system. In addition, details are provided regarding how the most commonly used transaction data in embedded PP-DS is transferred between the two sides of the SAP S/4HANA system. The representation of different transaction data objects in PP-DS, such as in-house production orders, external procurement orders, stocks, batches, sales orders, inspection lots, and plant maintenance orders, are also covered in this chapter.

- **Chapter 5: Production Planning**

  This chapter starts with an overview of the planning process and introduces the specific business scenarios in which PP-DS planning is required because such features cannot be attained by the ERP-side planning processes in the SAP S/4HANA system. The basic functions of the PP-DS planning processes, such as pegging, net requirement calculation, and source determination, are covered. Functionalities of different planning and service heuristics are discussed as well. The steps to trigger a PP-DS planning run and the options available to perform production planning in embedded PP-DS are provided. We also explain monitoring and evaluation of planning runs, as well as the results of the PP-DS planning runs.

- **Chapter 6: Detailed Scheduling**

  The specific features of the PP-DS scheduling processes and advantages of using PP-DS detailed scheduling are covered in this chapter, followed by detailed coverage of the PP-DS strategy settings and strategy profiles. We discuss how various detailed scheduling heuristics function, including the SAP Fiori apps and steps required to perform detailed scheduling in embedded PP-DS. Optimizing the production schedule using the PP-DS optimizer is also covered in this chapter.

- **Chapter 7: The Alert Monitor**

  In this chapter, we cover the creation of alert profiles in embedded PP-DS. In addition, we discuss the various options to monitor the alerts, such as monitoring the alerts from the alert monitor, generating alerts in the background, and monitoring alerts from various PP-DS apps.

- **Chapter 8: Advanced PP-DS Features**

  This chapter covers some of the commonly required advanced PP-DS features that can be leveraged in many industries, including shelf-life planning, product interchangeability, characteristics-dependent planning (CDP), block planning, and push production.

- **Chapter 9: Administering PP-DS with SAP S/4HANA**

  This chapter covers the basic administration requirements to operate embedded PP-DS efficiently. We also explain CIF queue monitoring, CIF postprocessing management, and the CIF compare and reconciliation tool. The application activities required to operate and reconcile SAP liveCache data and the administration required for certain master data objects are also covered in the chapter.

- **Chapter 10: Migration to Embedded PP-DS**
  This chapter provides an overview of activities required for transitioning to the SAP S/4HANA system and the options to bring PP-DS data in the transition scenarios, such as new implementation, system conversion, and landscape transformation-based migration.

Throughout the book, we've also provided several elements that will help you access useful information.

Tips and Tricks

Boxes with this symbol provide you with recommendations as to how you can simplify your work.

Notes

Boxes marked with this symbol contain additional information or important content that you should keep in mind.

Examples

Boxes marked with this symbol provide practical scenarios and explain how particular functions can be applied.

Conclusion

Reading this book will provide you with a comprehensive review of processes, data, and integration for the embedded PP-DS solution. The topics covered in this book will enhance or reinforce your knowledge of PP-DS.

Let's get started with Chapter 1, where we'll introduce planning and scheduling, discuss options for deploying PP-DS in different SAP software solutions, and explain the architecture behind embedded PP-DS.

Chapter 1

Introduction to PP-DS
with SAP S/4HANA

To start our journey through production planning and detailed scheduling (PP-DS), we'll begin with the basics: What is production planning, what is detailed scheduling, and how have they changed with SAP S/4HANA?

SAP's enterprise resource planning (ERP) software, in its different forms, is widely used by companies around the world across different industries. The various releases of the software over years have culminated in the latest two supported releases: SAP ERP and SAP S/4HANA (the focus of this book). SAP ERP supports many relational databases from different vendors, whereas SAP S/4HANA is the latest version, tailored for SAP HANA (the in-memory database created by SAP) and offering many new features.

Since the earliest releases of SAP ERP, SAP has provided solutions for production planning, capacity, and scheduling resources. In the SAP ERP software, tools such as sales and operations planning (S&OP), demand management, master production scheduling (MPS), material requirements planning (MRP), capacity scheduling, and leveling enable the production planning and scheduling functions.

As businesses and manufacturing processes evolved, a need emerged for more complex planning and scheduling algorithms to tackle such complexities. In response, SAP introduced SAP Advanced Planning and Optimization (SAP APO), which later became part of the SAP Supply Chain Management (SAP SCM) suite. With SAP APO, the demand planning, supply network planning, and PP-DS tools were introduced to solve complex forecasting, planning (long-term, mid-term, and short-term), and scheduling challenges. With the evolution of the SAP Integrated Business Planning for Supply Chain (SAP IBP) cloud solution, support was provided for S&OP, demand planning, and supply and response planning. SAP IBP is the long- to medium-term demand and supply planning tool.

In the SAP ERP suite on SAP HANA and, later, in SAP S/4HANA, the classic MRP solution was enhanced with the power of SAP HANA to perform the complex MRP calculations in the SAP HANA database layer, thus making multiplying the speed of access to the MRP results. In combination with the forecasting and long- to medium-term planning capabilities of SAP IBP, MRP Live in SAP S/4HANA is the solution for short-term planning.

In 2016, SAP released the 1610 version of SAP S/4HANA software, and the PP-DS component of SAP APO was made available within the SAP S/4HANA core as PP-DS. This enables the SAP S/4HANA solutions capability not only to support the short-term planning via MRP Live but also to support advanced planning algorithms and detailed scheduling.

The SAP digital supply chain is part of the SAP intelligent suite. SAP IBP and PP-DS in SAP S/4HANA are key components of the plan and manufacture components of the design-to-operate process within the digital supply chain.

In this chapter, we'll introduce the concept of PP-DS using SAP systems. We'll also see how the solution landscape evolved over time, the deployment options available prior to SAP S/4HANA, and the simplifications made in PP-DS in SAP S/4HANA compared to the PP-DS component of SAP APO. Then, we'll transition into the detailed architecture of PP-DS in SAP S/4HANA.

1.1   What Is Production Planning and Detailed Scheduling?

SAP provides tools to support complete supply chain planning and execution, as well as integration with other processes and areas. One of the core processes within the supply chain is production planning. The primary objective of *production planning* is to ensure that the right product is available at the right time and the right place to be delivered to customers and ensure the raw materials are available for production.

Detailed scheduling supports the sequencing and scheduling of production operations by taking into consideration the available resource (machines and human resources) capacity and the availability of the materials. In addition, detailed scheduling is used to ensure the optimal usage of resources.

Let's take a closer look at each in the following sections.

1.1.1 Production Planning

The production planning process involves several steps. Let's walk through the traditional flow in SAP ERP, as follows:

1. **Sales and operations planning (S&OP)**

   The production planning process starts with an aggregated sales forecast in S&OP, which can be disaggregated and then transferred to demand management where it will become a concrete production plan, with a planning strategy defined.

2. **Master production scheduling (MPS)**

   This production plan will be the input for MPS, which is used to plan finished products and products using bottleneck resources. MPS will generate planned orders to cover the forecast by using different planning parameters for each material, but it won't consider capacity restrictions.

3. **Capacity leveling**

   After the MPS execution, capacity leveling should be executed for the generated planned orders, adjusting the planned order dates and ensuring that the production plan is feasible and won't exceed the capacity available in the work centers.

4. **Material requirements planning (MRP)**

   When all capacity issues are solved, it's time to execute MRP to plan the remaining products. MRP will generate planned orders to produce semifinished products and purchase requisitions to procure raw materials.

Even though SAP ERP offers this complete process for production planning, there are some limitations with the tools offered. For example, materials planning and capacity leveling are two separated steps: MPS or MRP will first generate planned orders with an infinite capacity, and the system will only consider finite capacity restrictions during capacity leveling. Another limitation is that MPS and MRP won't consider the expiration date of material batches, so the expiration must be controlled separately. These limitations are in place because these very complex planning scenarios would consume additional hardware resources during the planning run and could require more time to finish it.

SAP S/4HANA is basically an evolution of SAP ERP, and many of the older features are being redesigned or even replaced by new features. Although most of these features are still there in SAP S/4HANA, they are part of what is called the compatibility scope, which means they aren't considered future technology and should be retired in the future.

[»]

Note

When a new SAP S/4HANA release is launched, SAP delivers a document called the simplification list, which describes the major changes of the new release, including the features that are part of the compatibility scope. An SAP Note linking to the simplification list can be found in Appendix A.

In SAP S/4HANA, S&OP is gradually being replaced by cloud-based SAP IBP, and capacity planning is being replaced by PP-DS. Production planning in SAP S/4HANA is powered by MRP Live and forms the production planning part of PP-DS.

1.1.2 Detailed Scheduling

After the production planning process is complete, resulting in the production proposals for the in-house manufactured products, the next step is to identify the correct resources needed to execute the orders in the manufacturing shop floor where the detailed scheduling processes are used. The detailed scheduling tools should consider the availability of the materials for manufacturing and the available capacity of the machinery, tools, and human resources.

In SAP ERP, detailed scheduling is supported in the form of capacity planning, which comprises two major features: capacity evaluation and capacity leveling. Capacity planning supports long-term rough-cut planning, medium-term planning, and short-term detailed planning.

Capacity requirements are created by orders that are generated via the production planning tools, such as MPS and MRP. In addition, capacity requirements are created by networks in project systems and plant maintenance orders. The orders created by the planning tools are scheduled on the resources (also called work centers) based on the planning settings and using the routing master data. The routing master data defines the calculation of the duration for scheduling and the capacity required to execute a specific manufacturing step.

After the capacity requirements are created, the capacity evaluation tool can be used to analyze the capacity load on the resources based on the available capacity. The capacity leveling tools are also used to dispatch and deallocate operations on the resources based on the underload and overload situations.

For complex manufacturing scenarios, the SAP ERP capacity planning tools have challenges in optimizing the capacity use of the resources and adhering to the production schedule to minimize delays in manufacturing. These complex requirements for capacity planning and detailed scheduling are addressed in the PP-DS component of SAP APO.

1.2   PP-DS with SAP

To address those complex planning and scheduling scenarios, SAP created a new PP-DS tool, as mentioned previously. This tool was introduced a long time ago as part of SAP APO, which provides a set of advanced supply chain planning tools. Additionally, SAP APO could be integrated into one or multiple ERP systems, planning an entire supply chain together. SAP APO has the special dedicated SAP liveCache database, which was designed to handle very complex algorithms.

The objective of PP-DS is to cover the demand with procurement proposals in the short-term horizon for critical products and also create an optimized resource schedule for the resources in which the manufacturing operations are performed.

Key features in PP-DS include the following:

- Production planning heuristics
- Interactive planning tools
- Detailed scheduling heuristics
- PP-DS optimizer
- Interactive detailed scheudling tools
- Background planning and scheduling tools
- Planning procedures
- Pegging relationships

In this section, we'll take a closer look at the PP-DS component of SAP APO, see how it's been embedded in SAP S/4HANA, and walk through how PP-DS fits into SAP S/4HANA deployment and architecture.

1.2.1   SAP Advanced Planning and Optimization

With the SAP S/4HANA 1610 release, PP-DS was made available in the SAP S/4HANA core. In addition, a side-by-side usage of SAP APO is possible with SAP S/4HANA as the ERP system.

SAP introduced cloud-based SAP IBP (also SAP IBP for demand and SAP IBP for response and supply), which is expected to replace the SAP APO system. Therefore, the target architecture for the end-to-end planning and scheduling solution is to have SAP IBP as the demand and supply planning solution and SAP S/4HANA as the PP-DS system for critical products and components.

Whether it's SAP ERP or SAP S/4HANA, the configuration data, such as organizational structures and master data objects (e.g., material master, bill of materials [BOM], routings, production version, work centers or resources, capacities, vendors, and customers) are maintained in the ERP system. These data objects are transferred to the SAP APO system via the core interface (CIF).

Let's walk through the SAP APO basics, before comparing it to PP-DS in SAP S/4HANA (embedded PP-DS).

SAP APO with SAP ERP

In the SAP APO system, the processes start with the demand planning, where the historical sales and consumption data is used for forecasting the demand. The outcome of demand planning is the constrained forecast, which is used to perform supply planning. Supply planning is executed using supply network planning, which comprises complex algorithms in the form of heuristics and the optimizer to plan supplies against demand. Demand planning and supply network planning are executed for mid- to long-term horizons. The data and process flow between the SAP ERP and SAP APO systems is shown in Figure 1.1.

For the short-term planning horizon, procurement proposals from the supply plan in supply network planning are transferred to PP-DS. Within PP-DS, the plan is refined further.

Comparing the PP-DS component's capabilities in SAP APO with the tools available for planning in SAP ERP reveals that the basic structure behind the two solutions is similar; however, PP-DS provides advanced tools and features that aren't available in SAP ERP, such as the following:

- Materials planning with finite capacity planning
- Planning with exact times
- Forecast consumption with descriptive characteristics
- Planning runs with multiple planning algorithms

- Dynamic pegging and fixed pegging (assignment of receipt elements across BOM levels)

- Planning with custom heuristics (planning algorithm that executes the planning on selected objects)

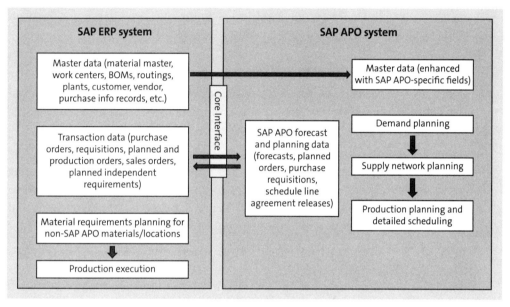

Figure 1.1 Planning Process and Data Flow between SAP ERP and SAP APO Systems

Some of these features are only possible in the PP-DS component in SAP APO, which uses the SAP liveCache database, designed to algorithmically handle complex data and runtime-intensive functions. SAP liveCache is an object-based and enhanced SAP MaxDB database.

SAP APO connects directly with SAP ERP, and data is transferred though the CIF. For each piece of master data to be transferred from SAP ERP to SAP APO via the CIF, you'll need to create and activate an integration model, so that the master data can be sent through the integration queues. After planning in SAP APO, the planning results are also integrated into SAP ERP via the CIF, and any record stuck in the integration queue can lead to major integration problems between the systems or lead to data inconsistencies.

In planning scenarios where there are planning runs to be executed in different systems, namely, SAP ERP and SAP APO, multiple planning executions are involved, and a lot of dependencies are created due to the same product getting planned in multiple locations, For example, if the supply chain network consists of three plants—plants 1 and 3 planned in the PP-DS component in SAP APO and plant 2 planned in the SAP ERP system—and the product structure extends throughout these three plants, then three different planning runs need to be spread across the SAP ERP and SAP APO systems. In addition, the second and third planning runs need to wait for the planning results to be transferred to SAP ERP from SAP APO and vice versa.

SAP APO versus SAP S/4HANA

Embedded PP-DS brings the PP-DS features from SAP APO into the SAP S/4HANA system, enabling the SAP S/4HANA system as a comprehensive planning and scheduling solution for the short-term planning horizon.

From a usability perspective, all PP-DS transactions are available within the SAP S/4HANA system, allowing end users to perform all the planning and scheduling functions in one system. With the PP-DS component in SAP APO, users need to switch between the SAP APO and SAP ERP systems to accomplish the planning and scheduling tasks. In SAP S/4HANA, new SAP Fiori apps have been introduced for detailed scheduling that work seamlessly with the SAP Fiori apps delivered for MRP Live planning.

With SAP APO, the master data and transaction data needs to be transferred between the SAP APO and ERP systems because both systems need to be in sync in terms of master data. In addition, for certain master data fields that are only relevant for SAP APO planning, the data is directly maintained only in the SAP APO system. The master data also needs to be synced up frequently between the ERP and SAP APO systems to ensure that the data is consistent and that the planning results are correct in the SAP APO system.

In SAP S/4HANA, master data maintenance is greatly simplified by maintaining only one version of data for SAP S/4HANA as well as for embedded PP-DS. For most of the master data objects, there is no need to create an integration model and transfer the data from SAP S/4HANA to embedded PP-DS. Master data objects such as materials and work centers are maintained in SAP S/4HANA transactions and are flagged for use in advanced planning.

Note

Advanced planning is the term used in SAP S/4HANA to identify the objects and processes that use the PP-DS capability.

The fields relevant to PP-DS fields are also exposed to the SAP S/4HANA master data objects and can be maintained in one transaction. When the data is stored in the database tables, it's saved only in SAP S/4HANA tables, and data duplication is avoided wherever applicable.

Similarly, transaction data such as planned independent requirements (PIRs), planned orders, production and process orders, purchase requisitions and orders, and sales orders are transferred to embedded PP-DS without any need for an active integration model. The relevant transaction data objects are marked as relevant for transfer in Customizing, and if the corresponding master data object is also marked as active for advanced planning, the transaction data is transferred to embedded PP-DS and from SAP S/4HANA and vice versa. Because embedded PP-DS also uses the SAP liveCache, the order objects need to be re-created in the SAP liveCache upon transfer to embedded PP-DS.

In scenarios involving multiple locations that require MRP and advanced planning, in SAP S/4HANA, just one MRP Live planning run can plan all the materials and locations, including those in PP-DS. There is no need to set up separate PP-DS planning runs to generate the procurement proposals for the advanced planning material locations. The planning run results are synced between SAP S/4HANA and embedded PP-DS in real time, so the risk with the CIF queue failures are greatly reduced.

> **Note**
>
> Although most of the planning and scheduling features are available in embedded PP-DS, certain features of the PP-DS component of SAP APO aren't available in embedded PP-DS. The critical simplification items are covered in the next section, and the complete list is available in SAP Note 2517109 – Simplification List: Production Planning and Detailed Scheduling for SAP S/4HANA 1709 (up to date through 1909).

1.2.2 Key Simplifications in PP-DS for SAP S/4HANA

In this section, we'll cover the key differences between the features of the PP-DS component of SAP APO and the embedded PP-DS features. These simplification items are dependent on the release version of SAP S/4HANA (this book is based on release 1909). We'll also cover specific impacts of the simplification items in the relevant chapters; in this section, we cover the simplification items that aren't covered in the other chapters.

Embedded PP-DS can't function as a planning hub. If there are multiple ERP systems, such as SAP ERP or SAP S/4HANA, in the solution landscape, the embedded PP-DS of one SAP S/4HANA system can't act as a central planning and scheduling system for all the ERP systems in the landscape. Only the planning data that is part of an SAP S/4HANA system can be used by embedded PP-DS of the same system. Standalone SAP APO systems can work alongside embedded PP-DS, but the data should be segregated in a way that the same set of data isn't planned by embedded PP-DS and the PP-DS component of SAP APO. A scenario in which a product location is planned in the SAP APO system for supply network planning and the same product location is planned in embedded PP-DS isn't supported in the standard delivered SAP S/4HANA software; however, custom interfaces may be used to support such a scenario.

Let's walk through the key simplifications, as follows:

- **Production versions**

  In the SAP ERP system, production-related master data such as BOM and routings are created and are linked via the master data object called the production version. These production versions, when transferred to the SAP APO systems, are created as production process models (PPMs) or as production data structures (PDSs) in the SAP APO system. While PPMs are based on older data models, PDSs are the new objects that can replace PPMs in SAP APO. However, in the SAP APO system, both PPMs and PDSs are supported.

  In embedded PP-DS, only PDSs are supported; if you're using PPMs in your existing SAP APO systems and plan to use embedded PP-DS, the usage of PDS is mandatory. If you have any enhancements implemented for the transfer of PPM in the SAP APO or SAP ERP systems, these need to be evaluated and adapted to the enhancements related to PDSs. We'll cover more about this in Chapter 2.

- **Simplified master data maintenance**

  In SAP APO systems, it's possible for local material masters and resources within SAP APO to be used in the PP-DS component of SAP APO. However, with embedded PP-DS, because one of the principle objectives is to reduce data duplication, it's not possible to create materials and resources just in PP-DS; instead, the materials and work centers (resources) should be created in SAP S/4HANA in the corresponding transactions and should be marked for advanced planning. This will make these materials and resources available in the PP-DS transaction in the SAP S/4HANA system.

■ **MRP-based detailed scheduling**
There is a functionality in the SAP APO system called MRP-based detailed scheduling, where MRP is executed in the ERP system (e.g., SAP ERP or SAP S/4HANA) and the PP-DS component of SAP APO is only used for detailed scheduling features. The orders created in the ERP system via MRP execution are transferred to the SAP APO system where the detailed scheduling is performed. After the detailed scheduling step, the new schedule with the new order dates is transferred back to the ERP system. However, with embedded PP-DS, this MRP-based detailed scheduling functionality isn't available. After a material is activated for advanced planning, it must be planned and scheduled with embedded PP-DS.

■ **MRP execution**
In the planning solution with SAP ERP and SAP APO systems, it's possible to execute MRP in SAP ERP even though the material is planned by the PP-DS component of SAP APO. This option isn't available in embedded PP-DS because MRP Live will always plan the advanced planning materials in PP-DS and not use the MRP algorithm in SAP ERP.

■ **Planning areas**
The demand planning and supply network planning components of the SAP APO system use a data object called the planning area. All the demand planning and supply network planning data is stored at the planning area level. Some PP-DS functionalities, such as deployment planning in SAP APO, use the planning area data object as well.

In embedded PP-DS, the demand planning and supply network planning components of SAP APO aren't available, so the planning areas concept doesn't exist in SAP S/4HANA, and the PP-DS component features of SAP APO that are dependent on the planning area aren't available in SAP S/4HANA. Therefore, functionalities such as capacity reservation, PP-DS deployment, and time-dependent safety stock aren't supported in embedded PP-DS.

■ **Global available-to-promise (GATP)**
GATP is a tool in SAP APO that can be triggered during the sales order creation process in the ERP system to check for the availability of the product and commit an availability date to the sales order. Similarly, capable-to-promise (CTP) is another availability check tool in SAP APO that checks for product availability; if there is no availability, the CTP tool creates a temporary planned order in SAP APO by considering the available capacity of the resources and then proposes an availability date back to the ERP system.

The GATP and CTP tools aren't part of embedded PP-DS, so these checks during the creation of sales orders aren't available in SAP S/4HANA. However, for planned orders and production orders, the native available-to-promise (ATP) tool of SAP S/4HANA is integrated for the availability check of planned and production order components. If a planned order is created or converted into a production order in embedded PP-DS, the corresponding order created in SAP S/4HANA triggers the ATP check for the components.

- **Custom sort profiles**
  In the SAP APO system, the order conversion and fixed pegging functionalities can use custom sort profiles to define the sequence of orders using the available order properties. These custom sort profiles are based on the GATP functionality. Because GATP isn't supported in embedded PP-DS, the custom sort profiles also aren't available in SAP S/4HANA.

- **Capable-to-match (CTM)**
  CTM is another tool in the SAP APO system used to plan the demands in multiple levels of the supply chain finitely. This tool isn't part of SAP S/4HANA because embedded PP-DS is no longer bundled with other SAP APO components such as demand planning or supply network planning.

- **PP-DS optimizer**
  The PP-DS optimizer is a powerful scheduling optimizer that creates an optimized plan according to the objective functions defined for optimization. In the PP-DS component of SAP APO, the optimizer can create new supply elements (e.g., planed orders) if there is a supply shortage. In embedded PP-DS, on the other hand, the PP-DS optimizer can't create planned orders. It can only schedule production orders and planned orders.

- **Data transfer**
  When master data is transferred between the SAP APO and the ERP system via the CIF, there are multiple enhancement options (e.g., user exits and business add-ins [BAdIs]) available to add additional fields and to enhance the master data. Such enhancements cover material masters and classification data (classes and characteristics). If these enhancements are used in the existing SAP APO system, you need to adapt those to the corresponding enhancement options available in the SAP S/4HANA system. In embedded PP-DS, it's possible to use the extensibility features to add additional fields to the material master so that any additional fields created in SAP APO can be made available in the SAP S/4HANA material master.

1.2.3   Deployment

In this section, we'll cover the deployment options available for PP-DS. To understand the reduced complexity of the deployment of embedded PP-DS, we'll discuss the various deployment options available for the PP-DS component in SAP APO and in SAP ERP as an add-on.

PP-DS with SAP APO

When introduced, SAP APO was a standalone system on the Basis platform, which is now the SAP NetWeaver platform. The underlying database can be any database system, such as SAP HANA, Oracle, DB2, DB6, or MSSQL. The SAP APO system requires a separate database for high-speed processing of the planning component, which is SAP liveCache. SAP APO also supports the optimization of planning problems, and the optimizer server can be also connected to the SAP APO system for executing optimizations in the areas of supply network planning, CTM, transportation load builder, and PP-DS, among others. The optimizer engine software is installed in a server that is connected to the SAP APO system via TCP/IP. The standalone SAP APO deployment option is depicted in Figure 1.2.

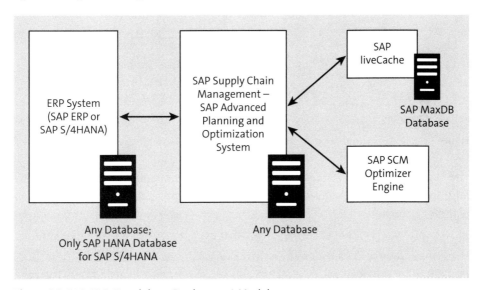

Figure 1.2 SAP APO Standalone Deployment Model

SAP liveCache in SAP APO is loaded with the time-series data that is relevant for demand planning and supply network planning, as well as order data that is used by supply network planning and PP-DS. In addition, SAP liveCache has an ATP time-series data object that is used by the GATP functionality.

SAP APO also contains a business warehouse environment, which is primarily used by the demand planning component of the SAP APO system to store historical data that is used in the forecasting process.

As Figure 1.3 shows, with the SAP APO system running on the SAP HANA database, SAP liveCache built-in to the SAP HANA database can be used by the SAP APO system. This eliminates the requirement to have a separate database system maintenance for SAP liveCache.

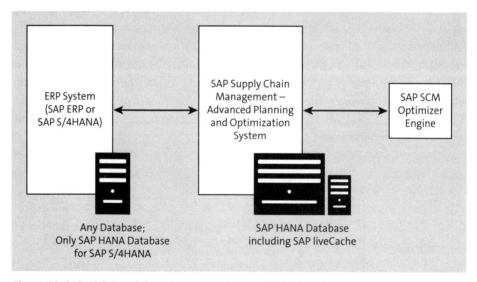

Figure 1.3 SAP APO Standalone Deployment on an SAP HANA Database

The standalone SAP APO deployment model is recommended for large and extra-large installations that require a lot of hardware resources to execute the SAP APO planning processes.

As of SAP SCM 7.0 EHP 3, SAP APO can be deployed as an add-on to the SAP ERP system. This add-on is installed on the existing SAP ERP system, and the SAP APO functionalities are provided with the switch activation framework. In addition, the base configuration for the SAP APO components in the form of business configuration sets (BC sets). Upon activation of the SAP APO switch and the BC sets installation, the SAP APO features are available in the SAP ERP system. The services parts planning component and maintenance and service planning component of SAP APO aren't available in SAP APO for SAP ERP as an add-on version. This deployment option is shown in Figure 1.4.

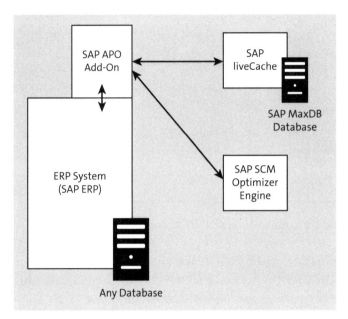

Figure 1.4 SAP APO as an Add-On to an SAP ERP System

SAP APO and the SAP ERP version reside in one SAP system and share a common SAP NetWeaver platform. When upgrading SAP APO and/or SAP ERP to a newer version or EHP, there are technical dependencies; the combination of SAP NetWeaver, SAP APO, and SAP ERP versions must be released for SAP APO add-on deployment. For example, updating the SAP APO add-on to a newer version may require SAP NetWeaver to be updated and require SAP ERP to be updated so that all components are on compatible versions.

The SAP ERP add-on deployment model is recommended for small and medium deployments. As the same hardware is shared by SAP ERP and SAP APO processes, the system should be sufficiently sized to cover the additional load.

For SAP ERP systems running on the SAP HANA database, the SAP APO add-on also has embedded PP-DS features and simplifications related to master data and the CIF. This deployment option is shown in Figure 1.5.

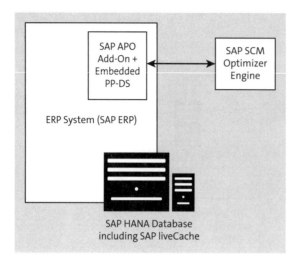

Figure 1.5 SAP APO as an Add-On to the Suite on SAP HANA System

This option of the SAP APO add-on for the SAP Business Suite on SAP HANA system is available from the SAP SCM 7.0 EHP 4 version and SAP ERP 6.0 EHP8 version. This option also supports MRP Live features and SAP Fiori apps.

Embedded PP-DS

SAP S/4HANA 1610 introduced embedded PP-DS. No other features of the SAP APO system are part of the SAP S/4HANA system. A standalone deployment of the SAP APO system can be used along with the SAP S/4HANA system. However, if embedded PP-DS is used, the same data can't be used for planning in the SAP APO system. Integration of orders generated out of standalone SAP APO systems can't be integrated into embedded PP-DS. Figure 1.6 shows the embedded PP-DS deployment option.

In embedded PP-DS, SAP liveCache is also embedded in the SAP HANA database on which the SAP S/4HANA system runs. It's recommended to install the optimizer engine in a separate server and connect to SAP S/4HANA using TCP/IP. The detailed architecture of embedded PP-DS is covered in the next section.

The new SAP S/4HANA core architecture sets the base for the feature innovations and simplification of the data, processes, and usability. The SAP S/4HANA platform is critical for enabling the Industry 4.0 features in the supply chain to enable and integrate the intelligent technologies such as the Internet of Things (IoT) and machine learning. Embedded PP-DS leverages the power of the SAP S/4HANA for simplifying the data, usability, and simplifications in the CIF.

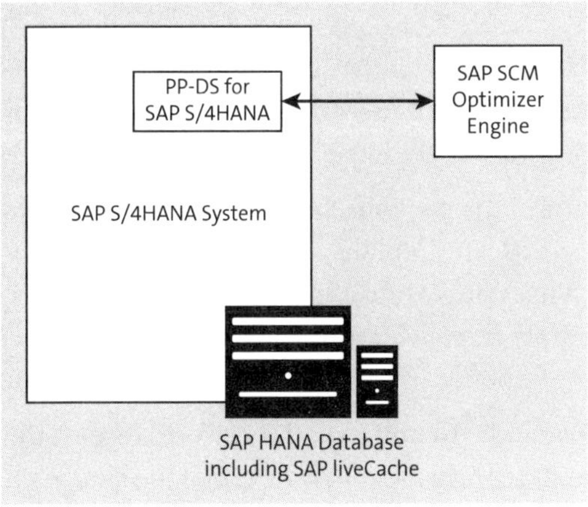
PP-DS for
SAP S/4HANA
SAP SCM
Optimizer
Engine
SAP S/4HANA System
SAP HANA Database
including SAP liveCache

Figure 1.6 Embedded PP-DS Deployment

As a target architecture, deployment of SAP S/4HANA, including the activation of embedded PP-DS integrated with cloud-based SAP IBP, should be targeted for the end state architecture of the SAP digital supply chain solution. The standalone SAP APO solution is currently supported with SAP S/4HANA, but all the future innovations for the planning and scheduling solutions will be delivered in SAP IBP and SAP S/4HANA.

Figure 1.7 shows the transformation of features and functionality in SAP SCM. The comparison of the SAP ERP and SAP APO solution capabilities to the SAP S/4HANA and SAP IBP solution capabilities are shown.

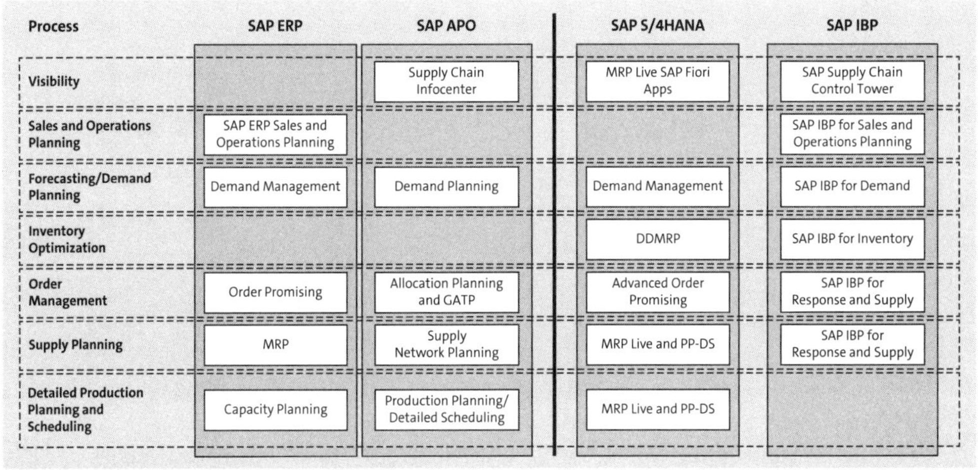
Process
SAP ERP
SAP APO
SAP S/4HANA
SAP IBP
Visibility
Supply Chain Infocenter
MRP Live SAP Fiori Apps
SAP Supply Chain Control Tower
Sales and Operations Planning
SAP ERP Sales and Operations Planning
SAP IBP for Sales and Operations Planning
Forecasting/Demand Planning
Demand Management
Demand Planning
Demand Management
SAP IBP for Demand
Inventory Optimization
DDMRP
SAP IBP for Inventory
Order Management
Order Promising
Allocation Planning and GATP
Advanced Order Promising
SAP IBP for Response and Supply
Supply Planning
MRP
Supply Network Planning
MRP Live and PP-DS
SAP IBP for Response and Supply
Detailed Production Planning and Scheduling
Capacity Planning
Production Planning/ Detailed Scheduling
MRP Live and PP-DS

Figure 1.7 SAP SCM Solution Transformation

1.2.4   Architecture

SAP S/4HANA has a new, simplified architecture to remove any redundancies in technologies, applications, and data. In this section, we'll cover the general architecture of the SAP S/4HANA system and the architecture of embedded PP-DS.

SAP S/4HANA simplified the architecture of the previous ERP versions. The principle of one is applied in the new architecture, which simplifies any duplicate functionalities and the need to save the same data in multiple tables for performance purposes. From a technical perspective, the multiple frameworks available with the ERP systems to realize functionality have been simplified in SAP S/4HANA.

In the ERP systems running on any database, to optimize the performance of the applications, the data is aggregated at different characteristics levels of the data, such as periods (daily, weekly, monthly), and aggregated at certain organizational levels. However, with the power of SAP HANA, these aggregations can be performed on the fly, and there is no need to create the redundant data in the database tables. With SAP S/4HANA, the applications can use the SAP HANA database to perform complex calculations. An example of how the inventory data storage is simplified in the SAP S/4HANA architecture is shown in Figure 1.8. In this example, the data is stored in more than 25 tables in ERP systems, whereas this is simplified to just two tables in the SAP S/4HANA system.

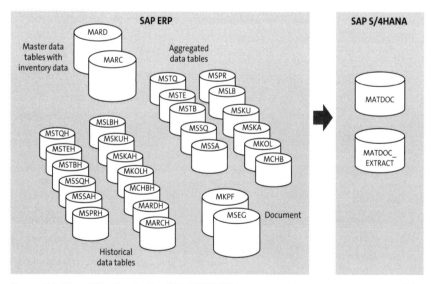

Figure 1.8 Simplification in the SAP S/4HANA Inventory Management Data Model Architecture

Another simplification in the architecture from the usability perspective is in the user interface (UI). For many business process areas, there are new, enhanced role-based SAP Fiori apps delivered with the SAP S/4HANA system that provide the end user with a unified and seamless UI irrespective of the device being used.

SAP S/4HANA also has embedded analytics to bring in the real-time transaction data and provide context to the transaction data with the master data within the transactional SAP Fiori apps. In addition, there are standalone SAP Fiori analytics apps that use the core data service (CDS) views to process the data during the runtime and provide powerful analytics.

The SAP S/4HANA architecture also makes the platform future-ready for innovations and integration to other cloud solutions. To enable the simplifications in terms of data, usability, analytics, and future readiness, the technical architecture of SAP S/4HANA system is designed as shown in Figure 1.9. The SAP HANA database layer consists of the database tables, and the CDS views enable simplified access to combined data from multiple tables. The SAP S/4HANA layer contains the transactional and analytical business logic and enterprise search, which simplifies and enhances the search capability in the SAP S/4HANA system. SAP Gateway is the communication layer between the SAP S/4HANA system and the SAP Fiori UI. The SAP Gateway layer contains all the technical artifacts to bring the data from the SAP S/4HANA system to the SAP Fiori apps.

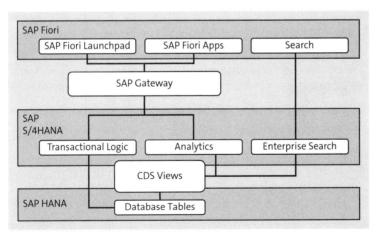

Figure 1.9 SAP S/4HANA Technical Architecture

In terms of data model simplifications in master data, integration of master data and transaction data, and usability simplifications, the simplicity and feature-rich SAP

S/4HANA architecture is also used by embedded PP-DS. In addition to the SAP S/4HANA core, which now is embedded with the PP-DS application functionalities, PP-DS also requires SAP liveCache to execute the complex planning and scheduling algorithms. SAP liveCache is part of the SAP HANA database in the SAP S/4HANA architecture. Figure 1.10 shows the difference between the standalone SAP APO and SAP ERP solution architecture and that of embedded PP-DS.

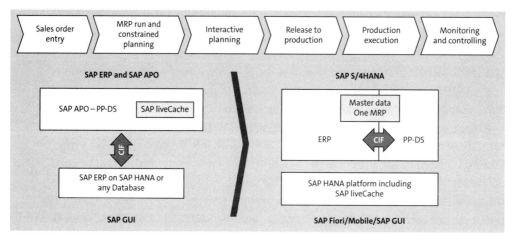

Figure 1.10 Simplified Embedded PP-DS Architecture

Embedded PP-DS has a simplified master data architecture. The master data is maintained in SAP S/4HANA and is visible and available for embedded PP-DS. The material master and work center are activated for advanced planning, which makes it available for embedded PP-DS. For the resource master data, the corresponding SAP liveCache time stream is also generated.

For PP-DS master data, such as the PDS, a generation report is provided, which will generate and save the PDS in the PP-DS tables by using the self-system remote function call (RFC). The business partner data (customers and vendors) and the organizational structure data (plant, shipping points, and MRP areas) are transferred to embedded PP-DS using a generation report. The variant configuration classes created in SAP S/4HANA is available for embedded PP-DS without a need to create any specific integration model.

For master data elements such as purchase info records, contracts, and scheduling agreements, an integration model is required to generate the external procurement relationship master data in embedded PP-DS. In addition, the characteristics-dependent planning (CDP) class type, which is specific to embedded PP-DS and not relevant for SAP S/4HANA, also requires an integration model for the transfer to embedded PP-DS.

The transaction data created in SAP S/4HANA is also transferred to embedded PP-DS and saved in SAP liveCache and in the mapping tables to ensure the consistency of the data in SAP S/4HANA and SAP liveCache. Similarly, the planning data created in embedded PP-DS is saved in SAP liveCache and sent to SAP S/4HANA. The transaction data includes planned orders and production orders for in-house manufacturing, purchase requisitions, purchase orders, scheduling agreement releases for external procurement, sales orders, forecast elements, and PIRs. The data architecture for most commonly used master and transaction data is shown in Figure 1.11.

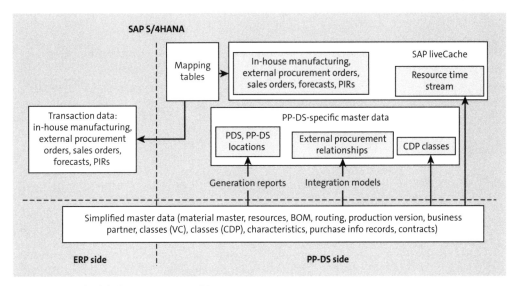

Figure 1.11 Embedded PP-DS Data Architecture

1.3   Summary

In this chapter, we introduced the basics of production planning, detailed scheduling, deployment options, and architecture of the PP-DS component for SAP APO and embedded PP-DS solutions. We also covered the evolution of the PP-DS architecture in the SAP systems and the embedded PP-DS data architecture in detail.

As we discussed in this chapter, the cloud-based SAP IBP system and embedded PP-DS will eventually replace the on-premise SAP APO system for the demand, supply planning, and PP-DS functionalities.

In the next chapter, we'll cover the critical master data objects required to operate embedded PP-DS for executing the PP-DS processes.

Chapter 2
Master Data

Now that we've covered the PP-DS basics, it's time to move on to the master data. In this chapter, we'll dive into the integration model and provide step-by-step instructions for setting up the master data objects.

In this chapter, we'll cover the master data objects in detail, beginning with the concept of integration models. Then we'll cover the individual master data objects such as materials, work centers, in-house production source of supply (e.g., production data structures [PDSs]), external procurement relationships (e.g., purchase info records, contracts, and scheduling agreements), classes, and characteristics.

For material master and work centers (resources), there is no need to create an integration model. But for certain master data objects, such as external procurement relationships, it's still required to create integration modes with the self-system destination. We'll also cover the concept of the integration model and all the master data objects required to execute the planning and scheduling in PP-DS in SAP S/4HANA (embedded PP-DS).

2.1 Integration Models

An integration model is an object used to transfer certain master data objects from SAP S/4HANA to embedded PP-DS. These integration models use the simplified core interface (CIF) in the SAP S/4HANA system. The CIF is a real-time data exchange framework using the queued remote function call (qRFC) communication technology. Typically, there are source and target systems involved in transferring data from an ERP system to the PP-DS system. Because both ERP and PP-DS are part of the same system in SAP S/4HANA, the source and destinations are the same for the integration model.

There are two steps involved in transferring the data via the integration model:

1. **Create the integration model**

   The process starts with creation of an integration model where the basic identifiers, such as the integration model name, the SAP Advanced Planning and Optimization (SAP APO) application name, and the logical systems, are defined. In addition, the selection and filter criteria for the master data objects are defined.

2. **Activate the integration model**

   The second step in transferring the master data to embedded PP-DS using the integration model is the activation of the defined integration model. During the activation, the data defined in the selection criteria for the integration model is packaged into the RFC queues and transferred to embedded PP-DS.

We'll walk through both steps in this section.

2.1.1   Create the Integration Model

The creation of an integration model is executed via Transaction CFM1 via menu path, **SAP Menu · Logistics · Central Functions · Supply Chain Planning Interface · Core Interface Advanced Planner and Optimizer · Integration Model · Create**.

As shown in Figure 2.1, the **Model Name**, **Logical System**, and **APO Application** uniquely identify the integration model. We'll cover the logical system definition and the technical details in Chapter 3.

Note

SAP S/4HANA can also be used as the ERP system with the SAP APO system. Therefore, the SAP S/4HANA integration model also supports creation of an integration model for standalone SAP APO systems. In this case, the integration model is created with the logical system defined for the SAP APO system, so you'll see all the master data objects that can be integrated via the CIF in the integration model transaction. After SAP S/4HANA is selected as the logical system, only the master data objects that still require an integration model in embedded PP-DS are available for selection in the integration model transaction.

The material-dependent master data objects (e.g., contracts and purchase info records) and the material-independent master data objects (e.g., setup groups and classes) can also be transferred to embedded PP-DS from SAP S/4HANA using the integration model.

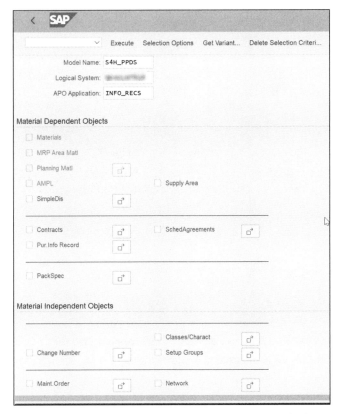

Figure 2.1 Creation of Integration Model: Definition and Selection Options

After the logical system is entered, and if it's the one defined for the same SAP S/4HANA system, the system shows only the master data objects that are transferred through the integration model. Other master data objects are transferred to embedded PP-DS via generation reports or by setting the **Advanced Planning** checkbox in the master data objects (which we'll discuss throughout this chapter).

The material-dependent selection, as shown in Figure 2.2, is relevant for the master data objects listed under the **Material Dependent Objects**, and when one of these objects is selected as part of the integration model, the selection criteria defined under **General Selection Options for Materials** is considered for the selection. In addition, the object-specific filter is applied. In the example shown in Figure 2.2, the purchase info record (**Pur.Info Record**) is the data object selected for the integration model, and the filter options specific to the purchase info records are displayed. There is also a button ❶ you can use to access additional filter options.

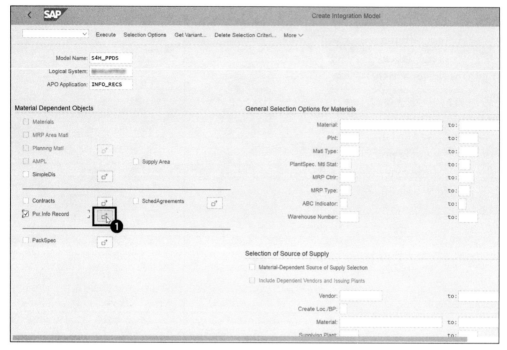

Figure 2.2 Selection and Filter Options in Integration Model Creation

After the appropriate selection and filter options are set, the **Execute** function on the screen is used to perform the data selection per the selection and filter values.

In the next screen, as shown in Figure 2.3, the integration model is generated, which then packages the selected data into the model. The **Generate IM** option is used to create the integration model, and the **Consistency Check** button is used to make sure that the packaged data doesn't have any inconsistencies.

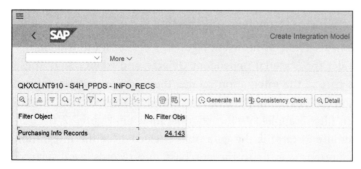

Figure 2.3 Integration Model Generation

2.1.2 Activate the Integration Model

After the integration model is generated, the model needs to be activated. This step will process the data and send it to embedded PP-DS from SAP S/4HANA. This step also maps the data to the PP-DS master data objects.

The activation step fetches all the data from SAP S/4HANA and then executes the mapping logic in the CIF. For example, the purchase info records from SAP S/4HANA are fetched and filled into the corresponding CIF structures. Within embedded PP-DS, when the queue is processed, the data from SAP S/4HANA is mapped against the structures of the external procurement relationships in embedded PP-DS. In addition, the corresponding enhancement spots in SAP S/4HANA and in embedded PP-DS are evaluated and applied during this process.

The activation of the integration model is executed from Transaction CFM2 via menu path, **SAP Menu · Logistics · Central Functions · Supply Chain Planning Interface · Core Interface Advanced Planner and Optimizer · Integration Model · Activate**.

As shown in Figure 2.4, the integration model name, the logical system, and the application are the possible selection options in the integration model activation transaction.

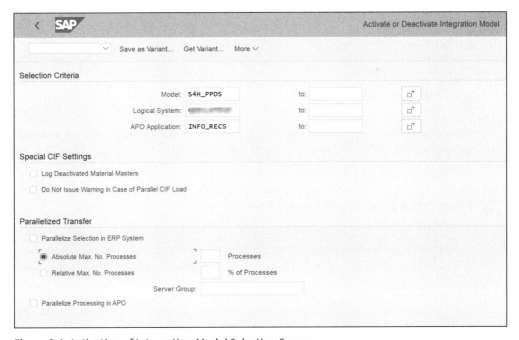

Figure 2.4 Activation of Integration Model Selection Screen

The **Special CIF Settings** tab provides additional options specific to material master deactivation and parallel CIF loads. In embedded PP-DS, there is no integration model for the material masters, so the **Log Deactivated Material Masters** option isn't applicable. The **Do Not Issue Warning in Case of Parallel CIF Load** option is also not very relevant for the SAP S/4HANA system as there are no integration model-based data transfers executed for the transaction data.

The **Parallelized Transfer** section of the selection screen, as shown in Figure 2.4, is used to optimize the performance of the data selection from SAP S/4HANA and processing of the data in embedded PP-DS. This can be used when the data to be transferred via one integration model is huge, and executing this in a single threaded process would take a longer time to process. By activating the parallel processing and entering the number of processes that can be used by the system, it will execute multiple threads for selecting SAP S/4HANA data and also process the queues in parallel within embedded PP-DS.

Out of the master data and transaction data objects that are supported by the CIF framework, only the external procurement relationships (info records, contracts, and scheduling agreements) objects are relevant for parallel processing in embedded PP-DS.

Note

The SAP S/4HANA system can also be used as the ERP system along with a standalone SAP APO system, so certain options such as the special CIF settings are still present in the SAP S/4HANA system to support the data transfer to a standalone SAP APO system via the CIF.

After the selection criteria for the integration model are entered, click the **Execute** button. In the next screen, the details of the integration model are displayed, as shown in Figure 2.5. An integration model can be activated and deactivated any number of times, so the previous status and the new status that will be executed upon clicking the **Start** action are shown in the screen.

Based on the selection, all the relevant integration models are listed in the left side of the screen, and when you select a specific integration model, the details are loaded on the right side of the screen. A consistency check can be executed by using the **Check** button in this screen.

To set the status of the integration model (whether activate or deactivate), you use the **Active/Inactive** button.

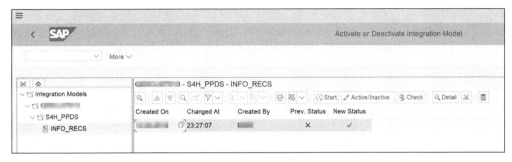

Figure 2.5 Activation of Integration Model: Details Screen

Tip [+]

In addition to creating and activating the integration model, Transaction CFM4 can be used to display it as well. Transaction CFM5 can be used to search for the integration model that a particular master data object is part of. In addition, Transaction CFM7 is used to delete integration models.

All the master data objects transferred from SAP S/4HANA to embedded PP-DS are assigned to the model 000 and version 000, which are the active model and version in the embedded PP-DS system. We'll cover the details of the model and version in Chapter 3.

We'll cover the technical settings required to work with the integration model in Chapter 3. The technical monitoring of the integration models will be discussed in Chapter 9.

2.2   Locations

In this section, we'll cover the different location master data types relevant for embedded PP-DS and how this data is transferred into embedded PP-DS from SAP S/4HANA. In addition, we'll cover the PP-DS settings that need to be maintained in the location master data.

In embedded PP-DS, the definition of locations includes plants, material requirements planning (MRP) areas, vendors, customers, and shipping/receiving points. The structure of these data objects isn't the same in SAP S/4HANA because plants and MRP areas are customizing data, whereas vendors and customers are created as master data. The PP-DS location master doesn't differentiate between SAP S/4HANA classification of the data, such as customizing or master data, and treats the location as a master data object in embedded PP-DS.

The ABAP program /SAPAPO/CREATE_LOCATION is delivered in the SAP S/4HANA system as of version 1809 to transfer the location data from SAP S/4HANA to embedded PP-DS. In SAP S/4HANA systems older than 1809, an integration model is required to transfer the locations. You can use the ABAP program /SAPAPO/UPD_LOC_SP_PL to update the location data in embedded PP-DS when changes are performed to the corresponding data in SAP S/4HANA.

In the ABAP program /SAPAPO/CREATE_LOCATION, the selection of relevant location data (e.g., plants, MRP areas, shipping points, and business partners representing customers and vendors) is entered as shown in Figure 2.6. When this report is executed, the data is fetched, processed, and sent to embedded PP-DS.

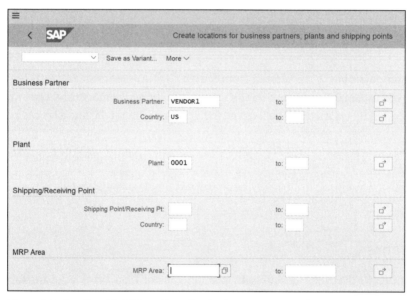

Figure 2.6 Creating PP-DS Locations for Business Partners, Plants, MRP Areas, and Shipping/Receiving Points

The locations transferred from SAP S/4HANA to embedded PP-DS can be edited in embedded PP-DS to enhance the location master with PP-DS data such as calendars and resources. The following enhancement options are also available for the integration of location master data:

- **/SAPAPO/LOC_CREATE**
  Create business partner locations on saving a business partner.
- **/SAPAPO/LOC_DETAILS**
  Change the location details.

In the SAP APO system, the customer master data is transferred from the ERP system to SAP APO as a customer location (location type 1010), and the vendors are transferred as a vendor location (location type 1011). With SAP S/4HANA, business partner is the master data object that replaces the vendor and customer master data. Therefore, in embedded PP-DS, the location types 1010 and 1011 are replaced by the location type 1021, representing the business partner master data object.

Although a plant is an organizational structure data object created in the Customizing of SAP S/4HANA, it's transferred to embedded PP-DS as a master data element. As shown in Figure 2.7, the basic information of the plant is defined in the SAP S/4HANA system.

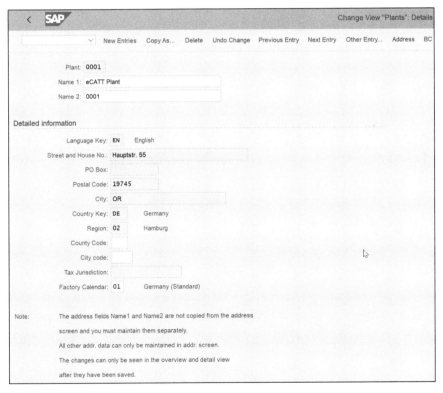

Figure 2.7 Definition of a Plant in SAP S/4HANA Customizing

After the report for transferring the plant location is executed, the plant location of location type 1001 – production plant is created in embedded PP-DS. The basic data, such as the name, address, time zone, and regions, is transferred to the location master data. The PP-DS data is maintained in the PP-DS transaction for the location master. The location master can be accessed from Transaction /SAPAPO/LOC3 or via menu path, **Logistics · Advanced Planning · Master Data · Location · Location**. The **Location** and **Location Type** are entered, as shown in Figure 2.8. Select the **Change** button to change and add additional PP-DS information to the location master.

Figure 2.8 PP-DS Location Master Data: Initial Screen

As shown in Figure 2.9, the general data settings, including the administrative data such as **Created** and **Changed**, are in the **General** tab. The basic data transferred from SAP S/4HANA is updated in the **Address** tab.

[»]

Note

In embedded PP-DS, all the master data and transaction data are assigned to a supply chain model and version. Versions can be created to simulate any planning relevant parameters. 000 is the active model, and 000 version is the active version. The master and transaction data integrated into embedded PP-DS from SAP S/4HANA is always assigned to the 000 version.

For maintaining the PP-DS calendars, click on the **Calendar** tab and maintain the **Production Calendar** for scheduling the production activities and the **Display Calendar (PPDS)** for controlling the display of the periodic views in PP-DS planning tools such as the production planning table.

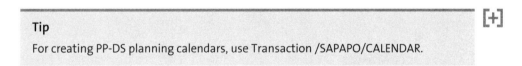

Figure 2.9 Location Master in Embedded PP-DS

> ## Tip
> For creating PP-DS planning calendars, use Transaction /SAPAPO/CALENDAR.

[+]

The handling resources in the location master is used by the goods receipt (GR) and goods issue (GI) processing operations. To support GR and GI processing times assigned in the product masters, the handling resources must be assigned in the location master. To maintain the resources, click on the **Resources** tab, and maintain the handling resources as shown in Figure 2.10. **Resource Inbound** is used in scheduling the GR activities when GR processing is assigned in the material master, and **Resource Outbound** is used in scheduling GI activities.

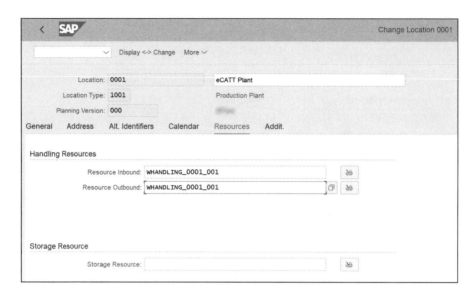

Figure 2.10 PP-DS Location Master: Handling Resource Assignment

The business partner master data is created in SAP S/4HANA, and depending on the role of the business partner, the role-specific data is added in SAP S/4HANA. Depending on whether the business partner is a vendor or customer, the same entity acts as a vendor and customer. In embedded PP-DS, the location mater data is used in transaction data objects. For example, the plant location data is used in in-house manufacturing orders such as planned orders and production orders, and the vendor and customer location master data is used in the purchasing documents and sales documents, respectively. The context for the transaction data is enhanced with the location master data details in embedded PP-DS.

2.3   Product Master

In this section, we'll cover the details of the product master in PP-DS in SAP S/4HANA and how the material master maintained in the SAP S/4HANA system is transferred to embedded PP-DS.

In the SAP S/4HANA system, the material master holds the information about the materials that a company manufactures, procures, and stores in its premises.

Depending on the usage of the material in the company, different material types are defined. And based on the type of material, such as raw material, semifinished material, or finished product, the relevant information is stored in the material master data.

In the PP-DS component of SAP APO, the material master created in the ERP system must be transferred to the SAP APO system via the CIF. In addition, the integration model is required to transfer the material master to the SAP APO system. Change pointers are also implemented to send the material master changes to the SAP APO system when a change is made in the ERP system. The material master data in SAP APO is called as the product master, and any product master data from the PP-DS component of SAP APO is directly maintained in the SAP APO system. Due to the presence of the CIF layer between the SAP APO and ERP systems, there are challenges in monitoring the queues for any errors and correcting them to ensure the data consistency between the ERP and SAP APO systems.

In embedded PP-DS, there is no need to create an integration model for the material master. As PP-DS is part of the SAP S/4HANA core, the material master created in SAP S/4HANA is available for PP-DS by activating the material for advanced planning. There is a new view in the SAP S/4HANA material master where the PP-DS specific master data can be maintained. Therefore, the maintenance of the material master is only possible from the ERP side transaction within the SAP S/4HANA system, and the PP-DS product master is a display-only view.

As shown in Figure 2.11, from the material master Transaction MM01 (Create Material) or Transaction MM02 (Change Material), navigate to the **Advanced Planning** tab, and check the **Advanced Planning** checkbox on the material master. This checkbox immediately makes the material master available for PP-DS planning. In addition, activating **Advanced Planning** will populate the mandatory fields, such as the **PP Plng Procedure** in the material master.

Any additional PP-DS master data that is relevant for specific planning scenarios within PP-DS can be maintained in this **Advanced Planning** tab. As shown in Figure 2.12, the PP-DS data is stored in SAP S/4HANA material master table MARC. The PP-DS database tables (e.g., table /SAPAPO/MATLOC) are just a view of the data stored in table MARC, and they don't persist the data.

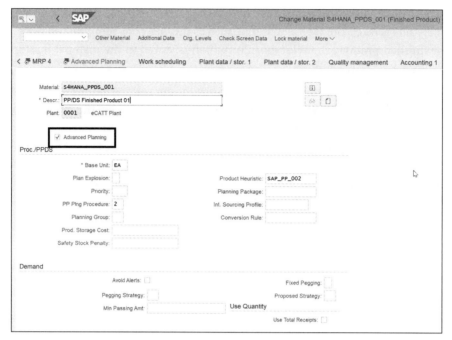

Figure 2.11 Activation of Advanced Planning in SAP S/4HANA Material Master

Field	Key	Initia...	Data element	Data Type	Length	Decimal...	Short Description
.INCLUDE			PRD_S_SCM_MARC	STRU	0	0	SCM Specific MARC Structure
SCM_MATLOCID_GUID			/SCMB/MDL_MATID	RAW	16	0	Internal Key for Product
SCM_MATLOCID_GUID			/SAPAPO/MATLOCID	CHAR	22	0	Internal Number (UID) for Location Product
SCM_GRPRT			/SAPAPO/GRPRT	DEC	11	0	Goods Receipt Processing Time
SCM_GIPRT			/SAPAPO/GIPRT	DEC	11	0	Goods Issue Processing Time
SCM_SCOST			/SAPAPO/SCOST	DEC	13	3	Product-Dependent Storage Costs
SCM_RELDT			/SAPAPO/RELDT	DEC	3	0	Replenishment Lead Time in Calendar Days
SCM_RRP_TYPE			/SAPAPO/PPS_PLANN	CHAR	1	0	PP Planning Procedure
SCM_HEUR_ID			/SAPAPO/PROD_HEUR	CHAR	12	0	PPC Heuristics
SCM_PACKAGE_ID			/SAPAPO/PROD_HEUR	CHAR	12	0	Planning Package to Which Product Belongs
SCM_SSPEN			/SAPAPO/SSPEN	DEC	13	3	Penalty Costs for Safety Stock Violation
SCM_GET_ALERTS			/SAPAPO/GET_ALERT	CHAR	1	0	Alert Relevance of Product
SCM_RES_NET_NAME			/SAPAPO/RESNET_NE	CHAR	40	0	Resource Network
SCM_CONHAP			/SAPAPO/SNPCONHAP	QUAN	13	3	Handling Capacity Consumption in Unit of Measure (Gds Rcpt)
SCM_HUNIT			/SAPAPO/HUNIT	UNIT	3	0	Unit of Measure: Handling Capacity in Goods Receipt
SCM_CONHAP_OUT			/SAPAPO/SNPCONHAP	QUAN	13	3	Handling Capacity Consumption in Unit of Measure (Gds Issue)
SCM_HUNIT_OUT			/SAPAPO/HUNIT_OUT	UNIT	3	0	Unit of Measure: Handling Capacity in Goods Issue

Figure 2.12 PP-DS Fields in SAP S/4HANA Material Master: Table MARC

The activation of advanced planning in the material master assigns the material to the active PP-DS model and version. The product master can be displayed in the PP-DS Transaction /SAPAPO/MAT1. This is a display-only view, and no maintenance of data in the PP-DS transaction is possible. All the basic MRP and advanced planning data objects maintained in the material master are visible in the PP-DS product master, as shown in Figure 2.13.

Figure 2.13 PP-DS Product Master Data in SAP S/4HANA

Note

Direct creation of material in embedded PP-DS isn't possible for simulation purposes. Materials are always created and maintained in the ERP transaction and must be activated for advanced planning.

Materials are created and assigned to a plant in SAP S/4HANA, and the same assignment is available for the PP-DS product master data. Therefore, the location master data of the plant must be integrated before activating the material for advanced planning. If an advanced planned material is assigned to an MRP area within the plant, the material can be planned in the MRP area in PP-DS as well. However, the MRP area should be integrated as a PP-DS location prior to activation of advanced planning.

2.4   Work Centers and Resources

In this section, we'll cover resource and work center data in SAP S/4HANA and how that data is integrated into PP-DS. We'll also discuss the specifics of PP-DS resource master data.

Resources and work centers represent the machines, tools, and labor resources that are used to manufacture products. In industries that follow continuous or process manufacturing (e.g., the chemical industry), the term *resource* is used to represent the production resources, and in discrete manufacturing scenarios, the production resources are called *work centers*.

Work centers and resources hold basic information about their usage in the production process, capacity definition, and scheduling data. In SAP S/4HANA, the data related to the activity types, which are used to derive the cost of the resource usage, plays a crucial role.

In embedded PP-DS, the resource master data maintenance is simplified by eliminating the need to create an integration model for transferring the work centers and resources to PP-DS. For the purpose of this section, we'll see how a discrete manufacturing work center is integrated into embedded PP-DS.

Work centers are created in SAP S/4HANA by executing Transaction CR01 and are changed by executing Transaction CR02. After you execute Transaction CR01, enter a **Plant**, **Work Center** name, and **Category**, and then press ⌐Enter⌐ to arrive at the screen shown in Figure 2.14. In the **Basic Data** tab of the work center master data, select the **Advanced Planning** indicator.

After the **Advanced Planning** indicator is selected, the resource is transferred to embedded PP-DS. In embedded PP-DS, the following four resource types are supported:

- **Single activity resource**
  Only one activity can be performed at this resource at a given time. The available capacity is defined only as a dimension of time.

- **Multi-activity resource**
  Multiple activities can be performed at this resource in parallel. The available capacity is defined as the time dimension, along with the number of individual capacities available.

- **Production line**
  Line resources are typically used in rate-based manufacturing such as automotive assembly lines.

- **Calendar resources**
  These resources don't hold any capacity, but they are used for determining the schedule of the activity performed in these resources.

Figure 2.14 Activation of Advanced Planning in the SAP S/4HANA Work Center

The PP-DS properties (e.g., resource type, category, validity of the resource time streams, etc.) are defaulted from the customizing maintained in Transaction CFC9 under the **Initial Data Transfer and Change Transfer for Resource** section, as shown in Figure 2.15.

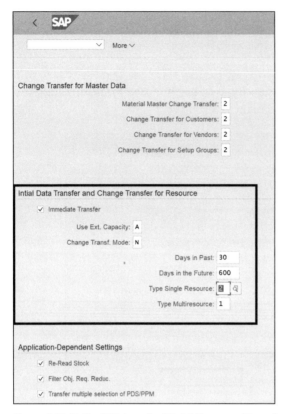

Figure 2.15 Default Values for PP-DS Resource Transfer

The default values for the PP-DS resource properties, such as the resource type, category, and validity of the resource time stream, can be overwritten in the work center master data in SAP S/4HANA. You can use the **APO Resource** button in the capacity header of the work center master data from Transaction CRO1 or Transaction CRO2 to define the work center-specific PP-DS resource properties, as shown in Figure 2.16. **Resource Cat.** (resource category) is a descriptive field for denoting the usage of the resource and doesn't have a scheduling functional significance. The time stream validity is determined by the fields **Days -** (days in past) and **Days +** (days in future) and the same is used to create the SAP liveCache time stream in PP-DS.

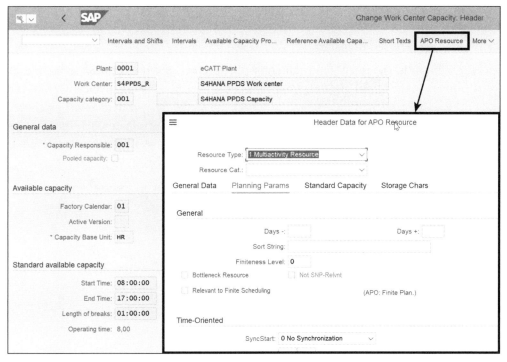

Figure 2.16 PP-DS Resource Properties in the SAP S/4HANA Work Center

> **Note**
>
> In the SAP S/4HANA work center, you'll still see fields and resource types relevant to the standalone PP-DS component of SAP APO scenario. In a side-by-side SAP APO and SAP S/4HANA system, these resource types are still relevant, so they are still present but not relevant for embedded PP-DS.

After the work center is transferred to embedded PP-DS by setting the **Advanced Planning** checkbox, the resource is available for maintenance of additional data in the PP-DS transaction. Execute Transaction /SAPAPO/RES01 to access the PP-DS resource master data. You can also follow the SAP menu path, **Logistics · Advanced Planning · Master Data · Resource · Resource**, to access the resource master.

Because the resources are created in PP-DS, they are assigned to planning version 000. There is also a version-independent resource that is created in PP-DS. Certain pieces of PP-DS resource data, such as the classification of the resources for characteristics-dependent planning (CDP), are maintained in the version-independent resource data.

As shown in Figure 2.17, you can enter the **Resource** and the **Location** in the initial screen. In the **Model and Plng Version** section, enter the **Planning Version** "000" for the active version of the resource, or check the **Model-Independent Selection** checkbox to access the model-independent version of the resource. Click the **Change Resource** button or the **Display Resource** button to change or display the resource details, respectively.

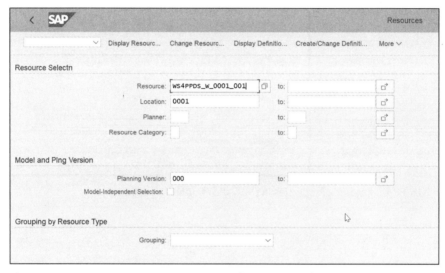

Figure 2.17 Resource Master in PP-DS in SAP S/4HANA: Initial Screen

Tip

When the work centers are transferred to embedded PP-DS, the work center name is prefixed with the letter "W", and the suffix of the location and the capacity category is added. For example, work center S4PPDS_W created in plant 0001 with capacity category 001 is created as WS4PPDS_W_0001_01 in PP-DS.

In the details of the PP-DS resource, the resource and basic information is displayed in list form ❶, and the details are available in the individual tabs as displayed in

Figure 2.18 ❷. Under the **PP/DS Bucket Cap.** tab, there is an option to set the PP-DS bucket capacity, which is used for planning capacity at a daily or shift-wise buckets, but that isn't valid for embedded PP-DS. The only bucket capacity supported in SAP S/4HANA is the block planning scenario bucket, which is set when the resource is enabled for block planning. We'll cover more details about block planning in Chapter 8, Section 8.3.2, when discussing advanced PP-DS features.

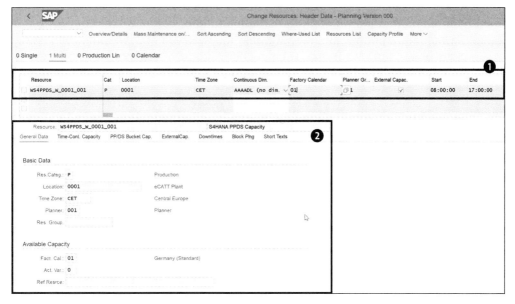

Figure 2.18 PP-DS Resource Master Data: Details

In the **ExternalCap.** tab, you can view the source of the capacity definition. If the **External Capacity** checkbox is selected, the capacity defined in the SAP S/4HANA work center is considered for the capacity definition. If the capacity definition needs to be maintained in embedded PP-DS, the **External Capacity** checkbox should not be selected.

The downtimes or nonworking times due to planned or repair maintenance of the resources can be directly maintained in the **Downtimes** tab of the resource master. In addition, when an SAP S/4HANA plant maintenance order can be integrated into PP-DS and a work center is assigned to the maintenance order, the maintenance duration is entered automatically as downtime in the PP-DS resource master.

2.5   Sources of Supply

In this section, we'll cover the various sources of supply supported in the SAP S/4HANA system and how these can be transferred to PP-DS for their usage in PP-DS planning.

The sources of supply in embedded PP-DS refers to how the material will be produced or procured. For in-house production of products, the sources of supply in SAP S/4HANA include bills of material (BOMs), routings, and production versions, which combine the BOM and routing for a specific product. In addition, for the process industries, the master recipe is the in-house source of supply that comprises the manufacturing steps in the form of operations and phases in production and the BOM.

Materials that are procured externally from suppliers and materials transferred between plants, which are the external procurement sources of supplies in ERP systems, include purchase info records, scheduling agreements, and contracts.

2.5.1   Production Data Structure

For the in-house sources of supply, in embedded PP-DS, the source of supply is called a production data structure (PDS), which contains all the basic, material, and scheduling information as defined in SAP S/4HANA BOMs, routings, and production versions. As shown in Figure 2.19, the validity of dates, lot sizes for which this production version can be used, and the BOM and routing information are maintained in the production version master data.

Execute Transaction CURTOADV_CREATE to create the PDSs in embedded PP-DS by processing SAP S/4HANA master data. You can also navigate to the SAP menu path, **Logistics · Production · Master Data · PDS for Advanced Planning · PDS Transfer (PP/DS)**, to execute the transfer.

The material for which the PDS is being transferred must be flagged for advanced planning. If multiple material components are part of the BOM, only the material components flagged for advanced planning will be created as the components in the PDS data in embedded PP-DS.

Similarly, the operations to which the work centers assigned to the routing operations must be flagged for advanced planning. Standard value key—the scheduling and capacity requirements formula—should be maintained in the work center data.

2

The routing operation must also have a nonzero activity time calculated during the scheduling, and the control key assigned to the operation should allow scheduling.

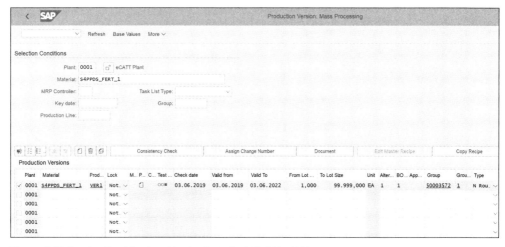

Figure 2.19 Production Version Master Data in SAP S/4HANA

> **Note**
>
> In SAP S/4HANA, it's mandatory to have production versions for the consideration of BOMs and routings in the MRP run and source of supply determination. You can use report CS_BOM_PRODVER_MIGRATION02 to create production versions in an automated manner.

The selection screen of the PDS transfer is shown in Figure 2.20. The PDS must be available in the PP-DS active version, so enter the value "000" for **Pl. Version in APO**, and then enter the selection options for which you need to transfer the PDS to embedded PP-DS under **Selection Criteria**.

PDSs are also used to manage the component requirements in the subcontracting scenarios, where a product is manufactured completely or partly by a third-party vendor, and the plant sends the components to the vendor to complete the manufacturing process. In these cases, a production version for manufacturing is linked to the purchase info records or scheduling agreements, and the corresponding PDSs also can be created in embedded PP-DS. You can define the relevance of the PDS for the subcontracting scenario in the **PDS Type** section of the selection screen.

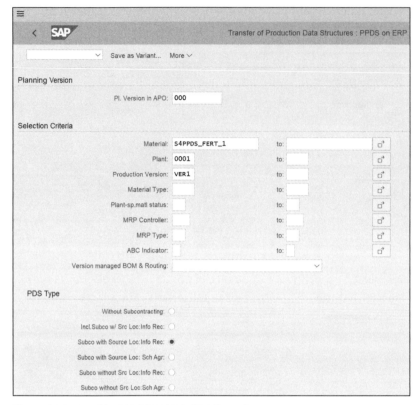

Figure 2.20 PP-DS in SAP S/4HANA: PDS Transfer

You can see more options for the PDS transfer by scrolling down the screen, as shown in Figure 2.21. You can use the **Extended Consistency Check** checkbox to ensure the consistency of the PDS data in embedded PP-DS. Because this performance-intensive option does a lot of checks and validations, don't use the **Extended Consistency Check** setting for transferring the PDS data periodically.

When errors are generated in embedded PP-DS during the PDS transfer, the changes in master data aren't transferred from SAP S/4HANA to embedded PP-DS. However, the PDS will continue to be used in the PP-DS planning. If you want to avoid this situation, select the **Lock PDS in error case** checkbox in the options. This will lock the PDS and avoid its usage in planning until the PDS integration is successfully completed.

Checking the **Absolute Transfer** checkbox to perform a complete transfer of the PDS data to PP-DS will regenerate the PDS based on the date from SAP S/4HANA. Conversely, the **Change Transfer** option is used for sending the changes made to SAP

S/4HANA master data, such as BOMs, routings, and production versions, after the PDS is transferred to PP-DS.

‹ **SAP** Transfer of Production Data Structures : PPDS on ERP	
⌄ Save as Variant... More ⌄	
Subco without Src Loc:Info Rec: ○	
Subco without Src Loc:Sch Agr: ○	
Options	
Extended Consistency Check: ☐	
Lock PDS in error case: ☐	
Transfer Deletion Flag: ☑	
☐ Delete PDS Despite Usage	
Absolute Transfer: ○	
Change Transfer: ●	
☐ Only Change Pointers Older Than Date	31.12.9999 23:59:59
☐ Only Change Pointers Older Than	0 Minutes
Test Mode: ☐	

Figure 2.21 PP-DS in SAP S/4HANA: PDS Transfer Options

> **Tip**
>
> Use Transaction CURTOADV_CRT_FOCUS for creating PDSs corresponding to order or work breakdown structure (WBS) BOMs in SAP S/4HANA. Because the WBS and order BOMs are specific to the sales order documents and WBS elements in the project system, a separate transaction is provided for selecting the order and WBS BOMs.

The PDS transfer can be executed in interactive mode using Transaction /SAPAPO/ CURTOADV_CREATE or can be scheduled as a background job with a selection variant defined for this transaction. The transfer logs are displayed immediately in the interactive mode, and the transfer log can be viewed from the application logs in background mode via Transaction SLG1 by entering the "CIF" in the **Object** field.

In embedded PP-DS, Transaction /SAPAPO/CURTO_SIMU is used to select and display the PDS data. As shown in Figure 2.22, after executing the transaction, you enter the **Product Number**, **Location**, and **Planning Version** in the selection screen to filter the PDS selection. Additional selections are also possible by providing an **Order Number** in embedded PP-DS where the PDS is used.

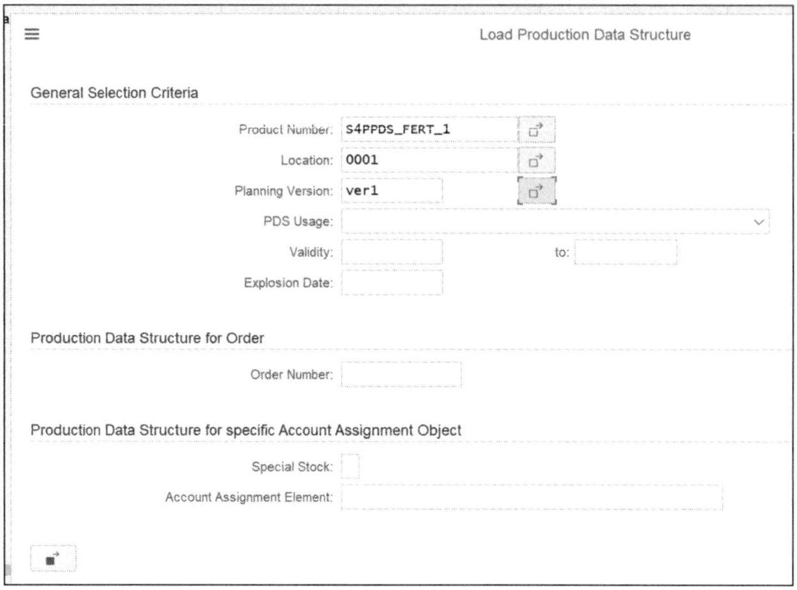

Figure 2.22 PP-DS PDS Selection Screen

In addition, for the PDSs that have a specific account assignment, such as a sales order, the **Special Stock** and **Account Assignment Element** fields can be used for selection with the sales document number. These sales documents should be transferred before the PDSs are generated with reference to them. Click the **Execute** button to display the list of PDSs selected per the selection criteria provided.

In the next screen, the list of PDSs is displayed, as shown in Figure 2.23. To view the details, double-click on the corresponding PDS in the list. In the list view on the first section of the screen, the basic details from the SAP S/4HANA production version are displayed. The validity dates and lot sizes are copied from the production version data.

The PDS details are shown in multiple sections and tabs, as shown in Figure 2.23:

- **Components**
  The **Components** tab shows all the material components that are transferred from the BOM linked to the production version. The header of the BOM is listed as an output component, and the components of the BOM are listed as input components.

- **Operations**
  The operations that are relevant to PP-DS are transferred to the **Operations** tab of

the PDS. For master recipes, the operations and the phases under the operations are also listed in the PDS **Operations** tab.

- **Activities**

  One operation can contain multiple activities, such as the setup, production, and tear-down activities. The activities for all the operations are listed under the **Activities** tab. The lot size dependency of the operation and also the base quantity defined in the operation in the routing are transferred to the individual activities in the PDS. The duration of the activities are calculated by the standard values for the activities defined in the routing operations.

- **Activity Relationships**

  The activities belonging to different operations form relationships in the PDS based on the relationships defined in the routing operations. For example, activities following a sequence will have an end–start relationship. The relationships of all the operations activities are listed under the **Activity Relationships** tab.

Figure 2.23 PDS Display in PP-DS

In embedded PP-DS, the PDS is only available for display, meaning the information can't be changed. For the data that originates from the SAP S/4HANA master data (e.g., the BOM, routing, and production version), the source of truth is the SAP S/4HANA master data and can't be changed in the PDS.

However, some of the PP-DS PDS data can be maintained in Transaction PDS_MAINT in SAP S/4HANA. Procurement priority of the PDS for the source of supply selection during the planning run or the costs associated with the individual PDSs can be maintained in Transaction PDS_MAINT. After such PP-DS PDS data is maintained via the maintenance transaction, the PDS needs to be retransferred to embedded PP-DS using Transaction CURTOADV_CREATE to reflect the changes there.

2.5.2   External Procurement Sources of Supply

In SAP S/4HANA, the sources of supply for external procurement include the following:

- **Purchase info records**
  Purchase info records in the SAP S/4HANA system represents the purchasing relationship of a material with its supplier. The purchase info record contains the information-specific procurement lead times, quantity restrictions, and pricing conditions, which are valid for the material and the vendor. The info records are defined at the purchasing organization level and can also have the plant level information. In addition, the info records can be classified as standard info records or subcontracting info records, among other types.

- **Scheduling agreements**
  Scheduling agreements are documents created at a plant level for procurement of material vendors on an agreed schedule. After the scheduling agreement is in place, the schedule line releases can be manually created, or the system can create schedule line releases via planning runs.

- **Contracts**
  Contracts or outline agreements are documents created with a negotiated value or quantity of a material and follow-on purchasing documents such as purchase orders or schedule lines created to initiate the procurement.

In embedded PP-DS, the purchase info records, contracts, and scheduling agreements are supported as external procurement relationships, which can be used by the PP-DS planning to determine the source of supply. The transfer of the external procurement relationships to embedded PP-DS requires creation and activation of integration models as of release SAP S/4HANA 1909. As discussed in Section 2.1, an integration model is created using Transaction CFM1.

You'll arrive at the **Create Integration Model** screen, as shown in Figure 2.24. Enter a name for the integration model in the **Model Name** field, and enter the **Logical System** and **APO Application** fields. The logical system in embedded PP-DS is the same as the logical system defined as the SAP S/4HANA system, as this is a self-system integration model generation. You may choose to create multiple integration models based on the plants or other filtering criteria (for object-specific selection, click the button ❶) to manage the volume and to trigger retransfers periodically to embedded PP-DS.

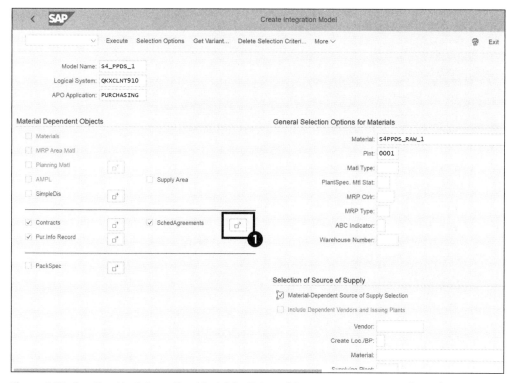

Figure 2.24 Creating the Integration Model for External Procurement Sources of Supply

Under **Material Dependent Objects**, select the checkboxes for the relevant source of supplies. In the **General Selection Options for Materials**, enter the selection criteria with which the sources should be selected. In the **Selection of Source of Supply** section, select the **Material-Dependent Source of Supply Selection** checkbox to filter out the source of supplies per the selection entered in the **General Selection Options for Materials** section. Click on the **Execute** button to trigger the selection for the integration model.

In the next screen, as shown in Figure 2.25, the sources of supplies are selected, and you can navigate to the selected sources by clicking on the count of the selected sources under the **No. Filter Objs** column. Click on the **Generate IM** button to complete the generation of the integration model.

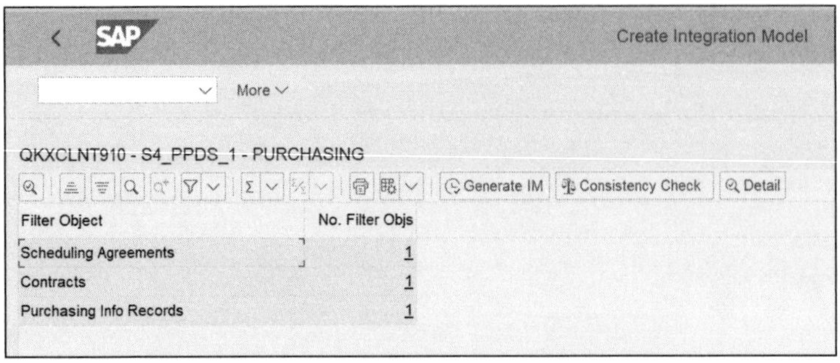

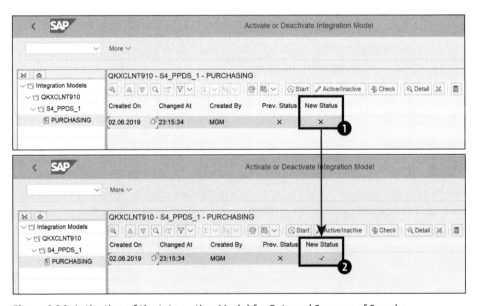

Figure 2.25 Integration Model Generation in SAP S/4HANA

After the integration model is generated, use Transaction CFM2 to activate the integration model (refer to Section 2.1.2). After entering the integration model details in the initial screen of Transaction CFM2, change the status of the integration model from inactive to active by clicking the **X** in the **New Status** box or by clicking on the **Active/Inactive** button, as shown in Figure 2.26 ❶. After the status is set as active ❷, click on the **Start** button to start the transfer of data to embedded PP-DS.

Figure 2.26 Activation of the Integration Model for External Sources of Supply

Queue failures may occur during this integration model activation. In interactive mode, where you execute the activation of the integration model as explained in this section, the queue errors are displayed on the screen. In background mode, the queues should be analyzed form the queue monitor to troubleshoot the errors and reprocess them. It's also possible to activate the integration model in background mode by using the ABAP program RIMODAC2. We'll cover queue monitoring and troubleshooting in Chapter 9 for administration of embedded PP-DS.

After the integration model is activated, and the queues are successfully processed, the external sources of supplies are available for PP-DS planning. These sources are called external procurement relationships in embedded PP-DS and can be accessed using Transaction /SAPAPO/PWBSRC1 or from the SAP menu path, **Logistics · Advanced Planning · Master Data · External Procurement Relationship · Display**.

The **Change External Procurement Relationship** screen appears, as shown in Figure 2.27. In the left part of the screen, the procurement relations are listed per the selection criteria and are grouped by the type of procurement relationship. Double-click on the item number of any procurement relationship to display the details of the specific source. In the **General Data** section, the organizational data (**Purchasing Org**, **Dest. Loc** [plant]) and the basic information (validity dates and source/destination locations) are displayed. The **Source Loc.** is the location of the vendor, and the **Dest. Loc.** is the location of the receiving plant.

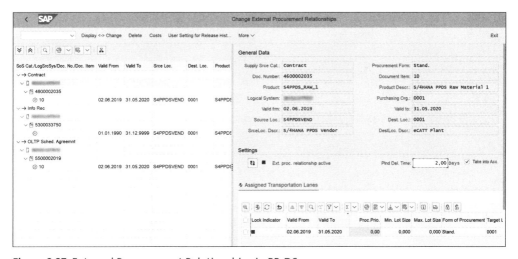

Figure 2.27 External Procurement Relationships in PP-DS

You can click on the **Display<->Change** button to make the sources editable. To overwrite the planned delivery time sent from SAP S/4HANA, the **Plnd Del. Time** is an editable field, and the source can be made active or inactive by selecting the **Ext proc. relationship active** checkbox under the **Settings** section.

As you can see in Figure 2.27, there is a **Assigned Transportation Lanes** sequence in the sources. Transportation lanes are master data generated by the system during the transfer of external procurement sources to embedded PP-DS and are assigned to the corresponding products. The procurement parameters also can be maintained at the transportation lane, and a mode of transport can be assigned to the transportation lane to ensure that the exact dates are calculated during planning for the procurement and transportation of materials from the vendor to the receiving plants.

You can execute Transaction /SAPAPO/TL1 to display or change the transportation lanes. In the selection screen of this transaction, enter the **Model Name** "000", which is the active PP-DS model, and all the transportation lanes integrated via the source of supply integration model are always created in the 000 model. In addition, enter the **Start Location** and **Dest. Location**, as shown in Figure 2.28.

Figure 2.28 Transportation Lanes in PP-DS: Selection Screen

Choose **Display** or **Change**, depending on the action you want to perform, and in the next screen, the details of the transportation lane are displayed. As shown in Figure 2.29, the products and the procurement relationships using the same transportation lanes are listed in the top section of the screen ❶. Selecting one of the sources will display the details of the procurement on the right side of the screen; in change mode, the information specific to PP-DS can be edited and isn't transferred back to SAP S/4HANA.

A means of transport, such as rail, truck, or air, and the corresponding data can be maintained by creating a new means of transport under the **Means of Transport** section ❷, where the means of transport common to all products in the transportation lane are located. It's also possible to define multiple means of transport and assign specific means to specific products ❸.

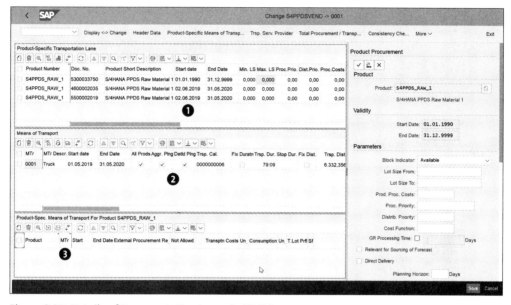

Figure 2.29 Details of Transportation Lanes in PP-DS

2.6   Classes and Characteristics

In this section, we'll discuss the usage of classes and characteristics in embedded PP-DS as well as how the classes and characteristics are maintained in the system.

A characteristic denotes a specific attribute of a product, such as color, capacity, usage, and so on. Characteristics that define a set of attributes of a product are grouped under a class.

In the PP-DS planning, there are two ways to use the classification system:

- **Characteristics dependent planning (CDP)**
  CDP is used in in-house manufacturing processes to match the characteristics of the demand element, such as sales order or dependent demand, to a supply element that has the same characteristics value assignment (also called characteristics valuation). The CDP scenario supports both make-to-stock (MTS) and make-to-order (MTO) planning scenarios.

- **Variant configuration (VC)**
  VC is used for complex configurable products mainly in MTO scenarios where the specification of the product in the sales order drives the manufacturing processes.

Either in CDP or VC scenarios, the classes and characteristics play the major role in transferring the configuration of the product from the demand level to the manufacturing level. Class types are defined in the SAP S/4HANA system to allow them to be used in a specific scenario. We'll cover the configuration schema (CDP vs. VC) of the PP-DS system in Chapter 3 when we discuss configuration.

You can execute Transaction CT04 to create, change, and delete characteristics master data, as shown in Figure 2.30.

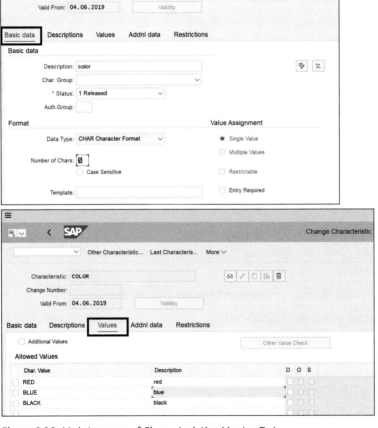

Figure 2.30 Maintenance of Characteristics Master Data

The basic data fields, such as the **Description** and **Status** of the class, are maintained in the **Basic data** tab, and the allowed values for this characteristic can be maintained in the **Values** tab. For complex configuration scenarios, a cross-reference to a specific table reference can be done in the **Addnl data** tab.

Classes are created using Transaction CL01 and can be maintained from Transaction CL02. The characteristics are assigned to the class.

Class of type 300 is used in VC scenarios, and the same is available for PP-DS in the VC scenario. There is no need to create an integration model for making the class of type 300 to be available for PP-DS. The class assignment to the material in the VC scenario is done in the SAP S/4HANA material master in the classification view, and the same can be displayed in embedded PP-DS when the material is marked for advanced planning. As shown in Figure 2.31, you can display the product master data in embedded PP-DS using Transaction /SAPAPO/MAT1.

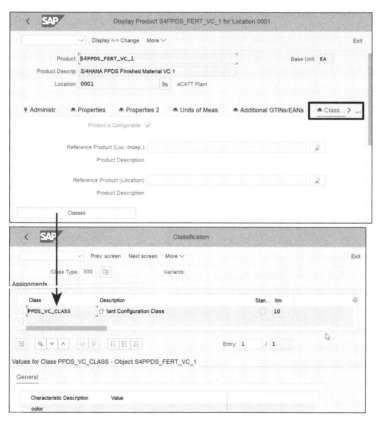

Figure 2.31 Display of Classification Data in the PP-DS Product Master

From the **Classification** tab, click on the **Classes** button to display the classes assigned to the material master, which is visible to PP-DS. Here, you can see **Class Type 300**.

When the configuration schema is set to CDP in embedded PP-DS, class types 023 (batch class) and 300 (variant class) need to be integrated to embedded PP-DS. This will create a new class with type 400 (CDP class) with the same class name in embedded PP-DS.

To integrate the classes of type 023 and 300 using an integration model, follow these steps:

1. Define an organizational area in the Customizing Transaction O1CL. In this transaction, select the entry for **MARA**, and select the **Organizational Areas** folder, as shown in Figure 2.32. Make entries for the relevant class types and enter an organizational area (in the **O** column). Organizational area can be any character with one-character length. This organizational area is the selection criteria available for the integration model generation for transferring the class data to PP-DS for CDP.

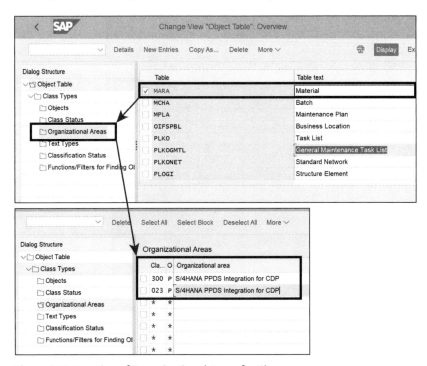

Figure 2.32 Creation of Organizational Areas for Classes

2. As shown in Figure 2.33, enter the organizational area information in the class master data, which needs to be transferred to PP-DS for CDP. This can be performed from the transaction for class maintenance—Transaction CLO2. Enter the **Organizational area** under the **Basic data** tab. In addition, enter the organizational area in the **Char.** (characteristics assignment) tab in the class master data as well.

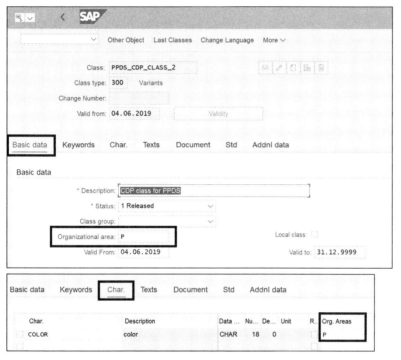

Figure 2.33 Maintenance of Organizational Area Data in Class Master Data

3. Finally, create an integration model with the selection of classes and characteristics, and then activate the integration model. First, access the **Create Integration Model** screen by executing Transaction CFM1, as shown in Figure 2.34.

4. Select **Classes/Charact** under the **Material Independent Objects**, and in the object-specific selection, enter the **Org.area ind,** which is assigned to the classes. Activate the integration model to transfer the classes to embedded PP-DS (see Section 2.1.2).

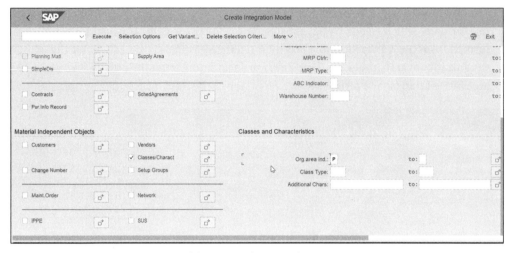

Figure 2.34 Integration Model Creation for CDP Classes

After the integration model is activated, it will create a class of type 400 (CDP class) in embedded PP-DS with the same class name.

2.7   Summary

In this chapter, we covered the basic and commonly used master data objects in embedded PP-DS. In addition, we covered the various methods to integrate the different master data objects from SAP S/4HANA to embedded PP-DS.

The material master and resource masters are transferred by simply activating the **Advanced Planning** checkbox in the master data in SAP S/4HANA. For locations and PDSs, the ABAP programs are executed to initiate the transfer of the data to embedded PP-DS. For external procurement, integration models need to be created and activated to transfer the master data for source supplies, such as purchase info records, scheduling agreements, and contracts, as well as classes used in the CDP scenario.

Other master data objects are specific to certain scenarios such as setup groups, setup matrix, interchangeability groups, and so on. We'll cover the details of these master data objects in Chapter 8 where we discuss the advanced PP-DS capabilities.

In the next chapter, we'll cover the configuration for setting up and operating embedded PP-DS.

Chapter 3
Configuration

*To get started using PP-DS, you first need to configure it in your
SAP S/4HANA system per your organization's requirements. You'll get
the step-by-step instructions to do so in this chapter, including both
basic and advanced settings.*

In this chapter, we'll discuss the configuration required to activate and operate PP-DS in SAP S/4HANA (embedded PP-DS). We'll start with the basic prerequisites for setting up SAP liveCache and then cover the detailed steps required to activate embedded PP-DS.

Though the PP-DS is now part of the SAP S/4HANA core, it requires the interface configured using the core interface (CIF) framework to transfer certain master data objects and transaction data. We'll cover the details of the CIF configuration required for working with embedded PP-DS.

All the planning features, functionalities, and tools depend on the configuration or Customizing settings made in the system. Apart from covering the basic configurations for operating the PP-DS system, we'll also cover the Customizing settings behind the commonly used functionalities and features.

3.1 Activating PP-DS in SAP S/4HANA

In the SAP S/4HANA system, the PP-DS functionality isn't activated in the standard delivered software. Explicit activation of the PP-DS functionality is done in the configuration in the SAP S/4HANA system. Certain SAP Fiori apps that are relevant to the PP-DS functionality are usable only within the activation of PP-DS.

Activating PP-DS will enable all advanced planning features as well as the following SAP Fiori apps:

- Monitor Capacity Utilization
- Production Scheduling Board
- Create Optimal Order for Shipment

There are technical prerequisites for activating PP-DS in the SAP S/4HANA system, and we'll cover them at a high level as these activities are related to the installation of the SAP liveCache application software and setting up the database to enable the SAP liveCache connections. Appendix A provides the notes to the detailed setup guide for the integrated SAP liveCache in an SAP HANA database.

The technical prerequisites are as follows:

- Installation of SAP liveCache in the SAP HANA database
- Creation of SAP liveCache connections and enabled execution of SAP liveCache procedures
- Execution of initialization reports /SAPAPO/OM_LIVECACHE_SETUP_S4H or reports SLCA_INIT_FOLLOW_UP and /SAPAPO/OM_CREATE_LC_TABLES to prepare the SAP liveCache and create all the required database tables
- Setup of the remote function call (RFC) connection for all the clients in the SAP S/4HANA system that are relevant for SAP liveCache

After the technical prerequisites are performed, execute Transaction /SAPAPO/OM13 to do a basic health check on SAP liveCache. As shown in Figure 3.1, the **Checks** tab shows the result of the individual checks, and the information on the warnings and errors can be displayed by clicking on the information button next to them.

Execute Transaction /SAPAPO/OM03 in the system to test the SAP liveCache, and you should see a success message.

The next step is to activate PP-DS in Customizing. To perform this, execute Transaction SPRO, and then follow the menu path, **SAP Customizing Implementation Guide • Advanced Planning • Basic Settings • Activate Advanced Planning and Scheduling • Activate Advanced Planning and Scheduling**.

As shown in Figure 3.2, select the **Activate Advanced Planning and Scheduling** checkbox, and click the **Save** button. This will complete the activation of the PP-DS advanced planning features in the SAP S/4HANA system.

After advanced planning is activated, you can set up the basic settings as explained in the next section of this chapter.

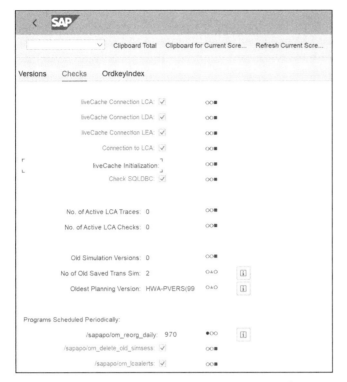

Figure 3.1 SAP liveCache Health Check Report in SAP S/4HANA

Figure 3.2 Activation of PP-DS in SAP S/4HANA

3.2   Basic Settings for Embedded PP-DS

In this section, we'll cover the basic settings required to set-up embedded PP-DS. These settings aren't specific to any functionality or features, but are required to execute any PP-DS functions in the SAP S/4HANA system.

3.2.1   Model Version Management

In embedded PP-DS, similar to the SAP Advanced Planning and Optimization (SAP APO) system, all the master data objects are assigned to the supply chain model. All the master data elements should be assigned to a model for the system to consider this data in the planning and scheduling functions and tools.

Embedded PP-DS only supports the model 000, which is the default active model in the system. All the master data integrated from SAP S/4HANA using the transfer programs, **Advanced Planning** checkboxes, or integration model are always assigned to the model 000.

The version is a subsection of the model. There can be multiple versions created under the model 000 in embedded PP-DS. The 000 version is the active version in PP-DS. Other versions can be created for carrying out planning simulation with changed master data settings, if required.

As part of the embedded PP-DS setup, the model and version must be created in the system. To create a model, you can use Transaction /SAPAPO/MVM or use the SAP menu path, **Logistics • Advanced Planning • Master Data • Planning Version Management • Model and Version Management**.

You'll arrive at the **Model and Version Management** screen, as shown in Figure 3.3. Click on the **Create** button, and select **Model**. Enter the model **Name** as "000", enter a description for the model (here, "Active Version"), and click on the **Create and Save** button to save the model.

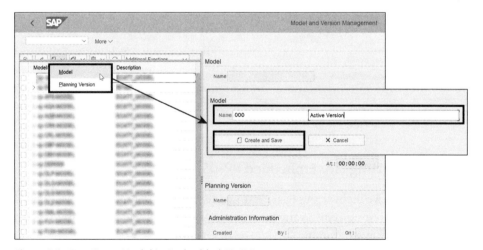

Figure 3.3 Creating a Model in Embedded PP-DS

After the model is created, the next step is to create the planning version as 000, which is the active version under the active model 000. To do so, click the **Create** button again, and select **Planning Version**. As shown in Figure 3.4, create the planning version "000", and enter a description for the version.

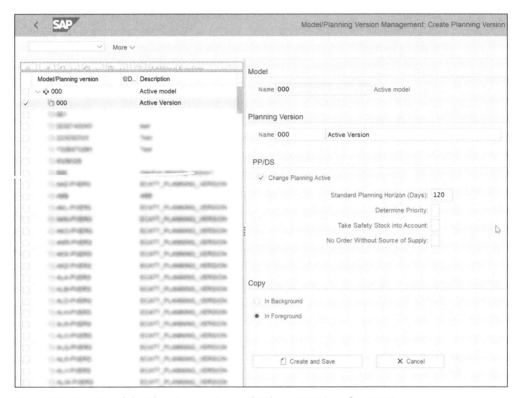

Figure 3.4 Creation of the Planning Version and Relevant Settings for PP-DS

Select the **Change Planning Active** checkbox, and make the following key settings:

- **Standard Planning Horizon (Days)**
  The PP-DS horizon in days defines the number of calendar days within which the PP-DS system is allowed to create, change, and delete procurement proposals during a planning run execution. Beyond the PP-DS horizon, it's possible to create procurement proposals manually using the PP-DS transactions. There is no option to set any material-specific planning horizon in embedded PP-DS, and all the advanced planning products will use the PP-DS horizon defined in the planning version settings.

- **Determine Priority**

  In PP-DS, it's possible to assign priorities to the procurement proposals (e.g., planned orders). These order priorities are used in PP-DS functions such as scheduling heuristics to reduce the delays in manufacturing an order that has higher priority. Click on the value help button in the **Determine Priority** field, and you'll see the following options:

  - **In make to order from sales order otherwise from product**
    With this setting, the priority of the orders that are created to cover a sales order requirement is derived from the priority assigned to the sales order. If the requirement element isn't a sales order, the priority is derived from the value maintained in the product master.

  - **Always adopt from requirement**
    With this setting, the priority of the order created by PP-DS is always derived from the requirement element such as sales orders or orders belonging to higher level planned orders to which the particular order is linked. This linkage of orders in PP-DS is called *pegging*. Planned independent requirements (PIRs) or forecast elements don't have any priorities assigned to them, so no priority is assigned to orders pegged to such requirement elements. It's also possible that one order is pegged to multiple requirements; in that case, a planning algorithm can be executed to reprioritize the orders. We'll cover the details of this planning algorithm (heuristics) in Chapter 5.

  - **Always adopt from the product**
    With this setting, the orders will always derive the priority from the product master, irrespective of the priority assigned to the requirement element.

> **Note**
>
> The priorities in PP-DS are defined from numbers 0–255, with 1 as the highest priority. The priority 0 is equal to the least priority 255.

- **Take Safety Stock into Account**

  Safety stock is the requirement element used in the plan to cover any unplanned demand that may result in a stock-out situation. PP-DS supports safety stocks in planning. Click on the value help button in the **Take Safety Stock into Account** to see the following options:

- **Don't Consider Safety Stock**
  The safety stock requirements aren't considered in PP-DS, and no safety stock specific alerts are created in PP-DS.

- **Consider Virtual Safety Stock Elements**
  In the SAP S/4HANA system, the safety stocks are only virtual elements, which means that the safety stock elements aren't created as orders in SAP liveCache. Therefore, these safety stock elements are used only in calculation of the net requirements and aren't pegged to an order or a receipt element.

- **No Order Without Source of Supply**
  In PP-DS, when orders are created, the source of supply, such as a production data structure (PDS) or an external procurement relationship (e.g., info records), is assigned to the orders. If there are no suitable sources of supply found, the orders can still be created, but the order dates can't be correct as the source of supply determines the duration it takes to procure or produce a material. In the planning version, you can define whether you want to create orders when no suitable source of supply is available or how the system should react when no source of supply is determined. In this field, click on the value help to select from the following options:

  - (Blank) **Order Without Source of Supply Allowed**
  - **E - No Order Without Source of Supply with In-House Production**
  - **F - No Order Without Source of Supply with External Procurement**
  - **X - No Order Without Source of Supply Generally**

Then click the **Create and Save** button to create the planning version.

The **Change Planning Active** option is required for using the PP-DS functions productively. When there is a planning-relevant change, such as creation, change, or deletion of any receipt or requirement data, or a planning-relevant master data is produced in the system, the system reacts according to the planning procedures customized and assigned to the product master. We'll cover the details of the planning procedure in Section 3.4.

3.2.2   Integration Settings

In the SAP S/4HANA system, to enable the transfer of master data and transaction data from SAP S/4HANA to embedded PP-DS and vice versa, you must make the following basic CIF settings, which we'll discuss in this section:

- Activate the business transfer event (BTE) indicator.
- Create a system landscape.
- Set up CIF user parameters.
- Activate postprocessing.
- Register the CIF queues.

Activate the Business Transfer Events Indicators

Changes to master data and transaction data in SAP S/4HANA that need to be transferred to embedded PP-DS via online transfer without executing an explicit job or program to transfer the data uses the BTE framework. In the embedded PP-DS, the BTE indicators new dimension integration (NDI) and new dimension-advanced planning and optimization (ND-APO) need to be activated for enabling the online transfer of data.

To enable these BTE indicators, execute Transaction BF11 (Change View "BTE Application Indicator"), and set the application active indicator for the applications **ND-APO** and **NDI** by checking the corresponding boxes in the **A** column, as shown in Figure 3.5.

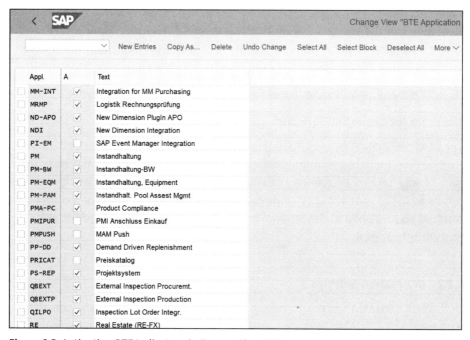

Figure 3.5 Activating BTE Indicators in Transaction BF11

Create System Landscape

In SAP S/4HANA, setting the landscape for the transfer of data between SAP S/4HANA and embedded PP-DS is achieved via the CIF framework. The CIF works based on the definition of the logical system, which represents the system ID of the SAP S/4HANA system and the client in which the transactions are performed.

You can define the logical system via the Customizing menu path, **SAP IMG Menu • Integration with Other SAP Components • Advanced Planning and Optimization • Basic Settings for Setting Up the System Landscape • Name Logical System**. You'll arrive at the screen shown in Figure 3.6, where you can define a **Name** for the logical system, and click on the **Save** button to save the data.

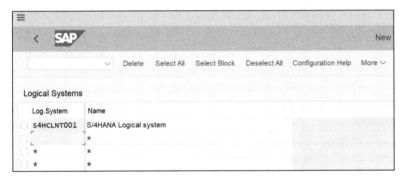

Figure 3.6 Defining the Logical System for the CIF

After the logical system is defined, it must be assigned to the client to which it corresponds. To assign the logical system to the client, use the menu path, **SAP IMG Menu • Integration with Other SAP Components • Advanced Planning and Optimization • Basic Settings for Setting Up the System Landscape • Assign Logical System to a Client**. Then, link the client to the defined logical system by entering the client name in the **Client** field and the logical system defined in the previous step in the **Logical system** field, as shown in Figure 3.7.

> **Tip**
> There are other SAP S/4HANA applications that require the usage of logical systems, so if there is already a logical system defined in the SAP S/4HANA system for the system ID assigned to the client, that logical system can be used for the CIF as well.

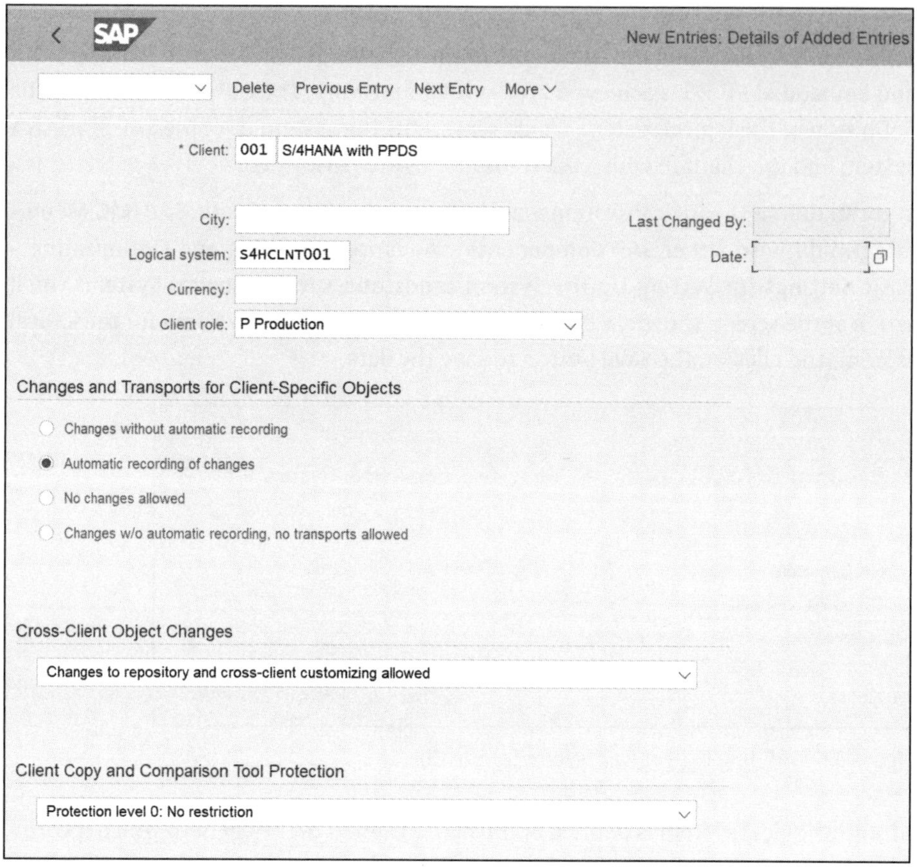

Figure 3.7 Assigning a Logical System to the Client

When data is transferred between SAP S/4HANA and embedded PP-DS, the system needs to recognize the software version of PP-DS in SAP S/4HANA for technical reasons. To define this, use the Customizing menu path, **SAP IMG Menu · Integration with Other SAP Components · Advanced Planning and Optimization · Basic Settings for Setting Up the System Landscape · Specify APO Release**. Here, enter the **Log.System** as the SAP S/4HANA logical system defined, **Syst.Type** as "SAP_APO", and **Release** as "713", as shown in Figure 3.8.

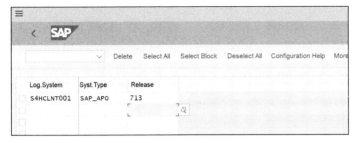

Figure 3.8 Specifying SAP APO Release for Embedded PP-DS in the CIF

Note

The SAP S/4HANA system can also act as an ERP system alongside a standalone SAP APO system; in that case, the Customizing settings need to be maintained for the standalone SAP APO system. In addition, for SAP SCM applications such as SAP Transportation Management (SAP TM) and SAP Extended Warehouse Management (SAP EWM), separate entries with the corresponding system details need to be maintained.

Set Up the Core Interface User Parameters

User settings in the CIF Customizing define how the data transfer is handled in terms of activating or deactivating the data transfer for users, the level of logging for the data transfer, and technical settings to stop the execution of the transfer for debugging purposes.

To define the user settings, use the Customizing menu path, **SAP IMG Menu · Integration with Other SAP Components · Advanced Planning and Optimization · Basic Settings for Data Transfer · Set User Parameters**. Click on the **New Entries** button, and you'll arrive at the screen shown in Figure 3.9.

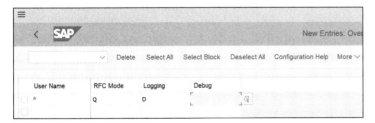

Figure 3.9 User Settings for CIF in Embedded PP-DS

There is no need to maintain the user settings for all user names in the SAP S/4HANA system. A generic wild card entry (*) can be made instead, as shown in Figure 3.9. Maintain the **RFC Mode** as "Q", which activates the transfer of data using the queued RFC (qRFC) protocol via the defined RFC destinations. For embedded PP-DS, the RFC destination will point to itself (self-system). The **Logging** can be set to the required level of logging from the following available options:

- **[blank] (no logging)**
  No logs are written to the application logs for the transfers.

- **X (normal)**
  Only the number of records is recorded in the log.

- **D (detailed)**
  The number of records as well as the content of the data are logged.

The **Debug** setting can be used only for troubleshooting any problems in the data transfers; it should be switched off otherwise.

[»]

Note

The CIF settings from SAP S/4HANA are maintained under the Customizing menu path, **SAP IMG Menu • Integration with Other SAP Components • Advanced Planning and Optimization**. The settings for embedded PP-DS are maintained under the Customizing menu path, **SAP IMG Menu • Advanced Planning • Integration via Core Interface**.

Activate Postprocessing

From embedded PP-DS, it's recommended to activate the postprocessing so that any if any transaction data transferred between SAP S/4HANA and embedded PP-DS fails for any reason, the data is logged in the Post Processing Framework (PPF) for reprocessing instead of the queues going into error mode and causing backed up queues.

To activate postprocessing, use Transaction /SAPAPO/C2 under embedded PP-DS CIF Customizing, and select **1 Postprocessing for Errors, No splitting of LUWs** in the **Err. Hndlg** column for the corresponding SAP S/4HANA logical system, as shown in Figure 3.10.

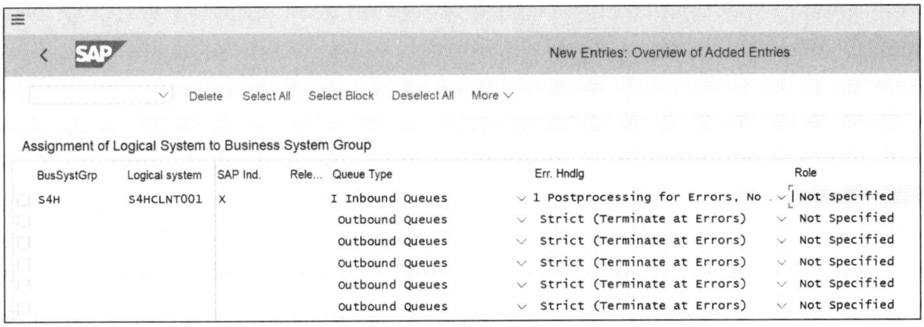

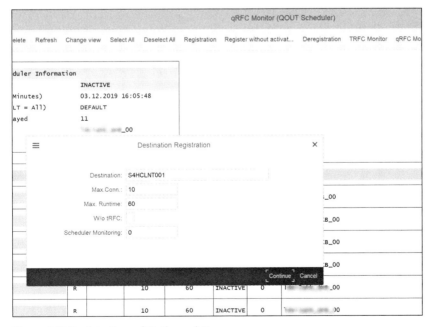

Figure 3.10 PP-DS CIF Settings: Activating Postprocessing

Register the Core Interface Queues

The technical activation of queue processing can be performed from Transaction SMQS (QOUT Scheduler) and Transaction SMQR (QIN Scheduler). Activation of the inbound and outbound queue schedulers is required for the automatic processing of the CIF queues.

To register the outbound queues, execute Transaction SMQS, and click on the **Registration** button to arrive at the screen shown in Figure 3.11.

Figure 3.11 Registration of Outbound Queues

Here, enter the **Destination** as the logical system defined for the SAP S/4HANA system. The maximum connection (**Max.Conn**) defines the number of parallel processes the outbound scheduler can use in the system and is defaulted to **10**. The maximum runtime (**Max. Runtime**) defines the number of seconds the outbound scheduler runs when it's activated and is defaulted to **60**. Click on the **Continue** button. This completes the registration of outbound queues.

To register the inbound queues, execute Transaction SMQR, and click on the **Registration** button. This will take you to the screen shown in Figure 3.12. Because all the queue names start with "CF", enter the value "CF*" in the **Queue name** field to find the queue names. The **Mode** field is defaulted to value **D** representing that the queues are processed in the system using dialog work processes. The **Max. Runtime** is the number of seconds the queue scheduler is active and is set at **30** by default. If there is a queue failure due to communication issues, for example, the value defined in the **Attempts** field (defaulted to **10**) determines how many times the system tries to execute the queue. Between each retry, the system will wait for the number seconds defined in the **Pause** field (defaulted to **120**). Click on the **Continue** button to complete the registration of the inbound queues.

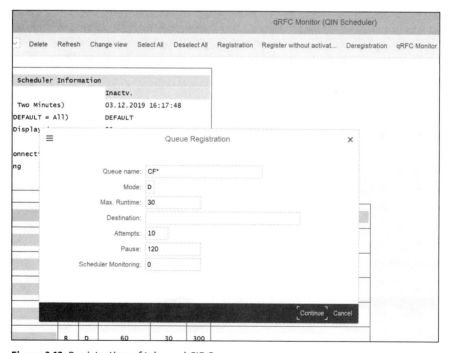

Figure 3.12 Registration of Inbound CIF Queues

3.2.3   Transaction Data Transfer

In embedded PP-DS, the system internally uses the CIF framework for transferring the transaction data between SAP S/4HANA and embedded PP-DS, which is why the basic CIF settings were required to be set up as detailed in the previous section.

However, unlike the SAP APO system integration, there is no need to create an integration model for the commonly used transaction data for embedded PP-DS. The activation of the transaction data transfer is performed as a Customizing setting.

To activate the transfer of transaction data, use the Customizing menu path, **SAP IMG Menu · Advanced Planning · Basic Settings · Settings for Data Transfer**. You'll arrive at the screen shown in Figure 3.13, where you can select all the transaction data objects that need to be transferred between SAP S/4HANA and embedded PP-DS and then click the **Save** button.

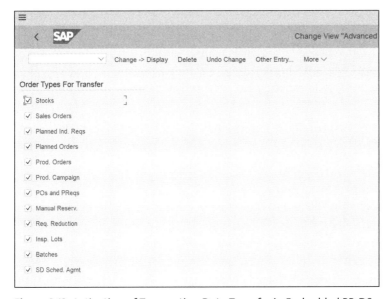

Figure 3.13 Activation of Transaction Data Transfer in Embedded PP-DS

Note

The activation of the transaction data transfers along with the activation of the **Advanced Planning** checkbox in the material master determine which transaction data is automatically transferred between SAP S/4HANA and embedded PP-DS.

Material-independent transaction data, such as plant maintenance orders, requires an integration model creation and activation to transfer the data from SAP S/4HANA to embedded PP-DS.

3.2.4   Configuration Schema of the PP-DS System

Configurable materials have classes and characteristics assigned that can be configured to specify product specifications or characteristics when sales orders are entered or production orders are created.

In the material master, the materials are marked as configurable and the corresponding classes and characteristics are assigned. For the variant configuration (VC) scenario, a configuration profile is created and assigned to the material.

Example

A motorcycle with different body styles, engine capacities, and colors can be modeled as a configurable material so that at the time of order entry, the specific values for the characteristics (body style, capacity, and color) are selected.

Embedded PP-DS supports configuration schemas similar to the SAP APO system. As we touched on in Chapter 2, Section 2.6, the supported configuration schema settings are as follows:

- **Characteristics-dependent planning (CDP)**
  CDP is used in scenarios where the requirements, such as sales orders or PIRs, have the configuration values, and the system matches the configuration characteristics values to an existing supply element (e.g., planned order or production order) during planning. The system can also create a new receipt with the corresponding classification information to fulfill a demand. CDP can be used in make-to-stock (MTS) or make-to-order (MTO) scenarios. The CDP scenario uses class type 400 in PP-DS. Class types 300 and 023 are used in SAP S/4HANA, and they need to be transferred to embedded PP-DS via an integration model. Upon transfer of these classes, class type 400 is created in embedded PP-DS.

- **Variant configuration (VC)**
  VC is used in MTO scenarios, where the sales orders are created in SAP S/4HANA with the product configuration (assigned values for characteristics values), and the

same is transferred to embedded PP-DS. Receipt elements, such as planned orders, are generated with the characteristics value in embedded PP-DS during the planning process.

The configuration schema for embedded PP-DS is set via the configuration menu path, **SAP IMG Menu · Advanced Planning · Basic Settings · Define Configuration Schema (CDP or Variant Configuration)**.

Select the required **Settings**, as shown in Figure 3.14. The configuration schema can be changed at any time, but it's not recommended to switch the schema after transferring data from SAP S/4HANA to embedded PP-DS as this may lead to data inconsistencies with respect to the classification system data in embedded PP-DS.

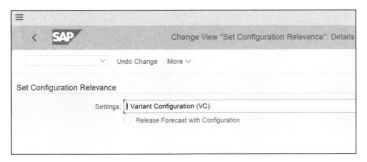

Figure 3.14 Setting Up the Configuration Schema in Embedded PP-DS

3.2.5   Global Parameters and Default Values

PP-DS global parameters and default values are the parameters used by the PP-DS system when there is no overriding setting made in the master data or in the individual planning and scheduling tools. These parameters are delivered by default and can be changed depending on the usage of the PP-DS system. In this section, we'll cover some of the important settings and the significance of these settings in the PP-DS system.

You can execute Transaction /SAPAPO/RRPCUST1 or follow the Customizing menu path, **SAP IMG Menu · Advanced Planning · Global Settings · Maintain Global Parameters and Defaults**, to display and change the default delivered settings in the PP-DS global settings. The PP-DS global parameters are displayed in Figure 3.15.

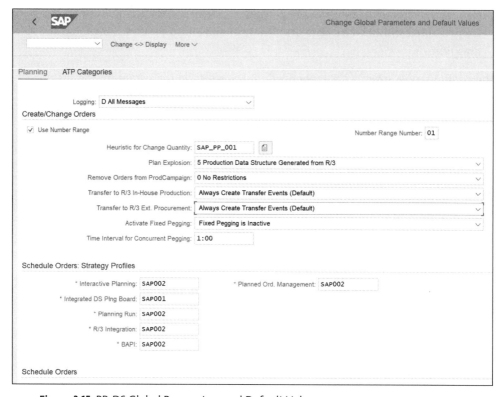

Figure 3.15 PP-DS Global Parameters and Default Values

Logging determines the level of information generated in the application logs from the PP-DS planning and scheduling tools. There are three options available:

- **No logging**
- **N Only Errors Terminations and Warnings**
- **D All Messages**

The **N Only Errors Terminations and Warnings** option is recommended to avoid the log tables getting filled with PP-DS application log data quickly and requiring frequent reorganization jobs to delete the old log messages. However, the logging level can be changed from the planning tools to override this global setting.

The **Use Number Range** checkbox makes the PP-DS system use a specific number range for the orders generated in the PP-DS transactions that aren't yet synced up with SAP S/4HANA. If the PP-DS number range isn't selected, the system will generate receipt elements without any external number, which means you can't see an explicit order number in the PP-DS transactions. After the data is saved, the system syncs this order number with the SAP S/4HANA order number and updates the corresponding transaction screens.

In embedded PP-DS, only the PDS is available as the source of supply for in-house manufacturing orders, so the value **5 Production Data Structure Generated from R/3** is set by default for the **Plan Explosion.**

The settings for the **Transfer to R/3 In-House Production** and **Transfer to R/3 Ext. Procurement** determine the timings of the transfer of the PP-DS orders to SAP S/4HANA when an order is created or changed in embedded PP-DS. The available options are as follows:

- **Do Not Create Transfer Events**
  With this setting, the PP-DS orders aren't transferred to SAP S/4HANA. For in-house production planned orders, if the orders aren't available in SAP S/4HANA, no further planning of dependent components that are not set with advanced planning is possible in SAP S/4HANA.

- **Create Transfer Events from Conversion Indicator**
  With this setting, the orders are only transferred to embedded PP-DS when the conversion indicator is set to the order. For in-house production, the conversion indicator means the planned order will be converted to a production order; for external procurement, the purchase requisitions will be converted to purchase orders after the conversion indicator is set. Until the order is set with the conversion checkbox, it's not available in SAP S/4HANA for planning any lower level components that aren't advanced planned.

- **Always Create Transfer Events (Default)**
  This default setting is commonly used in planning and scheduling scenarios. With this setting, the planned orders and purchase requisitions created in embedded PP-DS are required to be available in SAP S/4HANA. This option will always transfer the orders to SAP S/4HANA when the orders are created or changed.

Embedded PP-DS supports both dynamic and fixed pegging. Pegging is the relationship created between a receipt element, such as stocks, planned/production orders, purchase requisitions, and so on, and a requirement element, such as sales orders, PIRs, and so on. The system always creates a pegging relationship to dynamically link a receipt and requirement element, which is called dynamic pegging.

With dynamic pegging, when the planning situation changes, the requirement element can be pegged to a new receipt element other than the originally pegged element if the original pegged element is no longer available. These dynamic pegging relationships can be changed to fixed pegging relationships in the PP-DS system. After a fixed pegging relationship is in place, the original pegging is retained as long as the supply element isn't deleted, irrespective of the planning situation.

When the supply elements, such as planned orders and purchase requisitions, are fixed pegged to the requirement element and the order is converted to production orders or purchase orders, the fixed pegging relationships are lost. If you want the fixed pegging to be retained even after the order conversion, set the **Activate Fixed Pegging** (**Retain Fixed Pegging for Product on Document Change**) accordingly. This setting can be overridden with the material master setting. You can change this setting in the material master by using Transaction MM02 for the material and plant and then navigating to the **Advanced Planning** tab, as shown in Figure 3.16.

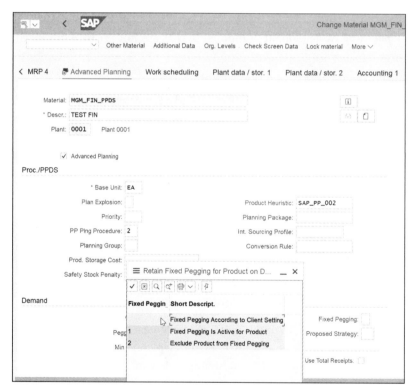

Figure 3.16 Material Level Fixed Pegging Setting in the Advanced Planning View

A strategy profile is a collection of settings regarding how an order will be scheduled when it's created, changed, or scheduled using PP-DS planning and scheduling tools.

The individual planning and scheduling tools can have their own strategy profiles when you use those tools. But in the PP-DS global parameters under the **Schedule Orders: Strategy Profiles** section (refer to Figure 3.15), the default strategy profiles are maintained so that they can be used by default if the specific planning or scheduling tool or transaction doesn't have an assigned strategy profile. In addition, the background processes, such as transferring an order from SAP S/4HANA to embedded PP-DS, use these default strategies set in this Customizing.

Let's move on to the **ATP Categories** tab in the PP-DS global settings and defaults. These settings map SAP S/4HANA-specific available-to-promise (ATP) elements (receipt and requirement) to the PP-DS specific elements. For example, a planned order is represented as category "PA" in SAP S/4HANA, and the same planned order, depending on if it's firmed or ATP confirmed, will have a corresponding category in embedded PP-DS.

As shown in Figure 3.17, for certain categories, such as planned orders and purchase requisitions, the default delivered category mapping can't be changed, but for some elements, it's possible to map a different ATP category in embedded PP-DS other than the standard delivered mapping. In most cases, however, the standard delivered ATP category mapping is enough to execute the planning in embedded PP-DS.

Figure 3.17 ATP Categories in PP-DS Global Settings and Defaults

Tip

The detailed mapping of the PP-DS and SAP S/4HANA ATP category mapping can be displayed from the /SAPAPO/V_ATP03 view via Transaction SM30.

3.2.6   Master Data Settings

In embedded PP-DS, for master data specific to PP-DS, it's possible to maintain the configuration settings that can be used by the integrated master data objects. However, because embedded PP-DS is an integrated system, most of the values for the master data fields are read or transferred from SAP S/4HANA to embedded PP-DS, and the settings available within embedded PP-DS are very limited.

Activate for Change Documents

Master data objects such as locations, transportation lanes, and quota arrangements, which also can be maintained in the PP-DS transactions, can be activated for change documents. The activation of the change documents for these master data objects will log every change made.

To activate the change documents in embedded PP-DS for such master data objects, you can use the Customizing menu path, **SAP IMG Menu · Advanced Planning · Master Data · Location · Activate Change Documents**. You'll arrive at the screen shown in Figure 3.18, where you select the checkboxes for the elements under the location master data, such as **Header Data**, **Mapping**, **Location Text**, and **Location Address**. The change documents can be activated for other master data objects as well, such as the transportation lanes and quota arrangements.

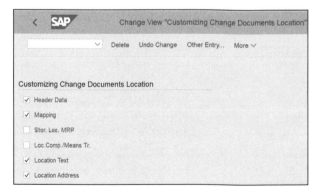

Figure 3.18 Activation of Change Documents for Location Master Data in PP-DS

Create the Planner

The product master in PP-DS includes the reference to the planner who is responsible for planning a specific product location displayed in the administration view of the product location master. This planner corresponds to the material requirements planning (MRP) controller in SAP S/4HANA master data. The customizing data of the MRP controllers isn't transferred to embedded PP-DS. If you want to use the planner field in the PP-DS transactions, the value help F4 for this field doesn't show the list of available MRP controllers.

You can create the person responsible in PP-DS Customizing under the Customizing menu path, **SAP IMG Menu · Advanced Planning · Master Data · Specify Person Responsible (Planner)**. On the screen that appears, click the **New Entries** button, as shown in Figure 3.19, to arrive at the screen where you can maintain entries corresponding to the MRP controllers in SAP S/4HANA. Select the **Prod. Planner** checkbox to denote that the entry being created is for a production planner, enter a name for the production planner in the **Name** field, and enter a description of the name or the full name of the production planner in the **Full name** field.

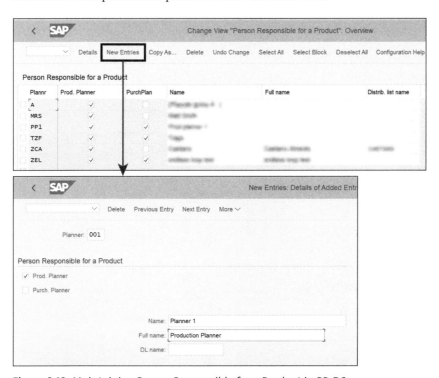

Figure 3.19 Maintaining Person Responsible for a Product in PP-DS

Tip

Even without maintaining the PP-DS person responsible, the **Planner** field in the PP-DS transactions can be used, and the products associated can be found using the corresponding **MRP Controller** value defined in the material master. However, the MRP controllers aren't visible in the value help F4 for the **Planner** field in PP-DS transactions where this field is available as a selection option.

Maintain Transportation Mode

In the transportation lane master data, you can maintain the transportation mode (road, rail, or air) and also the means of transport (a specific transportation provider). Either way, the lead times for the transportation are maintained in the master data of the transportation lane itself from Transaction /SAPAPO/TL1, as described in Chapter 2, Section 2.5.2. In the Customizing shown in Figure 3.20, it's possible to maintain additional modes and means of transport if required.

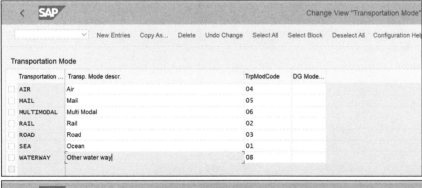

Figure 3.20 Mode and Means of Transport Customizing for Transportation Lane Master Data

> **Note** [«]
>
> In the means of transportation, the fields relevant to transportation scheduling aren't used by PP-DS in the SAP S/4HANA system.

3.3 Heuristics Configuration

In this section, we'll cover the details of the heuristics technical settings available in embedded PP-DS. Heuristics are algorithms that contain the logic for how a planning or scheduling problem is resolved by the system. Heuristics can't be compared with the PP-DS optimizer because heuristics will execute the set algorithm once and produce the result, whereas the PP-DS optimizer tries to iterate the results to find the best possible result.

In PP-DS, there are three types of heuristics:

- **Planning heuristics**
  These heuristics are used to resolve supply and demand problems.

- **Scheduling heuristics**
  These heuristics are used in resolving capacity problems and optimizing resource usage.

- **Service heuristics**
  These heuristics don't resolve any planning or scheduling problems, but they help to achieve the correct results for the planning or scheduling problems.

3.3.1 Heuristics Settings

The planning heuristics in PP-DS are planning functions or algorithms that can be used to create receipt elements such as planned orders for in-house produced materials, purchase requisitions, and stock transfer requisitions for materials that are externally procured.

These heuristics can also be used for performing other planning tasks, for example, aligning the dates of the receipt and requirements elements to avoid delays.

The scheduling heuristics operate on the resources and the orders and operations objects. These heuristics can be used to schedule the operations on a specific resource by respecting the settings and constraints maintained in the heuristics and the strategy settings maintained in Customizing. The strategy settings are covered in Chapter 6.

In this section, we'll cover some of the important technical settings that are required in heuristics. The functionality and the operations of these heuristics will be covered in Chapter 5 and Chapter 6.

You can use Transaction /SAPAPO/CDPSC11 or the Customizing menu path, **SAP IMG Menu · Advanced Planning · Heuristics · Maintain Heuristics**, to access the Customizing settings for the PP-DS heuristics.

As shown in Figure 3.21, the heuristics delivered by SAP are available in this Customizing transaction. If you want to alter any settings of these heuristics, you can copy and create a heuristic by clicking on the **Copy As** button and entering a new name in the customer name space (starting with "Z" or "Y") and change any specific settings to meet your planning and scheduling needs.

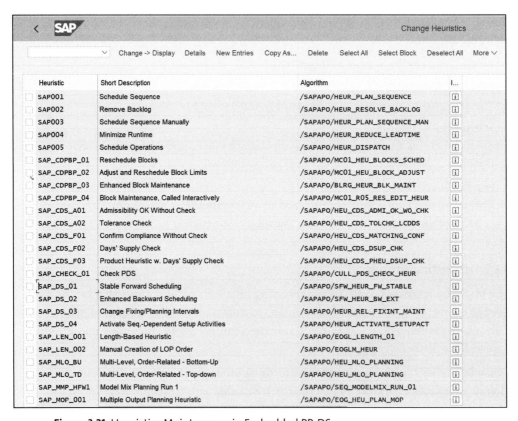

Figure 3.21 Heuristics Maintenance in Embedded PP-DS

When you double-click and navigate to any of these heuristics, you'll notice that the available settings are different for each one. These heuristics settings are customizable. But the logic of the algorithm is derived from the ABAP code and structures behind the algorithm assigned to the heuristics.

Note

It's also possible to create a new custom heuristic with a customized algorithm by copying the template function group /SAPAPO/RRP_HEUR_TEMPLATE in ABAP programming, copying the corresponding function modules, and adapting the code according to your requirements. Detailed instructions for this process are beyond the scope of this book.

As an example, the commonly used MRP heuristics can be copied to a custom heuristic in the customer name space. As shown in Figure 3.22, the SAP_MRP_001 heuristic is copied into **YSAP_MRP_001**, and here all the settings can be changed. If you change the algorithm assigned to this copied heuristic, the available settings will be changed accordingly.

Figure 3.22 Copying and Creating a New Heuristic with the SAP Standard Algorithm

3.3.2   Heuristics Profiles

Heuristics profiles are collections of heuristics that can be used in the planning and scheduling tools within PP-DS. In the interactive PP-DS planning tools, such as the detailed scheduling (DS) planning board, order views, and production planning table (which we'll discuss later in this chapter), it's possible to execute the heuristics depending on which tool is being used. For example, from the order views, the planning heuristics can be executed to resolve any demand and supply problems. In the DS planning board and in the production table, which are used to monitor and manage the scheduling problems, the scheduling heuristics can be executed.

The heuristics that can be executed from these interactive planning tools are defined via the heuristics profiles. These heuristics profiles are assigned to the tool-specific overall profile. To create a heuristics profile, you can follow the Customizing menu path, **SAP IMG Menu · Advanced Planning · Heuristics · Maintain Heuristic · Profiles**. You'll arrive at the screen shown in Figure 3.23. The list of profiles is displayed in this transaction, and new profiles can be created by clicking on the **New Entries** button.

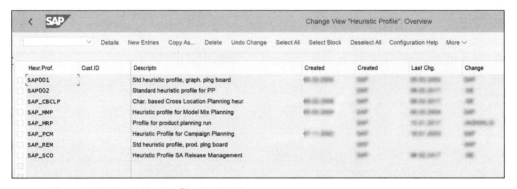

Figure 3.23 Heuristics Profiles in PP-DS

The heuristics are maintained in the heuristics profile, as shown in Figure 3.24. The **Customizing ID** field is used to differentiate a generic planning profile from the same one customized for a specific user. For example, if the value "user1" is entered in the **Customizing ID** field for heuristics profile ZSAP001, when the user named user1 launches a planning tool that has profile ZSAP001 in use, the settings from profile ZSAP001 with the **Customizing ID user1** are loaded. For other users, the system will load the list of heuristics from profile ZSAP001 without any **Customizing ID** assigned.

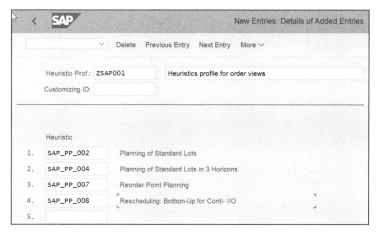

Figure 3.24 Maintaining a List of Heuristics in a Heuristics Profile

3.4 Planning Procedures

In PP-DS, the planning procedures determine the reaction of the system when a planning-relevant event takes place. In this section, we'll walk through the Customizing settings for planning procedures, before seeing how to configure the execution of a production planning run.

3.4.1 Planning Procedure Settings

The planning procedure is assigned to the material master in the **Advanced Planning** view. SAP delivers standard planning procedures in embedded PP-DS. The planning procedure Customizing can be accessed from the Customizing menu path, **SAP IMG Menu · Advanced Planning · Maintain Planning Procedures**. As shown in Figure 3.25, the list of available planning procedures is given here.

The planning procedure definition has a heuristic assigned to it. The **Confirmed Qty** column defines the quantity that is relevant for pegging. For customer requirements elements such as sales orders, there are two quantity fields available. One is the desired quantity, which is the quantity entered in the sales order and requested by the customer, and the other quantity is the confirmed quantity, which is the quantity confirmed by the ATP process after checking the availability of the quantity against the defined check rules. In the planning procedures, if the **Confirmed Qty** is selected, then the ATP confirmed quantities are considered by the planning procedure for pegging. The **Fix. Pegging CTP/ATP** column isn't relevant for embedded PP-DS.

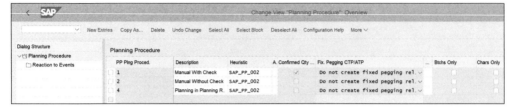

Figure 3.25 Planning Procedure Customizing in PP-DS

When you navigate by selecting one of the planning procedures and then clicking the **Reaction to Events** folder, you'll see a list of events and the reaction of the system and corresponding systems. As shown in Figure 3.26, every planning procedure has the **Reaction to Events** area that contains a list of events and the corresponding **Action**, **Reuse Mode**, and **SchedSttus** (scheduling status). The **BOP PlngFlEntry** column isn't relevant in embedded PP-DS.

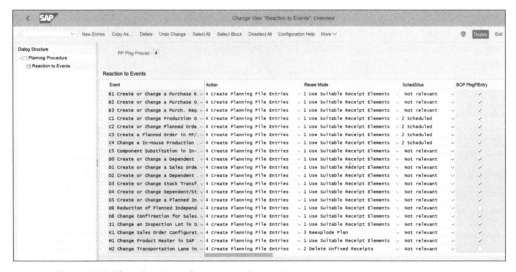

Figure 3.26 Planning Procedures: Reaction to Events

Let's walk through each of the columns, as follows:

- **Event**
  The **Event** signifies any planning-relevant changes, either triggered from SAP

S/4HANA or a change made in embedded PP-DS directly. These events may include master data changes, transaction data creation/change/deletion (e.g., orders), forecast elements, stocks, and so on.

- **Action**

  The system reaction to the event is defined here. The following actions are available:

  - **Do Not Carry Any Action**

    The system doesn't take any action for the specific event to which this action is assigned.

  - **Cover Dependent/Stock Transfer Requirements Immediately with Existing Receipts**

    When a planned order is created that will create/change dependent requirements for the components used in the production, this action will try to cover the dependent demand created with the existing receipt elements in the system, such as existing orders or stock elements. If the system isn't able to cover the dependent demand with an existing supply element, it will stop the creation of the original order.

  - **Cover Dependent/Stock Transfer Requirements Immediately If Possible**

    This action is similar to the previous action, but with this action the system will create a new supply element to cover the dependent demand even if the dependent demand can only be covered with a delay. The original order will be created irrespective of the delay in the coverage of the dependent demand.

  - **Cover Dependent/Stock Transfer Requirement Immediately**

    This action is similar to the previous action. But if the dependent demands can't be covered by the existing or new receipts on time, the original order creation will be stopped.

  - **Create Planning File Entries**

    This action will add a checkbox to the planning file entry table. Planning file entry is a record in the PP-DS system that stores the planning relevance of the product/location and is evaluated during a planning run.

  - **Start Product Heuristics Immediately**

    With this action, the heuristics assigned to the material master data are executed immediately when the assigned event occurs in the system.

- **Reuse Mode**

  The **Reuse Mode** determines how an existing receipt element, such as a planned order, purchase requisition, or stock transfer requisition, is treated when the action assigned to the event is triggered. The available options are as follows:

- **Use Suitable Receipt Elements**
  With this reuse mode, any of the existing receipt elements can be reused if the receipt elements are in excess of the supply. A net requirements calculation is made in which the receipt quantities and requirement quantities are netted out. If there are excess receipt elements that can be used to fulfill the new demand element, they will be reused with this mode.

- **Delete Unfixed Receipts**
  With this reuse mode, the receipt elements that aren't fixed are deleted and re-created to fulfill the demand. In PP-DS, it's possible to fix or firm the receipt elements manually or by using heuristics. These fixed receipts aren't changed by the system automatically, for example, in a planning run.

- **Re-Explode Plan**
  This is similar to the **Use Suitable Receipt Elements** reuse mode except that all the receipt elements are re-exploded irrespective of whether they are fixed or not fixed. Re-explosion is the process of rereading the corresponding PDS master data and adjusting the order data to align with the latest master data. For a change event in PDS data, this reuse mode can be used to update the orders with the new changes in the PDS data.

- **Delete Unfixed Receipts and Explode Fixed Receipts Again**
  This mode is a combination of the previous two reuse modes. The receipts that aren't fixed are deleted, and the fixed receipts will be re-exploded to update the order with the latest PDS data.

> **Note**
>
> When the in-house manufacturing orders have the statuses of **Released**, **Started**, **Partially or Finally Confirmed**, or **Date/Input Confirmed**, these orders can't be re-exploded because the re-explosion of PDSs may result in a change in input components and dates. The order statuses are set by the system according to the processing stage of the manufacturing orders.

- **SchedSttus**
  This column determines how the scheduling status of the order is set in case of an action related to in-house manufacturing orders. The in-house manufacturing

orders (planned orders and production orders) have the following possible scheduling statuses:

- **Scheduled**
  The order and all the operations are assigned with a resource, and the operations are already scheduled on a resource consuming the available capacity of the resource.

- **Deallocated**
  These orders are created in the PP-DS system, and the operations have a resource assigned, although they aren't yet dispatched or scheduled on the resource. These operations don't consume any available capacity of the resource.

- **Retain Scheduling Status**
  The system, depending on the value set in this Customizing for the event and action, can set the scheduling status as **Scheduled** or **Deallocated**. With the **Retain Scheduling Status** option, the same scheduling status is retained when the corresponding event is executed in the system.

3.4.2   Settings for Production Planning Runs in PP-DS

In the PP-DS system, there are several ways to execute production planning runs. One of the options is to execute the MRP heuristics in production planning runs within PP-DS. This process will execute the product heuristics or a heuristic assigned to the MRP heuristics in all the bill of material (BOM) levels.

There are customization settings related to the PP-DS planning run. The important customization settings to support the MRP planning in PP-DS are covered in the section.

Planning groups are defined to execute the planning for all the products belonging to a specific group together. Planning groups are evaluated by all the heuristics in the production planning run. If there are multiple products assigned to one planning group, when any one of these products is selected in the production planning run, the planning is executed for all products in the planning group irrespective of which defined materials are selected.

The planning groups can be defined in the Customizing menu path, **SAP IMG Menu • Advanced Planning • MRP Planning • Run Maintain Planning Groups**. Click the **New Entries** button, and you'll arrive at the screen shown on the top portion of Figure 3.27.

Here, provide a name and a description. The planning group is then assigned to the material master by executing Transaction MM02 and navigating to the **Advanced Planning** tab. Under the **Proc./PPDS** section, enter the **Planning Group** value, as shown on the bottom portion of Figure 3.27.

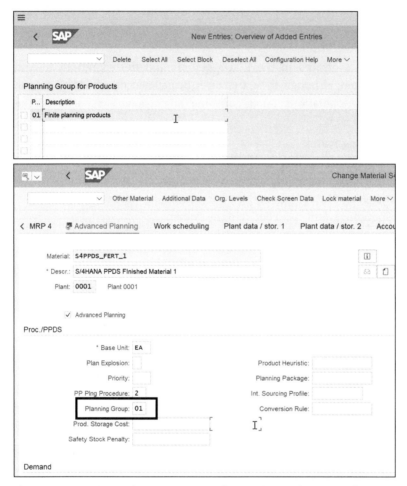

Figure 3.27 Creating a Planning Group and Assigning to the Material Master

Propagation ranges are used in the planning runs to determine which material location combinations are allowed apart from them the ones defined in the selection criteria for the planning run. If MRP planning heuristics are executed for one material, and there are multiple dependent materials due to the BOM component structure, all these dependent components should be part of the propagation range for the system to plan them.

To maintain propagation ranges, you can follow the Customizing menu path, **SAP IMG Menu · Advanced Planning · MRP Planning Run · Maintain Propagation Ranges**. For production planning runs, the standard delivered propagation range (**Prop.Range**) "SAPALL" can be used. The SAPALL propagation range includes all product locations and resources. By using this propagation range, the materials defined in the selection criteria are planned in MRP heuristics, along with all the dependent materials and all materials included in the planning run due to the linkage of the materials via planning groups.

If you want to restrict the planning run per specific set boundaries of materials, locations, or other characteristics of the material, a new propagation area can be defined, which can be used during the planning run.

As shown in Figure 3.28, the defined propagation ranges are listed in this Customizing transaction, and custom propagation ranges can be defined by clicking on the **New Entries** button.

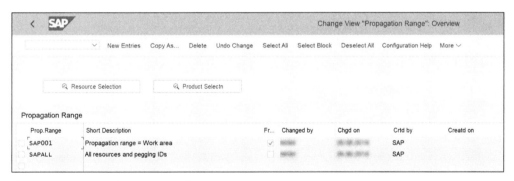

Figure 3.28 Propagation Range Maintenance

When creating a new entry, a **Prop.Range** name and a **Short Description** are entered, as shown in Figure 3.29. Click on the **Product Selectn** button to bring up the **Select Conditions** popup window.

All the available options are listed on the right side of this popup window. Select and move the required entries from the **Queue** to the **Selection** side by clicking the arrow buttons, and then you'll be prompted to enter the specific selection values for the selected fields. In the example shown in Figure 3.29, the **Production Planner** field is selected, and the value **001** is defined as the restricting criteria.

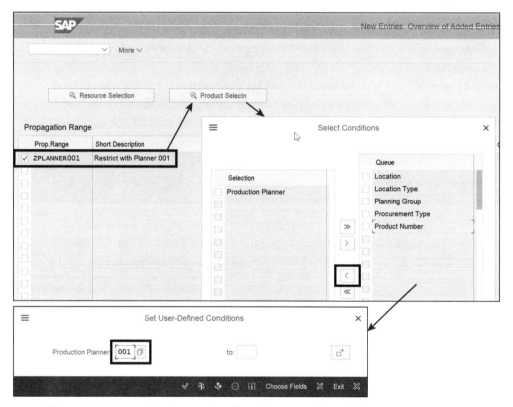

Figure 3.29 Propagation Range: Creating New Entries

The planning runs are resource intensive in nature, and the number of materials and locations involved can make the runtimes longer. In a PP-DS planning run for MRP, it's possible to set up parallel processing so that the system will package a certain number of materials and trigger multiple tasks to plan the materials in parallel. This will shorten the time required for the PP-DS planning run considerably. The package size is set and the parallel processing is activated in the heuristics settings, as shown in Figure 3.30 (see Chapter 5, Section 5.3.4, for more details).

The number of parallel processes the system can use and the SAP application servers or the remote function call group servers (RFC groups) in which they can request these parallel tasks are defined in the Customizing menu path, **SAP IMG Menu •**

Advanced Planning · MRP Planning Run · Maintain Destinations for Parallel Processing.

Figure 3.30 MRP Heuristics Settings for Parallel Processing

As shown in Figure 3.31, in this Customizing transaction, you select an RFC group or a list of allocation servers and then enter the number of parallel processes the system can use for MRP planning in parallel in the **Number** field.

Figure 3.31 Defining Destinations for MRP Parallel Processing in PP-DS

3.5   Order View Settings

In embedded PP-DS, planning results can be evaluated and planning runs can be triggered for the selected materials and locations in order views. In this section, we'll cover the important settings required for using these transactions.

The overall profile combines the individual settings and all the individual profiles that the order views use when the user launches an order view transaction. The commonly used order views and transactions are as follows:

- **Product view**
  Found in Transaction /SAPAPO/RRP3, the product view is similar to the stock requirements list in SAP S/4HANA. It lists all the receipts and requirements and allows you to navigate to the product master data and pegging relationships.

- **Receipts view**
  Found in Transaction /SAPAPO/RRP4, the receipts view lists all the receipt elements, such as in-house and external procurement orders, for the given selection.

- **Requirements view**
  Found in Transaction /SAPAPO/RRP1, the requirement view lists all the requirement elements, such as dependent demands, planned independent requirements/forecast elements, sales order requirements, and stock transfer requirements.

When you execute one of these transactions the first time in embedded PP-DS, the system prompts you to set a variant that refers to an overall profile. As shown in Figure 3.32, the system prompts you to select the overall profile and save it as a variant for the user by entering a user value in the **Save as User Variant** field and a **Variant Name**.

Tip

To delete the assigned profiles to the users or to copy the user settings from one user to another for the PP-DS tools, you can use the ABAP program /SAPAPO/PT_USER_PARAMS_MAIN.

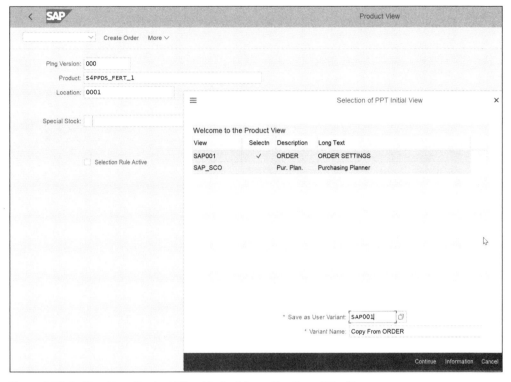

Figure 3.32 Setting Up a Product View Variant from the Overall Profile

The overall profile for the order views can be maintained from the Customizing menu path, **SAP IMG Menu • Advanced Planning • Order View • Define Overall Settings**. The overall profile is assigned with an application, which determines the relevance of this overall profile to specific PP-DS tools. As the Customizing settings are specific to the PP-DS tools, there are different customization transactions available for the tools/applications. From this Customizing transaction, it's possible to maintain the overall profiles only for application RRP_ORD, which is the order view.

As shown in Figure 3.33, multiple profiles are assigned to the selected overall profile **SAP001**. The standard delivered profiles can be copied to new profiles by clicking on the **Copy As** button, entering a name for the profile, and then entering the individual profile names in the **Master Profile** section of the screen (shown on the lower portion of Figure 3.33).

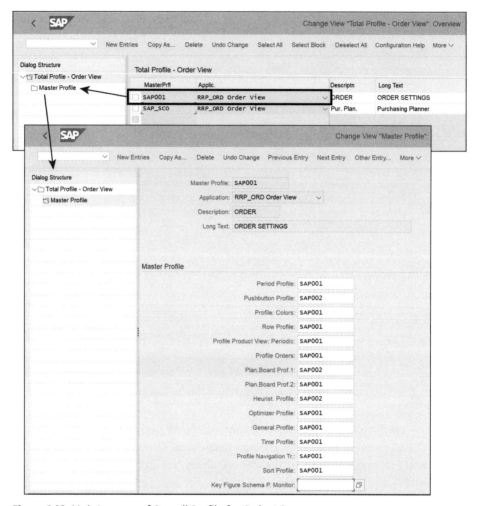

Figure 3.33 Maintenance of Overall Profile for Order Views

In the order view, one of the most often customized settings is the day's supply setting and the calculation associated with it. Day's supply is the value calculated as the number of days until the current receipt elements can cover the demand elements for the product location, for example, if there are 100 quantity of stock available and a sales order requirement.

In the day's supply calculation, the order categories involved in this calculation are defined. SAP standard delivers two day's supply types:

- **SAP1 – Day's Supply**

  This day's supply calculation includes only the stock as the receipt element, and this quantity is netted against all the requirement elements and the day on which the netted quantity falls negative. The difference from the current date and the date on which the quantity falls negative is calculated as the day's supply.

- **SAP2 – Receipt Day's Supply**

  This day's supply calculation includes the stock and all the receipt elements, and this quantity is netted against all the requirement elements and the day on which the netted quantity falls negative. The difference from the current date and the date on which the quantity falls negative is calculated as the receipt day's supply.

Table 3.1 shows the difference between the SAP1 and SAP2 day's supply calculation logic.

Date	Receipt/ Requirement	Element	Quantity	Net Calculated Quantity
June 1st, 2019	Stock	Stock	100	100
June 3rd, 2019	Requirement	Sales order	−100	0
June 5th, 2019	Requirement	Sales order	−10	−10
June 6th, 2019	Receipt	Production order	50	40
June 7th, 2019	Requirement	Dependent demand	−120	−80
June 9th, 2019	Receipt	Planned order	20	−60

Table 3.1 Day's Supply Calculation Logic: Example

Using the SAP1 day's supply calculation, only the stock element with quantity 100 is considered as the supply element. The requirement elements (sales orders and dependent demands) are reduced from the stock quantity. As the net calculated quantity falls below zero on June 5th, 2019, the day's supply is calculated as the difference between the June 1st, 2019 and June 5th, 2019, which is 4 days.

Using the SAP2 day's supply calculation, the stock quantity and the receipt quantities (from the planned order and production order) are netted against the requirement elements (sales orders and dependent demand). Because the net requirement is negative after June 7th, 2019, the day's supply is calculated as the difference between the current date (June 1st, 2019) and June 7th, 2019, which is 6 days.

The day's supply can be customized to suit the requirements. For example, in planning scenarios where the certainty of the dates in the purchase requisitions aren't trusted until the purchase orders are created and sent to the supplier, the day's calculation can be configured not to include the purchase requisitions in the day's supply calculation. Thus, the planner is alerted to the supply situation depending only on the purchase order receipts expected.

The day's supply calculation customization can be accessed from the Customizing menu path, **SAP IMG Menu · Advanced Planning · Order View · Define Days' Supply Types**, arriving at the screen shown in Figure 3.34. You can copy the standard delivered day's supply types and create your own types to include or exclude specific stock, receipts, requirements, and forecast elements.

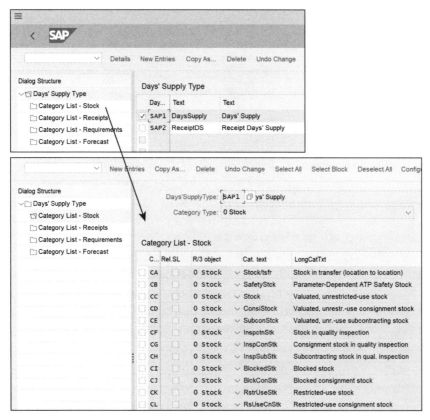

Figure 3.34 Customization of Day's Supply Types

As shown in Figure 3.34, the day's supply types are displayed in this transaction. You can copy and create a new type by using the **Copy As** function. In the left side of the screen, navigate to the category list folders to add or remove the categories from the calculation of the day's supply by checking or unchecking the boxes.

After the customization of the day's supply is maintained, this can be assigned to the general profile of the order view, which is assigned to the overall profile.

To customize the general profile of the order view, you can use the Customizing menu path, **SAP IMG Menu · Advanced Planning · Order View · Set Layout**. As shown in Figure 3.35, the general profiles are listed under the **Maintain General Settings** folder section of this Customizing transaction. You can create your own by using the **Copy As** function and assigning the day's supply type defined in the corresponding **Days' Supply Type** fields.

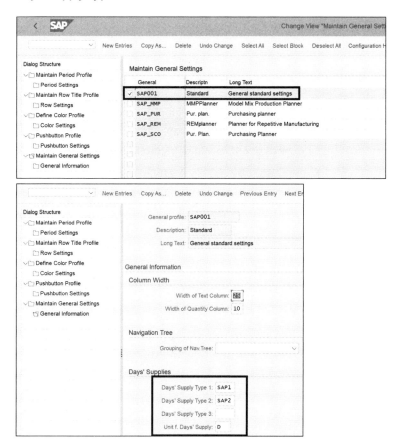

Figure 3.35 Assignment of Days' Supply Type to the General Profile

Different unit of measurements of time dimension can be used for the day's supply such as hours, days, weeks, etc. As PP-DS is a detailed scheduling tool, the day's supply is calculated in two decimal points calculated from the exact time stamp of the current time and the time stamp of the first negative quantity.

> **Tip**
>
> When there is a change in the customization of the profiles of the overall order view profile or the profiles assigned to the overall profile, the user settings need to be refreshed using the ABAP program /SAPAPO/PT_USER_PARAMS_MAIN in order for the changes to be reflected in the PP-DS transactions for the users.

Similar to the day's supply types creation and assignment to the general profile and then to the overall profile, you can copy other settings and assign them to the corresponding profile and then to the overall profile.

3.6   Detailed Scheduling Planning Board

In PP-DS, the DS planning board is a commonly used graphical board where various charts can be loaded to represent the stock levels, capacity consumption, orders, operations, and relationships between the orders and operations.

As the DS planning board has graphical objects, it's possible to color-code different objects. You can also customize the available action buttons on the screen of the DS planning board so that for frequently used actions, the user can easily perform those instead of navigating to the menu paths within this transaction. We'll cover the important profiles required for selecting the data for the DS planning board and also how the color-coding and the toolbar options can be customized.

3.6.1   Overall Profile

The DS planning board is launched by executing Transaction /SAPAPO/CDPS0 in embedded PP-DS. As shown in Figure 3.36, the **Overall Profile** is selected and that determines the **Time Profile** and **Work Area**. In addition, by clicking on **Profiles** in the menu bar, you can see all other profiles assigned to the overall profile, such as the **Plng Board Profile**, **DS Strategy Profile**, **Heuristic Profile**, and **More Profiles**, which are required to use the DS planning board.

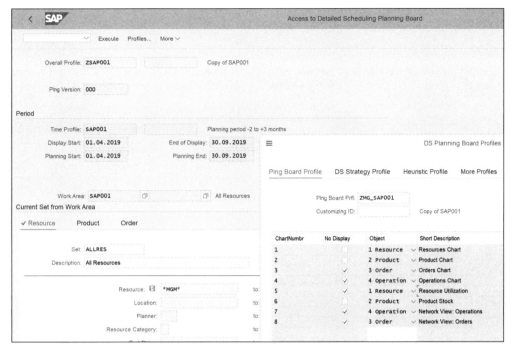

Figure 3.36 DS Planning Board Initial Screen

The overall profile can be customized to include other profiles that are customized. You can navigate to the customization of the overall profile using the Customizing menu path, **SAP IMG Menu · Advanced Planning · Detailed Scheduling · Maintain Overall Profiles**. As shown in Figure 3.37, the list of overall profiles is displayed here; you can create a new profile by copying an existing profile using the **Copy As** button in the menu bar.

All the **Subprofiles** assigned to the overall profiles are visible by double-clicking on the overall profile, and the entries here can be changed with the required individual profiles. The **Planning Version** can be defaulted by maintaining the same in the **Specific Settings** section.

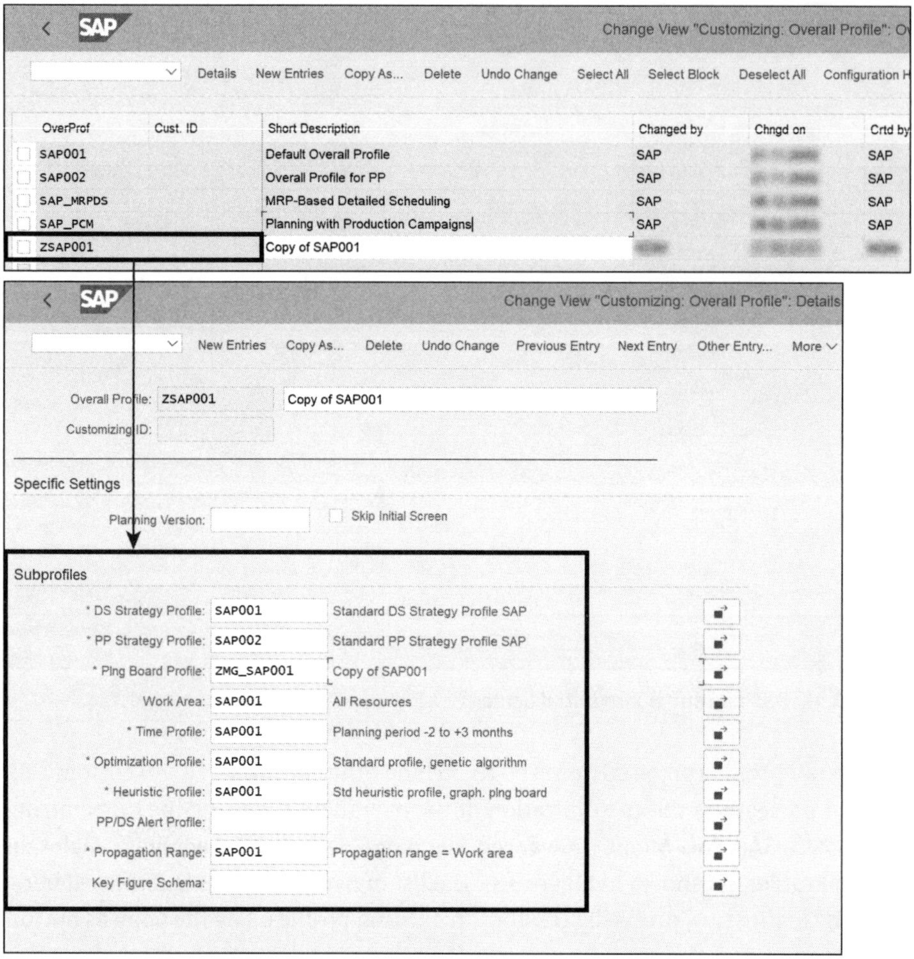

Figure 3.37 Customization of the DS Planning Board Overall Profile

3.6.2   Time Profile

The **Time Profile** determines the duration for the selection of objects for display in the DS planning board, and the **Planning Period** determines the duration within which the objects loaded on the DS planning board can be involved in a scheduling action. The display and planning periods, as shown in Figure 3.36, are calculated as relative dates as set in the Customizing. You can use the Customizing menu path, **SAP IMG Menu · Advanced planning · Detailed Scheduling · Maintain Time Profiles**, to maintain the time profile.

You'll arrive at the top screen shown in Figure 3.38. Double-click on the entries in the list to navigate to the bottom screen shown in Figure 3.38, where the period profile customization can be set as a relative period or as absolute periods.

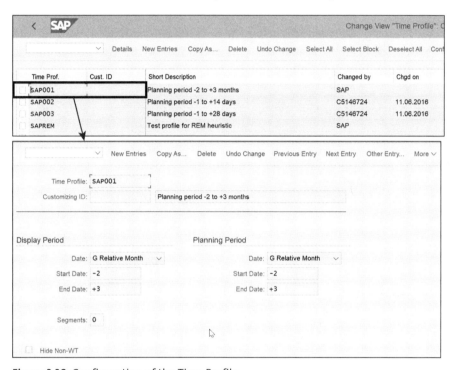

Figure 3.38 Configuration of the Time Profile

The start and end of the duration are defined. The **Segments** field defines the number of individual sections the display period can be split into for performance reasons. For example, if the total **Display Period** is 6 months, 3 **Segments** are defined (2 months per segment), only 1 month is displayed at launch, then the system will process the data only for the first segment (2 months). When the user scrolls through the time bar, the data is loaded for the next segments. This is purely a performance measure.

3.6.3   Work Area

The work area is the preset selection of resources, products, and orders for the selection and display of objects on the DS planning board. It can be customized to include a set of resources and products belonging to a manufacturing unit that a scheduling user is responsible for so that the user need not set the selection conditions every time he or she launches the DS planning board as the conditions are preloaded.

The work area can be customized under the Customizing menu path, **SAP IMG Menu · Advanced Planning · Detailed Scheduling · Maintain Work Areas**. As shown in Figure 3.39, the work area can be created from this transaction, and the resources, orders, and products selections are defined under the **Dialog Structure** folders.

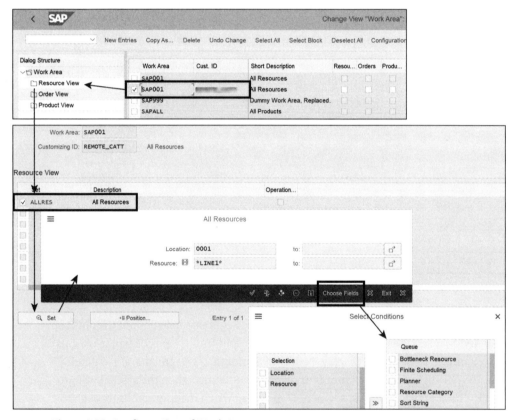

Figure 3.39 Configuration of Work Areas

For setting up the work area with resource selection, select the **Resource View** folder under the **Dialog Structure** panel on the left side of the screen. Select the entry from the **Set** column, and click on the **Set** button to open the **All Resources** popup box. Here, click on the **Choose Fields** button, select the required fields from the **Queue** column, move them to the **Selection** column, and press Enter. The selected fields will appear in the **All Resources** popup, and you can enter the values for the selected fields, such as the **Location** and **Resource**. Click on the **OK** (green checkmark) button and then the **Save** button to save the data maintained.

These steps can be repeated for the **Order View** and **Product View** as well, if you want to define the work area with respect to orders and products, respectively.

3.6.4   Planning Board Profile

The layout, color-coding of objects in the DS planning board, and the toolbar menu option customizations are grouped under the DS planning board profile. The DS planning board profile customization can be accessed from the Customizing menu path, **SAP IMG Menu · Advanced Planning · Detailed Scheduling · Settings for the Detailed Scheduling Planning Board · Maintain Planning Board Profiles**.

As shown in Figure 3.40, you'll see the list of the DS planning board profiles in the initial screen and the list of settings associated with the profile on the left side of the screen in the **Dialog Structure**. You can create a new profile by copying an existing entry using the **Copy As** button. Double-clicking on any profile will take you to the details of the basic color settings of the DS planning board. The settings made in this screen are valid for the DS planning board layout itself and the individual **Charts** that can be displayed in the DS planning board. The color-coding of the **Graphical Objects** and the **Toolbar: Displayed Functions** are configured by navigating to the corresponding folders in the dialog structure.

The **Marking Color** and the **Color of Guide** are configured in the DS planning board profile as shown in Figure 3.40. The marking color is the color used when an object on the DS planning board is clicked on or selected. When dragging and dropping an object within the DS planning board for rescheduling, the guide lines help the user determine the position of the timeline in the board.

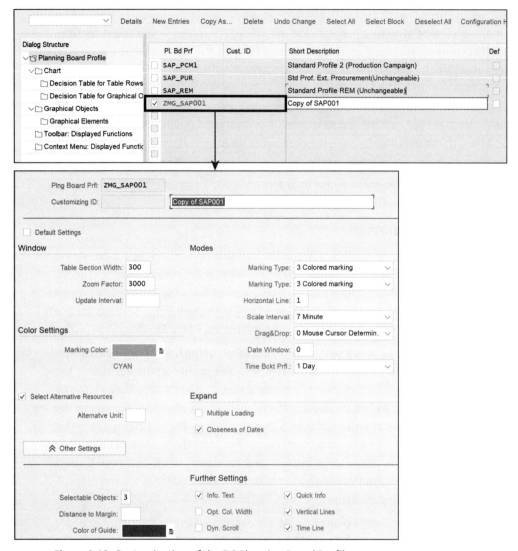

Figure 3.40 Customization of the DS Planning Board Profile

In Figure 3.41, the different elements of the DS planning board are marked so that you'll be able to follow the significance of the Customizing settings under the DS planning board profile that impact its display. After the selection is entered and executed in the initial screen of the DS planning board in Transaction /SAPAPO/CDPS0, the transaction will take you to the screen shown in Figure 3.41. The details of the DS planning board selection screen are covered in Chapter 6. The type of charts allowed, the objects displayed on the charts, and the color-coding of the individual objects and the buttons displayed in the task bar are driven by the Customizing of the DS planning board profile. Note the following:

❶ Task bar with actions

❷ Guidelines

❸ Selected object (in **Marking Color**)

❹ Order objects with color-coding

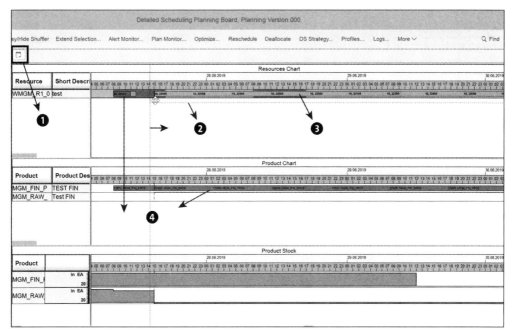

Figure 3.41 Objects in the DS Planning Board

The allowed charts and the graphical objects are customized under the DS planning board profile. We've already covered the guideline and the marking color configuration in the profile.

The order of the charts and elements operations is displayed in the chart, and the shape and color of the elements are configured in this step. To configure the decision table for the graphical objects, double-click on the **Chart** folder in the **Dialog Structure** panel on the left side of the screen. Select the **Resource Chart** by setting the checkbox in the **Chart** column, and double-click on the **Decision Table for Graphical Objects** folder under the **Dialog Structure**. This will open the screen shown in the bottom of Figure 3.42, which shows the list of decision groups. Here, you can identify the graphical object ID in the **Then** column.

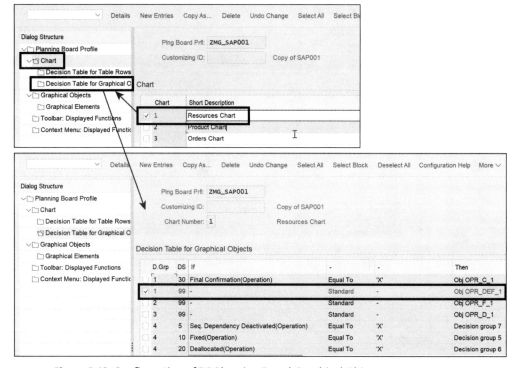

Figure 3.42 Configuration of DS Planning Board Graphical Objects

In the decision table, you can define conditions to identify an object from its properties in the **If** column and define the reaction for the condition in the **Then** column. In this example, the decision is defined as the assignment of **Obj OPR_DEF_1** for the standard operation objects by default without any special conditions.

Now, go to the **Graphical Objects** dialog structure, where the graphical object with **ID OPR_DEF_1** is defined in the example shown in Figure 3.43. Select the graphical object by setting the selection checkbox in the **Object ID** column, and double-click the **Graphical Elements** folder. This will take you to the screen displayed in the bottom of

Figure 3.43. In our example, there are four subelements defined to represent the different segments of a PP-DS order operation: **Setup**, **Process**, **Teardown**, and **Queue Time**.

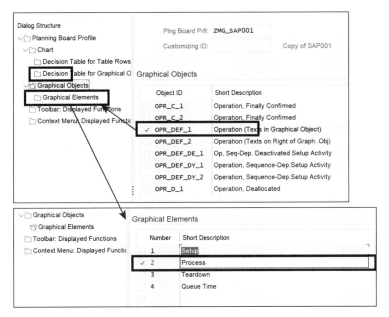

Figure 3.43 Configuring the Graphical Elements

Now, double-click on the element for which you want to define the color and shape settings in the list of graphical elements shown in Figure 3.43. This will take you to the screen shown in Figure 3.44. Here, under the **FORM Routine** section, select the **Element Type** radio button of the required shape and then select the color from the **Graph.El. Color** dropdown.

> **Note**
>
> The resource planning table (Transaction /SAPAPO/RPT) is another PP-DS tool that is used for managing the products and resources in a tabular form. The profiles and settings defined for the DS planning board can also be used for the resource planning table.

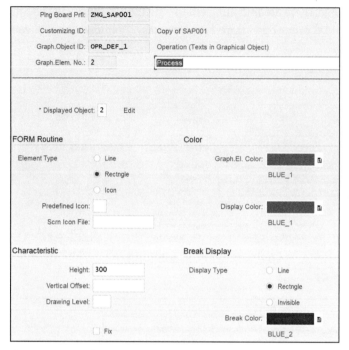

Figure 3.44 Configuring the Color and Shape of the Graphical Object

3.7   PP-DS Optimizer Settings

In this section, we'll cover the technical setup of the PP-DS optimizer. The setup of PP-DS optimizer profiles that are used to optimize the schedule will be covered in Chapter 6 during our discussion of detailed scheduling.

The PP-DS optimizer is an optional component of embedded PP-DS. The PP-DS optimizer is installed on its own server running the Windows operating system with a standalone SAP Gateway installed. Another option is to install the PP-DS optimizer in the same server as the SAP application server for the SAP S/4HANA system. The usual deployment method is to have a standalone server for PP-DS optimizer that is sized according to the workload expected to be handled by the PP-DS optimizer server and not sharing the load with any other applications.

In the PP-DS optimizer server, it's possible to install more than one PP-DS optimizer software instance because the same PP-DS optimizer server can be used by multiple systems, including the SAP APO system. The same PP-DS optimizer server may contain the software executables for supply network planning, capable-to-match (CTM), and so on. The PP-DS optimizer installed executable can be used by embedded PP-DS.

After the PP-DS optimizer executables and the required SAP Gateway components are installed in the standalone server, an RFC destination of type TCP/IP is created in the SAP S/4HANA system, as shown in Figure 3.45.

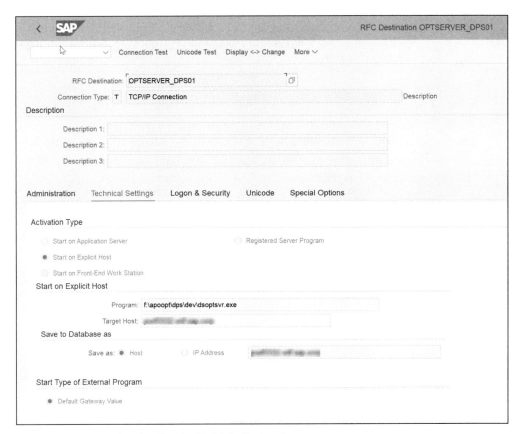

Figure 3.45 RFC Destination for the PP-DS Optimizer Server

Note

For further information, refer to the installation guide for the SAP SCM optimizer found at *http://s-prs.co/v495100*.

To create the RFC destination, execute Transaction SM59 and click on the **Create** button. Enter a name for the destination in the **RFC Destination** field, and select the **Connection Type** as **T – TCP/IP Connection**. Under the **Technical Settings** tab, select the **Start on Explicit Host** option under the **Activation Type**. Enter the **Target Host**, which is the server in which the PP-DS optimizer is installed. In the **Program** field, enter the path of the PP-DS optimizer executable file in the PP-DS optimizer server.

After the RFC destination is set up, the configuration of the PP-DS optimizer is maintained under the Customizing menu path, **SAP IMG Menu · Advanced Planning · Basic Settings · Optimization Basic Functions · Maintain Master Data for Optimization Server**.

In this Customizing transaction, click the **New Entries** button. Set the **Dest. ID** as "DPS01" and the **Appl.** as "DPS", as shown in Figure 3.46. If there are multiple PP-DS optimizer servers available, and you want to prioritize one of the servers, enter a number in the **Pri...** (priority) field that is lower than the other entries. The entry with the lowest number in the **Pri...** field gets the first preference when the embedded PP-DS application requests the connection to an PP-DS optimizer server.

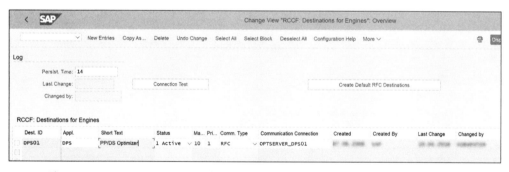

Figure 3.46 PP-DS Optimizer Technical Settings

The maximum number of slots (**Ma...**) determines how many CPU processing cores the PP-DS application can request at once when running an optimization operation. In Figure 3.46, the maximum number of slots is defined as "10". Next, enter the RFC destination that is created for the PP-DS optimizer server in the **Communication Connection** field. When you're done, click the **Save** button to save the PP-DS optimizer settings.

3.8   Summary

In this chapter, we covered in detail the activation and setup of embedded PP-DS, including the technical setup of the PP-DS optimizer. Embedded PP-DS requires explicit activation and the SAP liveCache installed and setup on the SAP HANA database that the SAP S/4HANA system is connected to.

For most of the transaction data, transfers between the ERP and PP-DS side of the SAP S/4HANA don't require an integration model. But, it internally uses the CIF framework to transfer the data, so the basic setup of the CIF is required in the SAP S/4HANA system. For PP-DS master data elements, the Customizing is maintained under the advanced planning Customizing settings.

We also covered the important settings and profiles required to use the PP-DS application tools in embedded PP-DS, such as the order views and the DS planning board.

In the next chapter, we'll cover the details of the transaction data in embedded PP-DS and how that data is transferred between SAP S/4HANA and embedded PP-DS. We'll also cover how the transaction data is represented in embedded PP-DS, as well as the version management in PP-DS for simulating the master data changes and its impact on transaction data.

Chapter 4
Data Transfer for Transaction Data

Part of the PP-DS setup is to configure the data transfer for trans-action data to PP-DS. In this chapter, we'll go through how each trans-action data object is treated within PP-DS and cover any restrictions in integrating these objects.

In this chapter, we'll cover the important transaction data that is relevant for planning and scheduling in PP-DS for SAP S/4HANA (embedded PP-DS). We'll discuss the data transfer methods for the transaction data and the representation of the PP-DS data for the corresponding SAP S/4HANA objects.

There are changes in the available enhancement points for the transaction data integration in embedded PP-DS compared to the PP-DS component of SAP Advanced Planning and Optimization (SAP APO). Wherever applicable, we'll also cover some of the enhancement options available for the transaction data in this chapter.

We'll discuss the integration of in-house and external procurement orders, quality management (inspection lots), plant maintenance orders, and forecast elements in detail.

4.1 Activating the Integration of Transaction Data

In embedded PP-DS, there is no integration model-based data transfer present for most of the transaction data objects that are based on a material number in PP-DS for planning and scheduling. For these material-dependent objects, the activation of data transfer is performed in the Customizing settings as a one-time activity.

For certain objects that are material independent, such as plant maintenance orders and network orders resulting from SAP S/4HANA project systems, the integration to PP-DS is based on an integration model.

To activate the data transfer for the material-dependent objects, you can navigate to the Customizing menu path, **SAP IMG Menu · Advanced Planning · Basic Settings ·**

Settings for Data Transfer. You'll arrive at the screen shown in Figure 4.1, where the material-dependent objects list is displayed. Select the checkboxes for the objects you want to integrate the data from SAP S/4HANA to embedded PP-DS and vice versa.

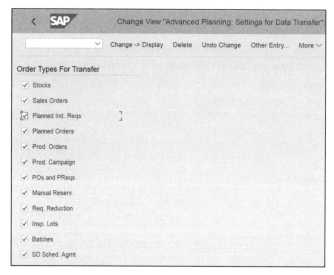

Figure 4.1 Activation of Transaction Data Transfer in Embedded PP-DS

The activation alone won't integrate all transaction data unless the material is activated for advanced planning. If the material is flagged for advanced planning, then during the transaction data creation in SAP S/4HANA, the system checks for the PP-DS relevancy of that transaction data object from the Customizing setting and sends the data to embedded PP-DS. Even though there is no integration model present for the transfer, the SAP S/4HANA to embedded PP-DS transfer internally uses the core interface (CIF) queues to perform the transfer.

For planned orders, production orders, purchase requisitions, and purchase orders, the data updated in embedded PP-DS is simultaneously updated in SAP S/4HANA. So for these objects, the transfer from embedded PP-DS to SAP S/4HANA doesn't involve the CIF-based transfer.

For the transfer from SAP S/4HANA to embedded PP-DS, if there are any problems encountered in embedded PP-DS during the transfer, the CIF queues will fail; these can be monitored and reprocessed if there are errors.

In PP-DS, the following transaction data objects are internally treated as orders. In other words, the PP-DS system creates an object of type order in the SAP liveCache, and the different objects, per their classification from SAP S/4HANA (e.g., sales orders, planned orders, etc.), are represented as order categories in SAP liveCache.

- Stocks
- Planned orders, production orders
- Project orders, maintenance orders
- Purchase requisitions, purchase orders
- Stock transport requisitions
- Stock transfer reservations
- Reservations
- Sales orders
- Planned independent requirements (PIRs)

The stocks and sales orders always originate in SAP S/4HANA, and they can't be changed in embedded PP-DS. Within PP-DS, the planned orders, purchase requisitions, stock transfer reservations, and requisitions can be created or changed by the PP-DS planning runs automatically or manually via any of the planning and scheduling tools.

In PP-DS, the term *manufacturing order* is used to represent both the discrete manufacturing production orders and the process industry process orders. In the Customizing setting, as shown in Figure 4.1, when the transfer of **Prod. Orders** is activated, this also applies for the process orders. The manufacturing orders and orders originating from SAP S/4HANA project systems (project orders) can be changed in embedded PP-DS, and the same is transferred to SAP S/4HANA.

The purchase orders, reservations, plant maintenance orders, and quality management inspection lots are always transferred from SAP S/4HANA to PP-DS and can't be changed in embedded PP-DS. These objects can only be changed in SAP S/4HANA.

4.2   Planned Independent Requirements

Planned independent requirement (PIR) elements in SAP S/4HANA represent the demand quantity coming in from the forecasting process. The PIRs can be maintained directly using SAP S/4HANA transactions, or they can be integrated using the standard delivered business application programming interfaces (BAPIs).

PIRs are transferred to embedded PP-DS without an integration model and with the activation of the data transfer in Customizing. The PIR data can only be maintained in SAP S/4HANA. It's possible to directly enter a forecast element in the PP-DS transactions, but these aren't integrated back to SAP S/4HANA.

In SAP S/4HANA the PIRs are managed in Transaction MD61 for creation and Transaction MD62 for change. As shown in Figure 4.2 on the bottom screen, in Transaction MD61, the PIR is created, and the **Reqmts type** (**LSF**) is derived from the planning strategy (**Strategy Group 10**) assigned to the material master on the top screen. Upon saving, the PIR element is transferred to embedded PP-DS.

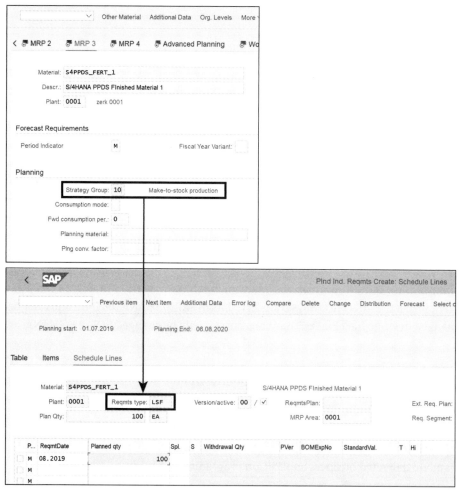

Figure 4.2 Creation of PIRs in SAP S/4HANA

The requirement type for the planning strategy assigned to the material master is set in the Customizing settings in the SAP S/4HANA system under the Customizing menu path, **SAP IMG Menu · Production Planning · Demand Management · Planned Independent Requirements · Planning Strategy · Define Strategy**. As shown in Figure 4.3, the requirement type for the PIRs is assigned to the strategy.

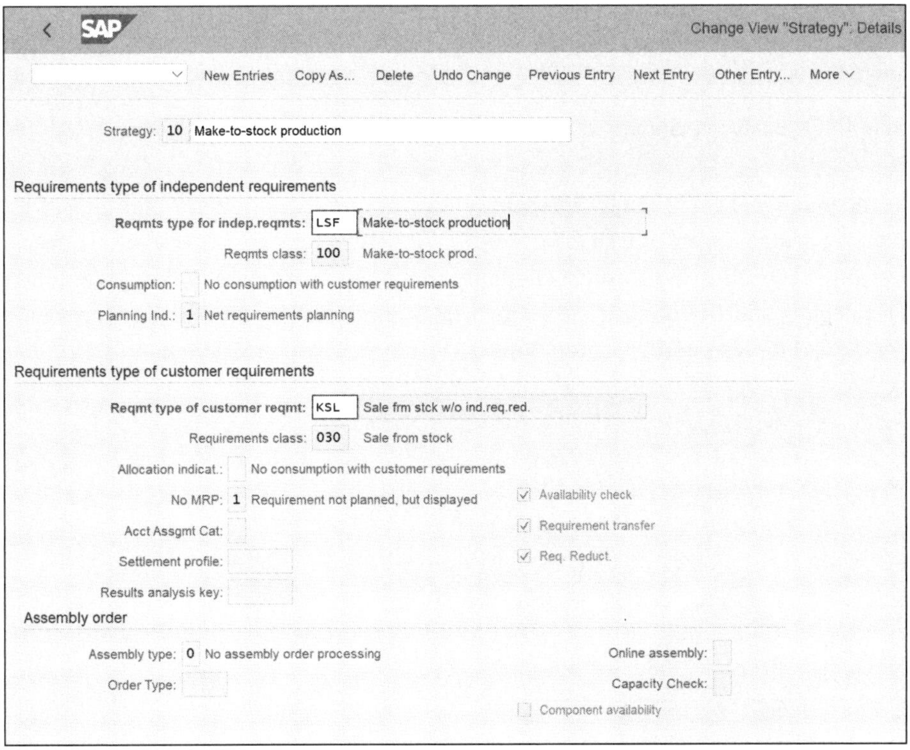

Figure 4.3 Requirement Strategy Settings in SAP S/4HANA

The SAP S/4HANA planning strategy and the PP-DS requirements strategy are mapped by default during the transfer. The PIR quantities are consumed by incoming demand elements, such as dependent demand coming in from a higher-level material in the BOM structure, sales order demand, stock transfer demand, and so on. The requirements strategy settings allow the incoming demand quantities to consume the PIR quantities. The PIR quantities are reduced by the corresponding demand elements, and the unconsumed demand can be deleted in periodic intervals.

The mapping of the planning and requirements strategy between SAP S/4HANA and embedded PP-DS is mapped by default, as shown in Table 4.1.

Planning Strategy in SAP S/4HANA	Requirements Strategy in PP-DS
10: Make to stock	10: Make to stock
40: Planning with final assembly	20: Planning with final assembly
50: Planning without final assembly	30, 35 (depending on material configurability): Planning without final assembly
60: Planning with a planning material	40: Planning with planning product

Table 4.1 Mapping of Planning Strategies

In embedded PP-DS, the PIR is represented as a forecast element in the planning tools such as product view (Transaction /SAPAPO/RRP3) or requirements view (Transaction /SAPAPO/RRP1). The forecast elements are shown as orders with the corresponding category and the quantity. As shown in Figure 4.4, the PIR element from SAP S/4HANA is represented as **FC. req** (forecast requirement in embedded PP-DS).

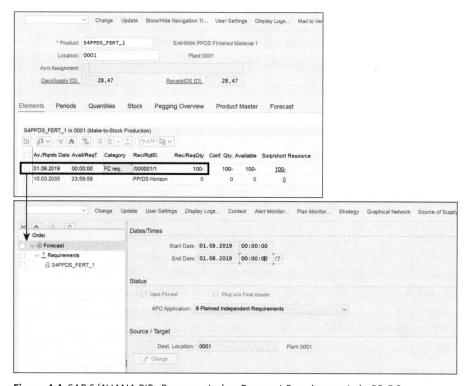

Figure 4.4 SAP S/4HANA PIRs Represented as Forecast Requirements in PP-DS

> **Note**
>
> The PIRs created from SAP S/4HANA can't be changed or deleted from embedded PP-DS. These PIRs are managed in SAP S/4HANA in terms of periodic reorganization of the unconsumed PIRs.
>
> The PIRs created manually and the PIRs loaded into SAP S/4HANA using the standard delivered BAPIs are integrated into embedded PP-DS.

4.3   Planned Orders

Planned orders are the procurement element for the in-house production of materials. Planned orders can be created manually and automatically by the system during a production planning run. As planned orders are proposals and not confirmed orders, they can be created and changed both in SAP S/4HANA and embedded PP-DS.

If a material is activated for advanced planning, and the Customizing for advanced planning transaction data transfer is activated for planned orders, the planned orders are transferred between SAP S/4HANA and embedded PP-DS as soon as they are created or changed. As the planning tools available in SAP S/4HANA and embedded PP-DS can change the planned orders during the planning run, it's recommended to set the material requirements planning (MRP) type as X0 (without MRP, with bill of materials [BOM] explosion) in the material master, so that the MRP runs in SAP S/4HANA don't create or change planned orders, and only the PP-DS planning (as part of MRP Live or PP-DS planning runs) is responsible for planning the material.

A planned order comprises basic information necessary to manufacture a product, such as the quantity to be produced, the start and end date of the order, and the components required to manufacture the product.

In SAP S/4HANA, a planned order uses the production version (BOM and routing) to derive the components from the master data, and the dates can be entered manually or can be determined by the planning tools according to the demand date and other constraints supplied to the planning tools. Planned orders can be created or changed in SAP S/4HANA via Transaction MD11 or Transaction MD12.

A planned order in SAP S/4HANA is shown in Figure 4.5. The **End** date was manually entered, and the **Start** date was derived using the in-house production duration from the material master. The **GR Processing Durn** is also copied from the material master to the order. The **Firming** checkboxes determine if the order can be changed by the system automatically or not. If the order is set by choosing the **Planned Order** check-box under **Firming**, the system can't change or delete the order. All the data is sent to embedded PP-DS from the SAP S/4HANA planned order after you save the planned order by clicking on the **Save** button.

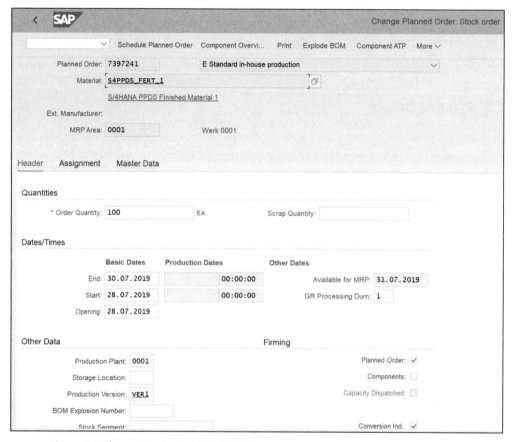

Figure 4.5 Planned Order in SAP S/4HANA

In embedded PP-DS, the planned order is represented with the following three major elements:

- **Receipts**
  This is the output of the planned order (the header material in the SAP S/4HANA planned order).

- **Requirements**

  These components are required to produce the material (derived from the production data structure [PDS] master data in PP-DS).

- **Operations**

  These are the operations and activities, the resources in which the activities are performed, and the calculated duration of these activities derived from the PDS master data.

The planned orders can be displayed or changed in embedded PP-DS using the product view (Transaction /SAPAPO/RRP3) or other planning tools. As shown in Figure 4.6, the header information of the planned order is displayed on the right side of the screen, and the **Receipts**, **Requirements**, and **Operations**/activities are displayed on the left side in the tree structure.

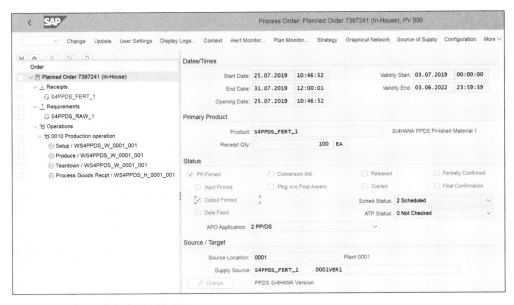

Figure 4.6 Planned Order in PP-DS

The goods receipt (GR) processing time from SAP S/4HANA is created as an activity in the PP-DS planned order, and the inbound handling resource assigned to the location master data is used for this activity.

The status, like the firming indicator, is also transferred to the PP-DS order. The **Sched. Status** is determined by the integration strategy maintained in the PP-DS global settings in Customizing.

The source of supply for the planned order is selected during the transfer of the planned order in embedded PP-DS, and the selected PDS is used as the **Supply Source**. The component and operations are derived from the explosion of the PDS master data.

The transfer of the planned order from SAP S/4HANA to embedded PP-DS internally uses the CIF queue mechanism, so if any problems are encountered during the planned order creation in embedded PP-DS, the CIF queues will fail. The transfer of the PP-DS planned order to SAP S/4HANA is done synchronously, so if the system encounters any problems in creating the planned order in SAP S/4HANA during the transfer from embedded PP-DS, the corresponding error is logged in PP-DS, and the system stops the change from being saved in PP-DS.

To create a planned order in embedded PP-DS manually, you can use the product view for the product and location. In the product view (Transaction /SAPAPO/RRP3), enter planning version "000" in the **Plng Version** field, enter the **Product** and **Location** information, and press ⌜Enter⌝ to navigate to the **Product View** screen. Then, click on the **Change** button to use the product view in change mode, enter a quantity in the **Rec/ReqQty** column and a date for the order in the **Avail/ReqD** column, and the system will generate a planned order, as shown in Figure 4.7, assigning a PP-DS planned order number. Upon saving the product view, it's transferred to SAP S/4HANA, and the SAP S/4HANA planned order number is updated back in PP-DS. You can use the **Update** button on the screen to refresh the data displayed in the product view. The system decides the order type (planned order or purchase requisition) based on the procurement type of the material. For in-house produced materials, the system will generate a planned order; for externally procured materials, a purchase requisition will be created.

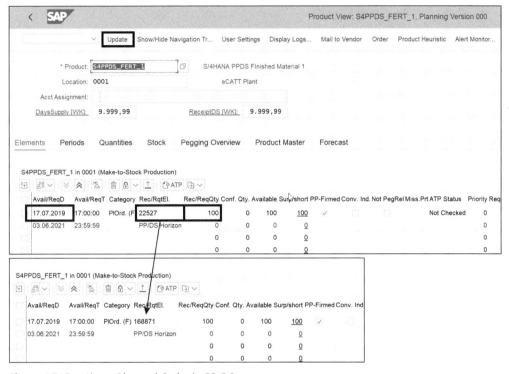

Figure 4.7 Creating a Planned Order in PP-DS

It's possible to enhance the integration of the planned orders using customer exits and business add-ins (BAdIs) delivered in the SAP S/4HANA system. Some of the important enhancement options are as follows:

- APOCF004
  This embedded PP-DS enhancement is for inbound processing of in-house orders.

- APOCF020
  This embedded PP-DS order interface is for customer-specific fields (after posting in SAP liveCache or to the database).

- CIFORD01
  This SAP S/4HANA enhancement is for order inbound interfaces (PP-DS to SAP S/4HANA).

- CIFORD02
  This SAP S/4HANA enhancement is for the transfer of customer-specific order fields (SAP S/4HANA to PP-DS).

4.4   Production Orders

Production orders are the executable in-house manufacturing orders used to instruct the shop floor to perform the manufacturing activities. In discrete industries, the term *production order* is used, and in process industries, the term *process order* is used. There are functional differences between these orders in SAP S/4HANA, but in PP-DS for planning and general scheduling purposes, both the production orders and process orders are treated the same.

Production orders can be created manually from SAP S/4HANA or can be created via the conversion of a planned order into a production order. The **Conv. Ind.** checkbox can be set in SAP S/4HANA and in embedded PP-DS or by using the unified conversion report for both SAP S/4HANA and PP-DS planned orders.

For the PP-DS planned orders, it's recommended to set the **Conv. Ind.** checkbox from within embedded PP-DS, use the unified conversion transaction (Transaction /SAPAPO/ PROD_ORD_CNV), or use the SAP menu path, **Logistics · Production · MRP · Planned Order · Convert to Production Order · Batch Conversion of Planned for Adv Planning · Production Order Conversion**. This transaction can be used for planned orders created in SAP S/4HANA or in embedded PP-DS for materials relevant to advanced planning.

After the **Conv. Ind.** checkbox is set, the planned order is converted into a production order, and the information (e.g., material, dates, quantity, and selected master data [production version]) is used for creating the production order. The production order is then also transferred to embedded PP-DS.

To set the **Conv. Ind.** checkbox for the planned order from the PP-DS product view, execute Transaction /SAPAPO/RRP3 to arrive at the screen shown in Figure 4.8. Then, select the **Conv. Ind** checkbox, and save the data by clicking the **Save** button. After the **Conv. Ind.** checkbox is set and saved, the production order is created and updated in PP-DS. You can refresh the product view using the **Update** button on the screen, which will display the production order number as shown in the bottom of the screen in Figure 4.8.

The creation of a production order is a transfer without a queue, so if issues are encountered in SAP S/4HANA during the creation of the production order, they are logged in PP-DS, and the order conversion is terminated in embedded PP-DS.

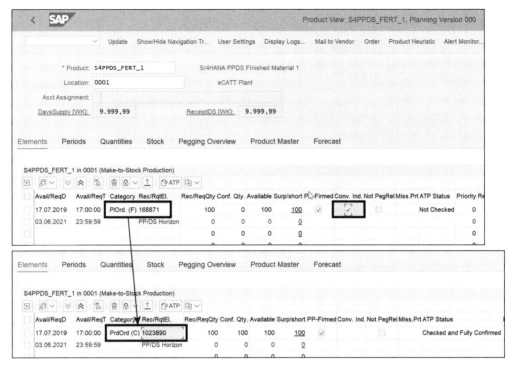

Figure 4.8 Conversion of Planned Order in the PP-DS Product View

A production order object in SAP S/4HANA has all the components and operations derived from the production version (BOM, routing), and the component materials of the production order, which are activated for advanced planning, are only available in embedded PP-DS for further planning. In addition, only the operations of the production order, which has resources relevant to PP-DS, are available in the PP-DS planning and scheduling tools.

After the planned order **Conv. Ind.** checkbox is set in embedded PP-DS, the production order is created in SAP S/4HANA, and then the production order is transferred to embedded PP-DS. The transfer of the production order to embedded PP-DS may change the production order dates in embedded PP-DS because of the scheduling of the production order. This change is also sent back to SAP S/4HANA. These changes are reflected in SAP S/4HANA with the production order status. This sequence of change is illustrated in Figure 4.9.

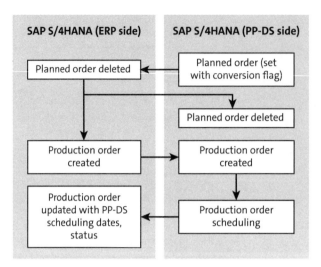

Figure 4.9 Production Order Conversion: Data Transfer between the ERP Side and Embedded PP-DS Side in SAP S/4HANA

For the retransfer to be performed by embedded PP-DS to SAP S/4HANA for orders, the Customizing settings needs to be created in Transaction /SAPAPO/CP3 in the SAP S/4HANA system for in-house production. In addition, the retransfer settings are relevant for external procurement orders. The production orders created by setting the **Conv. Ind.** checkbox in embedded PP-DS are set with the statuses **EXPL External Conv.of Planned Order** and **EXTS Changed by external system**, as shown in Figure 4.10.

Figure 4.10 Status of Production Orders Converted from PP-DS

The operations scheduled by PP-DS are set with the operation system **Status** as **DSEX**.

The changes in production order with respect to the quantity and dates are transferred from SAP S/4HANA to embedded PP-DS. If there are any date changes performed by the PP-DS scheduling tools, those are also updated back to SAP S/4HANA in the production order.

When a production order has the SAP S/4HANA status **CRTD – Created**, it can be deleted in the PP-DS transactions. This will set the **Deletion** checkbox in SAP S/4HANA for the production order and set the status **DLFL – Deletion Flag**. After the order is released in SAP S/4HANA (status **REL**), the order can't be deleted in embedded PP-DS.

The production order confirmations are created using transactions such as Transaction CO11N or Transaction CO15 when the production orders are executed in the shop floor to produce the products. After the production orders are confirmed in SAP S/4HANA, the status is updated in embedded PP-DS, as shown in Figure 4.11.

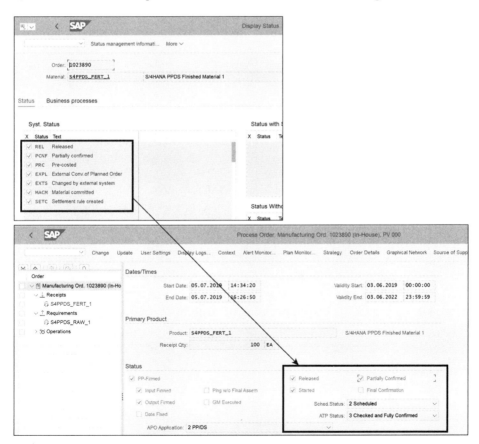

Figure 4.11 Production Order Status in SAP S/4HANA and in Embedded PP-DS

In addition, the quantity reduction of the production order due to GR posted against the production order in SAP S/4HANA is transferred to embedded PP-DS. If the production order is in a future date and a confirmation is posted on an earlier date, the production order in embedded PP-DS will be rescheduled to the confirmation date. This rescheduling can be stopped by certain enhancements, if required.

After the production orders are confirmed in SAP S/4HANA, the status checkbox of **Partially Confirmed** and **Started** are set in embedded PP-DS. After the **Started** checkbox is set in embedded PP-DS, the order can't be rescheduled manually or by PP-DS scheduling tools. To do any scheduling changes in the system, the production order needs to be set with an "interrupt" action in the scheduling tools, such as the detailed scheduling (DS) planning board where the **Interrupt** option is available on the context menu of the production order.

If the production order is set with any of the following statuses in SAP S/4HANA, the order is deleted from embedded PP-DS:

- **DLV – Delivered**
  The full order quantity is delivered.

- **TECO – Technically Completed**
  The order is technically completed in SAP S/4HANA.

- **DLFL – Deletion Flag**
  The order is set with a **Deletion** checkbox.

- **CLSD – Closed**
  The order is set with the **Close** checkbox in SAP S/4HANA.

4.5   External Procurement Orders

External procurement orders are for procuring materials from a vendor or from another plant (stock transfers). The procurement data transfer is activated via the same basic settings for advanced planning in Customizing. Activating the purchase orders and purchase requisitions in Customizing will activate the transfer of the following objects between SAP S/4HANA and embedded PP-DS:

- Purchase orders
- Purchase requisitions
- Online transactional processing (OLTP) scheduling agreement delivery schedules
- Advanced shipping notifications (ASNs) and purchase order acknowledgements

The external procurement proposals, such as the purchase requisitions and stock transfer requisitions, can be created in embedded PP-DS manually or automatically by a production planning run (see Chapter 5, Section 5.5).

When the orders are created manually in embedded PP-DS, if there are multiple sources of supply valid for the order, the system interactively provides an option to select the source of supply, as shown in Figure 4.12. In the **Admissible Sources of Supply** section, you can check the applicable sources for your order. During the automatic planning run in PP-DS, the system will select the source of supply with the minimal delay in fulfilling the demand.

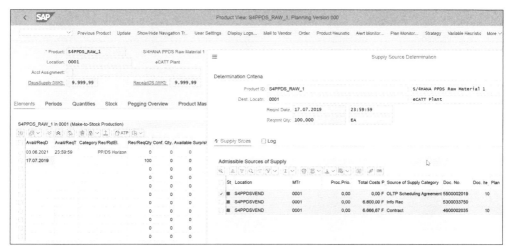

Figure 4.12 Manual Creation of External Procurement Order and Source of Supply Selection in PP-DS

If there is a GR processing time maintained in the material master, an activity is created in the purchase requisition for scheduling this time. This activity won't be transferred to SAP S/4HANA. Only the dates and the quantity are transferred to SAP S/4HANA.

The structure of the purchase requisition in PP-DS has the receipts, which represent the materials ordered in the requisition. If GR processing is involved, a GR activity is created in the order. Expand the **Activities** node in the left panel of the screen, and double-click the **Process Goods Recpt** activity to navigate to the GR activity, as shown in Figure 4.13. Click the **Save** button to save the purchase requisition.

For subcontracting purchase requisitions, the order will have the list of components to be provided to the vendor under the **Requirements** section of the purchase requisition. For stock transfer requisitions, where the sending and receiving locations are planned in PP-DS, the purchase requisition will also have a **Requirements** section in PP-DS that will show requirements created for the material in the sending location (**Plant**).

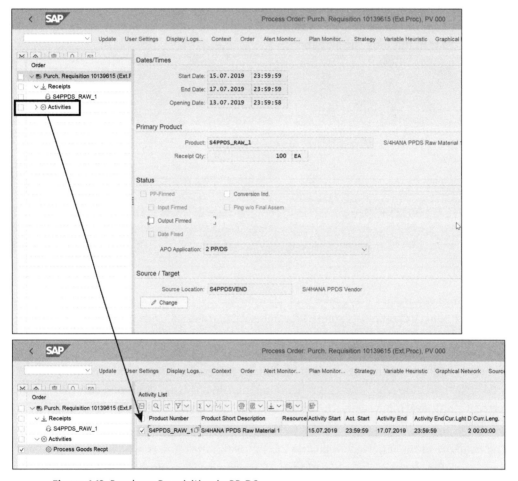

Figure 4.13 Purchase Requisition in PP-DS

Similar to planned orders, from the product view, select the **Conv. Ind.** checkbox to for purchase requisitions. Depending on the type of source of supply selected in the purchase requisition, the following types of orders for external procurement can be created:

- Purchasing info record: Purchase order
- Scheduling line agreement: Schedule line
- Contract: Purchase order with assignment to contract

In SAP S/4HANA, if a release procedure is in place for purchase requisition approval, the purchase requisition conversion must be executed in SAP S/4HANA because purchase order creation from the **Conv. Ind.** checkbox set in embedded PP-DS will fail if the purchase requisition isn't completely released in SAP S/4HANA.

In addition, if the SAP S/4HANA procurement process requires multiple purchase requisitions to be consolidated into one purchase order, conversion of the purchase requisitions to a purchase order should be executed in SAP S/4HANA. Setting the **Conv. Ind.** checkbox in embedded PP-DS will create one purchase order per purchase requisition.

4.6   Stocks and Batches

The inventory data in SAP S/4HANA includes the stocks and the associated batches. The stock information is transferred to embedded PP-DS along with the batch information if the material is batch managed.

The stocks are maintained at the plant level, and for planning purposes, the stock is considered at the MRP area level in SAP S/4HANA if an MRP area is assigned to the plant.

The plant-level stock will be transferred as the stock to the PP-DS plant location, and the stocks at the MRP area in SAP S/4HANA are transferred to the MRP area location in embedded PP-DS. The batch associated with the stock is transferred to embedded PP-DS; they are referred to as *versions* in the PP-DS planning tools.

The concept of stock update counters was introduced in SAP APO for improving the performance of the CIF transfer of inventory data and to avoid inconsistencies in the stock data being updated by a queue with older values of stocks. In embedded PP-DS, the stock update counters are activated by default and can't be turned off. The stock data transferred to embedded PP-DS uses the relative stocks, which refers to the delta between the current stock and the stock to be received or issued. The initial transfer of stock can be triggered by the CIF reconciliation tool (Transaction /SAPAPO/CCR) or the initial transfer report (Transaction /SAPAPO/PPDS_DELTA_ORD_TRANS). Whenever a stock posting happens in SAP S/4HANA, it's immediately transferred to embedded PP-DS, along with its batch and storage location information.

The stocks maintained in special scenarios, such as stock assigned to customers in make-to-order (MTO) scenarios, are also transferred to PP-DS and displayed under the customer segment in the PP-DS product view. The stocks are also represented as an order in PP-DS with the category "CC". As shown in Figure 4.14, the batch information displayed in SAP S/4HANA from Transaction MMBE for the material and plant is represented in the PP-DS product view (Transaction /SAPAPO/RRP3) as versions.

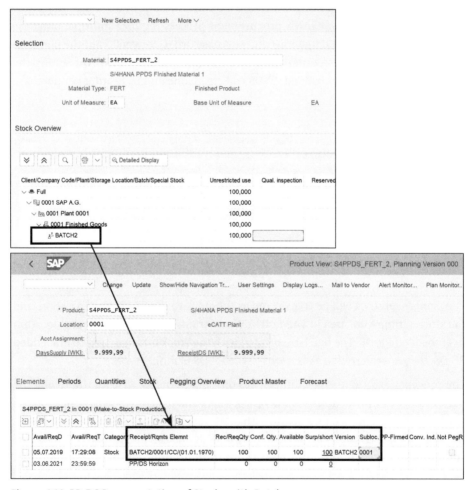

Figure 4.14 PP-DS Representation of Stocks with Batch

The **Version** column in the product view is the name of the batch from SAP S/4HANA, and the sublocation (**Subloc.** column) is the corresponding storage location in SAP S/4HANA. If the MRP area is associated with the storage location, the stock will be displayed only in the MRP area location (location type 1007 – Storage Location MRP Area) in PP-DS.

> **Note**
>
> As the stock update counters are used by embedded PP-DS by default, you can use the ABAP program /SAPAPO/STOCKUC_REORG to delete the obsolete stock update counters from embedded PP-DS.

4.7 Inspection Lots

Inspection lots in SAP S/4HANA are created in the quality management process. The inspection lot data includes the quantity, material, and plant. In the SAP S/4HANA system, the quantity under the inspection is considered quality stock.

In embedded PP-DS, for materials and plans for which the advanced planning is activated, the inspection lot is transferred to embedded PP-DS. Within PP-DS, the inspection lots are represented as an order with receipt, but not as a stock element. In PP-DS, the inspection lot will have only one receipt that corresponds to the material and location assigned to the inspection lot in SAP S/4HANA. No activities or requirements are attached to the inspection lot order in embedded PP-DS.

In SAP S/4HANA, the inspection lot is usually linked to an order (e.g., a production order) during in-process inspection, to a purchase order during procurement GR inspection, or to a sales order. This linkage isn't sent to PP-DS. Only the release status of the inspection lot is transferred to embedded PP-DS. The inspection lot in SAP S/4HANA ❶ (inspection lot displayed from Transaction QA03) and the same in PP-DS ❷ (the inspection lot displayed as **QM lot** in the product view) are shown in Figure 4.15.

The inspection lot is represented as an order in embedded PP-DS with an order category of BU – Insp Lot; this is represented as the **QM lot** in the **Category** column in the product view, as shown in the bottom screen of Figure 4.15. The inspection lot order is deleted from embedded PP-DS when the inspection quantity is set to 0, the usage decision is posted, the stock is moved to unrestricted quantity, or the inspection lot is canceled in SAP S/4HANA.

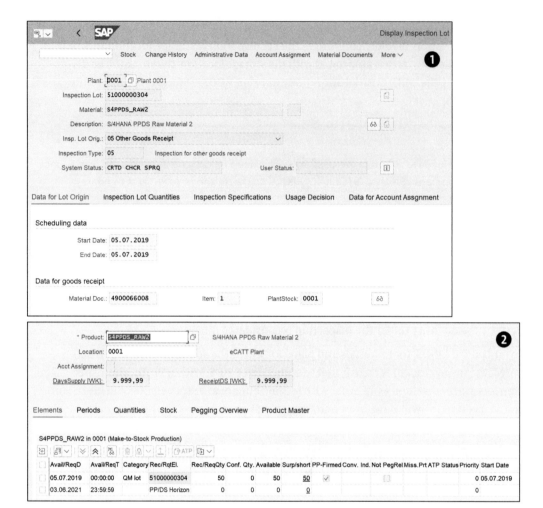

Figure 4.15 Inspection Lots in SAP S/4HANA and Embedded PP-DS

In PP-DS, the inspection lot can't be changed or deleted. Its date and output are fixed by default, as shown in Figure 4.16 (see the **Date Fixed** and **Output Firmed** checkboxes), so that PP-DS planning runs don't change the inspection lots.

Tip [+]

In embedded PP-DS, all the receipt elements are set with a time stamp so that they can be pegged by the requirement elements with the allowed pegging interval. As the inspection lot doesn't have a time in SAP S/4HANA, it's set with a time of **00:00:00** on the inspection lot start and end date. You can use the user exit QAP00003 to change this time stamp.

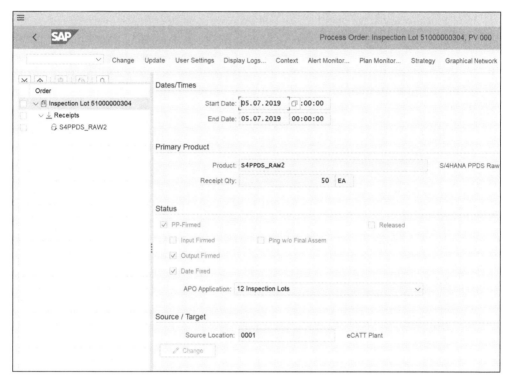

Figure 4.16 Inspection Lot Represented as an Order with Date/Output Firmed in PP-DS

4.8   Maintenance Orders

Plant maintenance orders in SAP S/4HANA are used for planning and executing the maintenance activities on the equipment and assets in the plant. Maintenance orders can be created for preventive or malfunction maintenance.

The maintenance orders in SAP S/4HANA can contain material components required for the maintenance and also operations required to perform the maintenance activity. These activities are scheduled on the maintenance work center. The equipment being worked on can be represented by the functional location, which can be assigned with a production resource or work center going through the maintenance activity.

In PP-DS, the maintenance order is only considered for the requirements generated by the maintenance order due to material components assigned to the order that are relevant to advanced planning. To block the availability of the resource on which the maintenance is being performed, a downtime can be created in the resource master data. This blocks the resource capacity for consumption by any planned orders or production orders, and any orders scheduled on the resource during this time will be rescheduled by the system.

For integrating the plant maintenance order to embedded PP-DS, an integration model needs to be created and activated because the plant maintenance order is a material-independent transaction data object. As shown in Figure 4.17, you can create an integration model using Transaction CFM1 and activate the integration model from Transaction CFM2 (refer to our discussion in Chapter 2, Section 2.1). Select the **Maint. Order** checkbox, and click the **Special Restrictions** button next to the **Maint.Order** field to enter the **Order Type** and **Plant** of the maintenance orders for which the integration model is being created.

Note

If a plant maintenance order has material components assigned that are relevant for advanced planning, material reservations are created for those components in SAP S/4HANA and are transferred to embedded PP-DS even without an active integration model for the maintenance orders.

When maintenance orders are created on production resources, they can't be available for production for the duration of the maintenance. The unavailability of resources for reasons such as maintenance is referred to as downtimes in PP-DS.

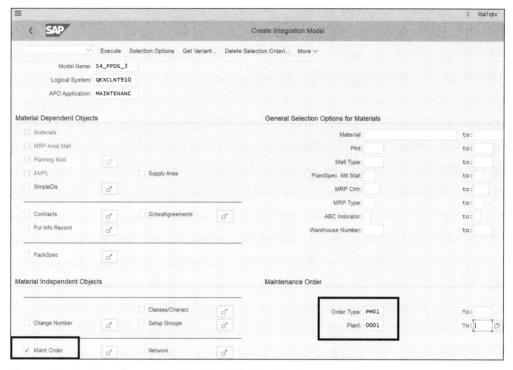

Figure 4.17 Creation of an Integration Model for Plant Maintenance Orders

Maintenance orders are created in Transaction IW31. For the plant maintenance orders to create downtime on the PP-DS resources, the following prerequisites must be met:

- The resource on which the maintenance is performed and on which in PP-DS the resource downtime creation is expected should be assigned to the functional location or the equipment entered in the maintenance order, as shown in Figure 4.18. The functional location is defined in Transaction IL01 by entering the work center name in the **Work center** field ❶. In the maintenance order, enter the functional location in the **Func. Loc.** field ❷.

- The maintenance order should be assigned with a system condition field (**Syst-Cond**) ❸, which is marked by the active checkbox in the **Reservatn** column (production work center reserved by plant maintenance) in the **System Condition** selection options screen, as shown in Figure 4.18 ❹.

159

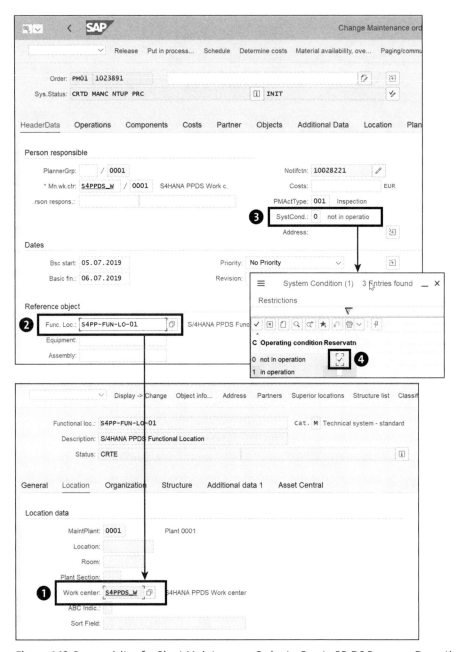

Figure 4.18 Prerequisites for Plant Maintenance Order to Create PP-DS Resource Downtime

The components entered in the maintenance order are transferred to embedded PP-DS as reservations if the components have are marked as active for advanced planning. These reservations can't be changed in embedded PP-DS and are always managed by SAP S/4HANA transactions such as goods issue (GI) so the order from the reservation will update the quantity in embedded PP-DS.

As shown in Figure 4.19, the component reservation is represented in embedded PP-DS with an order object that is input firmed, date firmed without any receipt elements, and can't be edited or deleted from embedded PP-DS.

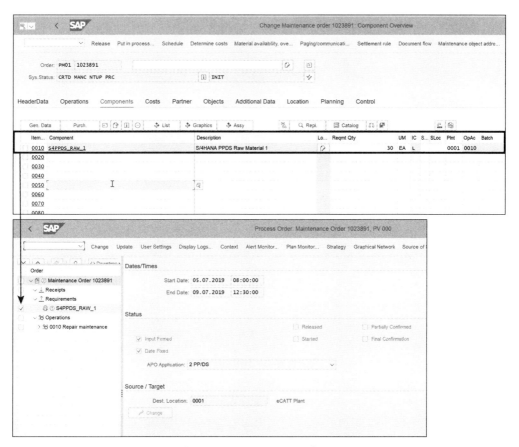

Figure 4.19 Plant Maintenance Order Components in SAP S/4HANA and Embedded PP-DS

After the component is completely issued to the order or the maintenance order is closed, the reservation is deleted from embedded PP-DS. As plant maintenance orders aren't dependent on materials, the reports to retransfer the PP-DS orders can't be used to transfer individual maintenance orders. The complete retransfer can be triggered by executing reactivation of the integration model, which is defined on the basis of the maintenance order types.

The operations in the plant maintenance order hold the information of the resource, which is used to perform the maintenance task and the duration of the work. The start date/time and end date/time are calculated based on the scheduling calculations. The start time and end times of the maintenance order can be displayed from the **Operations** tab of the maintenance order, as shown in Figure 4.20. The **Earl start date** and **Earl start time** columns have the start date and time of the maintenance operation, and the **EarliestEndDate** and **Earliest finish time** columns show the end time of the maintenance operation.

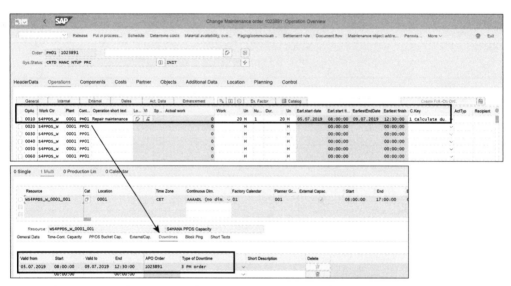

Figure 4.20 Maintenance Order Creating Downtime in the PP-DS Resource

The start and end times of the operation are used for calculating the downtimes in the PP-DS resource, as shown on the lower part of Figure 4.20. The downtimes of the resource in PP-DS can be displayed from the resource master data using Transaction /SAPAPO/RES01. Enter the **Resource** name and **Location**, and press ⌑Enter⌑. Then, navigate to the **Downtimes** tab. Here, you'll see an entry with the value "PM order" in the **Type of Downtime** column. If you want to change the data transferred to embedded PP-DS from SAP S/4HANA, the BAdI BADI_CIF_PM_ORDER can be used in SAP S/4HANA, and the BAdI /SAPAPO/MNT_INBOUND can be used in embedded PP-DS.

> **Tip**   [+]
>
> The PP-DS resource downtimes created by SAP S/4HANA maintenance orders can be listed by using report /SAPAPO/MNT_DOWNTIMES_FIND.

4.9   Sales Orders

Sales orders are the objects in SAP S/4HANA that represent the orders entered to fulfill customer requirements. The sales order can also have configurable materials for which the configuration of the product is entered at the time of order entry.

Depending on the planning strategy of the material in SAP S/4HANA, sales orders can be created in the make-to-stock (MTS) segment or MTO segment. The sales orders will consume the PIR quantities at the time of order entry or at the time of delivery, depending on the consumption strategy assigned to the planning strategy.

Sales orders are transferred to embedded PP-DS for the materials that are activated for advanced planning. The MTO sales orders will be created in the customer order segment in PP-DS. For configurable materials, the configuration entered during the order entry is transferred to the PP-DS sales order, which can be used by PP-DS in planning. The activation of the sales order transfer is set in Customizing for advanced planning, and no integration model is required for sales orders. Activating the sales order data transfer in Customizing also activates the following transaction data:

- Sales orders
- Deliveries
- Quotations
- Customer-independent requirements

Depending on the configuration schema set for the PP-DS system, the characteristics assigned to the sales order items are considered by the planning tools in PP-DS to fulfill the demand by supply elements with the same configuration.

In PP-DS, the material and location combination creates an object called the *pegging area*. The pegging area is also created in SAP liveCache and is the unique identifier for the location and material in the SAP liveCache level. For MTS materials, the pegging area is at the material/location level, and for MTO materials, individual sales orders, material, and location make up the pegging area. In PP-DS tools such as the product view, the sales order for MTO materials is shown under the corresponding segment (pegging areas), as shown in Figure 4.21. In the product view when there are multiple planning segments present, they are displayed on the left side of the screen under the **Planning Segments** panel. In the MTO scenario, the planning segments are displayed as shown in Figure 4.21 ❶. In the MTS scenario, there is only one planning area, which represents the product and location, as shown in Figure 4.21 ❷.

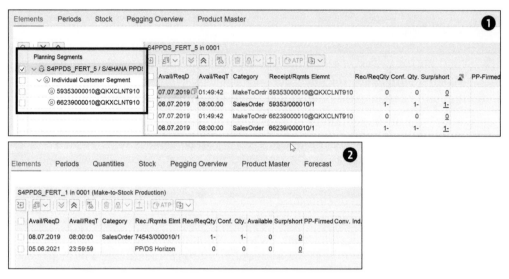

Figure 4.21 MTO versus MTS Sales Orders in PP-DS

Apart from the material, location, quantity, and the customer segment for the MTO scenarios, another important piece of information that sales orders bring into PP-DS is the order priority. Order priorities are used by PP-DS scheduling tools (e.g., detailed scheduling heuristics) and by the PP-DS optimizer to avoid delays in scheduling receipts for the sales orders with higher priorities.

In PP-DS, the order priority can be entered manually or can be automatically derived from the sales order or the priority set in the material master.

The order priority can be entered in the sales order item and be transferred to embedded PP-DS. During PP-DS planning, the order priority of the sales order can be propagated to the receipt elements, such as planned orders, and then to the production orders.

The source of the order priority is defined in the model version master data configuration in Transaction /SAPAPO/MVM. The options for setting the order priority determination were already covered in Chapter 3, Section 3.2.1.

If the model/version master data is set with the option **0 – In Make to Order from Sales Order Otherwise from Product** for the order priority, the MTO segment planned orders derive the priority from the sales order priority. The sales order priority can be set in the sales order (Transaction VAO2) item details via the **Shipping** tab in the **Delivery Prior.** field. The sales order priority is copied to the planned order and is displayed in the **Priority** column of the product view, as shown in Figure 4.22.

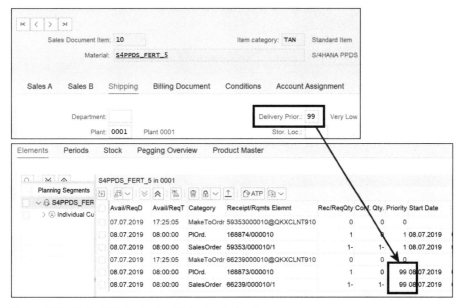

Figure 4.22 Order Priority in the Make-to-Order Scenario

If the model/version master data is set with option **0 – In Make to Order from Sales Order Otherwise from Product**, and the planning scenario is MTS, the order priority is derived from the priority set in the material master. In the material master (Transaction MMO2), navigate to the **Advanced Planning** tab, and under the **Proc/PPDS** section, enter the priority in the **Priority** field. The same is copied to the planned order. The planned order priority can be displayed in the product view under the **Priority** column in the **Elements** tab, as shown in Figure 4.23.

> **Note**
>
> In PP-DS orders, the priority value can range from 0 to 255, with 1 as the highest priority, and 255 as the lowest priority. Value 0 or no value is treated as 255, which is the lowest priority.

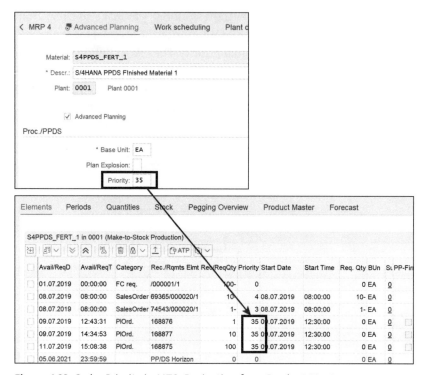

Figure 4.23 Order Priority in MTS: Derivation from Product Master

Materials with MTS planning strategies, where the PIRs aren't consumed by the sales order (e.g., planning strategy 10 in SAP S/4HANA) at the time of the sales order creation, are set with the **Not relevant for pegging** checkbox in embedded PP-DS. In addition, these orders can't participate in planning runs. The requirement quantity from such sales orders aren't considered for the calculation of the net requirement of the material location. Only the PIRs are considered for the net requirement calculation for such materials. The sales order requirements with **Not relevant for pegging** selected aren't pegged with any receipt element and are displayed in PP-DS transactions for information purpose.

When deliveries are created against the sales order and in planning strategies where the deliveries can consume the PIRs, the PIR consumption and the deliveries are transferred to embedded PP-DS.

4.10 Summary

In this chapter, we covered the important aspects of the transaction data during the integration between SAP S/4HANA and embedded PP-DS.

We also discussed the details of in-house manufacturing orders, external procurement orders, stocks, batches, sales orders, PIRs, inspection lots, and plant maintenance orders. Out of these, for the material-independent objects, there is a need to create and activate integration models, and for the other material-dependent transaction data objects, the transfer of data between SAP S/4HANA and embedded PP-DS is activated in Customizing.

For the commonly used transaction data objects, such as the planned orders, production orders, purchase requisitions, and purchase orders, the data is transferred via synchronous remote function call (sRFC) transfer from PP-DS to SAP S/4HANA, which minimizes the effort required to monitor the SAP S/4HANA inbound queues, and the errors are entered in the PP-DS planning logs.

We'll cover the technical aspects of the transaction data within SAP liveCache in Chapter 9, where we'll discuss administration of embedded PP-DS, including SAP liveCache.

So far, we've covered the basic required and commonly used configuration, master data, and transaction data details. In the next chapter, we'll discuss how the production planning functionality is executed in embedded PP-DS.

Chapter 5
Production Planning

In this chapter, we'll dive into the production planning process with PP-DS, from evaluating your requirements, to using heuristics, to evaluating the results of the planning run. You'll see how the process is impacted by integration with other planning solutions as well.

The SAP S/4HANA system has multiple options when it comes to planning materials for in-house or external procurement. SAP S/4HANA has sales and operations planning (S&OP), basic forecasting, demand management, long-term planning (LTP), and materials requirement planning (MRP). Some of these components, such as S&OP and forecasting, are no longer in further development, and SAP's next-generation supply chain planning tool, SAP Integrated Business Planning for Supply Chain (SAP IBP), takes over these components. In the SAP S/4HANA system, the traditional SAP ERP-based LTP and MRP went through a lot of improvements to simplify the way these processes are executed in SAP S/4HANA.

Apart from the improved enterprise resource planning (ERP) tools, the SAP S/4HANA system also has the PP-DS component in its core, which provides another option when complex planning problems arise that can't be solved by the SAP S/4HANA planning tools. The PP-DS planning is closely integrated to the SAP S/4HANA planning process via the new MRP Live function in the SAP S/4HANA system.

In this chapter, we'll start with the differentiators of PP-DS production planning compared to the SAP S/4HANA planning tools such as LTP and MRP, and then we'll cover the basic concepts in the PP-DS production planning process and the planning process itself, including the various heuristics for performing planning and the transactions and tools available in the PP-DS system for material planning. In addition, we'll discuss how PP-DS, MRP Live, and SAP IBP work in the SAP S/4HANA system, along with the tools available in the PP-DS system to evaluate the planning results and monitor the planning runs.

Any specific Customizing settings covered in previous chapters will be referred to here when they influence the PP-DS planning. Any new Customizing settings and the functionality behind them, such as the specific planning heuristics settings and planning tool settings, also will be covered as required.

5.1   Determining When PP-DS Should Be Used for Planning

In classic MRP, the basic concept is to fulfill the requirements with receipt elements by performing a net requirements calculation and calculation of the dates and quantities for the receipt elements per the set master data and Customizing settings. In addition, this process selects the source of supply for the receipt elements per the master data setup, such as quota arrangements and rules, validity dates, and lot sizes defined. The MRP functionality in SAP S/4HANA works with a set algorithm and provides flexibility in defining the MRP types that determine how the requirements and receipts are processed during the planning run, the lot sizing procedures that determine the quantity of the receipt elements, and various Customizing settings that can be used by the MRP algorithm during the planning run to handle planning situations. The MRP process guarantees material availability by balancing the inventory and receipts against the requirements.

If your manufacturing and procurement processes require more sophisticated features to optimize the plan, then the PP-DS planning brings in a lot of features covering requirements across industries and processes. The basic decision to use PP-DS planning depends on whether the material is critical to the supply chain and/or if the material is manufactured in a bottleneck resource. Let's walk through some of the specific functions required in the planning process that PP-DS can support and that aren't available in the SAP S/4HANA planning process, such as MRP:

- **Capacity-constrained production plan**
  MRP doesn't consider the capacity of the resources on which the receipt orders are going to be manufactured or handled. If a resource-constrained production plan is required, PP-DS can support this via the scheduling strategy assigned in the planning process. The production plan isn't generally required to be constrained with the resource availability, but PP-DS can support this process.

- **Shelf-life planning**
  PP-DS can be used if your materials are handled in batch management with shelf life defined, and you want the planning process to consider the shelf life. In PP-DS, the planning algorithm can consider the maturity time of the products received, the shelf life of the product, and the requirements of the maximum and minimum shelf life required to fulfill the requirements. The shelf life also can be propagated

throughout the order levels when there are multilevel orders present that handle materials with shelf life.

- **Variable lot sizes**
  In MRP, the lot sizing throughout the planning horizon is defined in the material master lot sizing procedure if you want to plan using different lot sizes for short-, medium-, and long-term horizons so that the supply elements are planned to the granular lot size level, such as daily for the short term and a more aggregated weekly or monthly for the medium term or long term. Materials that have such requirements are supported by PP-DS to achieve the desired results.

- **Characteristics-dependent planning (CDP)**
  In MRP, the planning run only considers the quantity during planning and can't ensure that components with the same characteristics values are netted against the demand elements that have characteristics values assigned to them. But with PP-DS CDP, it's possible to make sure the characteristics matching is executed during planning, and new receipt elements are created to fulfill the demand of the requirement elements with characteristics if there are no existing receipts with the same characteristics value available to fulfill the demand.

- **Realignment of supply and demand**
  In MRP in SAP S/4HANA, the planning is unidirectional and recursive only if the master data setup requires such planning. Therefore, after the MRP execution, it's possible that there are delays and earliness of receipts in covering the requirement elements. The MRP exceptions or the MRP Live cockpit needs to be reviewed manually to actively address these situations. With PP-DS, functionalities such as top-down and bottom-up rescheduling can be used to realign the demand and receipt elements. PP-DS can be used for critical materials for which the alignment of the demand and supply needs to be ensured through the order network.

- **Optimization**
  Critical materials, which require optimization from a production plan, and the scheduling perspective, which needs to be planned by PP-DS, the PP-DS optimizer can be used to optimize the plan to reduce setup costs and times, reduce delays, and optimize the production plan and schedule for the defined objective functions in the PP-DS optimizer.

- **Multistep planning**
  The PP-DS planning run need not be just a one-step planning execution like MRP. In one planning run, multiple steps can be defined to execute multiple planning algorithms in sequence. For example, MRP PP-DS heuristics can be followed by a

top-down or bottom-up rescheduling heuristics to realign the newly created and changed receipts from the MRP heuristic. Scheduling heuristics or even an PP-DS optimizer run can be scheduled in one planning run. Materials requiring such special planning and scheduling apart from MRP planning in SAP ERP should be activated for advanced planning.

- **Push production**
  In push production in PP-DS, if materials with shorter shelf life are received or produced in excess, they should be used up in producing materials with longer shelf life. This is applicable in food, dairy, chemical, and pharma industries. Such materials can be activated for PP-DS planning, so that they can be processed with PP-DS push production to avoid wastage of raw materials. PP-DS push production can identify the materials that can be produced using the expiring materials based in the production data structure (PDS) master data setup, and the planners can interactively plan the quantity of such material to be produced.

- **Product interchangeability**
  PP-DS supports simple discontinuation, so that if there are materials that are discontinued and being replaced by new materials, certain PP-DS planning heuristics can support this by using up the old material before the requirements are passed on to the new material. Updating the master data, such as bills of material (BOMs) and PDSs, is the right way to handle material changes in production; however, during the interim, when there is existing stock available for the old material, PP-DS interchangeability can be used for such materials to support the transition from the old to new material without causing wastage of the old product inventory.

- **Industry-specific functions**
  PP-DS supports certain industry-specific functions such as order combinations where multiple orders going through the same operation can be combined, and a new order is created to simplify and optimize the planning and execution processes. As many of the industry solutions, such as discrete industry and mill products (DIMP), are part of the SAP S/4HANA core, PP-DS can be used to leverage the industry functions in SAP S/4HANA, which can be further optimized using PP-DS planning and scheduling functions.

- **Alerts-based monitoring**
  The MRP process in SAP ERP works based on exceptions in the planning situation that are preconfigured in the system. Limited options are available to enhance the exception management of MRP in SAP ERP. With MRP Live in SAP S/4HANA, the

MRP cockpit is a set of SAP Fiori apps that provide more insights into the planning situation based on key performance indicator (KPI) applications, which are based on material coverage and capacity consumption. PP-DS brings in a much more sophisticated alert framework that is customizable to add the tolerances for the alerts and can be embedded into almost all the planning and scheduling tools. The alerts can be configured for receipts, requirements, pegging, shelf life, capacity consumption, and so on, and the materials activated for advanced planning in SAP S/4HANA can leverage the alert monitor in PP-DS to manage the exceptions in planning and scheduling.

5.2 Basic Functions in PP-DS Planning

In this section, we'll cover the basic concepts in production planning within PP-DS. These concepts are used widely by most of the planning heuristics and planning processes in PP-DS. The basic task of any planning tool is to consider the receipt elements and the requirement elements, and then perform a net requirements calculation. Then, based on the delta quantity and the dates on which the net quantity falls below zero, the planning tools should create a receipt element based on the quantity restrictions (lot sizes) maintained in the master data.

In addition, this section will cover the terminology used in the PP-DS planning process. We've covered the planning procedures and day's supply calculation in Chapter 3, where we discussed the configuration. In this section, we'll cover the details about pegging, net requirements calculation, and source of supply selection concepts.

5.2.1 Pegging

Pegging in PP-DS is used to signify the relationship or the link between a receipt (supply) and a requirement (demand) element. By doing so for all the material BOM levels, the overall lead time for the finished material can be calculated. If there are any delays in fulfilling the requirements generated in any level of the BOM by the demand for the finished material, these delays can be identified, and an alert can be generated accordingly.

The pegging process is executed by the system after every planning run and after any planning-relevant change in data, so that the receipt and requirements elements are linked at all times. The alerts also can be determined when any planning tool is being loaded with the planning data for any product location.

PP-DS supports two kinds of pegging relationships:

- **Dynamic pegging**
  In dynamic pegging, the system creates the pegging relationship between the supply and demand element based on the current planning situation. If there is a change, or a new receipt or requirement is created manually or by the system in the planning process, the pegging relationship will be recalculated and re-created.

- **Fixed pegging**
  In fixed pegging, the dynamic pegging relationship created can be fixed so that any future planning situation change won't alter the fixed pegging relationship. Manually created fixed pegging can't be changed or deleted by the system automatically during production planning, but the fixed pegging relationship created by the system during a planning run can be later changed in a subsequent planning run. However, a mere change in the planning situation won't change the fixed pegging relationship created by the system.

[+]

Tip

The business add-in (BAdI) /SAPAPO/RRP_HEUR_DO can be used to create fixed pegging relationships during a PP-DS MRP run. However, the standard method for creating a fixed pegging relationship in planning is to execute the heuristics for creating fixed pegging as a subsequent step after the planning heuristics in the PP-DS planning run.

For the pegging to be executed between a receipt and requirement element, the following conditions must be met:

- **Same pegging area**
  The pegging area is the combination of a product and a location in a planning version with the account assignment if relevant. For example, for a make-to-stock (MTS) material in a plant, the pegging area in the active planning version 000 is the combination of the material and the location. For a make-to-order (MTO) material, every sales order from the customers forms a customer segment, and apart from the material and location, the sales order (as an account assignment object) also becomes a part of the pegging area. The receipt and requirement elements should be part of the same pegging area for them to get pegged to each other.

■ **Pegging interval**
The receipt elements, including the stock elements, will be pegged to the requirement element if they are within the pegging interval. The pegging interval is set by default as 277,000 hours, which is approximately 31.6 years. This is the maximum value technically allowed for this field. So in embedded PP-DS, the pegging interval is a rolling defaulted 31.6 years (calculated from the requirement element date) and can't be changed in the material master, as shown in Figure 5.1.

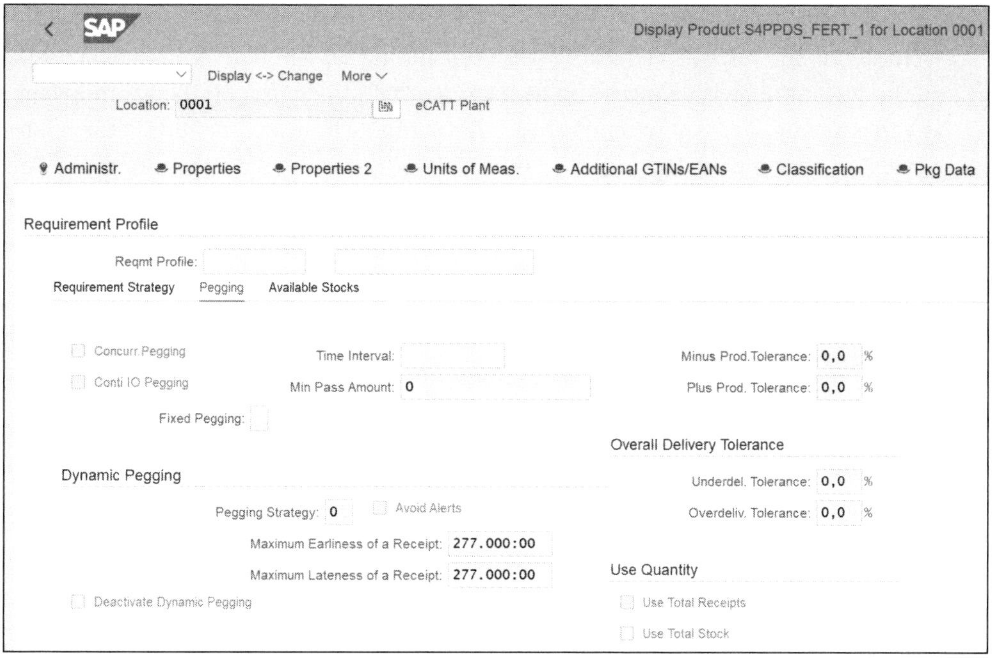

Figure 5.1 Default Values of Pegging Interval in the PP-DS Product Master

In CDP scenarios, the characteristics values of the receipt and requirement elements are checked for compatibility for pegging them.

For products that have a defined shelf life, minimum required shelf life, and maturation time after production, the dynamic pegging considers these values to make sure that when they are pegged to the requirement element, it's out of the maturity period of the product and complies with the minimum required shelf life.

5.2.2   Planning Horizon and Planning Time Fence

In PP-DS, either the demand can be transferred from a SAP planning system, such as SAP IBP, or a non-SAP system can send in the forecast in the form of planned independent requirements (PIRs) to SAP S/4HANA, which will be transferred to embedded PP-DS if the material is activated for advanced planning. A planning tool such as SAP IBP is responsible for forecasting and planning the mid- to long-term forecasting and supply planning. However, embedded PP-DS is a short- to mid-term planning tool, and PP-DS is used for short-term detailed scheduling.

To define the responsibility of PP-DS for planning only in the short term, a PP-DS planning horizon is defined. Any demand that falls under the PP-DS planning horizon is planned by PP-DS planning tools. The planning horizon is defined in the model version master data (Transaction /SAPAPO/MVM) (see Chapter 3, Section 3.2.1). The horizon defined here is considered by all the material locations. In a production planning run, the PP-DS planning heuristics only consider the demand and supply within this horizon for the calculation of the unfilled demand.

> **Note**
>
> In PP-DS for SAP S/4HANA (embedded PP-DS), the planning horizon can only be maintained at the model version level, and there is no possibility to maintain a material location-specific PP-DS planning horizon.

The PP-DS planning time fence is the shorter horizon in the planning horizon within which the system isn't allowed to make changes to the planning data during an interactive or background production planning run. Manual changes are allowed within the planning time fence. When the planners adjust the plan and finalize the schedule for the near-term shorter time horizon, the plan must not be altered by the system, and the planning time fence can be defined to such a duration. The PP-DS time fence is defined in the material master by using Transaction MM02 and navigating to the **MRP 1** tab, as shown in Figure 5.2. On the upper screen, you can see the **Planning time fence** value of "21" set, in our example. This value defined in the material master is also used by the PP-DS planning time fence if the material is activated for advanced planning, as shown in the lower screen in Figure 5.2.

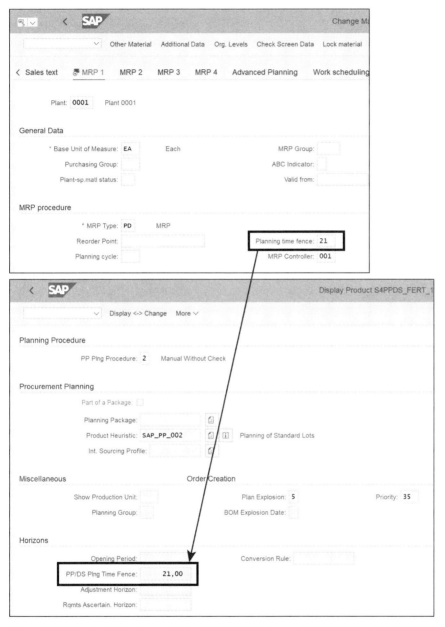

Figure 5.2 Planning Time Fence in the Material Master and in PP-DS Product Master Data

5.2.3   Net Requirements Calculation

Net requirements calculation is the process of balancing the demand and supply quantities and arriving at the missing quantities so that new receipt elements can be created to cover them.

In embedded PP-DS, it's possible to customize the way the receipts and requirement elements are treated by the net requirements calculation process. These customizations are made in the heuristics settings, so that when a planning heuristic is called in the planning run or interactive planning, the system uses the net requirements calculation procedure set in the heuristics to apply it on the planning.

The concept of pegging isn't to be confused with the concept of net requirements calculation. The pegging only links the available receipt and requirement element. But the role of net requirements calculation is to find out when the net quantity (sum of receipts and requirements) falls below zero and trigger a receipt creation at that point in time to fill the open demand.

During net requirements calculation, the system starts with the stock and the receipt elements and nets them against the open demand elements. The settings are made in the heuristics Customizing (Transaction /SAPAPO/CDPSC11), as shown in Figure 5.3. The following options are available to influence the netting:

- **FIFO**
  With the first in, first out (FIFO) netting procedure, the earliest available requirement element is assigned to the stock element or the earliest available receipt element, and the same chronological order is followed for netting throughout the PP-DS planning horizon.

- **Avoid Surpluses**
  This procedure will try to avoid new receipt elements creation by assigning the available receipt and stock elements to the requirement elements, irrespective of whether this assignment will cause a delay for the requirement element being fulfilled on time. This procedure divides the planning horizon into two sections, one for the elements within the PP-DS time fence and another section for the elements outside the planning time fence.

- **Avoid Delays**
  This netting procedure will try to avoid delays in fulfilling the requirement elements by assigning the stocks and fixed receipt elements to the requirements. If there is a delay, this procedure will propose creating a new receipt element. Thus, this procedure may lead to excess supply.

The other options available to influence the net requirements calculation are as follows:

- **Use Total Receipts**
  With this setting active, when one receipt element is pegged to a requirement element irrespective of the quantity being pegged to the requirement element, the complete receipt element is consumed. If there are partial available quantities from the receipt element, those are left open and are not assigned to any other requirement element.

- **Use Total Stocks**
  With this option, when the stock element is assigned to a requirement element during the net requirements calculation, then the stock element is completely consumed for the purpose of the net requirements calculation, and no other requirement element can be pegged to the stock element.

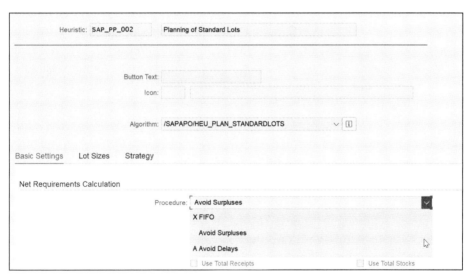

Figure 5.3 Net Requirements Calculation Procedures in PP-DS Planning Heuristics

5.2.4   Procurement Quantity Calculation

When the net requirements calculation determines when to create a receipt element, the procurement quantity calculation will determine for what quantity the receipt quantity should be created. This is determined by the lot size definition. The lot size can be defined in the heuristics-specific settings and in the material master's **Advanced Planning** tab.

The heuristics-specific settings for lot size provide options that are only relevant for that heuristic. The lot size data maintained in the **MRP 1** view and the **Advanced Planning** view of the material master are considered by the PP-DS planning heuristics, which needs to determine a quantity for order creation. The lot sizing information from the **MRP 1** view, such as lot sizing procedure, minimum and maximum lot sizes, and rounding factors, is considered by PP-DS in addition to the lot sizing unit of measure and other lot sizing-specific fields from the **Advanced Planning** view of the material master.

The standard planning heuristics, such as the planning of standard lots heuristics, support several lot sizing procedures in the standard embedded PP-DS system. You can access the following procedures in the **Lot Sizes** tab, as shown in Figure 5.4:

- **Lot-for-Lot**
  This procedure will propose a receipt quantity exactly the same as the requirement quantity per the net requirements calculation. However, this procedure will consider the minimum and maximum lot size settings and the rounding parameters maintained in the material master.

- **Fixed Lot Size**
  This procedure will propose receipt quantities per the fixed lot size defined in the material master, irrespective of the net requirements quantity. If one receipt can't cover the entire net requirements quantity, multiple receipts are proposed with the fixed lot size until the requirement can be covered with the new receipts.

- **By Period**
  In periodic lot sizing procedures, the net requirements are grouped together per period (day, week, etc.), and one receipt element is proposed per period. This procedure also respects the minimum and maximum lot size settings and the rounding settings.

- **Reorder Point**
  Embedded PP-DS only supports the **Reorder Point Method 2**, which is reorder supply from the material location master.

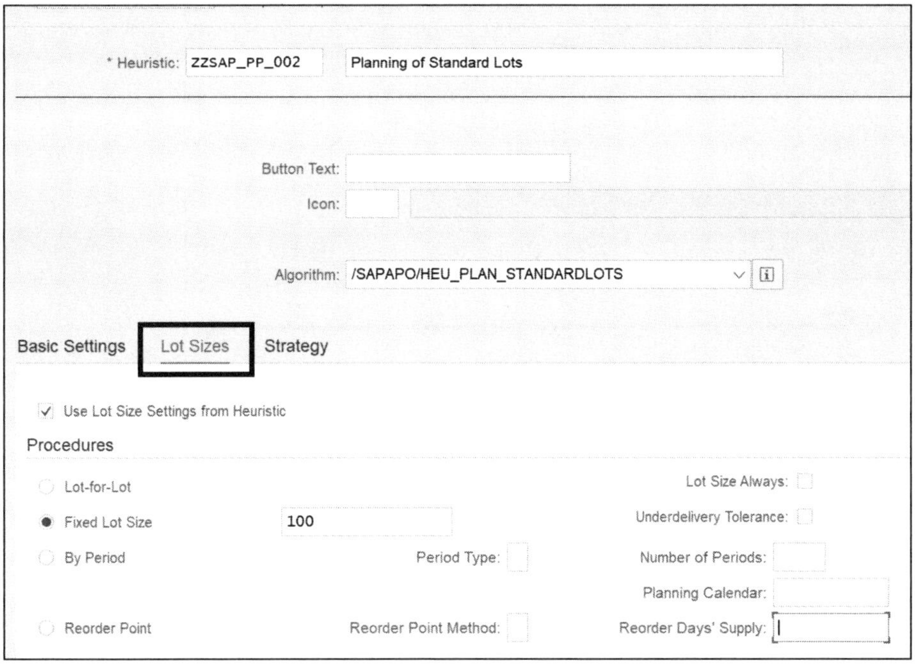

Figure 5.4 Lot Sizing Maintenance in PP-DS for Advanced Planned Materials

[+]

Tip

Irrespective of the lot sizing method maintained in the **MRP 1** view of the material master, if the reorder day's supply is maintained in the **Advanced Planning** view of the material master, then PP-DS planning heuristics will consider this material with a lot sizing procedure with the reorder order point method.

The minimum and maximum lot sizes are maintained in the material master (Transaction MM02) **MRP 1** tab in the **Minimum Lot Size** and **Maximum Lot Size** fields. In addition, the PP-DS specific lot sizing settings, such as the **Reorder Day's Supply**, is defined in the **Advanced Planning** tab under the **Lot Size** section, as shown in Figure 5.5.

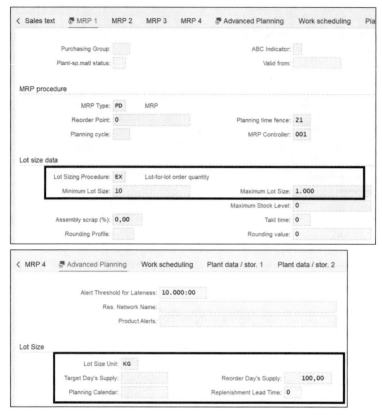

Figure 5.5 Lot Sizing Procedure Definition in MRP 1 and Advanced Planning Views

5.2.5   Source Determination

When the time and the quantity are determined by the netting and procurement quantity calculation processes, the next step is to determine the source of supply for the receipt element. Depending on the type of procurement, whether it's in-house produced material or externally procured material, the source determination process will determine either a valid PDS to produce the material or a valid external procurement relationship to procure the material.

For in-house produced materials, the system considers the available PDSs, and the PDS that can produce the material with the minimum delay is selected by the system to create the receipt element. In interactive planning, if the heuristics setting allows this, the user can select the source of supply manually from a ranked list of all the available sources.

For externally procured materials, the rankings of the source of supplies are calculated per the procurement priority, procurement costs assigned to the procurement relationships, and the quota. The system will look for the least costly and highest priority source that can fulfill the demand without any delay.

For PP-DS source determination in general, on-time delivery is the driving principle in selecting the source of supply.

5.3   Leveraging Planning Heuristics

In embedded PP-DS, the planning of a material can be executed in multiple ways, including MRP Live planning, PP-DS background planning runs, and interactive planning from the PP-DS planning tools. All these methods of executing the planning, end up calling a planning heuristic, and the heuristics settings, along with the various profiles used by different planning tools, determine the planning results. In this section, we'll discuss the features offered by the commonly used production planning heuristics.

The planning heuristics have an algorithm that can determine a shortage quantity and create a receipt to cover the shortage quantity. The algorithm is an ABAP function module that is designed to execute the specific planning task. The screens and the available settings in the heuristics Customizing are also part of the algorithm definition. Any of the production planning heuristics can be called in the MRP heuristic, which offer a mechanism to determine the BOM structure and execute the heuristics assigned to the MRP heuristic or the product heuristics following the low-level code of the material.

> **Note**
>
> Irrespective of the heuristics type (planning, scheduling, or service heuristics), it's always recommended to create a copy of the heuristics, and make the required changes to enable options and functionalities offered by the specific heuristics.

5.3.1   Planning of Standard Lots

Planning of standard lots is the most commonly used planning heuristic to fulfill uncovered demands. The standard heuristics are delivered with the name SAP_PP_

002 and the standard algorithm /SAPAPO/HEU_PLAN_STANDARDLOTS assigned to the heuristic.

The planning of standard lots heuristic executes the standard net requirements calculation and calculates the procurement quantity per the lot sizing definition from the material master or from the heuristic itself. Then, it executes source of supply determination per the standard logic. After the dates, quantities, and sources are determined, the receipt elements are created by this heuristic. When creating the planned orders for in-house produced materials, these planned orders need to be scheduled on the resources belonging to the PDS selected. Therefore, this heuristic provides options to control the scheduling parameters via the scheduling strategy assignment in the heuristic setting.

This heuristic can respect the characteristics values during net requirements calculation to evaluate the characteristics values of the requirement and receipt elements during the netting process. The shelf-life data, such as maturation time and minimum remaining shelf life, is also considered by this heuristic if the heuristics setting is made accordingly (see Chapter 8, Section 8.1).

To access this heuristic, execute Transaction /SAPAPO/CDPSC11 and double-click on the **SAP_PP_002** heuristic in the list displayed. You'll arrive at the screen shown in Figure 5.6. The basic settings of the **Planning of Standard Lots** heuristic has several areas, which we'll explore in the following sections.

Figure 5.6 Net Requirements Calculation Settings for the Planning of Standard Lots Heuristic

Net Requirements Calculation

As shown in Figure 5.6, in the **Net Requirements Calculation** section of the heuristics Customizing, the **Procedure** for the net requirements calculation is set. The **Group Past Requirements** checkbox can be used to cumulate all the requirement elements in the past (older than current date) and the requirements within the PP-DS time fence together and consider this as one demand element so that the procurement quantity calculation, including the lot sizing, is applied on this cumulated quantity. It makes sense to use this checkbox in planning situations where past demands are always present that weren't fulfilled on time and need to be fulfilled immediately. Grouping them together will reduce any excess quantities procured due to lot sizing restrictions.

For the consideration of the shelf-life restrictions, such as maturity time and the minimum required shelf life, the **Plan with Shelf Life** checkbox needs to be selected. In addition, the corresponding products must have the **Plan with Shelf Life** checkbox activated in the **Advanced Planning** tab of the material master.

In planning scenarios where the shortages outside the PP-DS horizon need to be planned within the PP-DS horizon, the **Consider Shortages Outside the PP/DS Horizon** option can be used. With this option, the system temporarily brings in the requirements outside of the PP-DS horizon for the duration defined under the **Period Outside the PP/DS Horizon** section. If there are shortages, then receipt elements will be created inside the PP-DS horizon.

Create New Receipt Elements

As shown in Figure 5.7, the order of the new receipt creation and the reuse mode is defined for the heuristics. The **Sort Procedure** has two options:

- **Chronological Order**
  When the heuristic needs to create several orders due to the dates, netted quantities, and lot sizing procedures, they are created in the order of the earliest order first.

- **Order Priority, Chronological**
  With this option, the orders with higher priorities are created first and then the earliest order within the priority is created first. Along with the scheduling profiles assigned to the planning of standard lots heuristic, this setting can help ensure that the higher-priority orders are created and scheduled first before other orders are created.

185

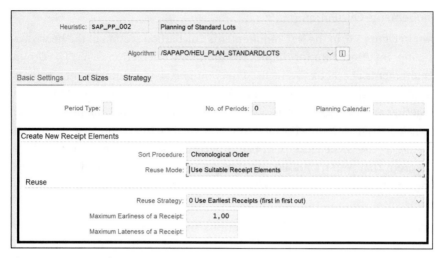

Figure 5.7 Settings for New Receipt Creation in Planning of Standard Lots Heuristic

The **Reuse Mode** within the heuristics setting controls how the existing fixed and unfixed receipt elements are treated during the execution of this heuristic. We covered the details of the reuse modes in Chapter 3, Section 3.4.1, where we discussed the PP-DS planning procedure customization.

When the **Reuse Mode** is set to **Use Suitable Receipt Elements**, the system also leverages the settings under the **Reuse** section. The **Reuse Strategy** defines how the existing receipt elements are used by this heuristic to cover open requirements. Following are the available options:

- **0 Use Earliest Receipts (first in first out)**
  Irrespective of the requirement date, use an existing receipt in chronological order (first in first out) when there is a shortage. This may lead to requirement elements covered too early or too late, as well as earliness and lateness alerts for pegging.

- **Use Timely Receipts**
  With this option, the system searches for a timely receipt within the reuse interval defined per the **Maximum Earliness of a Receipt** and **Maximum Lateness of a Receipt** fields. If there are no suitable receipt elements available within the reuse interval, this heuristic will propose a new receipt to be created.

Settings for New Explosion

As shown in Figure 5.8, the **Settings for New Explosion** section is relevant for the standard lot heuristics when the **Reuse Mode** is set to **Reexplode Plan**. With this reuse mode, the source of supply is re-exploded. When this happens for an in-house manufacturing planned order, this may lead to changes in the modes/dates and thus the resources used by the order. To ensure that the heuristics retain the same mode (and the resource) during a re-explosion of the PDS triggered by the planning of standard lots heuristic, the **Retain Mode** checkbox can be selected.

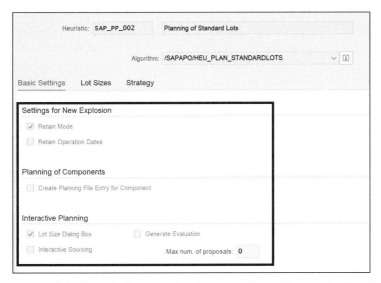

Figure 5.8 Settings for Re-Explosion, Components, and Interactive Planning in the Planning of Standard Lots Heuristic

Note

If the mode is no longer available due to a change in the PDS or the validity date of the mode is no longer under the validity of the order, a mode change can happen irrespective of the **Retain Mode** checkbox value.

A re-explosion of an in-house manufacturing planned order may lead to a rescheduling of the order, and, thus, the operation dates may get changed in this process. To retain the operation date as it appeared before the re-explosion, you can use the

Retain Operation Dates checkbox. When this is selected and the scheduling direction is set as backward scheduling, the operation end date is derived from the operation of the order before it's re-exploded. When the scheduling direction is set as forward scheduling, the operation start date is derived from the operation of the order before the re-explosion is triggered. (The details of the scheduling direction are covered in Chapter 6, Section 6.2.2.) However, because a finite scheduling strategy will lead to a change in the operation dates, it's generally recommended to perform the production planning run in PP-DS without finite scheduling.

Planning of Components

Creating new receipts by the planning of standard lots heuristic will create dependent demand for the components of the material being planned. According to the planning procedure set for the component materials, when the dependent demand is created or changed, the system reacts accordingly (no action, planning run immediately, create planning file entry, etc.). But if you want to override the planning procedure action and always create a planning file entry for the materials for which the dependent demand is created, you can select the **Create Planning File Entry for Components** checkbox in the heuristics settings. If the component material has a planning procedure with **Do Not Carry Out Any Action** defined as the **Action**, then no planning file entry will be created (see Chapter 3, Section 3.4.1).

Interactive Planning

The **Interactive Planning** section (refer to Figure 5.8) determines how the system behaves when the planning of standard lots heuristic is called from an interactive planning tool, such as the product view or order view. During interactive planning, you can change the lot size definition for just that heuristic execution in the planning tool; to allow this, select the **Lot Size Dialog Box** checkbox in the heuristics settings. With this setting, a dialog box with the current lot sizing procedure per the values from the material master or the values from the heuristics is defaulted on the screen, and the user has an option to change them manually.

To understand the planning elements the system has considered during the interactive execution of the planning of standard lots heuristic, you can select the **Generate Evaluation** checkbox in the heuristics settings. The evaluation contains the information of all the requirement elements, the fixed receipts, the receipts the heuristics has deleted, and the planning file entries created during the execution of the planning of standard lots heuristic in interactive mode.

In addition, you can select the **Interactive Sourcing** checkbox to manually select the source of supply for the external procurement receipts being generated by this heuristic. When there are more orders than the value defined in the **Max. num. of proposals**, the interactive sourcing isn't enabled.

Lot Sizes

The **Lot Sizes** tab of the heuristics settings has the same lot sizing settings that can be set from the material master **MRP 1** and **Advanced Planning** views (as you saw in Section 5.2.4). But if you want to override the lot size data maintained in the material master and use the one defined in the heuristics settings, select the **Use Lot Size Settings from Heuristic** checkbox, as shown in Figure 5.9.

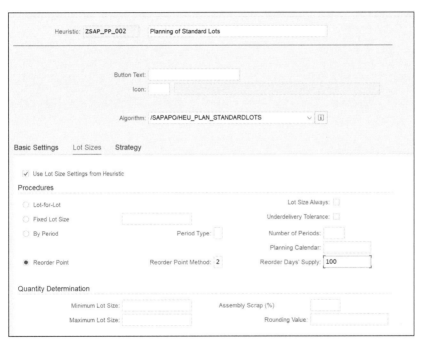

Figure 5.9 Heuristic-Specific Lot Sizing Overriding Material Master Lot Size Data

Strategy

As shown in Figure 5.10, the **Strategy** tab of the heuristics settings determines the scheduling parameters to be used for scheduling the receipt elements created by the planning of standard lots heuristic. The scheduling strategy options within the planning of standard lots heuristic are controlled, so that the heuristic can execute and created orders. For example, only the infinite scheduling strategy is available within the heuristics setting for the scheduling mode. However, the scheduling strategy also can be defined in the individual planning tools, which will take precedence over the strategy profile defined at this heuristic level. The following scheduling strategies are available in the **Sched. Mode** dropdown:

- **4 Infinite Scheduling**
- **7 Search for Bucket with Free Capacity**

When the scheduling strategy defined at the planning tool level isn't able to create the order due to scheduling constraints imposed by the strategy, the strategies defined at the planning of standard lots heuristic will act as a backup strategy and can create orders if allowed.

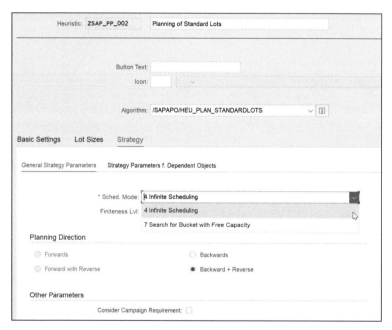

Figure 5.10 Scheduling Strategy for Planning of Standard Lots Heuristic

5.3.2   Reorder Point Planning

The reorder point planning heuristic is delivered in the standard embedded PP-DS system with the name SAP_PP_007 – Reorder Point Planning and with the algorithm /SAPAPO/HEU_REORDER_POINT_PLAN.

The reorder point maintained in the material master **MRP 1** tab is considered by this heuristic for refilling the stock up to the reorder point if the current stock level is below the reorder level maintained in the material master.

The net requirements calculation for this heuristic only considers the current stock level, the receipt elements, and the reorder point defined in the material master. No other requirement elements are considered for the net requirements calculation, which may lead to excess supply or supply shortage; therefore, this heuristic should be used for materials that are truly procured based on reorder point planning. In general, for such materials, advanced planning isn't necessary, and they can be planned in MRP Live in SAP S/4HANA. If such materials are produced in-house on a bottleneck resource, then those materials can be activated for advanced planning, and the reorder point planning heuristic can be assigned as the product heuristic for those products.

The heuristics settings for the reorder point planning heuristic are shown in Figure 5.11. In the **Basic Settings** tab, the **Delete Non-Fixed Receipt Elements** option will delete all the nonfixed receipt elements and re-create them if the net requirements calculation determines a shortage. If the **Delete Non-Fixed Receipt Elements** checkbox isn't selected, the excess nonfixed receipt elements won't be deleted by this heuristic.

Figure 5.11 Reorder Point Planning Heuristic Basic and Lot Size Settings

The example for the treatment of the nonfixed receipt elements is depicted in Table 5.1 and Table 5.2. Table 5.1 shows the current planning situation with a reorder point of 70 maintained in the material master.

Date	Time	Element	Number	Receipt/Requirement Quantity
05.07.2019	0:00:00	Stock	Stock	10
24.07.2019	12:00:00	Forecast requirement		−50
02.08.2019	17:00:00	Purchase requisition	10140086/00	100

Table 5.1 Example of Current Planning Situation

This situation would look the same without the **Delete Non-Fixed Receipt Elements** option selected. Because the nonfixed receipt element (purchase requisition) isn't deleted, the total available receipts (stocks + purchase requisition) quantity (10 + 100) is more than the reorder point defined in the material master (70).

However, with the option selected, the situation would look like Table 5.2 after the reorder point planning heuristic. As you can see, the nonfixed purchase requisition with quantity 100 is deleted, and a new purchase requisition is created with quantity 60 to balance the reorder point quantity of 70: stock quantity 10 + new purchase requisition quantity 60 = 70 (reorder point).

Date	Time	Element	Number	Receipt/Requirement Quantity
05.07.2019	0:00:00	Stock	Stock	10
24.07.2019	12:00:00	Forecast requirement		−50
02.08.2019	17:00:00	New purchase requisition	10140086/00	60

Table 5.2 Planning Situation after Reorder Point Planning (with Delete Nonfixed Receipts Option)

Referring back to the settings shown in Figure 5.11, the **Fill to Maximum Stock Level** checkbox will create a receipt element to fill up to the maximum stock level maintained in the **MRP 1** view of the material master when the net requirements calculation warrants the creation of a receipt element by the system.

> **Note**
>
> When maintaining the maximum stock level and reorder point in the **MRP 1** tab of the material master, the system will raise a warning or an information message saying the MRP procedure doesn't make use of these fields. But with advanced planning, PP-DS uses these fields when the reorder point planning heuristic is executed.

The **Lot Size** settings in the reorder point planning heuristic (shown on the lower area of Figure 5.11) only provide the option to define the maximum and minimum lot sizes because other settings, such as lot sizing procedure, aren't relevant for the reorder point planning scenario and are ignored by this heuristic.

The **Strategy** tab is like the planning of standard lots heuristic where the heuristic only has infinite scheduling modes available in the heuristics settings.

5.3.3 Planning of Standard Lots in Three Horizons

The planning of standard lots in three horizons heuristic is delivered in the SAP standard system with the name SAP_PP_004 and the standard algorithm /SAPAPO/ HEU_PEGID_PERIODIC_LOT.

The planning of standard lots in three horizons is the same as the planning of standard lots heuristic, except for the lot sizing procedure defined in the heuristics settings. The basic settings and the strategy settings are the same as the planning of standard lots heuristic.

This heuristic offers up to three different lot sizing procedures that can be used in certain periods. For example, week 1 is planned in lot-for-lot lot sizing procedure, week 2 to week 5 are planned using a daily (periodic) lot sizing procedure, and week 6 to the end of the PP-DS horizon are planned with a weekly (periodic) lot sizing.

As shown in Figure 5.12, the **Lot Size** tab of this heuristic offers the flexibility to enter three different lot sizes for different time horizons. The **Short-Term Horizon** starts from the date of the heuristics execution until the duration defined as the short-term horizon, and the **Medium-Term Horizon** starts at the end of the short-term horizon and runs for the duration defined in the heuristics setting. The **Long-Term Horizon** starts from the end of the medium-term horizon and runs through until the end of the PP-DS horizon. Following are the commonly used **Period Types**:

- **D** (day)
- **W** (week)
- **M** (month)
- **Q** (quarter)

Figure 5.12 Lot Sizing Settings for the Planning of Standard Lots in Three Horizons Heuristic

An example of the lot size calculation from the planning of standard lots in three horizons heuristic is illustrated in Table 5.3, Table 5.4, Table 5.5, and Table 5.6. Table 5.3 shows the current planning situation before the heuristic is executed.

Date	Element	Quantity
24/07/2019 (current date)	Forecast requirement	−10
24/07/2019	Dependent demand	−10
27/07/2019	Forecast requirement	−12
27/07/2019	Forecast requirement	−25
10/9/2019	Forecast requirement	−30
11/9/2019	Forecast requirement	−25
12/9/2019	Forecast requirement	−10

Table 5.3 Current Planning Situation

Because the short-term horizon is defined as three days in this example, and the lot-for-lot lot sizing procedure is used, the planned orders are created with the exact lot of the forecast requirements, as shown in Table 5.4.

Date	Element	Quantity
24/07/2019	Forecast requirement	−10
24/07/2019	Planned order	10
24/07/2019	Dependent demand	−10
24/07/2019	Planned order	10

Table 5.4 After the Planning of Standard Lots in Three Horizons Heuristic Execution: Short-Term Horizon 3 Days, Lot Sizing Lot-for Lot

Because the mid-term horizon is defined as 30 days in Table 5.5, and the daily lot sizing procedure is used, the planned order is created by combining the requirement quantities (12 and 25) of the same day in one planned order with quantity 37.

Date	Element	Quantity
27/07/2019	Forecast requirement	−12
27/07/2019	Forecast requirement	−25
27/07/2019	Planned order	37

Table 5.5 After the Planning of Standard Lots in Three Horizons Heuristic Execution: Mid-Term Horizon 30 Days, Lot Sizing: Daily (Periodic)

The long-term horizon has the weekly lot sizing procedure in this example shown in Table 5.6. Executing the planning of standard lots in three horizons heuristic combines all the requirement quantities from the week (-30, -25, and -10) and creates one planned order for the total quantity 65.

Date	Element	Quantity
10/9/2019	Forecast requirement	−30
11/9/2019	Forecast requirement	−25
12/9/2019	Forecast requirement	−10
10/9/2019	Planned order	65

Table 5.6 After the Planning of Standard Lots in Three Horizons Heuristic Execution: Long-Term Horizon, Lot Sizing: Weekly (Periodic)

5.3.4 MRP Heuristic

The MRP heuristic in PP-DS is an enabling heuristic that can execute a production planning heuristic assigned to the heuristics or the product heuristics assigned to the material in the **Advanced Planning** view of the material master. It's delivered in the standard PP-DS system with the name SAP_MRP_001 and with the standard algorithm /SAPAPO/HEU_MRP_PLANNING.

The MRP heuristic is classified as an enabling heuristic because it can't perform planning (net requirements calculation, procurement quantity determination, and source determination) on its own. However, because it can be used for executing planning heuristics, we're covering the details of the MRP heuristic in this section.

The MRP heuristic settings are very limited, as shown in Figure 5.13, to the extent of a few heuristics parameters and the technical settings for parallel processing to improve the performance of the PP-DS planning run.

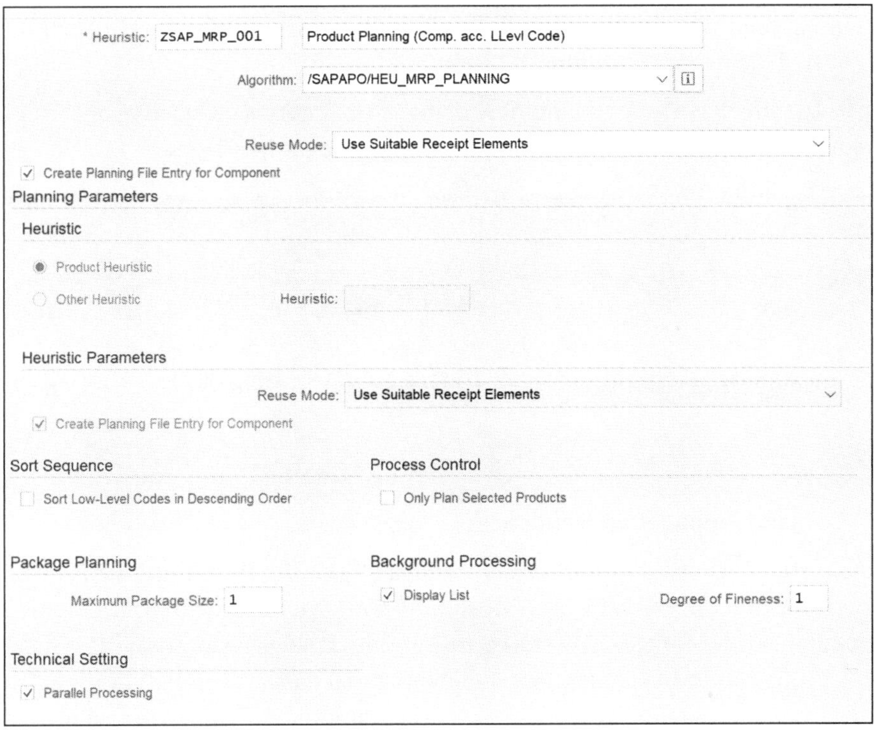

Figure 5.13 Settings for the MRP Heuristic

The **Heuristic** section of the settings determines if the MRP heuristic will execute the product heuristic or another heuristic assigned in the heuristics settings.

The heuristics parameters are the same as the planning of standard lots heuristic for the **Reuse Mode** and **Create Planning File Entry for Component**. The **Sort Low-Level Codes in Descending Order** setting will change the direction of the planning from the lowest level component to the top-level finished product. This can be useful when executing other service heuristics via the MRP heuristic to realign the higher-level requirement with the lower-level supplies. However, in a production planning run (using a planning heuristic), this checkbox must be deselected to avoid adverse impacts in the planning results.

The **Maximum Package Size** is relevant when **Parallel Processing** is selected for the MRP heuristic. The production planning runs handles a large data volume, and even with the power of SAP liveCache in the PP-DS, the performance can still be a concern. To reduce the runtime of the MRP heuristic, parallel processing can be activated in the heuristics settings. The technical setup of parallel processing for the MRP heuristic is covered in Chapter 3, Section 3.4.2.

The package size determines the number of material locations included in one package, which is dispatched to a parallel process to execute the heuristics.

Note

When the MRP heuristic is executed, if one of the materials in a planning package ends up with a termination, the planning of all the materials in the package are rolled back. Therefore, it's important to have a small number as the package size to reduce the impact and avoid one material in the package making the whole package fail.

5.3.5   Demand Propagation Heuristic

This heuristic is delivered in standard embedded PP-DS with the name SAP_PP_022 and the algorithm /SAPAPO/HEU_DEMAND_PROPAGATION. It can be used in external procurement scenarios where stocks are transferred between locations. This heuristic identifies all the locations that supply material to the material location for which the heuristic is being executed, and it propagates the demand to the supplying locations by creating procurement elements such as stock transport requisitions.

This heuristic can execute multilevel demand propagation according to the heuristics settings. As shown in Figure 5.14, when the **Multilevel** checkbox is set, it executes the heuristic across all locations of the material. The **Reuse Mode** and the **Create Planning File Entry for Component** function similar to the settings available in the planning of standard lots heuristic (refer to Section 5.3.1).

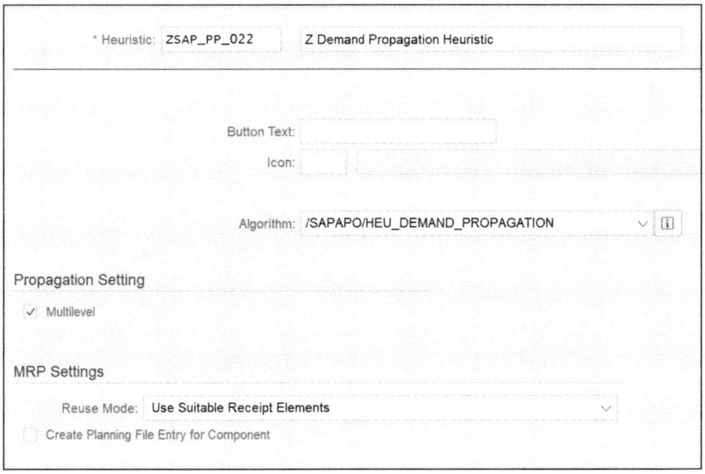

Figure 5.14 Demand Propagation Heuristic: Available Settings

5.4   Leveraging Service Heuristics

In embedded PP-DS, the service heuristics are the algorithms that can't directly be involved in planning or in scheduling but help in altering the planning data, which is later leveraged by the planning and scheduling heuristics. These heuristics can't create or change the quantity of the receipt or requirement elements.

Service heuristics, such as the fixed pegging creation or deletion, changing the order priorities, or new explosion, trigger a nonplanning or a nonscheduling action but can change the receipt elements with the task they are assigned to perform. We'll cover the details of the commonly used service heuristics in this section.

5.4.1   Bottom-Up Rescheduling

The bottom-up rescheduling heuristic is delivered in standard embedded PP-DS with the name SAP_PP_009 and the algorithm /SAPAPO/HEU_MIN_PEG_GIV_SUPPLY. The primary purpose of this heuristic is to ensure that the existing supplies that were planned as part of a production planning heuristic for the dependent demands can fulfill the demands with as little delay as possible. This heuristic evaluates the existing supplies and then shifts the requirement elements (dependent demands) closer to the availability date of the existing receipts, so that there is no or very little delay. As the components from the orders are assigned to an activity of the order under an operation, this heuristic needs to reschedule the activity to a newer date where the component requirements can be fulfilled with the existing receipts.

To keep the delays minimal, this heuristic takes the component availability date (the date of the existing receipt elements) and then reschedules the activity using forward scheduling. If there are related orders due to their BOM structure, depending on the settings made in the detailed scheduling (DS) strategy profile of this heuristic, it can update the availability dates of the related orders.

This heuristic can only shift the dependent demand date by rescheduling the corresponding activity of the order. However, it won't shift the customer requirement (sales order or customer-dependent requirement) dates or PIR dates. So, after the execution of this heuristic, even though the receipts and requirements at the lower-level BOM levels are aligned with no or little delay, at the top level (finished product level), there could be a delay in fulfilling the requirement.

The available settings for this heuristic are shown in Figure 5.15. We'll walk through them in the following sections.

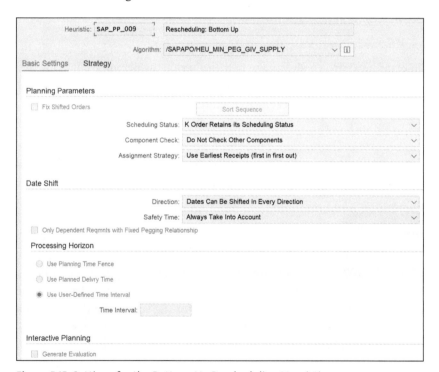

Figure 5.15 Settings for the Bottom-Up Rescheduling Heuristic

Planning Parameters

The **Planning Parameters** have the following functionality:

- **Fix Shifted Orders**

  If this checkbox is selected, then the orders whose activities are rescheduled by this heuristic will get the output firmed indicator so that no other planning run changes such orders automatically.

- **Sort Sequence**

  The sort sequence is the sequence in which the requirement elements are sorted for matching with an existing receipt element. The default delivered setting is to sort the requirement elements chronologically. Clicking the **Sort Sequence** button brings up a popup where the following list of available fields for sorting can be selected:

  - **Requirements Time**
  - **Deallocated**
  - **Order Priority**
  - **Output Firmed**

- **Scheduling Status**

  When the activities and the corresponding orders are rescheduled to the new dates by this heuristic, the orders can retain the scheduling status (scheduled on a resource or deallocated), or it can be set to either deallocate or set to reschedule on the same resource using the **Scheduling Status** heuristics settings.

- **Component Check**

  When the activities are rescheduled by this heuristic, that action may lead to other dependent activities of the order being rescheduled to maintain the order-internal relationship between the activities, which will then lead to a change in the requirement dates for the components assigned to those activities. To determine the behavior of the heuristics in the handling of other components of the same order, the following options are available in the **Component Check** setting:

  - **Do Not Check Other Components**

    With this setting, the heuristic doesn't check for the availability of the other components of the order and only works with the selected component's dependent demand dates.

  - **Check Component to Be Planned Immediately**

    For components that are critical in determining the order availability date, planning procedure 3 (immediate planning) is used so that the component is planned immediately instead of waiting for the PP-DS planning run. This helps in creating the required alerts as early as possible in the process and avoids any delays for the order. This mode for the component check in the heuristics setting considers all the components with planning procedure 3, checks for their availability, and realigns their requirement dates as well when the bottom-up heuristic is executed for any one of the components of the order.

- **Check Other Components**

  This option checks for the availability of all the components of the order, which may result in multiple activities being rescheduled. Depending on the number of components and activities of the order, this option can be very performance intensive, so it isn't recommended to have this setting for scenarios where many order activities and components are involved in the planning process.

- **Assignment Strategy**

  The **Assignment Strategy** is used to determine the receipt element that can be assigned to the requirement elements. This setting is similar to the settings available in the planning of standard lots heuristic (refer to Section 5.3.1).

Date Shift

The **Date Shift** settings determine the direction in which the activities of the requirement elements can be rescheduled. These activities can be rescheduled into a future date from the current requirement date or toward the current date from the requirement date. With the **Date Can Be Shifted in Every Direction** option, when the delay can be minimized for a requirement element, the activity can be rescheduled into the future or toward the current date of the heuristics execution.

Safety time in PP-DS is the time duration with which the requirement dates for a material are brought forward virtually during a planning run. This is defined in the material master. For the bottom-up heuristics, the safety time consideration during the determination of the requirement elements can be controlled by the **Safety Time** heuristics setting, which can be set on or off. In addition, a third option is available where the safety time will participate in the requirement date termination if there is no delay caused by considering the safety time in the calculation.

During the execution of the heuristics, the fixed pegging relationship between the receipt and requirement elements is always respected, and the heuristics bring the requirement date closer to the receipt date to reduce any delays. With the other receipt and requirement elements, it uses the **Sort Sequence** for the requirement elements and the **Assignment Strategy** for determining the receipt elements. By setting the **Only Dependent Reqmnts with Fixed Pegging Relationship** checkbox in the **Date Shift** settings, the receipt and requirement elements that aren't in a fixed pegging relationship aren't selected and processed by the heuristics.

Processing Horizon

For the bottom-up heuristics to select the receipt and requirement elements for aligning them, a specific period is required within which this matching and realignment needs to happen. It doesn't make much sense to execute this heuristic for the whole PP-DS planning horizon as the planning situation changes often for the mid- to long-term horizon. This heuristic provides the following options for the definition of time duration (**Processing Horizon**, as shown previously in Figure 5.15). If the start date of the activities of an order is within the processing horizon, these activities and the relevant components are selected by the heuristics for processing.

- **Use Planning Time Fence**
  The planning time fence defined in the material master is considered the horizon for processing the receipts and requirements.

- **Use Planned Delvry Time**
  The planned delivery time defined in the material master is set as the processing horizon.

- **Use User-Defined Time Interval**
  The previous two options are specific to the material location, and the other option available is **Use User Defined Time Interval**. The value is defined in the number of working days, and all the materials selected for the heuristics will use this value as the processing horizon.

Multilevel Planning

For enabling the bottom-up heuristics to work in the multilevel execution of a production planning run (consider the lowest level component of the BOM and work all the way up to the finished product), the bottom-up heuristics needs to be called within the MRP heuristic.

The **Heuristic** settings can be navigated by double-clicking the heuristics in the heuristics list available in Transaction /SAPAPO/CDPSC11. As shown in Figure 5.16, the bottom-up rescheduling heuristics can be assigned to the MRP heuristic by selecting the **Other Heuristic** option. As this heuristic needs to work from the lowest level first to the top level last, the **Sort Low-Level Codes in Descending Order** checkbox needs to be set in the MRP heuristic setting under the **Sort Sequence** section of the heuristics setting screen, which is created for executing the bottom-up rescheduling in a multi-level scenario.

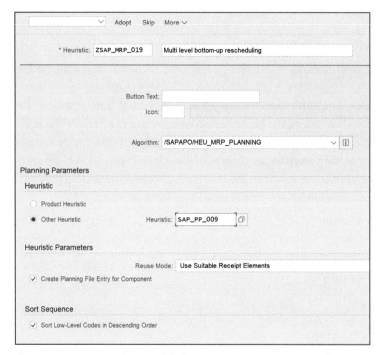

Figure 5.16 MRP Heuristic Enabled to Execute Bottom-Up Rescheduling Heuristics in Multilevel Scenarios

The DS strategy assigned to the bottom-up rescheduling heuristics offers infinite scheduling strategies so that the order activities with the requirements assigned can be scheduled with minimal delays and without capacity constraints during the planning to create a feasible plan.

The requirements from the orders that have the status **Date Fixed**, **Started**, **Confirmed** (**Partial** or **Final**), and **Delivered** (**Partial** or **Final**) aren't changed by this heuristic.

Interactive Planning

The bottom-up rescheduling heuristic also can be executed interactively from tools such as the detailed scheduling (DS) planning board. For performing such execution, the SAP_MLO_BU heuristic is delivered, and the bottom-up heuristic (SAP_PP_009)

is assigned to this heuristic. The SAP_MLO_BU heuristic is like the MRP heuristic, but it works based only on the orders as an object selected for executing this heuristic.

> **Note**
>
> When copied to another custom heuristic, the SAP_MLO_BU heuristic can be used for executing any heuristics that works based on order selection. However, in the standard system, it's only used for bottom-up and top-down rescheduling.

In interactive planning, using tools such as the DS planning board, the SAP_MLO_BU heuristics starts with the order selected in the planning tool and works all the way up to the finished product level based on the low-level codes. As shown in Figure 5.17, this heuristic is also set with **Sort low-level codes in descending order** checked, so that after the relevant materials and locations are identified by the order relationships, the heuristic starts with the lowest BOM level to apply the bottom-up rescheduling algorithm.

Figure 5.17 Multilevel Order Related Bottom-Up Heuristics Settings

5.4.2   Top-Down Rescheduling

The top-down rescheduling heuristic is delivered with the name SAP_PP_010 and with the standard algorithm /SAPAPO/HEU_MIN_PEG_GIV_DEMAND assigned to it.

The top-down heuristics can be used in planning situations where the planning run results in the receipt elements scheduled too far from the requirement elements. This heuristic tries to reduce the delay to the requirement element by shifting the receipt elements closer to the requirement date. This heuristic uses backward scheduling from the requirement date to schedule the shifted orders.

Other heuristics settings, such as the **Basic Settings** and the **Strategy** settings, are the same as the bottom-up rescheduling heuristic shown in Figure 5.18. The top-down heuristic derives the planning period from the time profile assigned in the production planning run (see Chapter 3, Section 3.6.2).

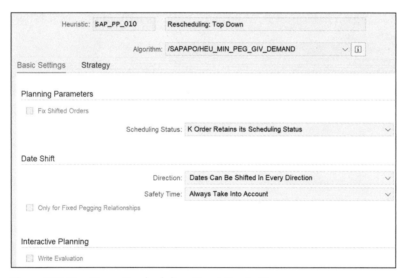

Figure 5.18 Top-Down Rescheduling Heuristics Settings

For executing the top-down rescheduling heuristic in a planning run, heuristic SAP_PP_010 can be called within the MRP heuristic. The **Sort low-level codes in descending order** checkbox must be deselected so that when the low-level codes are determined by the MRP heuristic, it starts with the topmost BOM level (finished materials) and works toward the lower-level components.

In interactive mode, this heuristic can be executed for an order at the top level of the BOM structure by calling the multilevel order heuristic SAP_MLO_TD. This heuristic calls the top-down heuristics for the selected orders from the top level to the bottom-most component level.

5.4.3   Change Order Priorities

In embedded PP-DS, the order priorities are considered during the planning to prioritize the higher priority orders for scheduling and avoid delay for these high-priority orders. In addition, the PP-DS optimizer can respect the order priority to reduce penalty costs for the high-priority orders by reducing the delays.

The priority for the orders are determined based on the setting maintained in the model and version master data in Transaction /SAPAPO/MVM (refer to Chapter 3, Section 3.2.1, for details). Especially in MTO scenarios, one receipt element can be pegged to multiple requirement elements. During a planning run, when the receipt and requirement elements are changed, this will lead to changes in dynamic pegging. Therefore, the order priorities assigned to the receipt elements before the planning runs are no longer valid as the pegging situation has changed.

The change order priority heuristics can be used in such cases to change the priority of the receipt element to the same as the pegged requirement element. This heuristic is delivered with the name SAP_PP_012 and the algorithm /SAPAPO/HEU_PRIO_CHANGE.

The heuristic checks for the priority of all the requirement elements that are assigned to a receipt element, and it sets the highest priority of the pegged requirement to the receipt element.

5.4.4   Create Fixed Pegging

In embedded PP-DS, the pegging structure is generated by the system to maintain the relation of the receipt and requirement elements within a pegging area (material/location/account assignment object). The structure comprises the order relationship across the supply chain network, including the in-house production and external procurement orders. These relationships are possible due to the relationship between various BOM levels, which is represented by the dependent requirement (demand) elements.

The pegging relationship can be displayed from the product view (Transaction /SAPAPO/RRP3), and the inter-order relationship can be displayed in tools such as the DS planning board (see Chapter 6, Section 6.4.1).

The pegging relationships can change when the planning situation changes; therefore, if you want to maintain the pegging structure permanently for the lifecycle of an independent requirement element such as a sales order or a PIR, you can create a fixed pegging relationship between the receipt and requirement elements.

The creation of fixed pegging relationships is delivered with a heuristic name SAP_PP_019 and the algorithm /SAPAPO/HEU_FIX_PEG_CREATE.

The available heuristics settings for the fixed pegging relationship heuristic are shown in Figure 5.19.

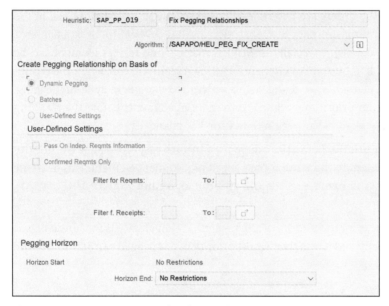

Figure 5.19 Heuristics Settings for the Fixed Pegging Heuristic

The **Create Pegging Relationship on Basis of** setting defines the basis for the pegging relationship, which will be converted to a fixed pegging relationship. The pegging structure is created with fixed pegging as well. The available options are as follows:

- **Dynamic Pegging**
  With this setting, the existing dynamic pegging relationship will be converted into a fixed pegging relationship.

- **Batches**
  For materials with batches when the requirement element and the receipt element has the same batch assigned, they will be fixed pegged to each other.

- **User-Defined Setting**
  With this setting, you'll have to define how the fixed pegging relationships are created between the receipt and requirement elements.

The **User-Defined Settings** contain the following options:

- **Pass on Indep. Reqmts Information**
  This checkbox is used to create fixed pegging in a multilevel fixed pegging creation scenario. The information, such as the available-to-promise (ATP) category of the independent requirement (sales orders, PIRs), is sent to the lower levels.

> **Note**
>
> The custom sort profiles in which the requirement elements can be sorted according to custom sort rules are only supported in the PP-DS component in SAP APO. This custom sort profile isn't supported in embedded PP-DS, as this functionality is based on global available-to-promise (GATP).
>
> You may use the BAdI `/SAPAPO/RRP_FIXPEG` to adjust the filter and sorting of the input and output elements during the heuristics execution.

- **Confirmed Reqmts Only**
  This checkbox will filter out the requirement elements based on their status. Confirmed requirement elements, such as the sales order, are only considered for filtering out the requirement elements, and other requirements aren't included in creation of the fixed pegging relationship.

- **Filter for Reqmts/Filter f. Receipts**
  You can use these fields to define specific requirement and receipt elements that need to be considered for the fixed pegging creation. The assignment strategy determines the order in which the selected receipt elements are assigned to the selected requirement elements for creating the fixed pegging relationship.

The **Pegging Horizon** settings are used to limit the duration in which the fixed pegging relationship is created by this heuristic. The start of the horizon is defaulted to **No Restrictions**, meaning all the receipt and requirement elements, even if they are older than the current date, will be selected by this heuristic. The **Horizon End** has the following options from where the number of days of the set parameter is added to the current date (date of the heuristics execution) to determine the end of the horizon:

- **No Restrictions**
  All the receipt and requirement elements irrespective of their dates are selected.

- **PP-DS Horizon**
  The PP-DS horizon set in the model version master data is considered as the end of horizon.

- **Planning Time Fence, Planned Delivery Time**
  These are dependent on the material location and are defined in the material master.

- **User Defined**
  A set value can be configured for the number of days that will be used by this heuristic to calculate the end of the horizon for fixed pegging.

- **ATP Check Horizon**
  The GATP features aren't supported in embedded PP-DS, and advanced available-to-promise (aATP) can also be used but it isn't yet integrated with embedded PP-DS. However, the value maintained for the **Tot. repl. lead time** (total replenishment lead time) field in the **MRP 3** view of the material master is considered the ATP check horizon value at the database table level for the material master. But because the ATP checking calendar can't be maintained in embedded PP-DS's material master, the value derived as the ATP check horizon is used as the number of calendar days and added to the current date to calculate the pegging horizon.

> **Note**
>
> When a specific setting is maintained for the determination of the pegging horizon and no value is maintained in the material master for the selected field, this heuristic won't be able to calculate a horizon end and won't create any fixed pegging relationship for such materials.

From the product view, you can create fixed pegging by executing the fixed pegging heuristics via the **Variable Heuristics** button. You then select the fixed pegging heuristics from the list of available heuristics in the **Variable Heuristics** screen and click the **Execute** button.

The fixed pegging created by the heuristics can be manually changed from the product view (Transaction /SAPAPO/RRP3), and the fixed pegging relationships can be manually created from the product view. As shown in Figure 5.20, to check the current fixed pegging relationships, navigate to the **Pegging Overview** tab. The quantity that is fixed pegged to the requirement and the corresponding receipt elements are listed here. The **FixPegQty** ❶ shows the quantity that is fixed pegged to the receipt automatically by the system. The second **FixPegQty** column ❷ is editable and can be used to create or delete fixed pegging relationships between the receipt and requirement elements. If you want to change the pegging type from fixed pegging to dynamic pegging, remove the quantity from the **FixPegQty** column ❷ and press Enter. When the fixed pegged quantity is 0, the system creates a dynamic pegging link.

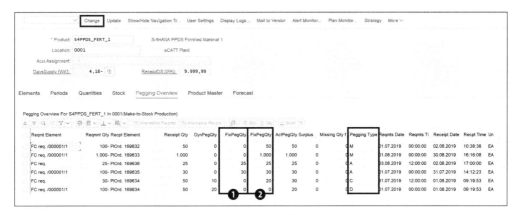

Figure 5.20 Working with Fixed Pegging Relationships from the Product View in Transaction /SAPAPO/RRP3

The **Pegging Type** column on this screen shows the type of pegging according to the way the pegging relationship was created. As shown in Figure 5.20, the available pegging types are as follows:

- **D**
  A dynamic pegging relationship is established.

- **M**
  The fixed pegging relationship that is manually created from the interactive planning tools sets the pegging type **M**.

- **A**
  The system automatically creates a fixed pegging relationship (e.g., the fixed pegging heuristics).

- C

  A combined pegging relationship is set when one requirement element is partially dynamically pegged and partially fixed pegged.

- [Blank]

  No pegging relationship has been established yet for the requirement element.

5.4.5   Delete Fixed Pegging

When the create fixed pegging heuristic is executed in the production planning run for creating a multilevel fixed pegging structure, it's recommended to delete any fixed pegging relationships created previously so that the current fixed pegging run will recalculate the pegging link and fix them.

To delete any previously created fixed pegging relationships, the heuristics for deleting fixed pegging named SAP_PP_011 is delivered with the algorithm /SAPAPO/ HEU_PEG_FIX_DELETE_NEW. This heuristics can be interactively called for one material location or can be called within the MRP heuristic in a production planning run.

The settings available for the delete fixed pegging heuristic is almost like the create fixed pegging relationship heuristic. As shown in Figure 5.21, under the **Delete Pegging Relationship** section, the heuristic can be set to **Automatically Created Fixed Pegging Relationships**, **Manually Created Pegging Relationships**, or both.

The **Filter for Pegging Relationship** section has the same options as the same section for the create fixed pegging relationship heuristic. The **Pegging Horizon** for the delete fixed pegging heuristic is the horizon in which the heuristic can delete the fixed pegging relationships. If you want the heuristic to delete the fixed pegging relationship only after the PP-DS planning fence, you can set the value accordingly in the heuristic. The end of the horizon for the deletion of the fixed pegging relationship is set as **No Restrictions** by default, and this value isn't changeable in the heuristics settings.

The delete fixed pegging heuristic deletes the fixed pegging relationship according to the heuristics settings maintained. If those elements can be dynamically pegged, the dynamic pegging relationship is established between the requirement and receipt element.

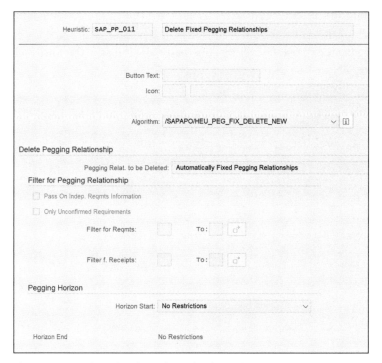

Figure 5.21 Settings for the Delete Fixed Pegging Heuristic

5.4.6   Stage Numbering

In PP-DS, the low-level codes determine the position of a material and location in the supply chain hierarchy. For example, for an in-house manufactured material, the low-level code is determined on its position in the multilevel BOM structure. For materials that are part of the BOM of multiple materials, the lowest position of the usage of the material among all the BOMs is determined as the low-level code for that material/plant.

Low-level code is very important for the PP-DS planning run, as it determines the sequence of the materials in the planning. If the sequence is incorrect, it may lead to a dependent demand created by a finished material as a semifinished material isn't fulfilled by creating a receipt element. The incorrect sequencing may plan the semi-finished material first and then the finished material. As shown in Figure 5.22, the position of a material in the BOM determines its low-level code, and the low-level code determines the sequence in which the planning is executed during a planning run. In the example in Figure 5.22, the Finished 1 material is at the top of the BOM level, so the low-level code (LLC in Figure 5.22) 0 is determined. For the material Raw 1, which is used in all the BOM explosion levels, the low-level code is determined as 3, as that is the lowest BOM explosion level for this material. Similarly, the low-level codes for other materials are also displayed in the example.

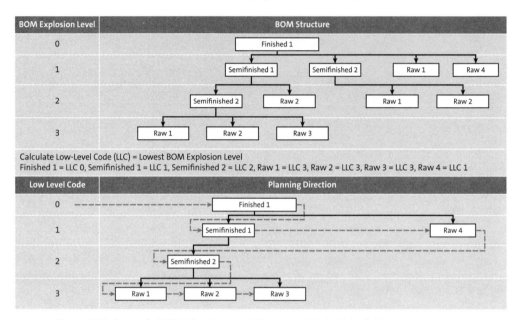

Figure 5.22   Example BOM Structure and Low-Level Code Calculation

When materials are activated for advanced planning in the SAP S/4HANA material master, they are made available for PP-DS planning. The low-level code determined in SAP S/4HANA is also transferred to PP-DS, which can be used by the PP-DS planning run. If the position of the material changes in the BOM structure or in the stock transfer scenarios, the change in the low-level code isn't updated back to embedded PP-DS from SAP S/4HANA. Therefore, it's important to recalculate the low-level code using the stage numbering heuristic in PP-DS if the PP-DS planning run is used as one of the planning tools.

[»]

Note

When MRP Live is used as the only tool for planning PP-DS materials in the SAP S/4HANA system, it uses the low-level code calculated in SAP S/4HANA. In these scenarios, the low-level code in embedded PP-DS doesn't need to be recalculated.

In embedded PP-DS, the stage numbering heuristic is delivered with the name SAP_ PP_LLC and the standard algorithm /SAPAPO/HEU_LOLVLCODE. Its settings are shown in Figure 5.23.

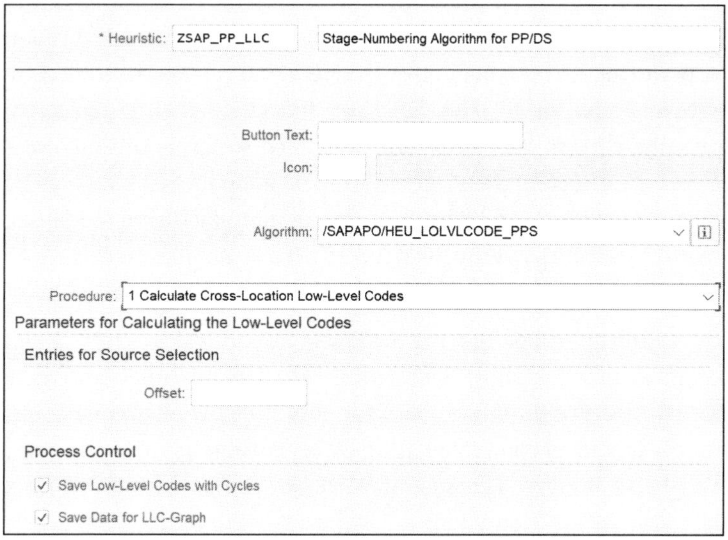

Figure 5.23 Settings for the Stage Numbering Heuristic

The calculation **Procedure** determines how the low-level code is calculated. Following are the available options:

- **0 Transfer Low-Level Code from R/3**
  With this option, the low-level code calculated in SAP S/4HANA is adopted in PP-DS.

- **1 Calculate Cross-Location Low-Level Codes**
  This procedure also considers the stock transfer relationship of components between locations and sets the low-level code accordingly.

- **2 Calculate Location Internal Low-Level Code**
  This option doesn't consider the stock transfer relationships. It can only be used if the planning is limited internally within a location. In addition, the planning run is executed per location, and the sequence of the location is done manually when scheduling the planning run in PP-DS.

This heuristic evaluates the sources of supply for determining the low-level codes. The sources of supply that are valid for the current date of the heuristic execution are considered by the heuristic. If you want to shift the current date (to the past or future) for determining the validity of the sources of supply, you can set the required (positive or negative) number of days in the **Offset** field.

In the supply chain model, cycles can occur when two locations are bidirectional (both source and destination) for the same material. In such cases, the low-level code calculation can't be performed. The behavior of the heuristic can be controlled by using the **Save Low-Level Codes with Cycles** checkbox, however. When it's selected, the heuristic will save the current low-level code calculated so far before the cycle occurred. If the option isn't selected, the system will write a log message and won't update the low-level code for such materials. In in-house manufacturing scenarios, recursive BOMs (the header material of the BOM is also used as a component) lead to cycles in low-level code calculation.

The **Save Data for LLC-Graph** checkbox records the low-level code calculation results in the system to generate a graph to show the relationship of the materials and their low-level codes and the corresponding sources of supplies. The low-level code graph can be accessed after the low-level code calculation by executing the ABAP program /SAPAPO/SHOW_LLC_GRAPH from Transaction SE38 or Transaction SA38. This report is also available in SAP APO, so you'll see some selection options related to SAP APO in the selection screen. For embedded PP-DS, only the selections relevant to PP-DS are valid.

As shown in Figure 5.24, the upper-left screen shows the selection options of the low-level code graphical display report. You can navigate to the source of supply details by double-clicking the link lines ❶ between the boxes with the material numbers. You can double-click on the material numbers ❷ in the graphical object to navigate to the product view. The highlighted numbers ❸ below the material numbers display the low-level code of the material.

> **Note**
>
> If materials are assigned to a planning group, all the materials in the planning group will get the same low-level code and will be planned together in a planning run.

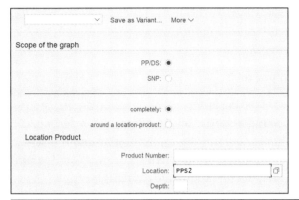

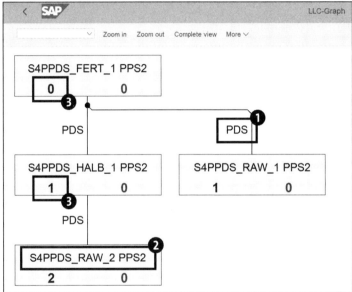

Figure 5.24 Low-Level Code Graph Generated from the Stage Numbering
Algorithm Heuristic

5.5   Triggering a PP-DS Planning Run

In SAP S/4HANA and in embedded PP-DS, triggering a planning run means making a
selection for the material that needs to go through the planning process. In PP-DS,
the planning run is passing the materials through one or multiple heuristics (algorithms) according to the business processes involved.

In embedded PP-DS, there are various ways to execute the production planning run, but these are the two major ways:

- Production planning run
- Interactive planning in the planning tools

We'll cover the step-by-step process of setting up and executing the planning process in embedded PP-DS in this section (and how to evaluate our results in Section 5.6). The transaction for the production planning run also can be used to perform scheduling and PP-DS optimizer runs. In this section, we'll focus on the settings and parameters required to execute the planning run for production planning.

5.5.1   Production Planning Run in Interactive Mode

The production planning run can be performed interactively for a very few number of materials and for a few steps. For larger data sets, it's always recommended to execute the planning run in background mode.

To execute the production planning run online, navigate to the transaction from the **SAP Easy Access** menu, **Logistics • Advanced Planning • Production Planning • Automated Production Planning and Optimization • Production Planning Run**, or execute Transaction /SAPAPO/CDPSBO to call the planning run transaction.

In the production planning run, you can execute multiple heuristics in sequence for the same set or different sets of data. A simple example of a planning run could be executing the following heuristics in sequence for the same set of data:

- **Stage numbering algorithm**
  Recalculate the low-level code for the materials.
- **Delete fixed pegging**
  Remove the fixed pegging constraints for planning.
- **MRP with the product heuristics**
  Plan supplies for the uncovered requirement using the product heuristics assigned in the material master.
- **Bottom-up rescheduling heuristics**
  Use for certain materials where the availability of the lower-level material is critical for on-time delivery of the finished product.

After you call up the production planning transaction, you'll see the screen shown in Figure 5.25. First, enter the **Planning Version**, which is the version on which the planning run is to be executed. It's possible to copy the active version 000 to an inactive version and plan them differently for simulation purposes.

The **Time Profile** determines the planning period within which the current planning run can reschedule or deallocate orders on the resources. However, for performing the production planning and certain service heuristics, the PP-DS planning horizon defined in the model version management (Transaction /SAPAPO/MVM) is used as the planning period. For example, a time profile is defined with -2 and +3 months (Transaction /SAPAPO/CDPSC4; see Chapter 3, Section 3.6.2) and if the PP-DS horizon defined in model version master data is 4 months, a planning heuristic will consider all the requirements within the 4 months of the PP-DS horizon and will create receipt elements within the 4 months horizon, if there are uncovered requirements.

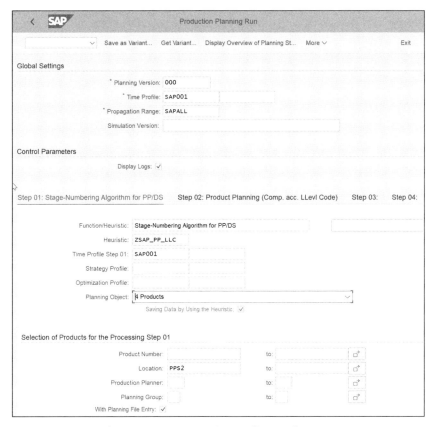

Figure 5.25 PP-DS Planning Run Transaction: Online Mode

The **Propagation Range** is a limiting factor for the selection of materials and locations determined by the heuristics. The configuration of the propagation range is covered in Chapter 3, Section 3.4.2. The propagation ranges defined in the configuration are available for selection by clicking on the value help button on the **Propagation Range** field in the **Production Planning Run** screen. For example, if a finished material is entered as the selection in the MRP heuristic in the planning run, and it creates or deletes orders at the finished material level, the MRP heuristic automatically determines (when the planning procedure allows) that the semifinished material for which the dependent demand is created also needs to be planned. But if the propagation range is created with only the finished material, then the planning will be limited to just the finished material. Even if a material and location are mentioned in the selection under the individual step, if the material is excluded in the propagation range, that material can't be planned.

For certain heuristics, it's possible to write the results of the planning run into a **Simulation Version** rather than writing the results back to the active version. This can be useful if you want to apply different detailed scheduling algorithms and save the results in simulation versions for analyzing and comparing them later before deciding on the algorithm to be executed on the active version 000. Not all heuristics allow you to save data in the simulation versions. If the **Saving Data by Using the Heuristic** checkbox is selected under the **Planning Object** field in the planning **Step** (see Figure 5.25), then such heuristics can't save data to a simulation version. For an allowed heuristic, when you enter a simulation version name, the system creates a new simulation version with the name you entered and writes the result of the planning run into the simulation version.

Because the **Simulation Version** field is at the header level of the production planning run and not at the individual step level, all the heuristics that are defined as steps in the production planning run should support saving results into the simulation version.

Tip

To identify the heuristics that allow the results to be saved to a simulation version, check the database table /SAPAPO/HEURFUNC. If a function module assigned to the heuristic has the value "X" for the **Impl. Commit** (IMPLICIT_COMMIT) field, the data will be saved to the planning version during or at the end of the algorithm by the function module. Therefore, such heuristics can't save data to a simulation version.

The **Display Logs** checkbox enables the display of logs immediately after the completion of the planning run in online mode. The planning logs will be generated by the system according to the settings maintained in the PP-DS global Customizing, but the immediate display of the log after the online production planning run is determined by this checkbox.

The **Global Settings** in the display log, which you see in the first half of the screen of the planning run transaction, are global to all the heuristics and functions that are executed in that planning run. In the bottom half of the screen, you'll see **Step 01** through **Step 10**. Within these steps, you can define the sequence of the heuristics and the data selection for the individual steps. Up to 10 steps can be defined in one production planning run.

Under the step, the heuristics defined in the Customizing (Transaction /SAPAPO/ CDPSC11) or the standard delivered functions that aren't defined as heuristics can be executed in the planning run. Following are the functions that aren't defined as heuristics but can be executed in the planning run:

- Deallocate
- Firm objects
- Interrupt operation
- Optimization
- Reschedule
- Unfirm objects

If you want to execute any of these functions, do a value help [F4] search on the **Function/Heuristic** field under the **Step** tabs.

After the heuristic or the function for the individual step is defined, a step-specific **Time Profile**, **Strategy Profile**, and **Optimization Profile** can be entered. For certain functions and heuristics, it's mandatory to use one or more of these profiles. For example, if you select the optimization function, then it's required to make an entry for the **Optimization Profile** under the step details.

The selection of the **Planning Object** is also dependent on the heuristic or function selected to be executed in the planning step. In general, for production planning heuristics, the allowed selection objects are products; for detailed scheduling heuristics, the allowed selection objects are resources, orders, and operations. The selection of objects can also be controlled by the user exit APOCDPS1. To select the objects via the user exit, select the **Copy Object** option from customer exit APOCDPS1 in the **Planning Object** field.

When the selection object of product, operation, order, or resource is selected, you can enter the selection criteria for the corresponding objects. For **Step 02** onward, you have the option of copying the selection data from the previous step (**0 Copy Objects from the Previous Processing Step**) to the current step, as shown in Figure 5.26. The heuristics in the second step can perform the required action only if the current step can work with the data from the previous step. For example, if **Step 01** has a detailed scheduling heuristic as the selection, and you execute a production planning heuristic (e.g., MRP heuristics) in **Step 02** with the selection object as **Selection from Previous Step**, the heuristic execution will end up with an error.

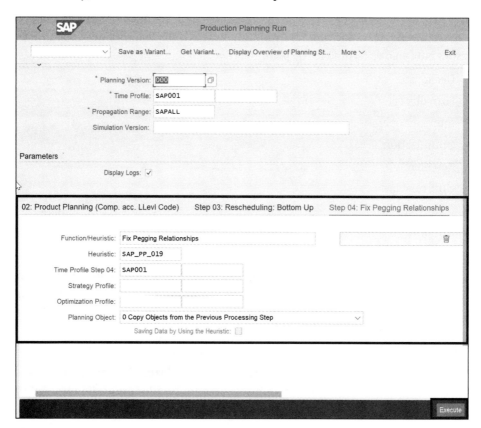

Figure 5.26 Executing a Production Planning Run: Online Mode

When the production planning heuristics are defined as the production planning run steps, the **With Planning File Entry** option is shown under the selection details of the selection objects. When this checkbox is selected, only products that have a valid planning file entry (a planning-relevant change for the material/location has updated the planning file entry per the planning procedure assigned to it) are selected for processing. So the behavior of the heuristic will be a net change planning when this checkbox is selected.

After you define the steps for all the planning tasks to be executed by the production planning run, you can save the steps and the selection in a variant by clicking on the **Save as Variant** option in the menu bar. The **Settings for Heuristics** menu button from the menu bar can be used to display the heuristics settings of the heuristic defined in the planning step.

As shown previously in Figure 5.26, to execute the planning run, click on the **Execute** button on the bottom-right part of the screen. After the planning run is completed, the system will automatically take you to the log screen, if you've set the **Display Logs** checkbox in the selection screen.

Figure 5.27 Working with Simulation Versions in the Production Planning Run

If you've used the option to save the results of the planning run into a simulation version, then the same information will be written in the planning log, as shown in Figure 5.27. You can see the name provided for the **Simulation Version** in the top-left corner ❶. The simulation version will be created, and you can see the recorded log in the middle of Figure 5.27 ❷. The simulation version can be accessed from Transaction /SAPAPO/CDPSS0 ❸. From this transaction, the data saved in the simulation version can be opened in the DS planning board or other allowed tools for working on the simulation versions.

Tip

If you want to work with simulation versions, keep the size of the simulation versions smaller by restricting the selection in the planning run, and delete the old simulation versions frequently to avoid overload of SAP liveCache.

5.5.2 Production Planning Run in the Background

When the data to be processed in the production planning is larger, the production planning run must be done in the background. By doing so, the system can execute the planning in a background job, and longer executions won't end up with timeout errors such as in online/dialog mode.

The background planning run can be scheduled from Transaction /SAPAPO/CDPSB1 or via the **SAP Easy Access** menu: **Logistics • Advanced Planning • Production Planning • Production Planning Run in the Background**.

The initial screen of this transaction displays the list of all the already saved variants, as shown in Figure 5.28.

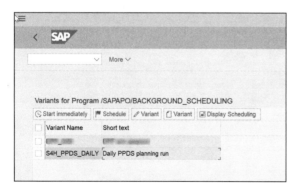

Figure 5.28 Initial Screen with Variants for PP-DS Planning in Background

The variants saved from the online production planning run discussed in the previous section (Transaction /SAPAPO/CDPSB0) are also displayed in this transaction and can be used to schedule background planning runs.

If you want to create a new variant, click on the **Variant** button on the screen. This will take you through a series of screens to complete the process of a new variant creation.

In the **ABAP: Variants** popup that appears ❶, enter a variant name for the new variant being created, and then click the **Create** button, as shown in Figure 5.29. For the screen assignment ❷, select the **For All Selection Screens** option so that all the screens of the transaction are visible for maintaining the selection criteria. The screen for creating the variant for background production planning is like the online planning run transaction except for the **Execute** option, which is only available in the online transaction.

After all the global data for the planning run and the individual steps with heuristics/ functions are defined (see our discussion in Section 5.5.1), navigate back from the screen, and you'll be prompted to save the newly created variant ❸. Click **Yes**. On the next screen, you can enter a **Description** of the new variant and then click the **Save** button ❹.

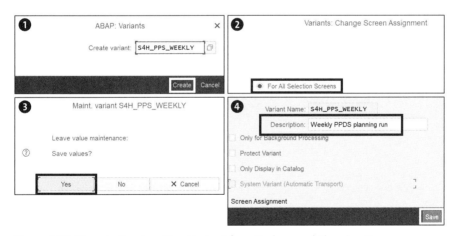

Figure 5.29 Steps to Create a New Variant for a Background Planning Run

The variants created for the background planning run can be scheduled immediately for execution of the background job or scheduled to be executed in periodic intervals. For example, a variant with net requirements planning can be scheduled to execute daily, and a more complex variant can be scheduled to execute every weekend.

To schedule a new job, click on the **Schedule** button on the initial screen of the background planning run (see top portion of Figure 5.30). In the next screen, **Background Planning Scheduling: Start Time** (see bottom portion of Figure 5.30), you have the options to enter the start time for the job. You set the execution date and time for the job, and if the job is to be executed immediately for one time, select the **Schedule once** option.

For periodic jobs, enter the start date, for example, a daily job that needs to start at 15:00:00 hours daily; enter the date from which the job needs to be scheduled and the time as "15:00:00"; and select the **Schedule periodically** option. In the **Period Duration** popup, under the **Repeat period** section, you have **Months**, **Weeks**, **Days**, **Hours**, and **Minutes** as options. For a job that needs to be scheduled every two days, select the **Days** option, and enter "2" as the value. After the job frequency is entered, click on the **Create** button in the **Period Duration** popup to create the job schedule.

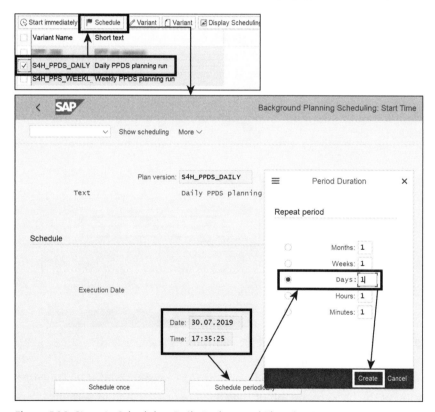

Figure 5.30 Steps to Schedule a Daily Background Planning Run

After the job is scheduled, it can be monitored from the background job monitor (Transaction SM37) or from the background planning run transaction itself. The job status will appear as **Released**; after it's executed, the status will change to **Completed**, and the system will automatically release the next job per the frequency (daily, weekly, etc.) in the scheduling settings.

From the initial screen of the background planning run (refer to Figure 5.28), select the variant for which you want to check the scheduling. Click on the **Display Scheduling** button. In the next screen shown on the left side of Figure 5.31, you'll see the list of the scheduled requests of the variant selected. The list will have all the past executions for the variant as well as the next scheduled execution details. You can select the completed executions and navigate to the **Log** to check the background job log. The **Results** option on this screen will navigate to the spool request created by the background job, which has the statistics and the results of the planning run. You can double-click on the spool button to navigate to the spool record that contains the results of the production planning run.

In addition, you can delete or change the schedule (start date, time) and the frequency of the scheduling by clicking the pencil icon shown on the left side of Figure 5.31. You can delete the scheduled executions by selecting a released line and clicking on the **Delete Job Definition** button.

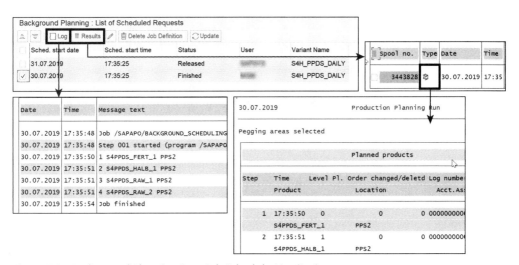

Figure 5.31 Background Planning Run: Job Schedule Monitoring

5.5.3   Interactive Production Planning

Many of the planning tasks scheduled as planning run steps within the production planning run can be executed interactively to evaluate the results of the planning. In addition, actions such as creating an order, changing or deleting an order, changing the sources of supply, re-exploding the source of supply, setting and removing firming indicators, setting the conversion checkbox, and changing or creating fixed pegging relationships can be executed from the interactive planning tools.

In embedded PP-DS, the following are the commonly used interactive planning tools used for production planning purposes:

- Product view
- Receipts view
- Requirements view
- Order processing view
- Product planning table
- Product overview

We'll cover the product view in detail in this section and also give an overview of the other tools and their specific use cases, if any.

Some of the tools can be used to perform the detailed scheduling actions as well. But in this section, we'll cover the functions related to production planning in the interactive planning tools.

Product View

The product view is the most commonly used transaction for interactive planning and evaluation of the planning results for individual material/locations. The product view can be accessed from the **SAP Easy Access** menu: **Logistics** · **Advanced Planning** · **Production Planning** · **Interactive Production Planning** · **Product View**. You can use Transaction /SAPAPO/RRP3 to access the product view as well.

The initial screen of the product view, as shown in Figure 5.32, has the **Plng Version**, **Product**, and **Location** options. Entering these three values is the basic minimum requirement. If you work with special stock scenarios, such as sales orders or project orders, you can use the **Special Stock** indicator and the account assignment object.

Figure 5.32 PP-DS Product View: Selection Screen

The **Selection Rule** can be specified to filter out the receipt and requirements displayed in the product view by period restrictions or by excluding certain order categories from displaying in the results.

For any action you perform within the product view, the system generates planning logs according to the PP-DS global settings. For performance reasons, the global settings may be set to just error messages. You can override this setting within the product view by setting the logging level via **More · Settings · Planning Log**, as shown on the right side of Figure 5.32, and setting the **All Messages** option in the dialog box. This setting is valid for the current session, and when you restart the product view transaction, it will be defaulted back to the original setting.

> **Tip**
>
> The product view selection rule can be customized from the Customizing IMG menu path: **SAP IMG Menu · Advanced Planning · Order View · Define Selection Rules for Product View**.

In addition, by using the **Create Order** button, the system will take you to the screen where you can create a new procurement element, such as a planned order or purchase requisition (depending on the procurement type of the material). After entering the required selection options, click on the **Continue** button or press Enter to view the result of the product view.

The results screen of the product view has multiple tabs and features, as shown in Figure 5.33. Click on the **Change** button on the menu bar to make the planning data editable in the product view. In edit mode, only the elements that can be changed in embedded PP-DS can be changed in the product view.

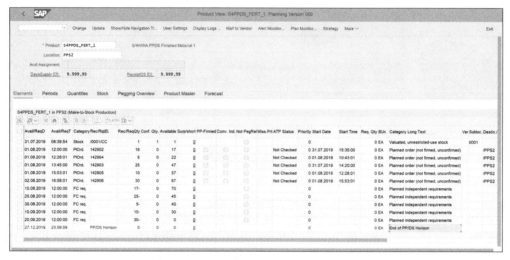

Figure 5.33 PP-DS Product View Details Screen

Following are the different tabs and the functionality and data contained in these tabs, which are used for interactive planning:

- **Elements**

  The **Elements** tab has the list of stock, receipt, and requirement elements displayed in chronological order. The PP-DS planning time fence and the PP-DS planning horizon are marked accordingly. The resources on which the orders are manufactured, the dates/times, quantities, and order categories are some of the important fields listed in the **Elements** tab. You can select individual or multiple orders (by pressing the ⌈Ctrl⌋ button and clicking on the **Order Selection** checkbox on the screen) to delete them.

  Double-clicking on the order will take you to the order details screen (see Figure 5.34) where you can perform actions such as setting or removing the firming checkboxes ❶ and setting the **Conversion Ind.** for converting the planned orders to production orders or the purchase requisitions to purchase orders ❷. For the manufacturing orders (production/process orders) the order status checkboxes are set according to their execution status in SAP S/4HANA ❸. The list of available sources of supply can be displayed by clicking on the **Change** source of supply button ❹. In addition, if required, a different valid source of supply can be selected for the order.

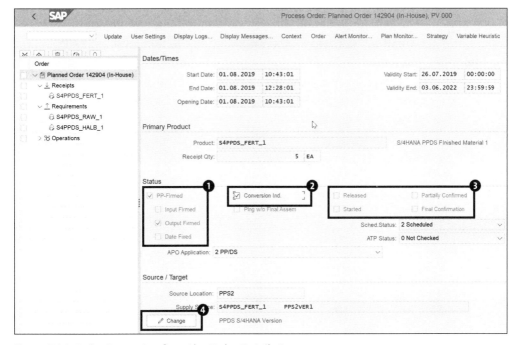

Figure 5.34 Order Processing from the Order Details Screen

> **Note**
>
> The product view, receipt view, and requirement view work based on simulation (sim) sessions. Until the user saves the data, all the changes are only saved in the sim session, which allows multiple planners to work in parallel if required. Therefore, all the heuristics execution and changes are temporary in the product view until the user explicitly clicks on the **Save** button.

- **Periods/Quantities**

  The **Periods** and **Quantities** tabs display the demand and supply situation in a periodic view. The **Periods** tab shows the data in a tabular periodic form with additional context, such as the day's supply calculated for all the displayed periods. The

Quantities tab shows the receipts supplies and the netted quantity in a graphical format.

- **Stock/Pegging Overview**
  The **Stock** tab shows the inventory availability of the material across all available locations. In the **Pegging Overview** tab, you can display the current pegging overview of the requirements and receipts. In change mode, you can create fixed pegging relationships or change already existing pegging relationships.

- **Product Master**
  The **Product Master** tab displays the embedded PP-DS product master of the material master maintained in SAP S/4HANA. This is a display-only feature, and no changes can be directly made to the material master from embedded PP-DS.

- **Forecast**
  The **Forecast** tab has the information about the requirements strategy master data. It also lists the forecasts (PIRs from SAP S/4HANA and forecast elements created in embedded PP-DS) and whether the forecasts are consumed by incoming sales orders or sales order deliveries according to the requirements strategy used.

The product view display of tabs, alerts, and available heuristics to be executed via the product view are determined by the user profile and other profiles assigned to the user profile. Settings can be maintained for controlling the display of the product view. As shown in Figure 5.35, you can click on the **User Settings** button on the screen to bring up the display variant per the Customizing settings. You can change the values on the user settings and save the variant as a **New Variant**, which will be loaded by default when you open the product view.

Note

You can use the ABAP program /SAPAPO/PT_USER_PARAMS_MAIN from Transaction SE38 or Transaction SA30 and choose the appropriate options to delete the variants saved for the user; this will also delete the variant saved by the user. When the product view is launched again, the system prompts you to choose a variant set in Customizing.

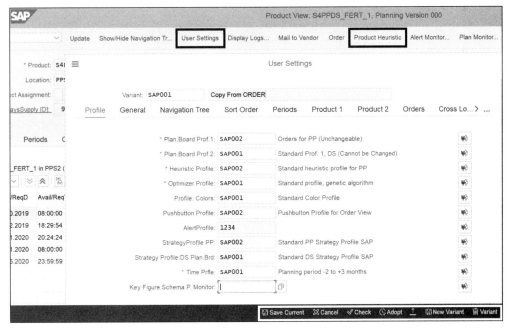

Figure 5.35 User Settings in Product View: Changing the Default Variant

In change mode within the product view, you can execute the product heuristics by clicking on the **Product Heuristic** button. Depending on the heuristics settings for interactive planning, it will execute the heuristics. By clicking on the **Variable Heuristics** button, you'll be taken to a screen where the list of allowed heuristics from the assigned heuristics profile is given. You can also change the default heuristics settings for execution from this screen. If you want to execute a heuristic that isn't in the list of heuristics, you'll have to assign a heuristics profile to the user setting that has the desired heuristic assigned.

When executing a heuristic, if the **Generate Evaluation** option is set as active in the **Settings** tab for interactive planning of the heuristic, then you'll see the **Evaluation** tab on the screen for executing the variable heuristics. This tab contains the details about the receipt and requirement elements the system has considered for planning. The details of the fixed receipts and the planning file entries generated by the system are recorded in the evaluation, as shown in Figure 5.36.

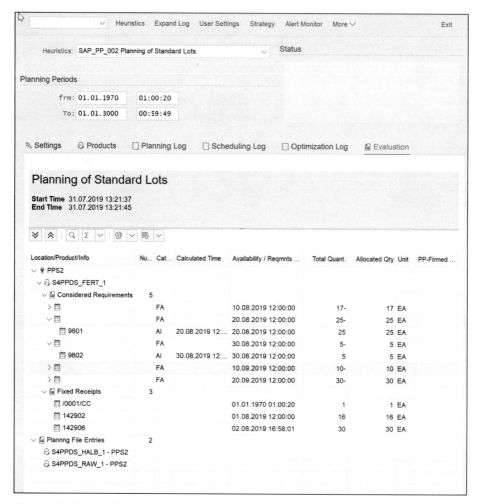

Figure 5.36 Execute Variable Heuristics: Evaluation in the Product View

[+]

Tip

By entering "GT_IO" on the transaction code box (top-left corner of screen) and pressing the ⌨Enter key, you can see the SAP liveCache representation of the elements displayed in the product view. The SAP liveCache order GUIDs and order categories can be seen from this option as well.

Other Interactive Planning Tools

Apart from the product view, the other interactive planning tools also can be used for changing PP-DS planning data interactively. Following are some of the commonly used tools and specific features they offer:

- **Receipts view (Transaction /SAPAPO/RRP4)**
  This view lists all the receipt elements for the given selection. This can be used to mass process the receipt elements and to set the conversion indicator for all the selected receipts when allowed by the order type and status. The order quantities and proprieties can be changed, and the variable heuristics can be used to execute heuristics (e.g., bottom-up and top-down rescheduling for the selected orders) from this view.

- **Requirements view (Transaction /SAPAPO/RRP1)**
  This view lists all the requirement elements for the given selection. In change mode, the requirement quantities can be created, changed, or deleted for the allowed requirement elements, such as forecast elements. Variable heuristics can be executed for the selected requirement elements as well.

- **Product planning table (Transaction /SAPAPO/PPT1)**
  This comprehensive planning tool allows all the production planning and detailed scheduling tasks to be performed in the tabular form of the data. In addition, the graphical DS planning board can be loaded into the planning table. Although it can be used for any planning scenario, it's commonly used for repetitive manufacturing planning as the production plan and the resource loads can be simultaneously performed from the product planning table.

  The product view, PP-DS optimizer, and periodic views for product and resource can also be loaded onto the planning table. Various profiles to be used for specific business scenarios are delivered in the SAP standard system, which has the charts and options configured for the specific scenarios. However, it's possible to tailor the planning table profiles in the customization and interactively within the planning table to add/remove additional charts and views, as well as adjust the display profiles.

- **Product overview (Transaction /SAPAPO/POV1)**
  This is another tool where the products and their planning segments (MTS or account assignment) are listed. In addition, the details about the last planning run can be accessed for the products via the planning run information in the product overview transaction.

5.5.4   Planning PP-DS Materials in MRP Live (One MRP Run)

The advanced planning materials also can be planned in the MRP Live planning run. MRP Live will call the PP-DS planning tools for planning the advanced planning materials.

When the requirement is to execute the product heuristics as part of MRP Live, this can be achieved by including the advanced planning materials in the MRP Live run. However, if there is a need to execute multiple heuristics in sequence, including the product heuristics in one step, this isn't possible from MRP Live planning. In such cases, a separate PP-DS planning run needs to be scheduled and executed.

When planning advanced planning and nonadvanced planning materials together in MRP Live, you must ensure that all the materials above the BOM level structure of the material are also planned in advanced planning. This makes sure that the dependent demand generated in one level by PP-DS is passed all the way to the last-level material that is relevant for advanced planning.

The MRP Live run executes the planning in sequence according to the low-level code set in SAP S/4HANA for the materials. So, if you have special planning situations where the PP-DS low-level code is critical for planning, such as usage of planning packages or interchangeability, they need to be planned in a PP-DS planning run.

For the advanced planning materials, it's recommended to have an MRP type similar to X0 (without MRP, with BOM explosion), so that if any older planning tools are used in SAP S/4HANA apart from MRP Live, the materials aren't planned. MRP Live will always call the PP-DS product heuristics when the material has **Advanced Planning** selected. If the MRP type is set to **No MRP**, then the material also isn't planned in PP-DS irrespective of the **Advanced Planning** checkbox.

MRP Live can be executed using Transaction MD01N or via the **SAP Easy Access** menu: **Logistics • Production • MRP Planning • MRP Live**. As shown in Figure 5.37, the **MRP Live** selection screen has fields for materials, plants, and so on. There are no specific settings required in the MRP Live run to plan the advanced planning materials.

For advanced planning materials, the product heuristics are maintained in the **Advanced Planning** tab in the **Product Heuristic** field of the material master in Transaction MM02. The settings maintained in the heuristics customization for the assigned product heuristics of the material derive the planning parameters, including the handling of the lower-level components and scheduling parameters.

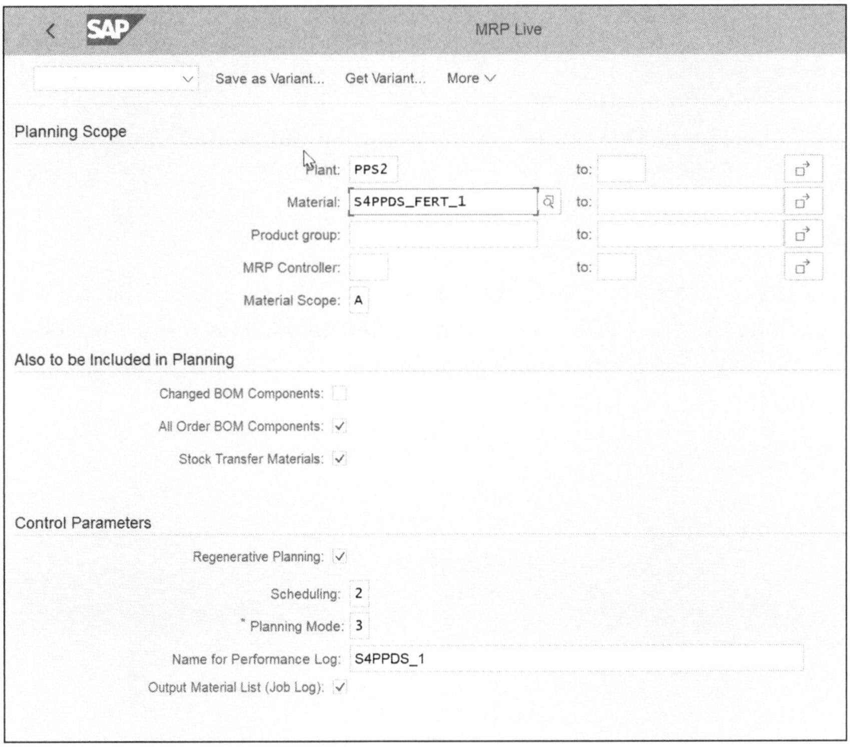

Figure 5.37 MRP Live Planning in SAP S/4HANA

MRP Live can be executed online in dialog mode or can be scheduled in the background job. The MRP Live log contains the level of materials planned and the number of PP-DS materials planned by the execution. Application logs are written for the PP-DS materials, which can be accessed from Transaction SLG1 (Application Logs).

5.6   Monitoring and Evaluating the Planning Runs

It's important to monitor the logs and the evaluations from the PP-DS planning runs, including the MRP Live run, to ensure that all materials are planned correctly and that there are no repeated errors or terminations that stop materials from getting planned correctly. In this section, we'll cover some of the tools used to evaluate the planning logs.

5.6.1   PP-DS Planning Log

When a planning-relevant action is executed via the interactive planning tools or from the online/background production planning run, the system generates application logs and records all the relevant information according to the PP-DS global settings. If the PP-DS global settings (Transaction /SAPAPO/RRPCUST1) are set for all messages, the application log will contain information, warning, error, and termination messages.

The central transaction to monitor all the logs system-wide for PP-DS can be accessed via Transaction /SAPAPO/RROLOG1 or from the **SAP Easy Access** menu: **Logistics · Advanced Planning · Production Planning · Reporting · Logs · Display Logs**. The selection screen of this transaction is shown in Figure 5.38.

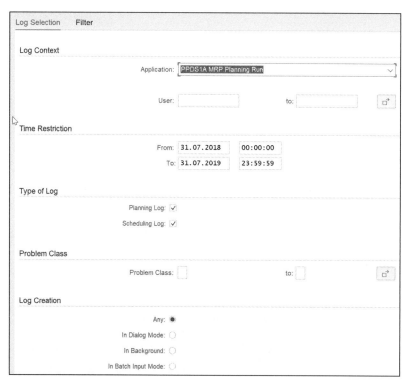

Figure 5.38 PP-DS Log Display: Selection Screen for Logs

The logs can be filtered by the **Application** that was used for planning. All the various applications, such as the product view, planning run, and planning table, are available as selection options. The **All Applications** option is available to read all the logs for the defined selection criteria irrespective of the PP-DS application used for planning. The user name is also available as a selection option under the **Log Context** area.

The log selection can be restricted by the date and time ranges in the **From** and **To** fields of the **Time Restriction** area. This transaction can list all PP-DS logs, including planning and scheduling logs. If you're only interested in a specific type of log (scheduling or planning), choose the appropriate checkbox.

The **Problem Class** can be used to select only error or termination messages. Especially if other selection options aren't very restrictive, the log list will be huge, making finding a specific message by scrolling on the log results a tedious activity. Typically, you should set the filter for the error and termination messages. Then, after the context of the error or termination is known from the result, that information (time stamps, user, etc.) can be used to rerun the log display to understand the complete context of the error or termination messages.

The **Log Creation** mode selection determines whether the system should read the logs generated by interactive tools or generated in the background mode, for example, in a background planning run, or both. The option for batch-input isn't relevant for PP-DS transactions.

The log display transaction selection also has a **Filter** tab that provides further filter criteria specific to the PP-DS data, as shown in Figure 5.39.

The active **Planning Version 000** is entered by default; however, if you work with any nonactive PP-DS planning versions for simulation reasons, you can set the planning version accordingly.

In PP-DS, the application log messages are grouped under exception groups. Some of these messages can also be customized. If you're interested in certain groups of messages in the logs, that can be done using the **Exception Group** in the filter.

> **Tip**
>
> The exception groups can be customized from the Customizing menu path: **SAP IMG Menu** · **Advanced Planning** · **Application Logs for PP/DS** · **Maintain Exception Groups**.

Under the **Message Context** area, it's possible to filter out the logs generated by specific heuristics or with the filter of the pegging area fields, such as the **Product**, **Location**, **Production Planner**, **Account Assignment Object**, and so on.

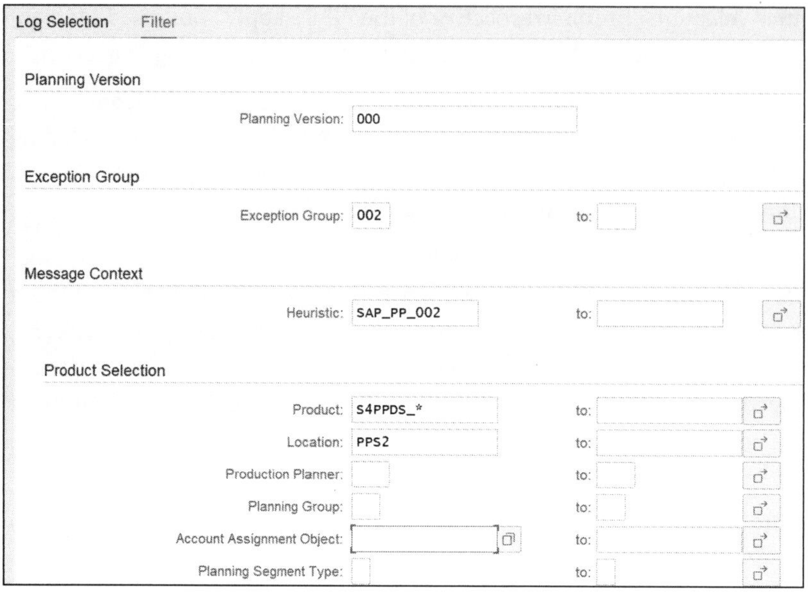

Figure 5.39 Filter Options in the PP-DS Log Display

5.6.2   Evaluate the MRP Live Execution

When MRP Live is executed in the background or in online mode, the system generates performance statistics apart from generating the application logs. While defining the variant for the MRP Live job in Transaction MD01N, you can enter a name for the performance log file so that it's easy to identify and analyze after the MRP Live planning run.

The MRP Live performance log can be accessed using Transaction MD_MRP_PER-FLOG. The selection screen for this transaction allows you to select the performance logs by the name of the log, by the user name who executed the MRP Live planning, or by the MRP start date, as shown in Figure 5.40.

Click the **Execute** button in the screen to see the list of performance logs according to your selections. The key metrics, such as the MRP Live runtime (**Tot.PlgTime**), number of materials planned (**Matls Plnd**), how many of the materials were planned in PP-DS (**PP/DS Matl**), how many PP-DS materials failed during the planning run (**PPDFailMat**), and the time spent in the PP-DS planning tools (**PP/DS Time**), are listed as columns in this screen (see Figure 5.41).

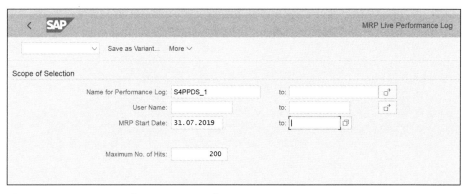

Figure 5.40 MRP Live Performance Log Selection Screen

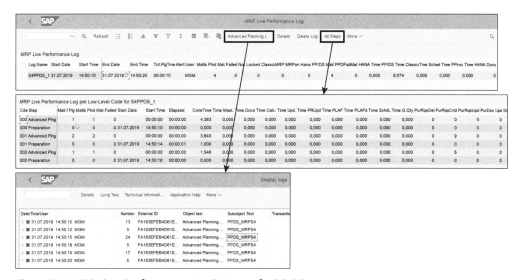

Figure 5.41 MRP Live: Performance Log Features for PP-DS

By clicking on the **All Steps** button, you can navigate to a detailed screen where the individual planning steps according to the low-level code and the planning tool (MRP Live on SAP HANA, classic MRP, or PP-DS) that planned the specific step are listed. The time breakdown for the overall runtime (only for materials that are not in PP-DS) and the number of documents (e.g., planned orders, purchase requisitions, etc.) created, changed, and deleted by each step are also listed here.

The PP-DS application logs can also be displayed for the MRP Live execution by selecting the **Advanced Planning Log** button in the **MRP Live Performance Log** screen.

> **Note**
>
> The PP-DS application logs generated from the MRP Live executions also can be accessed from Transaction SLG1. In the selection screen, enter "APO" for the **Object** and "PPDS_MRPS4" (only in SAP S/4HANA 1909) for the **Subobject**.

5.6.3   Evaluate the PP-DS Background Planning Run

The background PP-DS planning run can be monitored from the background planning transaction (Transaction /SAPAPO/CDPSB1) itself. But it's also possible to only create a variant for the background planning transaction. You can use the variant and program /SAPAPO/BACKGROUND_SCHEDULING in the external job scheduling tools to schedule the background planning runs in embedded PP-DS.

The externally scheduled jobs can also be monitored in the SAP background job monitoring Transaction SM37. You can use the job name or the program name /SAPAPO/BACKGROUND_SCHEDULING for filtering the PP-DS planning jobs.

From the job screen, clicking on the job log shows all recorded the messages raised during the background planning job. If there are any terminations, those are also available in the job log, which can also be reviewed and analyzed from the application logs (Transaction SLG1).

Depending on how the job is set up, there is a chance that the job is scheduled by a user name which is not the user name maintained in the job step. All the application logs are created under the user assigned in the step, so it's really important that you identify the right user who executes the production planning step in the background job, as shown in Figure 5.42. After selecting the correct **JobName**, click the **Step** button in the menu bar to display the steps defined in the job. The **User** column in the **Step List Overview** screen shows the user the system used to execute the job step.

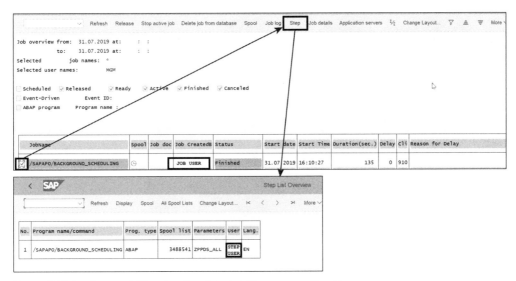

Figure 5.42 Background Planning Run Job: Job User versus Step User

You can navigate to the job log from the job overview screen by clicking on the **Job log** button. The spool request has all the statistics of the PP-DS planning run and the results for the individual materials with top CPU consumption to indicate if there are any warnings, errors, or terminations. The main usage of the background planning job spool is to review the statistics and the top CPU consuming materials to check if any specific master data or Customizing settings for these materials are causing any bottlenecks. For performing the application level analysis, the log display is a better tool because it has filtering capabilities, unlike the spool document. Some of the important statistics and information available in the planning job spool are shown in Figure 5.43.

The materials planned in the planning run are listed in the sequence they are planned in Figure 5.43 ❶. The number of records processed (e.g., the number of pegging areas selected and planned); the orders created, changed, and deleted; and the run time statistics of the planning job (e.g., the runtime, the CPU time consumed by the heuristics, and the CPU time to update the data) are displayed as shown in Figure 5.43 ❷. The materials that are the top CPU consumers are also listed in the spool (see Figure 5.43 ❸).

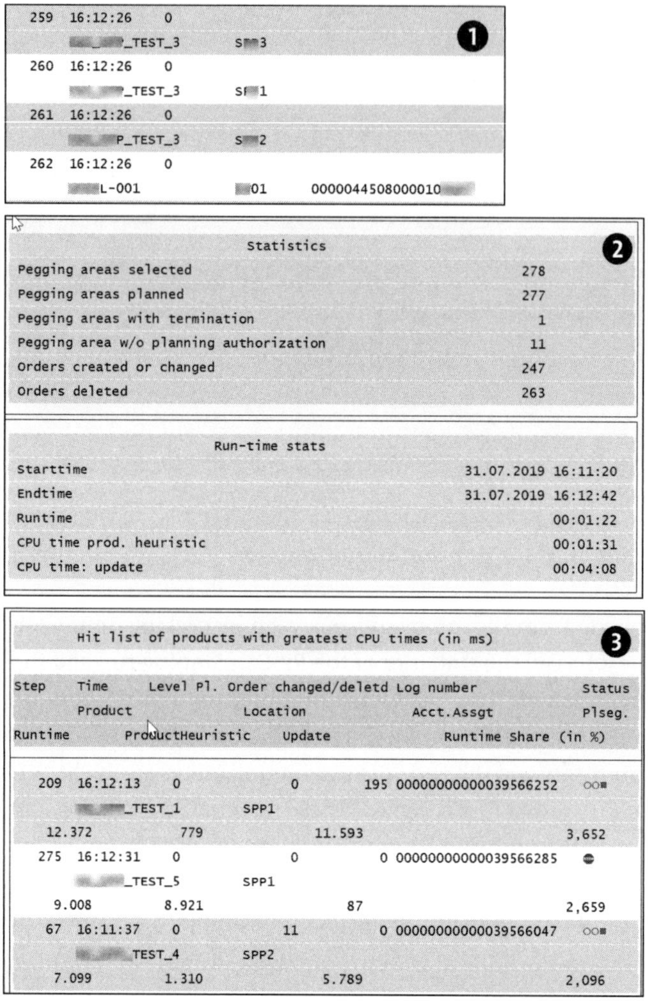

```
259  16:12:26    0
      ___P_TEST_3        S   3                          ❶
260  16:12:26    0
      ___P_TEST_3        SF  1
261  16:12:26    0
      ___P_TEST_3        S   2
262  16:12:26    0
      ___L-001           01    0000044508000010
```

	Statistics		❷
Pegging areas selected		278	
Pegging areas planned		277	
Pegging areas with termination		1	
Pegging area w/o planning authorization		11	
Orders created or changed		247	
Orders deleted		263	

	Run-time stats	
Starttime		31.07.2019 16:11:20
Endtime		31.07.2019 16:12:42
Runtime		00:01:22
CPU time prod. heuristic		00:01:31
CPU time: update		00:04:08

Hit list of products with greatest CPU times (in ms)   ❸

Step	Time	Level Pl. Order changed/deletd Log number		Status
	Product	Location	Acct.Assgt	Plseg.
Runtime	ProductHeuristic	Update	Runtime Share (in %)	
209 16:12:13 0		0 195 00000000000039566252		OO
___TEST_1 SPP1				
12.372	779	11.593		3,652
275 16:12:31 0		0 0 00000000000039566285		⊜
___TEST_5 SPP1				
9.008	8.921	87		2,659
67 16:11:37 0		11 0 00000000000039566047		OO
___TEST_4 SPP2				
7.099	1.310	5.789		2,096

Figure 5.43 Information Available in the PP-DS Background Planning Job Spool

5.6.4   Monitor Planning Results from MRP SAP Fiori Apps

In the SAP S/4HANA system, the MRP cockpit is a set of SAP Fiori apps that can handle both the MRP planned and advanced planned materials. The apps can manage and monitor material shortages, receipts, and requirements. From the MRP SAP Fiori apps, it's possible to trigger a PP-DS planning run for individual materials to resolve a planning problem. The advanced planning-specific SAP Fiori apps—such as the SAP

Fiori-based DS Planning Board app and the Monitor Capacity app—are only relevant for advanced planning resources and materials.

For the MRP SAP Fiori apps, the selection is based on the area of responsibility (AOR) assigned to the user in the app user settings. The AOR is the combination of the plant and the MRP controller. One user may be assigned to multiple plants and MRP controllers.

For working with the MRP SAP Fiori apps, authorization role SAP_BR_MATL_PLNR (Material Planner – External Procurement) and role SAP_BR_PRODN_PLNR (Production Planner) are delivered standard. After the roles are assigned and you open the SAP Fiori launchpad, you'll see the MRP cockpit apps.

The first time you open an MRP app, it will prompt you to enter the **Area of Responsibility**. From the user menu in the upper-right corner of the SAP Fiori launchpad, go to the **App Settings** to open the **MRP Settings** popup, as shown in Figure 5.44. Click the **Area of Responsibility** arrow to access the **Area of Responsibility** popup, where you can click the **+** button. In the subsequent **Add Plant and MRP Controller** popup, select your AOR, and click **OK**. If the user doesn't have authorization for the selected plant and MRP controller in the SAP S/4HANA system, no data will be loaded, and the message is logged.

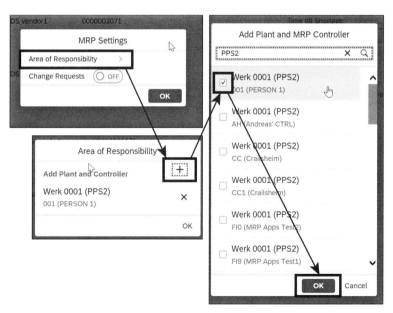

Figure 5.44 Assigning the AOR

Tip

In the SAP Gateway system, execute Transaction /N/UI2/FLP to open the SAP Fiori launchpad. The apps will be loaded per the authorization roles assigned to your user.

Monitor Material Coverage

The Monitor Material Coverage app is an important apps because it shows the material coverage per the shortage profile assigned in Customizing. To create and assign the shortage profile to users, follow the Customizing menu: **SAP IMG Menu · Production · Material Requirements Planning · Apps for Material Requirements Planning · General Settings · Define Material Shortage Profiles · Assign Material Shortage Profile to Users**.

This app will list all the materials per the AOR defined and any additional filters set within the app. The stock availability will be shown with negative stock availability marked in red so you don't have to scan through a huge list of materials and can focus on the materials with shortages. Filters can be applied by days till shortage, shortage quantity or day's supply, and so on. You can select the materials and trigger an MRP Live run from the app itself by clicking the **Start MRP Run** button, which will start MRP Live for the selected materials in the SAP S/4HANA system. If the materials are advanced planned, the product heuristics also will be called by MRP Live. As shown in Figure 5.45, you also can launch the Manage Materials app for the selected material by clicking the **Manage Materials** button and then clicking the **Start MRP Run** button from the subsequent screen.

In the Manage Material app, you can see all the demand and supply and change supply elements manually, and you can start an MRP Live run.

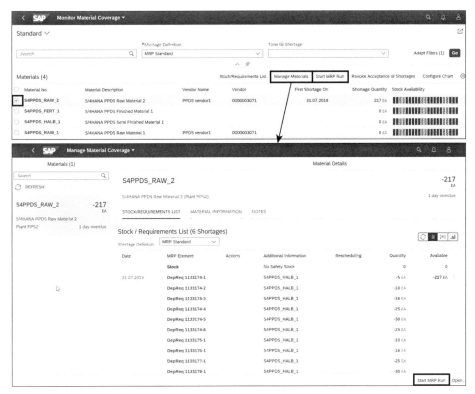

Figure 5.45 Monitor Material Coverage SAP Fiori App: Options

Display MRP Master Data Issues

Apart from monitoring the MRP Live planning run application logs from Transaction SLG1, the advanced planned materials that have failed in the MRP Live planning run also can be monitored from the Display MRP Master Data Issues app. This app lists all the materials with messages from the last MRP Live run for the AOR. You can set a filter on the category of the issues (information, warning, or error) or the source of the error (MRP Live, advanced planning).

You can set filters within this app by clicking the **Adapt Filters** button, as shown in Figure 5.46. You can then access **More Filters**, which will bring you to the **Select Filters** popup. For this example, select the **Source** filter, and click **OK**. Then, in the **Items** popup, select **Advanced Planning**. With the filters set correctly for the advanced planned materials, you can quickly see a list of materials with errors in the MRP Live planning that are relevant to advanced planning, as shown in Figure 5.47.

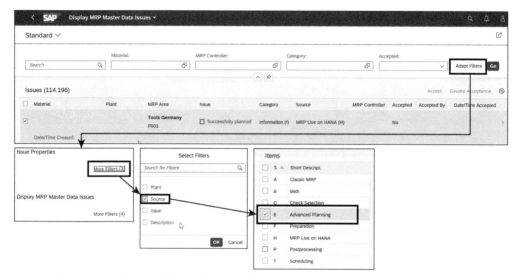

Figure 5.46 Advanced Planned Materials in Display MRP Master Data Issues SAP Fiori App

Standard * ∨								
Filtered By (1): Source								
□	.... ref product, green, GREEN	Plant 0001	Werk 0001	◇	∨	Default	Advanced Planning	PERSON 1
	13961004	0001	0001			Category	(E)	(001)
	Date/Time Created: 13.06.2019, 05:01:33							
□	....._VAR_AVC	Plant 0001	Werk 0001	◇		Default	Advanced Planning	PERSON 1
	....._VAR_AVC1	0001	0001			Category	(E)	(001)
	Date/Time Created: 13.06.2019, 05:01:33							
□	Finished product:........................	Werk Copy of 0001	Werk Copy of 0001	⟳ An error occurred for product &1 in location &2		Default	Advanced Planning	PERSON 1
	.._..., ...	....	....			Category	(E)	(001)
	Date/Time Created: 09.04.2019, 07:11:33							

Figure 5.47 Display MRP Master Data Issues App: Advanced Planning Materials with Errors

One other efficient way of monitoring the planning results from the business point of view is from the alert monitor where alerts can be configured for delays, resources, shelf life, and so on. We'll cover the alert monitor in Chapter 7.

5.7   Planning in PP-DS with SAP IBP

SAP IBP is the cloud-based supply chain solution from SAP that features different components such as S&OP, demand, supply, response and supply, and inventory. SAP IBP can integrate into SAP ERP or SAP S/4HANA and other ERP solutions.

Depending on the components used within the SAP IBP system, the result output from SAP IBP can be the constrained forecast, supply time series, or order data. The planning and forecasting results integrate back to the SAP S/4HANA system.

The system uses SAP HANA smart data integration (SDI) for order-based data, and it uses SAP Cloud Platform Integration for data services for time series data. The application system landscape of the SAP IBP system is shown in Figure 5.48.

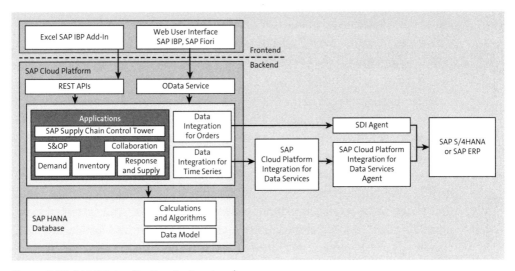

Figure 5.48 SAP IBP Application System Landscape

The master data is sent from the SAP S/4HANA system to the SAP IBP system via the integration model process, which uses SDI. The master data objects, such as materials, locations, business partners, external procurement source of supplies, PDSs, and transport lanes (generated from special procurement for materials), are sent to the SAP IBP system.

When the master data and transaction data are sent from SAP S/4HANA to SAP IBP or when SAP IBP sends the forecasting and/or planning results back to SAP S/4HANA, the communication is between the SAP S/4HANA system and the SAP IBP system. SAP IBP doesn't directly communicate with embedded PP-DS. However, as PP-DS is an integral part of the SAP S/4HANA system, for the advanced planned materials in the SAP S/4HANA system, the SAP IBP planning results updated in SAP S/4HANA are available for PP-DS too—if the integration between SAP S/4HANA and PP-DS is set up as described in Chapter 3 and Chapter 4.

Solution deployment of SAP IBP and SAP S/4HANA along with advanced planning varies due to the supply chain maturity of a business. But, in general, the following are the key deployment models:

- **Output of SAP IBP demand to PP-DS**
  SAP IBP for sales and operations planning and SAP IBP for demand are used to arrive at the constrained forecast whose data is sent to the SAP S/4HANA system as PIRs. The planned independent data can be made visible to embedded PP-DS for the advanced planned materials. PP-DS plans these materials and generates supplies to cover any uncovered demand.

- **Output of SAP IBP supply to PP-DS**
  In SAP IBP, the S&OP demand and supply planning are performed, and the time series supply data is sent to the SAP S/4HANA system. In such scenarios, the PDS explosion has been performed, and the supply data for the finished materials and the components that are part of the SAP IBP PDS are also determined in SAP IBP. If the supply data time series is brought to SAP S/4HANA as PIRs, then duplicate dependent demand will be generated when the PDSs are exploded in embedded PP-DS or the production version is exploded in SAP S/4HANA. Therefore, these time series can be created as planned orders in the SAP S/4HANA system. If these materials are advanced planned, these planned orders are also visible to PP-DS, and the advanced planning and scheduling tools can be used to fine-tune the supply plan.

  Because the time series data can't be mapped to specific planned orders in the SAP S/4HANA system, every time the planning data is refreshed, the planned orders need to be deleted and re-created in the SAP S/4HANA system, beyond the planning time fence.

- **Output of SAP IBP response to PP-DS**
  When the supply/response planning is performed in SAP IBP, the resulting order data can be brought into the SAP S/4HANA system via the SDI interface. This is a standard interface with the options to enhance the data using BAdIs within the SAP S/4HANA system. With this option, the order mapping between SAP IBP and embedded PP-DS is maintained; thus, delta transfers of the planned orders and purchase requisitions are possible.

In any of these cases, embedded PP-DS treats the advanced planned materials in the same way irrespective of whether those materials are integrated into SAP IBP or not. Therefore, the process design should consider the time horizon responsibility of all the planning tools involved in the overall solution to ensure that no two tools are planning the same time horizon and causing incorrect planning results.

5.8 Summary

In this chapter, we covered the use cases where PP-DS planning can help resolve planning problems that can't be handled by the SAP S/4HANA planning tools (e.g., MRP).

The basic concepts of production planning for the short term and how these concepts are realized within embedded PP-DS were also covered in this chapter. Various planning and service heuristics that are commonly used in PP-DS were discussed along with their use cases wherever applicable. We also delved into the technical settings of these heuristics that enable various functionalities.

The PP-DS planning run can be executed in interactive/dialog/online mode or in background mode. The various options, including the SAP Fiori apps, to analyze the PP-DS planning results and planning issues were discussed as well.

After the production planning is performed and a feasible plan is in place, the next step is to constrain the feasible plan against the available capacity to arrive at an executable plan. In the next chapter, we'll discuss the tools and features offered in embedded PP-DS for detailed scheduling and finite capacity planning.

Chapter 6
Detailed Scheduling

Now, let's move on to the second main process: detailed scheduling. In this chapter, we'll walk through the key detailed scheduling heuristics as well as how to trigger PP-DS scheduling. We'll also see how to use the PP-DS optimizer for optimizing the production schedule.

The main objective of any detailed scheduling tool is to reduce the lead time of manufacturing and avoid delays in fulfilling customer orders and internal dependent requirements while ensuring the productivity of the resources.

In the SAP S/4HANA system, tools such as capacity planning, capacity leveling, and scheduling can be used to plan the capacities of the resources and schedule orders. But for performing detailed scheduling of the orders, operations, and activities within the operations considering multiple other constraints, the detailed scheduling tools and algorithms delivered in PP-DS for SAP S/4HANA (embedded PP-DS), are the most efficient options.

Detailed scheduling functions and heuristics are delivered in standard embedded PP-DS, and these can fulfill most of the complex scheduling requirements. The heuristics can be customized and extended to realize any requirements that aren't delivered in the standard algorithms. Industry-specific algorithms are also delivered in the standard for repetitive manufacturing, process manufacturing, and discrete manufacturing.

The detailed scheduling part of embedded PP-DS leverages the power of SAP live-Cache in performing the scheduling efficiently. The time duration is calculated in seconds, so the accuracy of the routing and master recipe master data in SAP S/4HANA is critical for PP-DS scheduling.

Performing finite scheduling during production planning isn't recommended. Constraining the capacity during material planning may cause shortages and delays during the planning stage. Therefore, after a material feasibility plan is arrived at, then the capacity constraints can be applied to create an executable plan while ensuring the productivity of the manufacturing resources.

In this chapter, we'll explore the use cases where PP-DS scheduling can be used and the basic settings in the detailed scheduling (DS) strategy profile, which is the driving object for all the scheduling actions performed in the PP-DS system. We'll cover some of the important scheduling heuristics and the settings and options available in the scheduling tools, such as the detailed scheduling (DS) planning board and the PP-DS optimizer. The new SAP Fiori apps for monitoring/managing the capacities and the SAP Fiori-based DS planning board will be discussed as well.

6.1   Determining When PP-DS Should Be Used for Scheduling

The main objective of any detailed scheduling tool is to reduce the lead time of manufacturing and avoid delays in fulfilling customer orders and internal dependent requirements while ensuring the productivity of the resources. Following are some of the scenarios where the scheduling algorithms and tools offered in embedded PP-DS can help in resolving complex scheduling issues:

- **Flexibility in scheduling**
  PP-DS scheduling offers various models and scheduling tools to handle very simple scheduling requirements, to resolve simple scheduling issues, and address complex schedule and resource optimization issues. The tools offered by PP-DS are very flexible and customizable. If graphical scheduling and sequencing is required with automated scheduling, sequencing, and optimization, PP-DS has all the capabilities to fulfill these requirements.

- **Granularity of scheduling**
  For detailed scheduling scenarios on automated shop floors where concepts of just in time or just in sequence are implemented to feed the right materials to the right work stations, it's important that the schedule is accurate and planned up to the time stamp within seconds. In automotive manufacturers with automated assembly lines, such requirements are common, and PP-DS functionalities for repetitive manufacturing can be leveraged in such scenarios.

- **Resource and source of supply alternatives**
  Often in shop floors, alternative resources are available to handle additional volumes of product manufactured or when capacities aren't available due to planned or unplanned downtimes. In such cases, the requirement is to block the original

resource and load the alternative resource with the orders scheduled to be executed on the original resource. In addition, if there are capacity availability issues, the alternative resources can be used. In PP-DS, the use of alternative resources is supported with the right master data setup. The scheduling heuristics and tools in PP-DS support the use of alternative resources via the alternative mode selection during scheduling. Features such as multiresource scheduling in PP-DS also support automatic selection of alternative sources of supply if the initially chosen source of supply can't produce the materials without delays.

- **Characteristics-based setup matrix**
  The enterprise resource planning (ERP) systems support setup groups and matrices to improve the setup time required for sequencing the orders efficiently. However, in complex manufacturing processes with variant configuration (VC), a group of product characteristics determines the changeover times of the resources. Such cases lead to an enormous amount of manual work to create and maintain the master data in the SAP S/4HANA system. In these situations, the characteristics-based setup matrices can be generated in PP-DS, which requires only the changeover duration and costs to be maintained manually—all the possible characteristics combinations can be generated automatically by the system with the defined rules. These generated setup matrices are used by the PP-DS optimizer to optimize the setup time and setup costs.

- **Characteristics-dependent planning (CDP) and block planning**
  In industries such as mills (paper) and metal, the upstream planning processes define the products to be manufactured and their attributes during a certain period of time. In such cases, the production lines and resources need to be set up in a specific way to handle the manufacturing of the products during the defined time. This requires preassignment of resource capacities for products with specific characteristics. This process is called *block planning*. Embedded PP-DS supports block planning with CDP. The blocks can be created on the resources with preassigned capacities for the characteristics of the products to be manufactured. PP-DS scheduling tools will place the right order in the right block with compatible characteristics values.

- **Operation relationships**
  In PP-DS, when production data structures (PDSs) are created from SAP S/4HANA routings, the operation and activity relationships are also sent. For example, if there are wait times, queue times, and transportation times defined between the operations, and overlap and minimum send-ahead quantities are defined in the routing operation, these define the operation and activity relationships in the PDS

in PP-DS. In addition, if flexibility regarding consideration of these relationships is required during scheduling, PP-DS can support these requirements and such orders should be scheduled using PP-DS.

- **Pegging relationships**
  The SAP S/4HANA scheduling and capacity planning tools can't consider the order of relationships in terms of pegging. In SAP S/4HANA, the pegging structure isn't persisted, and the usage of the same isn't possible in scheduling. However, in embedded PP-DS, the pegging structure is persisted in SAP liveCache, and these relationships can be considered while performing scheduling so that the order relationship created after the planning can be respected during scheduling. This helps to avoid the introduction of any new shortages after the planning.

- **Capacity-driven order creation**
  When the resource capacities are precious in terms of costs and availability, every opportunity to use the capacity of such resources is required to ensure optimal usage. Capacity-driven order creation can be used on such resources to create orders or extend existing orders to use the available capacity to the maximum possible extent. Such resources and the corresponding materials should be planned and scheduled in PP-DS.

- **Production campaigns**
  In process industries, orders are grouped into campaigns based on the common attributes of the end products. Although production campaigns are possible in SAP S/4HANA, embedded PP-DS provides much more flexibility and supports complex requirements via the heuristics and interactive management of the campaigns using the DS planning board. In PP-DS, the production campaign can be created for one or more materials, whereas in SAP S/4HANA, the production campaign can only handle one material per campaign. For the campaigns created and managed in PP-DS, SAP S/4HANA also supports campaigns with more than one material per campaign.

- **Complex project and sales order-oriented scheduling**
  PP-DS supports complex project and sales order-oriented order networks by identifying and scheduling the critical paths and the corresponding operations and orders.

- **Optimization**
  The PP-DS optimizer is tool used to optimize the schedule based on defined objective functions for reducing manufacturing lead time, setup times and costs, and

delays. The PP-DS optimizer is an optional component of embedded PP-DS. However, for resources that handle complex operation structures and multiple changeover combinations, the PP-DS optimizer helps optimize the schedule.

Note

MRP-based detailed scheduling refers to the executing planning in SAP S/4HANA and performing only the detailed scheduling in the PP-DS component. This functionality is only supported in a side-by-side deployment of the PP-DS component in SAP Advanced Planning and Optimization (SAP APO) along with SAP S/4HANA. With embedded PP-DS, the MRP-based detailed scheduling isn't supported.

6.2 Creating a Detailed Scheduling Strategy

In PP-DS, detailed scheduling works based on DS strategies. In the order scheduling function, the order and the operations under the order go through the process of calculating their dates and times. The DS strategy is a set of settings and parameters that controls the order scheduling. The parameters the system needs to consider for the scheduling, such as the scheduling direction (forward or backward), the sequence in which the orders should be considered for scheduling, and the constraints the system needs to respect for scheduling (e.g., capacity and material availability) are maintained in the DS strategy profile.

In this section, we'll walk through how to set up strategy profiles and their parameters.

6.2.1 Strategy Profiles

The strategy profiles are defined as a group of DS strategies. Several strategies with different settings and parameters are grouped under one strategy profile. The system uses the first strategy defined in the strategy profile, and if it's not able to schedule the order successfully respecting the parameters and constraints defined in the first strategy, it will try to schedule the order with the next available strategy in the strategy profile.

In embedded PP-DS, the strategy profiles can be maintained from the Customizing menu path: **SAP IMG Menu · Advanced Planning · Global Settings · Maintain Strategy Profiles**.

As shown in Figure 6.1, the SAP standard delivered strategy profiles are listed in the transaction. You can create a new strategy by clicking on the **New Entries** button. In the **New Entries: Overview of Added Entries** screen, enter a name for the scheduling **Strategy Profile** and a **Short Description**. Then, select the newly added entry, and double-click on the **Strategies** folder. In the next screen, **Change View "Strategies":** **Overview**, click on **New Entries** to create and add a new scheduling strategy to the strategy profile, as shown in Figure 6.2.

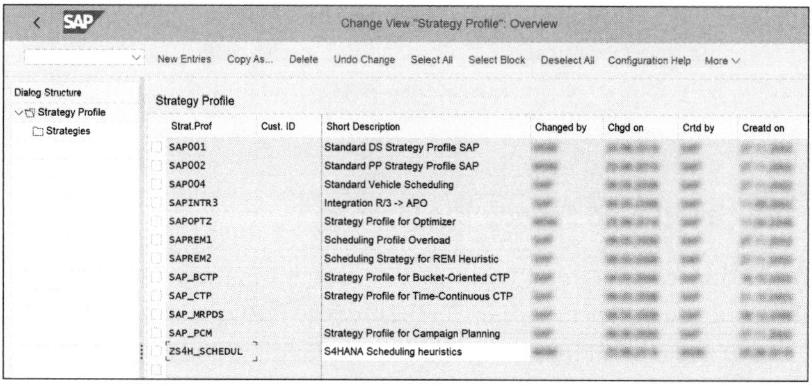

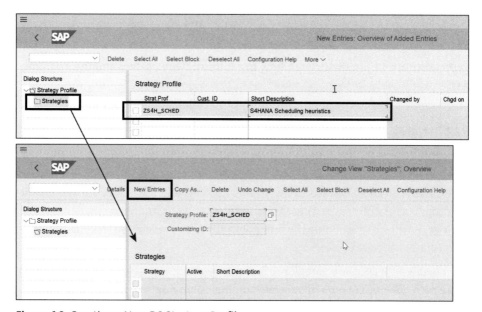

Figure 6.1 DS Strategy Profiles in SAP S/4HANA

Figure 6.2 Creating a New DS Strategy Profile

Now you'll be in the **New Entries: Details of Added Entries** screen, where you can maintain the details of the scheduling strategy, as shown in Figure 6.3.

The **Strategy Number** is the sort order of this strategy within the many strategies that can be maintained under a strategy group. The lowest strategy number will have the highest priority. Strategy number 1 will be used first by the system to schedule orders, and if it can't schedule the order by respecting all the settings and constraints, then the system will try the scheduling with the next strategy that has the next highest strategy number.

The **Cross-Strategy Parameters** are valid for all the strategies under one strategy profile. If a newly added strategy under a strategy profile has different values maintained for the settings under the cross-strategy parameters, it will overwrite the values for other strategies.

Figure 6.3 Maintenance of Scheduling Strategy Settings

The **Scheduling Offset** parameter under the **Cross-Strategy Parameters** signifies the number of minutes from the current time during which the system can start scheduling orders. This can be a positive value to allow order scheduling after the maintained number of minutes or a negative value to allow order creation before the maintained number of minutes. The before and after calculations are based on the current time of the system during which the scheduling operation is performed in PP-DS.

Example

If the current date and time is June 25th, 2019, 08:00:00, and the value -1440 is maintained as the offset parameter, then the system can start scheduling the affected order starting June 24th, 2019, at 08:00:00, that is, 1,440 minutes (24 hours) before the current date/time.

The **Desired Date** determines the order dates when a rescheduling is performed from the scheduling tools and production planning runs. The following is the significance of the available options:

- **Current Date**
  This is the assigned date of the order before the rescheduling is used as the desired date, and the system searches for an available date from this date to schedule the order. Depending on the planning direction in the strategy, the current end date is considered for backward planning, and the current start date is considered for forward planning.

- **Earliest Date**
  The system will schedule the order at the earliest possible date. In PP-DS, the earliest date can be the current date/time +/- the offset maintained.

- **Specified Date**
  When a rescheduling is performed, the system prompts the user to enter a desired date during which the user wants the system to schedule the order.

Note

The **Desired Date** setting is only relevant for the reschedule function in the detailed scheduling tools and for the background planning run. As the specified date option requires a user to enter a date manually, this setting isn't applicable for the production planning run.

The **Current Modes** setting allows or stops the usage of alternative modes for scheduling the operations, if there are alternative modes available. Alternative modes are used in scenarios where multiple work centers/resources can be used to perform the same activity; if the resource assigned to the operation doesn't have any available capacity, then the operation can be scheduled on one of the other alternative resources. These are modeled as alternative sequences and resources in the SAP S/4HANA routing master data and transferred to the PDSs as alternative modes. In addition, it's possible to assign priorities to the alternative modes that PP-DS scheduling can use to determine the next possible resource to schedule an operation if a mode with higher priority doesn't have the available capacity.

The available options for the **Current Modes** setting are as follows:

- **Retain**
  The scheduling strategy won't change the mode (resource) of the operation and will try to schedule the order on the same resource that is already assigned to the operation, possibly on a later date with a delay.

- **Select Any Mode**
  This setting allows the scheduling strategy to select any of the allowed modes (alternative modes in the PDS master data) to schedule the operation.

When there are multiple orders and operations selected for a scheduling function from the scheduling and planning tools, the **Scheduling Sequence** button can be used to sort the operations and orders per the sort definition maintained in the scheduling sequence setting. As shown in Figure 6.4, you can click on the **Scheduling Sequence** button to open the **Choose Fields** popup from which you can choose the fields from the standard provided list and assign a sort order to those fields.

As shown earlier in Figure 6.3, there are also two tabs in the **New Entries: Details of Added Entries** screen:

- **General Strategy Parameters**
  The parameters and constraints for the operations and orders being scheduled use the settings under this tab.

- **Strategy Parameters f. Dependent Objects**
  When operations are changed by the scheduling operation, other operations and orders may be linked to the operation being scheduled. The settings under this tab determine how the linked dependent objects (operations and orders) should be handled. For example, if an order has two operations, and the second operation is rescheduled to an earlier date than the first operation, it's logical to move the first

operation before the second operation because the second operation can't start before the finish of the first operation. In this case, the settings under this tab determine how the first operation is handled when the second operation is moved.

After a strategy is maintained and saved by clicking the **Save** button, you can add multiple other strategies to the same strategy profile. As shown in Figure 6.5, the strategies maintained under the strategy profiles can be activated and deactivated by checking the **Active** checkbox.

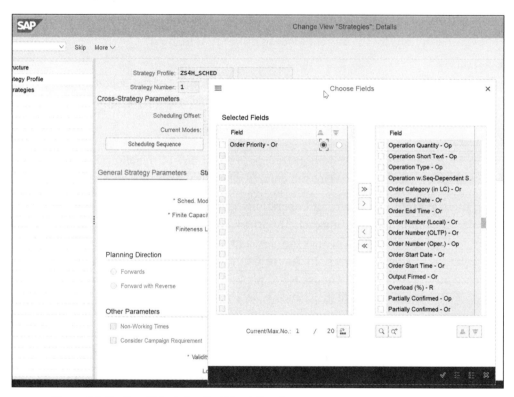

Figure 6.4 Sorting Objects for the Scheduling Sequence

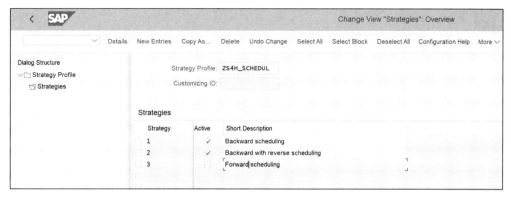

Figure 6.5 Multiple Scheduling Strategies in One Strategy Profile

6.2.2   General Strategy Parameters

In this section, we'll cover the individual settings and options available and the significance of these settings in detailed scheduling (referring back to the **General Strategy Parameters** tab in Figure 6.3). The details behind the settings will cover some of the fundamentals and basic concepts of the scheduling process as well.

Scheduling Mode

Scheduling modes determine how the operations are placed on resources. The resource availability is represented in SAP liveCache by a resource time stream, which is created according to the settings on the resources for the factory calendar, shift definitions, and capacity definitions. The same is also visible in the DS planning board where the resource time stream is represented graphically.

Apart from the infinite scheduling mode, all other schedule modes are finite schedules. In infinite scheduling, orders can be scheduled on a resource even if it doesn't have enough capacity to handle the order. In finite scheduling modes, the resources won't be overloaded beyond their available capacity. In single activity resources (resource type – single resource), only one activity can be scheduled at a time, and in multi-activity resources (resource type – multiresource), the number of activities that can be scheduled on the resource is based on the number of individual capacities available on the resource. The scheduling type of finite scheduling is driven by the scheduling mode (which should be a finite mode), and the resource must be activated for finite scheduling in the resource master data.

Example

If resource R1 isn't marked as relevant for finite scheduling in the capacity header view of the work center master data, usage of the find slot (a finite scheduling) mode may result in the resource being overloaded. This is because R1 is an infinite resource.

The following scheduling modes are supported by PP-DS:

- **Find slot**

  Find slot is a finite scheduling strategy where the system finds an available slot on the finite resource time stream to fit in the operation sufficiently without having to change any other operations already scheduled on the resource. The scheduling direction is also considered for finding the slot.

  The functionality and the impact of the scheduling direction on this scheduling mode is shown in Figure 6.6. The diagram shows the initial scheduling situation in the top row of operations (Opr 1 to Opr 5). When a new operation (New Opr) is scheduled on the desired date with the find slot scheduling mode, depending on the planning direction, the following behavior results:

  - **Scheduling direction – backward**

    The system checks for an available slot from the desired date (end date of the new operation) in a backward direction where the new operation can be inserted without impacting any of the existing operations. The search direction and placement of the new operation is shown in the left side of the middle row of operations. After the slot is identified, the new operation is scheduled, and the scheduling result is shown in the bottom row of operations.

  - **Scheduling direction – forward**

    Although similar to the backward scheduling direction backward, with forward scheduling, the system searches for an available slot in the forward direction (future) from the desired date (start date of the new operation). This is shown in the right side of Figure 6.6.

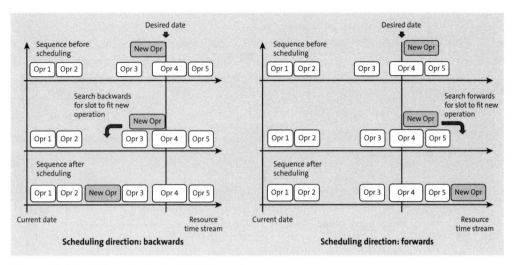

Figure 6.6 Scheduling Mode: Find Slot Example

- **Insert operation**

  Insert operation is a finite scheduling strategy in which the system creates a slot for inserting the operation on the desired operation data or as close as possible to the desired date. For creating the slot that can hold the operation, the system will push the operation before the slot backward or after the slot forward. How this scheduling mode works is shown in Figure 6.7. The insert operation scheduling mode can only be used on single-activity resources.

  The initial scheduling situation is shown in the first row of the operations in Figure 6.7. With the insert operation mode, when a new operation is to be scheduled on the desired date, the following behavior occurs:

  - **Scheduling direction – backward**

    The system will push the existing operations in the backward direction to make space for the new operation. The push starts from the operation (Opr 3) that has an end date before the end date of the new operation. So the operations 1, 2, and 3 are pushed backward, and the new operation is placed in the newly created slot.

  - **Scheduling direction – forward**

    Operations (Opr 5) with a start date after the start date of the new operation are pushed in the forward direction to make space for the new operation.

265

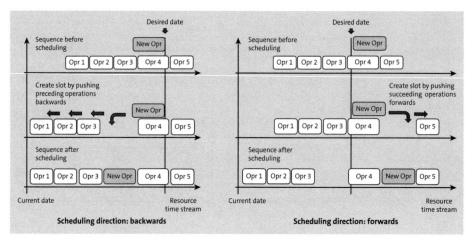

Figure 6.7 Scheduling Mode: Insert Operation Example

- **Squeeze in operation**

  With the squeeze in operation finite scheduling mode, the system will create a slot of the operation being scheduled by pushing the preceding operations backward and succeeding operations forward. This scheduling mode works only with single-activity resources. As the operations are pushed in both directions, the scheduling direction (backward or forward) doesn't make a difference with this scheduling mode, as shown in Figure 6.8.

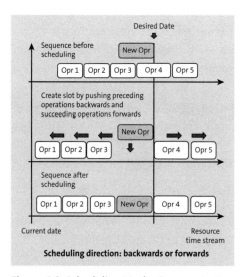

Figure 6.8 Scheduling Mode: Squeeze In Operation Example

Irrespective of the scheduling direction, the system will make space for the new operation by pushing the preceding operations (Opr 1, 2, 3) in the backward direction and the succeeding operations (Opr 4, 5) in the forward direction.

- **Insert operation and close gap to start/end**
Insert operation and close gap is a hybrid scheduling mode where the system works exactly as the insert operation scheduling mode but will close the gaps between the operations in the scheduling direction.

There is a distinction between using this scheduling mode—with and without block planning. In block planning, the scheduling of operations is limited within the block in which the operation is placed or being scheduled into. The newly created and deallocated operations when scheduled in a block planning scenario will get scheduled into the block that matches the block planning-relevant characteristics values of the operation.

If no block planning is used, this scheduling mode can only be used with forward scheduling mode. The system will push the succeeding operations forward to insert the new operation being scheduled. Then, if there are gaps in the forward direction, the system will close them by pulling the operations to the earliest possible time stamp so that the gaps are closed or minimized.

With block planning in use, both the scheduling directions can be used while closing the gap within the block in the scheduling direction. The system moves the operations to close the gap to the earliest date (earlier of the original date or the newly determined date).

- **Append operation**
The append operation is a finite scheduling mode that schedules the new operation at the end of the last operation scheduled on the finite resource.

- **Search for bucket with free capacity**
The bucket with free capacity is relevant for resources where a bucket definition is maintained in the PP-DS resource master. This can be maintained in the SAP APO resource view in the SAP S/4HANA work center master data. The duration of one bucket is defined by the bucket schema (days, weeks, etc.) in the resource data.

[Ex]

Example

For resource R1, the bucket is defined with a bucket schema of days and bucket definition of time-continuous capacity. If the resource is available for 8 hours per day, then D1, D2 . . . Dn buckets will be created with 8 hours capacity per bucket.

With this scheduling mode, the operations will be rescheduled only when the available bucket capacity is completely consumed. But the operations aren't scheduled on the resource time stream, so there could be several operations starting at the same start time within the bucket. However, as long as the total resource consumption of the operation doesn't exceed the bucket capacity, the operations will stay at the same position after rescheduling (same start time for multiple operations).

The concept of bucket capacity is mostly used in SAP APO's supply network planning component, but it's not widely used for PP-DS scheduling because the purpose of PP-DS scheduling is to arrive at a resource optimized and sequenced executable schedule.

In block planning scenarios in PP-DS, the resources can be defined with a bucket capacity derived from the block definition in the resource master data. In this scenario, the search for buckets with free capacity scheduling mode can be used.

- **Infinite scheduling**
  With the infinite scheduling mode, the operation is scheduled on the resource without taking the resource load into account, which can result in resource capacity overload.

- **Infinite sequencing**
  Infinite sequencing scheduling mode is similar to the infinite scheduling mode, but it can close the gaps between the operations selected to be rescheduled.

  The working model of infinite scheduling versus infinite sequencing is shown in Figure 6.9. With infinite scheduling (left side of Figure 6.9), operations 2, 3, and 4 are selected for rescheduling, but they are scheduled in the same place where they are at present because the system doesn't consider the available capacity of the resource. So before (top-left row of operations) and after rescheduling (bottom-left row of operations), there is no change in the schedule.

  With the infinite sequencing mode (right side of Figure 6.9), the system schedules the operations infinitely, but if there are gaps (G1 and G2) in between the selected operations (Opr 2, 3, and 4), the system closes these gaps. As shown in the bottom-right list of operations, gaps G1 and G2 are closed, and the operations are scheduled infinitely without considering the capacity of the resource.

With any of the preceding finite scheduling modes, the system tries to perform the scheduling action per the scheduling mode. But depending on the other constraints, moving other operations may not be possible. In such cases, you may need to relax the other constraints or switch to a scheduling mode that is less restrictive (e.g., append operation).

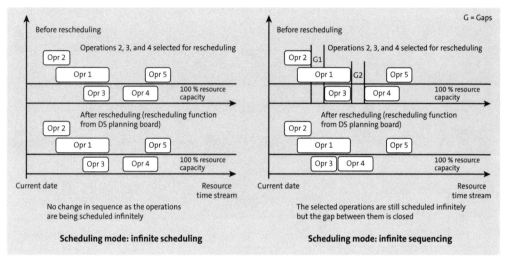

Figure 6.9 Scheduling Modes: Infinite Scheduling versus Infinite Sequencing Example

Finite Capacity

The next setting in the DS strategy is the **Finite Capacity**. This setting decides which capacity is considered for finitely scheduling the operations. In the resource master, the default value for the finite scheduling relevant capacity ❶ is defined as shown in Figure 6.10. If the bucket capacity is defined for the resource, it can be displayed from the resource master (Transaction /SAPAPO/RES01) **PP/DS Bucket Cap** tab by clicking on the **Bucket Capacity** button ❷; however, within the strategy settings shown in Figure 6.11, it's possible to override the resource master data setting and use **Time-Continuous Capacity** (scheduling on a resource time stream), the **Bucket Capacity** (only if the bucket definition is defined in the resource master data), or **As Specified in the Resource** for finite scheduling.

> **Note**
>
> If the **Sched. Mode** field is set as **Search for Bucket with Free Capacity**, then the finite capacity must be set as **Bucket Capacity** or as **As Specified in the Resource**, where the resource is set with the bucket capacity as the finite capacity.

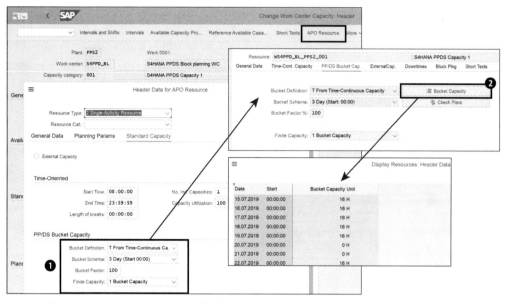

Figure 6.10 Bucket Capacity Definition in SAP S/4HANA and PP-DS Master Data and Options in the DS Strategy Profile for Finite Capacity

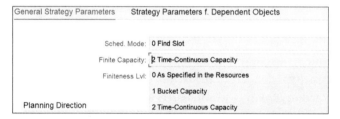

Figure 6.11 Options for the Finite Capacity Selection in General Strategy Parameters

Finiteness Level

The **Finiteness Lvl** in the DS strategy profile is the next level of control apart from the finite scheduling relevant indicator in the resource master and the scheduling modes in the DS strategy profile. If you have a number of finite resources and—depending on the application being used—you want some of them to be scheduled finitely and some of them infinitely, then the finiteness level can be used.

The finiteness level is a number between 0 and 9999. The system compares the finiteness level defined in the resource master against the finiteness level defined in the

DS strategy profile to decide whether or not to schedule the resource finitely. If the finiteness level defined in the detailed scheduling strategy is equal to or greater than the finiteness level defined in the resource, then the resource will be finitely scheduled in the application where this DS strategy is used. But for the resource to be scheduled, the prerequisites apart from the finiteness level check is that the resource is marked as finite scheduling relevant in the resource master and the scheduling mode being used in detailed scheduling is a finite scheduling mode. When the finiteness level in the resource is less than the one defined in the strategy profile, then the resource is infinitely scheduled.

The finiteness level values 0 and 999 have special functions. When the finiteness level 0 is assigned to the strategy profile, then only the resources with finiteness level 0 or resources with no finiteness level defined are scheduled finitely. With the value 999 set in the strategy profile, all the finite scheduling relevant resources will be finitely scheduled irrespective of the finiteness level defined at the resource master level.

Finiteness level needs to be configured before its used in the resources or in the strategy profile. To configure the finiteness level, follow the Customizing menu path: **SAP IMG Menu · Advanced Planning · Global Settings · Define Finiteness Levels for Resources**.

Tip [+]

The general resource master data can only be edited from the work center data SAP APO resource view in SAP S/4HANA. The finiteness level configured values aren't visible in the work center transactions (Transaction CR02), so you'll have to assign the valid values manually without value help F4 . The system won't allow saving the resource with a finiteness level value that isn't configured in PP-DS.

Planning Direction

Planning Direction is a basic setting in the strategy profile that directs the system to look for an available date for the operation being created or being rescheduled. The forward scheduling will search for availability on the resource schedule in the future (from the desired start date) for a possible order start date. The backward scheduling will search for an available schedule on the resource in the past from the desired date for a possible order end date.

Both the forward and backward scheduling directions have a reverse option too. With reverse, if the forward direction isn't able to find a schedule in the future, it will start to search for availability in the past.

How the four options work for the planning direction is shown in Figure 6.12.

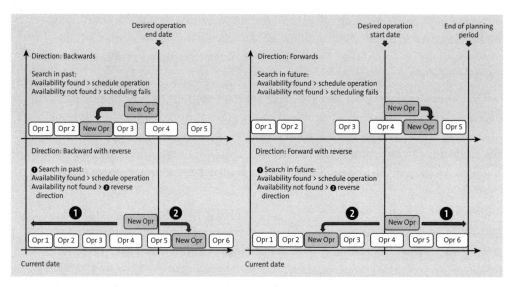

Figure 6.12 Planning Direction in Scheduling (Scheduling Mode: Find Slot Example)

Nonworking Times

The **Other Parameters** section in the strategy profile has further settings to add and relax more constraints in the scheduling process, as shown in Figure 6.13.

The **Non-Working Times** setting relaxes the scheduling constraints by considering the nonworking times, such as shift breaks, as available capacity. The consideration of the nonworking time is only applied to the operations/activities being scheduled manually or selected explicitly for the consideration for the scheduling action. The operations/activities that are scheduled due to their relationship (dependent operations and activities) to the operation being scheduled won't respect the **Non-Working Times** setting.

Figure 6.13 Other Parameters in the General Strategy Parameters

> **Note**
>
> The **Non-Working Times** setting won't consider the downtimes of the resource for marking them as working time. Only the unavailability due to nonworking days and shift breaks are considered working times with this setting. The available capacity for the nonworking time is calculated based on the immediately preceding working time.

Consider Campaign Requirement

In embedded PP-DS systems, production campaigns are used to minimize setup costs and storage costs. When there is a sequence of orders scheduled on resources belonging to the same or different product, production campaigns can be created so that orders with similar setup attributes can be brought together, and one setup order can be created at the start of the campaign. The profile for the campaign planning determines whether to create a clean-out order at the end of the campaign or a setup order at the start of the campaign. Production campaigns can be created manually or automatically by the campaign optimization. When selected, the **Consider**

Campaign Requirement checkbox in the strategy profile won't allow any other operations that are part of the campaign to get scheduled inside the campaign. This checkbox has a dependency on the **Campaign-Relevant** checkbox in the resource master data in PP-DS. For the system to respect the **Consider Campaign Requirement** option in the strategy profile, the **Campaign-Relevant** checkbox must be activated in the corresponding resource master data.

Production campaigns are used in production line manufacturing or process manufacturing where setup and storage are involved between the manufacturing of products.

> **Tip**
>
> The **Campaign-Relevant** checkbox in the resource master is also set in the SAP S/4HANA work center (Transaction CR02) or resource (Transaction CRC2) in the SAP APO resource view. This checkbox isn't editable in the PP-DS resource master (Transaction /SAPAPO/RES01).

Validity Periods of Order

The validity of the order created or transferred to PP-DS is determined by the validity of the source of supply, which is the PDS components and operations. When a PDS is used in an order, the latest of the validity starts among the operations and the components determine the start of validity of the order, and the earliest validity end among the components and operations determines the end of validity for the order. An example of the order validity is shown in Figure 6.14. You can see the PDS header validity dates ❶, the PDS **Operations** validity dates ❷, and the PDS **Components** validity dates ❸. The order validity dates are derived from these, as shown in Figure 6.15.

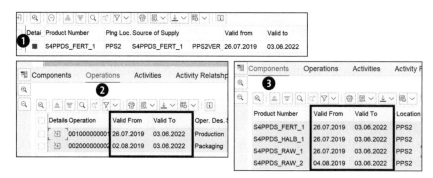

Figure 6.14 PP-DS Order Validity Derivation from PDS

Figure 6.15 Validity Dates in a PP-DS Planned Order

In the strategy profile, the **Validity Periods of Orders** setting checks the order validity and determines if the order can be moved out of the order validity period depending on the value defined under this setting. The options are as follows:

- **Consider Validity Period**
  The system will respect the validity period for the order being scheduled and the orders that are linked to this order by a pegging relationship. The orders can't be scheduled outside their validity periods.

- **Consider Only for Dependent Orders**
  If the strategy profile is set up to consider the pegging relationship of the orders, then with this option, the dependent orders can't be scheduled outside their validity periods. However, the order that is being scheduled is allowed to violate its validity while getting scheduled.

- **Do Not Consider**
  The order validity of the order and its dependent orders aren't considered for scheduling purposes.

Lowest Mode Priority

The PDSs in PP-DS can contain more than one mode under an activity that serve as alternatives. In the PDS, the operation in the SAP S/4HANA routing is transferred as operations to the PDS in PP-DS, the individual standard values within the routing operation are transferred as activities (setup, produce, and teardown) to the PP-DS PDS, and the resource consumption data is transferred as modes to the PDS.

There could be more than one mode that serves as alternatives in the PDS. The alternative modes can be modeled via alternative sequences in the SAP S/4HANA routing or by classification assignment to the resources and operations of the routing.

During scheduling with detailed scheduling heuristics, the alternative modes can be considered if the current mode of the operation/activity doesn't have enough capacity. The alternative modes in the PDS may have priorities assigned to them, and in the strategy profile, the **Lowest Mode Priority** is assigned. The mode priorities are defined from A (highest priority) to O (lowest priority). If you want the system to consider alternative modes up to only a certain priority of modes, you define the lowest of the value in the **Lowest Mode Priority** strategy setting. For example, if you set D as the lowest priority, the system will check for modes with priority A, B, C, and D for selecting the alternative if it needs to make a mode shift during scheduling.

Tip

The mode priorities can't be maintained in SAP S/4HANA routing. In embedded PP-DS, you can use Transaction PDS_MAINT to set the mode priorities manually or the PDS business add-ins (BAdIs) to set the mode priority values during the PDS transfer.

The mode priorities A–I represent the priorities A–I, and the numbers 0–5 represent J–O. The mode priority M is the manual priority mode, and activities can only be manually scheduled on the mode with priority M.

Resource Network

When the alternative modes are in use in the PDSs, there may be requirements to model some dependencies, so that when a specific mode of an activity is selected, a linked mode from another activity can be selected automatically. This can be modeled via mode linkages in the PDS. But for linking modes from different orders, the resource network can be used.

Example

In material M1 for order activity A1, the mode M1 with resource R1 is selected. The PDS for M1 has an alternative resource of R2. M2 is a semifinished material of M1, and it has activity A2 with alternative modes with resources R3 and R4. The dependency is that when R2 is selected for M1, R4 should be selected for the order for M2, and when R1 is selected for M1, R3 should be selected for M2.

In this example, a resource network can be created and assigned to the material master of the M1 and M2 materials. In addition, within the resource network, you can create a resource link for the resources R1 and R3 and for the resources R2 and R4. There could be multiple such dependencies, and priorities can be assigned to these resource links within the resource network.

You can create the resource network from Transaction /SAPAPO/RESNET, as shown on the left side of Figure 6.16, by clicking on the **New** icon under the **Resource Links** tab. Enter a **Resource From** and **Resource To** value, and assign a **Priority** for the resource link. Save the resource network by clicking on the **Save** button. You can then assign the resource network to the material master, as shown on the right side of Figure 6.16.

Figure 6.16 Resource Network Creation and Assignment to the Material Master

Then, in the **Other Parameters** section of the strategy profile shown in Figure 6.17, you can set the **Lowest ResNet Link Priority** setting accordingly.

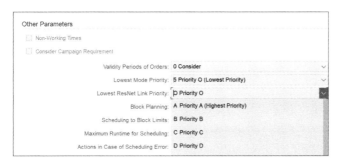

Figure 6.17 Other Parameters: Options for the Resource Link Priority

The priority is denoted by letters A to O. A is the highest priority, and O is the lowest. For example, if you set the lowest resource link mode as priority D, the system only considers modes with priorities A, B, C, and D.

Block Planning

The next two settings in the strategy profile are related to the block planning scenario. As we've discussed already, block planning refers to creating blocks on the resources for manufacturing orders with characteristics that match the block characteristics values. Blocks can be fixed so that no operation within the blocks can be moved during rescheduling. The **Block Planning** setting provides the option to consider the blocks during scheduling or to ignore the blocks during scheduling. If block planning is in use, it's always recommended to set **Take Into Account** for the block planning setting in the strategy profile. The block fixings are respected by default, and no operations within a fixed block can be rescheduled. This can be overridden with the **Consider Blocks and Ignore Block Fixings** option.

The operations scheduled within the blocks can be adjusted to align their operation and component dates/times with the block start and block end. This indicator is set at the block definition on the resource master data. This can be overridden by selecting **Do Not Take Into Account for Selected Operations** in the **Scheduling to Block Limits** setting in the strategy profile.

Maximum Runtime for Scheduling

Scheduling functions may be executed depending on the constraints modeled in the strategy and the consideration of dependent orders in the pegging network. In such cases, the performance of the scheduling will become a bottleneck, and this could add more workload to the application servers and the SAP liveCache scheduler. By default, the system will cancel the scheduling function after a certain number of steps are executed by the scheduler, which counts for approximately 10 minutes. After 10 minutes, the system will cancel the scheduling function if no value (value 0) is entered in the **Maximum Runtime for Scheduling** strategy setting. You can set the value for this timeout value for up to one day in seconds (86,400 seconds).

Actions in Case of Scheduling Error

When the system isn't able to schedule an operation, it returns an error message. The **Actions in Case of Scheduling Error** setting for the error handling in the strategy profile, as shown in Figure 6.18, decides how the system will react when the scheduling ends up in an error.

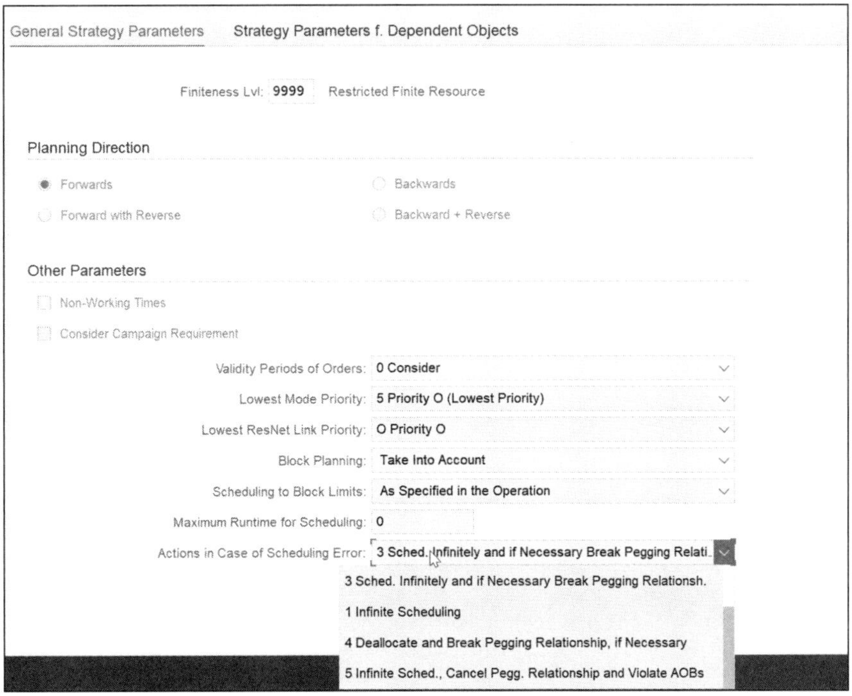

Figure 6.18 Options for System Reaction When Scheduling Returns an Error: Error-Tolerant Scheduling

The second attempt by the system to schedule the operations that can't be scheduled otherwise by respecting all the strategy profile constraints is called *error-tolerant scheduling*. The options for error tolerance are as follows:

- **1 Infinite Scheduling**
  In case of scheduling errors, switch the mode to infinite scheduling so that the capacity constraints are ignored, and the operations are scheduled infinitely.

- **2 Deallocate**
  When the scheduling ends up in an error, deallocate the operations that are being scheduled. You'll be able to see the deallocated objects in the DS planning board and can reschedule them manually if required.

- **3 Sched. Infinitely and If Necessary Break Pegging Relationships**
  This option has another constraint of the pegging relationships relaxed on top of

the infinite scheduling option. The operations will be scheduled infinitely, and pegging relationships will be ignored during the infinite scheduling if required.

- **4 Deallocate and Break Pegging Relationship, if Necessary/5 Infinite Sched., Cancel Pegg. Relationship and Violate AOBs/6 Deallocate, Cancel Pegging Relationship and Violate AOBs**

  These three options (**4**, **5**, and **6**) provide the maximum relaxed constraints wherein the system can break the pegging relationships and the order internal relationships between the activities of the operations.

Conversely, you can choose **Terminate Immediately** to provide no error tolerance. If any of the scheduling constraints are violated, and the scheduling must fail, the terminate option will write a termination message in the scheduling log and cancel the scheduling process.

> **Note**
>
> The PP-DS scheduling works via an all-or-nothing principle. If there are multiple operations sent for scheduling, and of one of them terminates, all the objects in the selection for scheduling are rolled back to their original dates.
>
> If there are multiple planning strategies in the strategy profile, and the first profile being used doesn't have an error-tolerant setting, the system will try to use the next strategy in the profile and will apply this profile to all the operations if it's able to schedule (or schedule with error tolerance) without any terminations.

6.2.3   Strategy Parameters for Dependent Objects

In the **Strategy Parameters f. Dependent Objects** tab of the strategy settings, the parameters are defined to control the behavior of the dependent objects of the operation being scheduled, as shown in Figure 6.19.

The dependent objects of the operation being scheduled are determined by the order-internal relationships and cross-order relationships. The order-internal relationships are defined by the relationship between the operation and activities of the same order, and the cross-order relationships are the time-dependent relationships between orders (especially in subcontracting where the manufacturing order in the subcontractor location has a time relationship with the subcontracting purchase order).

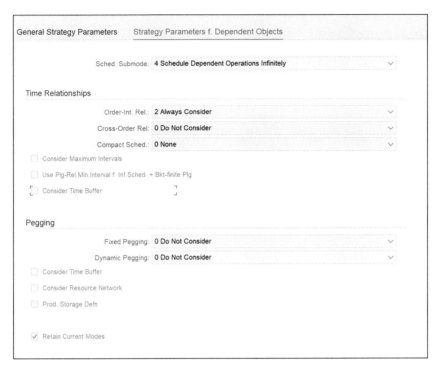

Figure 6.19 Strategy Parameters for Dependent Objects

Order-Internal Relationships

The operations and activities in an order are connected with each other via the order-internal relationship. These relationships are directed by the minimum and maximum intervals related to scheduling or planning and the relationship created by the time proximity of the activities (e.g., activities with end-start, start-start, etc., relationships). These interval relationships are created from the inter-operation times (wait, queue, and transportation times) maintained in the routing operation. Rules applied on these times are defined in the routing operation and translated into minimum and maximum intervals between the activities in the PDS master data.

There are two minimum intervals between the operations:

- **Process-related minimum interval**
  This is the exact interval between the operations that finite scheduling modes consider for placing the operations when the order-internal relationship is set as active in the strategy profile.

- **Planning-related minimum interval**
  This is an average interval rather than the exact interval, which can be used for planning purposes when using infinite scheduling.

For example, infinite scheduling for the dependent objects can be performed while considering the process-related minimum interval. This scheduling can be fine-tuned later when scheduling those dependent resources in finite scheduling mode. By doing this, the critical resources for the main operation are ensured in the first scheduling run (as the constraints are relaxed for the dependent objects), but they are kept closer to the main resources, and the overall lead time for the order is still closer to the one that will be achieved after fine-tuning the plan.

Following is the mapping of the different interoperation times maintained in the SAP S/4HANA routing and their representation in the PDS activity relationships:

- **Wait times**
  The wait time in the routing signifies the duration that can pass before the next operation starts. The wait times defined in the routing operation (minimum wait and maximum wait) are transferred as the process-related minimum and maximum intervals, respectively, to the PDS in PP-DS. The wait time belongs to a category called nonscheduled relationships. The intervals brought into the PP-DS PDS aren't scheduled using the resource calendar (resource availability).

- **Queue times**
  Queue time in the routing is the time the operation actively waits on the work center before the operation starts. The minimum queue time maintained in the routing operation is transferred as the minimum interval (process related) to the PDS. The minimum interval introduced by the queue time in the PDS activity belongs to the category of scheduled relationships (these intervals are calculated on the resource time stream per the resource availability).

- **Move times**
  The move time in the routing is the time required to move from one work center to another to perform the next operation. The behavior of the move time in the PP-DS PDS is the same as the queue time.

In the routing master data, navigate to the operation details by clicking on the operation number. As shown in Figure 6.20, in the **Interoperation times** area, you can see the wait times ❶, the queue times ❷, and the move times ❸.

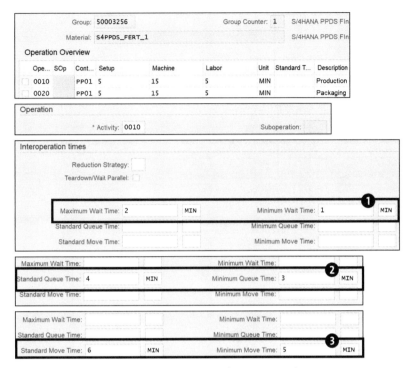

Figure 6.20 Interoperation Times in SAP S/4HANA Routing

The interoperation times (see Figure 6.21) from the routing are mapped to the PDS activities as follows:

- The minimum (1 min) and maximum wait times (2 mins) from the routing are mapped as **Min. Time** (60 seconds) and **Max. Time** (120 seconds), respectively, in the PDS activity ❶.

- The standard queue time (4 mins) and the minimum queue time (3 mins) from the routing are mapped as **Av. Time** (240 secs) and **Min. Time** (180 secs), respectively ❷.

- The standard move time (6 mins) and the minimum move (5 mins) time from the routing are mapped as the **Av. Time** (360 secs) and **Min. Time** (300 secs), respectively ❸.

Details	Preceding Act.	Succeeding Act.	Min. Time	Max. Time	Av. Time	Scheduling of Relationships	Relationship
⊞	001000000001P	001000000001T				No Scheduling Using Resource	End-Start Relationship
⊞	001000000001S	001000000001F				No Scheduling Using Resource	End-Start Relationship
⊞	001000000001T	002000000002S	60,000	120,000		No Scheduling Using Resource	End-Start Relationship
⊞	002000000002P	002000000002T				No Scheduling Using Resource	End-Start Relationship
⊞	002000000002S	002000000002F				No Scheduling Using Resource	End-Start Relationship

Preceding Act.	Succeeding Act.	Min. Time	Max. Time	Av. Time	Scheduling of Relationships	Relationship
001000000001P	001000000001T				No Scheduling Using Resource	End-Start Relationship
001000000001S	001000000001F				No Scheduling Using Resource	End-Start Relationship
001000000001T	002000000002S	180,000		240,000	Scheduling Using Resource of Predecessor Activity	End-Start Relationship
002000000002P	002000000002T				No Scheduling Using Resource	End-Start Relationship
002000000002S	002000000002F				No Scheduling Using Resource	End-Start Relationship

Preceding Act.	Succeeding Act.	Min. Time	Max. Time	Av. Time	Scheduling of Relationships	Relationship
001000000001P	001000000001T				No Scheduling Using Resource	End-Start Relationship
001000000001S	001000000001F				No Scheduling Using Resource	End-Start Relationship
001000000001T	002000000002S	300,000		360,000	Scheduling Using Resource of Predecessor Activity	End-Start Relationship
002000000002P	002000000002T				No Scheduling Using Resource	End-Start Relationship
002000000002S	002000000002F				No Scheduling Using Resource	End-Start Relationship

Figure 6.21 Routing Interoperations Mapped to PDS Minimum, Maximum, and Average Duration between Activities

When there is more than one interoperation time defined in the routing, the behavior of the mapping to the PDS will differ. These relationships and intervals are always between two consecutive operations of an order.

If wait time is defined, it will be considered for the minimum and maximum process-related interval, and any other interoperation times defined in the routing operation aren't transferred to the PDS.

The queue time and the move time, if maintained together, will be combined to calculate the minimum interval and the planning-related minimum interval (average time in PDS).

When operation overlap is defined in the routing operation, the produce activities will form a start-start relationship. In addition, if a send-ahead quantity is mentioned, then the production duration for the send-ahead quantity is calculated and incorporated into the intervals in the PDS.

As shown in Figure 6.22, when wait time is used, the queue and move times are ignored ❶. Conversely, when queue and move times are used, they are combined for the PDS interval calculation ❷.

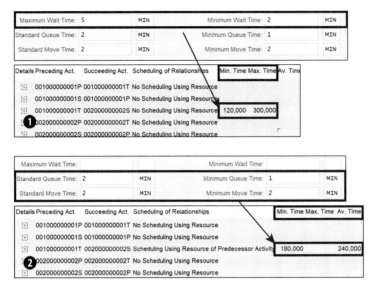

Figure 6.22 Combined Usage of Interoperation Times and the Representation of the Intervals in the PDS Activity

When the PDSs with minimum (**Min. Time**) and average (**Av. Time**) intervals are used in in-house orders such as planned orders, the **Min. Time** is copied to the order as the process-related minimum interval (**Proc. Min. Interval**), and the **Av. Time** is copied to the order as the planning-related minimum interval (**Plan. Min. Interval**), as shown in Figure 6.23.

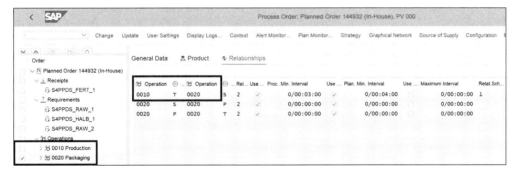

Figure 6.23 Representation of PDS Activity Interval Duration in a Planned Order

[»]

> **Note**
>
> The queue time can also be defined in the work center master data in the **Scheduling** tab. The queue times from the resource will be added to the queue times defined in the routing operation to calculate the total average and minimum interval durations in the PDS activity.

Scheduling Submode

Now, that we've covered the relationships between the operations of the order, let's review the settings available for handling the dependent objects in the strategy profile.

The scheduling mode that will be used for scheduling the dependent objects is called the scheduling submode (**Sched. Submode**, as shown previously in Figure 6.19). The following options are available:

- **Schedule Dependent Operations According to Scheduling Mode**
  The scheduling mode used for the operations are used for the dependent objects.

- **Schedule Dependent Operations Infinitely**
  Already scheduled dependent operations will be scheduled infinitely, and the deallocated dependent objects stay deallocated.

- **Find Slot in Sched. Mode 'Find Slot', Otherwise Infinitely**
  If the main scheduling mode for the higher-level operations is **Find Slot**, then the same is used for dependent objects; otherwise, the dependent operations will be infinitely scheduled (for already scheduled operations) and for the dependent objects that are deallocated, they stay deallocated.

- **Deallocate Dependent Operations**
  The dependent operations are set with deallocated status that needs to be scheduled separately.

- **Dispatch Dependent Operations Infinitely**
  All the dependent objects are infinitely scheduled irrespective of whether their previous status is scheduled or deallocated. They will be infinitely scheduled and will get the **Scheduled** status.

Time Relationships

The **Time Relationships** settings (refer back to Figure 6.19) define the consideration of the order-internal relationships and cross-order relationships when scheduling the dependent operations. The following settings must be made:

- **Order-Int Rel**

  This setting is for the order-internal relationships and is generally required be to set as **Always Consider**. Without this, the scheduling results can be incorrect. For example, if operations 10 and 20 are in an order with an end-start relationship, operation 20 can start before operation 10 if the order-internal relationship isn't considered. With the **Consider in Propagation Range** option, if the dependent operation belongs to resources that are within the propagation range definition, the relationship with the higher-level operation is evaluated and respected during scheduling for these dependent operations. **Do Not Consider** is the most relaxed constraint for the dependent operation, where the relationship and the minimum intervals between the operations aren't evaluated by the scheduling process.

- **Cross-Order Rel**

  This setting is for considering the relationship between different orders, such as time relationships or pegging relationships. Time relationships are only relevant for scenarios such as subcontracting, where the subcontractor manufacturing order is linked with the subcontracting purchase order and the in-house manufacturing order that triggered the subcontracting process. In general, apart from subcontracting, other manufacturing orders don't have a time relationship. The **Cross-Order Rel** setting is evaluated along with the **Dynamic Pegging** and **Fixed Pegging** settings under the **Pegging** section of the strategy settings.

- **Compact Sched.**

  Compact scheduling is the process of reducing the overall lead time for a manufacturing order by keeping the operations as close as possible by respecting the minimum intervals, if defined in the master data. The **For Deallocated Operations** option will only compactly schedule the dependent operation (closer to the higher-level operation) if the dependent operation is in **Deallocated** status. The **For Deallocated Operations and Selected Orders** option will attempt to compactly schedule the whole order whose operation is being scheduled. For the dependent operations from other orders, it will only try to perform compact scheduling if the operations of the affected dependent order are in **Deallocated** status.

- **Consider Maximum Intervals**

  This setting is only valid if the order-internal relationships are set to be considered. With the **Consider Maximum Intervals** setting, the maximum intervals defined in the PDS between the operations are taken into consideration while scheduling the dependent operations. The average interval from the PDS is used as the planning-related minimum interval, and by selecting the **Use PLG-Rel.Min.Interval f. Inf.Sched. + Bkt-finite Plg** checkbox, the planning interval can be set to be considered with the infinite scheduling submode setting for the dependent operations.

- **Consider Time Buffer**

  This setting is for considering the time buffer defined at the resource level between the operations within an order. If the time buffer is defined at the resource level of a succeeding operation, then the preceding operation should finish at least before this buffer duration. The buffer duration is defined in the work center master data in SAP S/4HANA under the **APO Resource** view.

In Figure 6.24, the minimum interval in the PDS activity is highlighted in the **Min. Time** column (top screen), and the **Time Buffer** is maintained in the resource master data **Time-Cont. Capacity** tab (bottom screen).

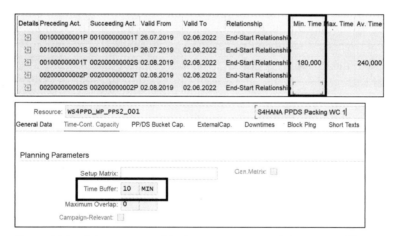

Figure 6.24 Minimum Interval in the PDS Activity and the Time Buffer in Resource Master Data

Figure 6.25 shows that the minimum interval (3 mins) and the buffer time (10 mins) is considered during scheduling, and the dependent operations are scheduled 13 mins apart. The two graphical objects shown in Figure 6.25 are subsequent operations of the same planned order. You can see the operation 10 end time ❶ (10.09.2019, 22:17:00) and the operation 20 start time ❷ (10.09.2019, 22:30:00).

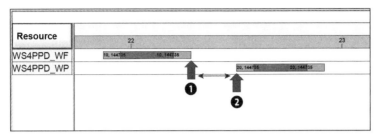

Figure 6.25 Interval between Operations due to Minimum Interval and Buffer Time

Now, let's see how this is reflected in the **Strategy Parameters f. Dependent Objects** section, as shown in Figure 6.26:

- **Order-Int. Rel.**
  The end-start relationship is respected, and the minimum interval is respected.

- **Cross-Order Rel**
  There is no maximum interval in PDS, so the maximum gap between the operations isn't a constraint.

- **Compact Sched.**
  The overall lead time is kept minimal by keeping the operations as close as possible.

- **Consider Time Buffer**
  The 10 minute buffer set in Figure 6.24 is added to the gap between the operations on top of the minimum interval.

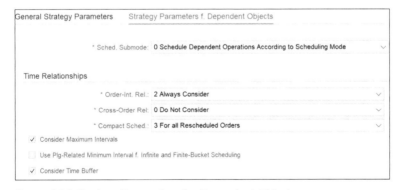

Figure 6.26 Strategy Parameters for Dependent Objects

Pegging

The next section in the strategy profile for the dependent objects is the pegging related settings. When the cross-order relationship is set to be considered, then the fixed pegging or dynamic pegging can also be considered if the corresponding check-boxes are set in the profile for the dependent objects. The options are as follows, as shown previously in Figure 6.19:

- **Do Not Consider**
  The pegging links can be broken, for example, an order for the dependent demand (D1) from a planned order (O1) can be scheduled after the planned order (O1) finishes.

- **Always Consider**
  Fixed and dynamic pegging relationships are respected by the system.

- **Consider within Propagation Range**
  When the dependent objects are for products and resources within the propagation range, then the pegging relationship is respected only for such dependent operations.

Buffer times are defined in the resource master. When **Consider Time Buffer** is activated in the strategy profile and there are orders linked by pegging relationships, if the succeeding order's (D1) resource (from the operation) has a buffer time defined, then the preceding order (O1) must at least finish before this duration.

Consider Resource Network needs to be selected if the resource links created by the resource networks need to be considered while scheduling the dependent operations. **Retain Current Modes** should be selected if you want the system to keep the same mode (resource) for the dependent operation. If this checkbox isn't set, the system may select any of the available alternative modes for the dependent operations to schedule them while respecting the constraints defined.

6.3   Leveraging Detailed Scheduling Heuristics

Similar to the planning and service heuristics, detailed scheduling heuristics are delivered in the standard embedded PP-DS system to facilitate the scheduling functions. The scheduling algorithms are delivered by the heuristics, but the DS strategy settings within these heuristics or defined at the applications are the driving factors in scheduling the objects following the heuristic algorithm's logic.

> **Note**
>
> The detailed scheduling heuristics settings have their own strategy parameters defined under the heuristics. When executing the heuristics, the parameters defined under the heuristics are considered for controlling the schedule.

In this section, we'll cover the details of some of the commonly used detailed scheduling heuristics.

6.3.1   Schedule Sequence

Schedule sequence is a basic detailed scheduling heuristic used to perform finite production scheduling for resources that are defined as finite resources. In the standard system, this heuristic is delivered with the name SAP001 and the algorithm /SAPAPO/ HEUR_PLAN_SEQUENCE.

This heuristic, as shown in Figure 6.27, can be used to performing a sequencing of the operation on resources following a defined sort order of the operation in the heuristics settings.

The strategy setting made under the heuristics settings will take precedence over the strategy profile set in the application. Certain settings in the strategy are hidden in the heuristics settings that the heuristic doesn't consider. The **Planning Direction** and **Finite Capacity** heuristics are defaulted and can't be changed. Only the scheduling modes of **Find Slot** and **Insert Operation** are supported by this heuristic.

This heuristic will deallocate all the operations per the selection and then sequence them based on the sort order. The operations are sorted with the operation start date ad start time in ascending order in the standard delivered heuristics.

The **Planning Direction** is set as **Forwards** by default, so the system looks for the earliest dates to start sequencing the operations and schedules them forward from their start date. The earliest date could be the current date or the current date adjusted (+/-) with the offset period defined in the heuristics settings. All the operations (within the planning period) on the resource (with resource selection) are selected and sequenced on the resource.

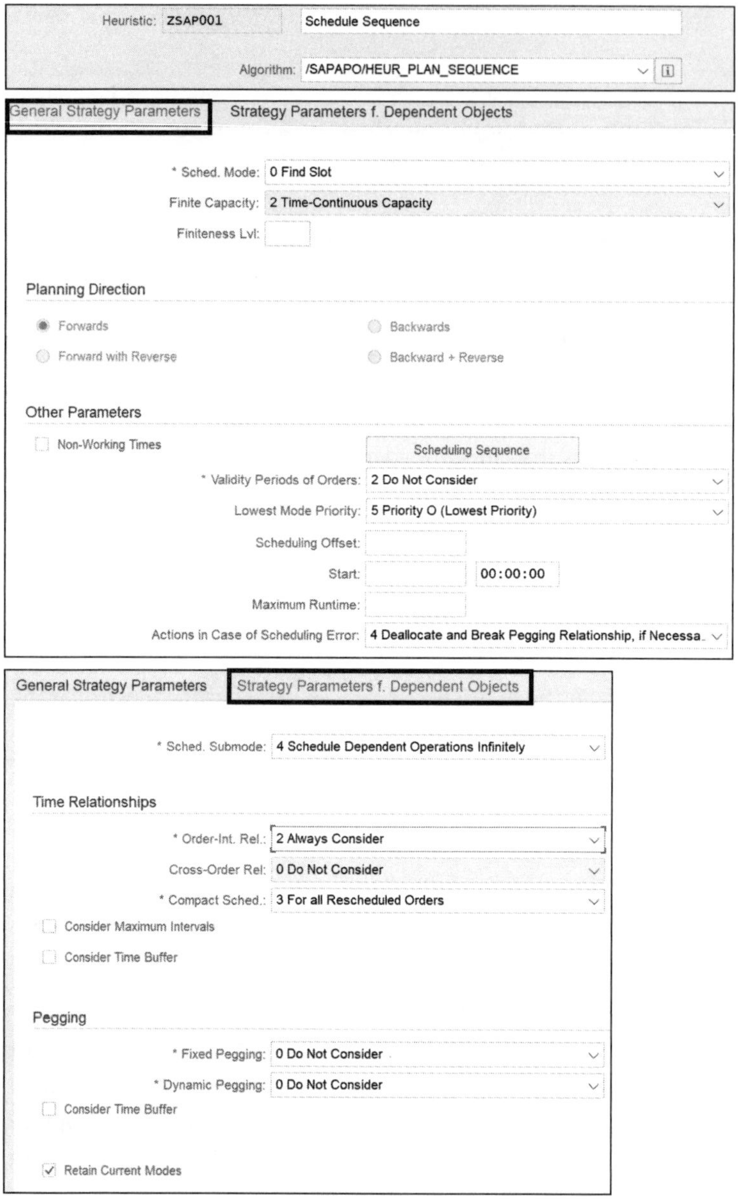

Heuristic:	ZSAP001	Schedule Sequence

Algorithm:	/SAPAPO/HEUR_PLAN_SEQUENCE

General Strategy Parameters   Strategy Parameters f. Dependent Objects

* Sched. Mode:	0 Find Slot
Finite Capacity:	2 Time-Continuous Capacity
Finiteness Lvl:	

Planning Direction

- ⦿ Forwards
- ◯ Forward with Reverse
- ◯ Backwards
- ◯ Backward + Reverse

Other Parameters

☐ Non-Working Times	Scheduling Sequence
* Validity Periods of Orders:	2 Do Not Consider
Lowest Mode Priority:	5 Priority O (Lowest Priority)
Scheduling Offset:	
Start:	00:00:00
Maximum Runtime:	
Actions in Case of Scheduling Error:	4 Deallocate and Break Pegging Relationship, if Necessa..

General Strategy Parameters   **Strategy Parameters f. Dependent Objects**

* Sched. Submode:	4 Schedule Dependent Operations Infinitely

Time Relationships

* Order-Int. Rel.:	2 Always Consider
Cross-Order Rel:	0 Do Not Consider
* Compact Sched.:	3 For all Rescheduled Orders

- ☐ Consider Maximum Intervals
- ☐ Consider Time Buffer

Pegging

* Fixed Pegging:	0 Do Not Consider
* Dynamic Pegging:	0 Do Not Consider

- ☐ Consider Time Buffer

- ☑ Retain Current Modes

Figure 6.27 Schedule Sequence Heuristic Settings

6.3.2   Remove Backlog

Another variation of the schedule sequence heuristic is the remove backlog heuristic, which is delivered as standard with the name SAP002 and with algorithm /SAPAPO/ HEUR_RESOLVE_BACKLOG.

The heuristic-specific strategy settings shown in Figure 6.28 are the same as for the schedule sequence heuristic except for the default scheduling mode (which is **1 Insert Operation**, in this heuristic).

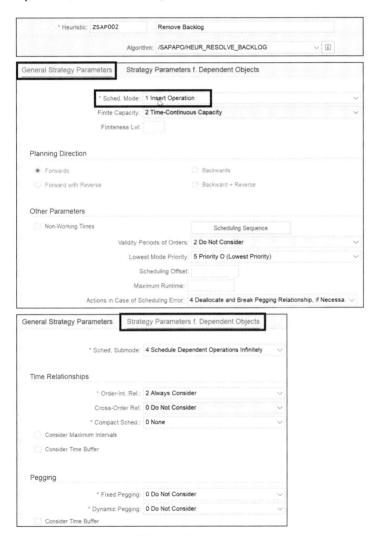

Figure 6.28 Remove Backlog Heuristic Settings

This algorithm looks for the operations that are currently in backlog (the start date of the operations are before the current date, or the current date is adjusted [+/-] with the offset period set in the heuristics). It then deallocates all the backlog operations and schedules them using the sort order for operations (ascending order of operation start date and time).

The scheduling mode used by this heuristic is **Insert Operation**, so the system will try to schedule the backlog operations as soon as possible closer to the current date by pushing the already existing operations in the future direction and placing the backlog operations there.

The remove backlog heuristic will only select the operations that are in backlog and then schedule them in the future, as shown in Figure 6.29. Here, you can see a working example of the remove backlog heuristic, both before execution ❶ and after execution ❷. The current date is represented by the dashed vertical line. Note the backlog operations ❸ and the operations scheduled in the future that are closer to the current date ❹. In addition, the operations that are moved by this heuristic to place the backlog operations are also finitely sequenced on the resource. Other operations on the resource that aren't impacted by the backlog operation rescheduling aren't changed, so resource overload situations could still occur in periods that are far from the current date.

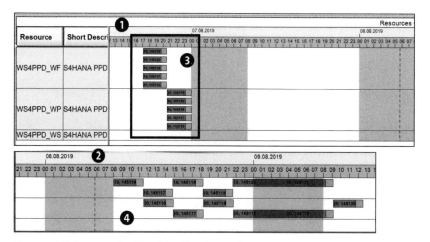

Figure 6.29 Remove Backlog Working Example

The schedule sequence and/or remove backlog heuristics can be used just after the production planning run or when planned orders are sent from an external planning system (e.g., SAP IBP) to sequence the order and resolve backlogs and capacity overload for the selected resources. The run can be fine-tuned by a PP-DS optimizer run or another detailed scheduling heuristic later.

6.3.3   Schedule Operations

The schedule operations (SAP005) heuristic can be used to schedule the deallocated operations (see Figure 6.30). Only the deallocated operations within the planning period defined are selected and then rescheduled according to the strategy profile assigned to the heuristic.

Figure 6.30 Schedule Operations Heuristic Settings

The schedule sequence (SAP001) heuristic doesn't schedule any deallocated operations on the selected resources; it only schedules operations with the **Scheduled** status. If there are business process scenarios where the production orders are created in SAP S/4HANA (e.g., via interfaces), then the production orders will be created with deallocated status in PP-DS by default. In such cases, the schedule operations (SAP005) can be executed as a first scheduling step to allocate resources to the orders and then do further finite scheduling as shown in our working example in Figure 6.31. Here, in the initial scheduling situation in the top portion, you can see the scheduled operations ❶ and the deallocated operations ❷. After the schedule operations heuristic is executed, shown in the middle portion, only the deallocated operations are scheduled ❸. Conversely, after the sequence operations heuristic is executed, shown in the bottom portion, all operations are scheduled ❹.

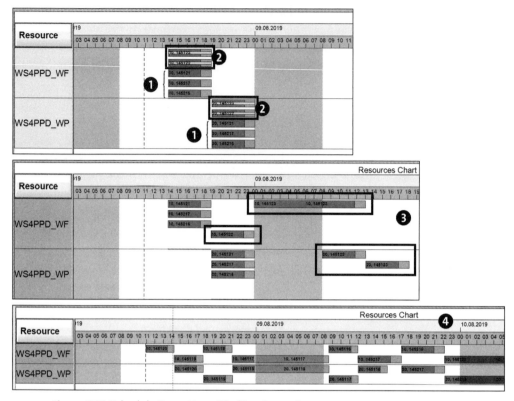

Figure 6.31 Schedule Operations Working Example

6.3.4   Minimize Runtime

Minimize runtime (SAP004) is another basic detailed scheduling heuristic that reduces the lead time of the orders. This heuristic can be executed for a resource. The operations on the resources will be fixed by the system during the execution of the heuristic. So that the operations that are selected for this heuristic stay where they are, only the dependent operations are moved to reduce the lead time.

If the operations on the selected resource are scheduled infinitely before the start of this heuristic, they remain in the same state after the execution too. Therefore, it's important that the schedule sequence heuristic or another finite scheduling heuristic is executed before the execution of the minimize runtime heuristic. From there, the system will move all other operations dependent on the fixed operation within the propagation range and will try to minimize any unnecessary gaps between these operations. After the best possible lead time reduction is achieved for all the orders, then the operations that were fixed initially are unfixed. All the operations must be in the planning period for this heuristic to schedule them closer to each other. If there are backlogs, those aren't rescheduled by this heuristic. The scheduling mode used by this heuristic is **Find Slot**.

Figure 6.32 shows the operations with gaps in the past ❶, followed by the current date ❷. Then, on the right side, you can see the operations with resource overload (on the resources selected for executing the heuristic) ❸. There are gaps between the operations in both order **145122** ❹ and order **145123** ❺.

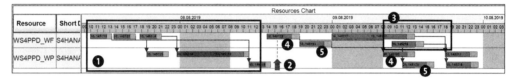

Figure 6.32 Minimize Runtime Heuristic: Initial Scheduling State Example

Figure 6.33 shows that after the heuristic is executed, the operations with gaps in the past remain as they are ❶. However, on the right side, you can see that the order lead time has been reduced by removing the gaps between operations of the same order **145122** ❷ and between the operations of order **145123** ❸ (the operations with resource overload remain the same, but the gaps are closed ❹).

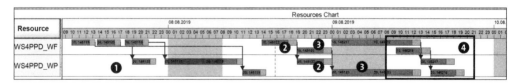

Figure 6.33 Minimize Runtime Heuristic: After Heuristics Execution Example

6.3.5   Multilevel Scheduling Framework Heuristics

The detailed scheduling heuristics we've seen so far can be used for scheduling backlogs, scheduling deallocated orders, and sequencing the operation on the finite resources.

After the production planning run and one or more heuristics from the schedule sequence, schedule operations, and remove backlog, the schedule can be fine-tuned further, for example, by the PP-DS optimizer (see Section 6.5). These steps can be executed every week as background jobs to ensure the demands are fulfilled on time with optimized resource utilization.

The multilevel scheduling framework offers heuristics that can navigate through the pegging structure and schedule the orders from the lowest level to the highest pegging level. The following heuristics are available in the multilevel scheduling framework:

- Stable forward scheduling
- Enhanced backward scheduling
- Change fixing/planning intervals

We'll discuss each in the following sections.

Stable Forward Scheduling

The stable forward scheduling (SAP_DS_01) heuristic is used to perform multilevel finite scheduling. Manufacturing schedule disruptions such as backlogs, capacity overloads, and violations of the minimum intervals for the orders can be corrected in several levels of production by this heuristic.

The heuristics parameters for the stable forward scheduling heuristic are shown in Figure 6.34.

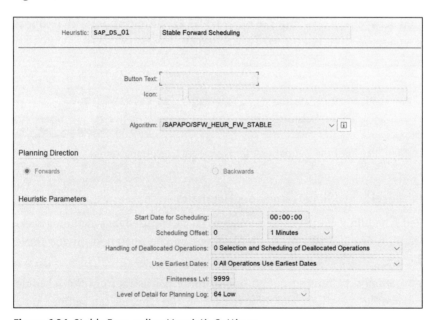

Figure 6.34 Stable Forwarding Heuristic Settings

The **Start Date for Scheduling** is the earliest date and time from which the system can start scheduling orders on the resource. This option, along with the **Scheduling Offset** option in the heuristics settings, has different behavior based on which dates and times are set in the heuristics settings.

If the start date time is entered for the **Start Date for Scheduling** field, and if a **Scheduling Offset** is entered, then the system ignores the scheduling offset. The start date for scheduling is set as the start date/time for scheduling.

Following is the behavior for other combinations of scheduling start date/time and offset time:

- **With only start time**
  Schedule start = Current date at the scheduling start time set.

- **With only start date**
  Schedule start = Start date at 00:00:00 hours.

- **With start time and offset**
  Offset is applied first to calculate the schedule start date, and the entered start time in the Customizing is set as the start time for the scheduled start.

If you select the value for the **Handling of Deallocated Operations** option as **No Selection** or **Scheduling of Deallocated Operations**, the deallocated operations aren't selected and therefore not scheduled. However, if operations on which these deallocated operations are dependent are rescheduled, then the deallocated operations will be updated with the date and time so that they stay closer to the operations being rescheduled.

The **Use Earliest Dates** setting has two options:

- **All Operations Use Earliest Dates**
  Irrespective of the start date/time of the operations, all operations are scheduled one after another on the resource starting the scheduling start date/time. There will be no gaps left on the resource after the heuristics execution with this setting. If your planning period has a longer horizon, this setting will reschedule all orders to start at the earliest possible date on the resource from which this heuristic is executed. You should use this setting only with a limited planning period (very short-term horizon).

- **Operations in the Past Use Earliest Dates**
  The operations that are backlogged (start date older than current date) will be rescheduled to start from the scheduling start date/time, and other operations on the resource won't be pulled toward the earliest date. The backlog operations

when rescheduled may cause resource overloads due to the already existing operations on the resource; in that case, the existing operations (which aren't backlogged) are also rescheduled.

Finiteness Lvl can be entered to decide which resources are finitely scheduled during this heuristic's execution.

This heuristic reads the whole pegging structure from the selected operation (and all operations of the same order) or the operations and all the orders of these operations when the heuristic is executed with resource selection. Then, forward scheduling is executed starting with the lower-level manufacturing orders (orders for the semifinished products first and then the higher-level orders). For the externally procured materials, this heuristic executes a postprocessing step to set the procurement order dates as close as possible to the manufacturing requirements. The propagation range must allow the heuristics to work across the pegging hierarchy. If orders/operations are outside the pegging hierarchy, an error message is raised during the execution of the heuristics.

The stable forward scheduling heuristic resolves the following issues in the schedule:

- **Backlogs**
  Resolve backlogs by scheduling forward from the current date.
- **Capacity overloads**
  Finite scheduling on all levels of the pegging structure ensures that capacity overloads are resolved.
- **Violation of minimum spacing between orders/operations**
  Violations of the minimum intervals between operations those are handled.

An example of the heuristic resolving the scheduling issues across the pegging structure is shown in Figure 6.35 and Figure 6.36.

In Figure 6.35, you can see the operations in the backlog (with a start date in the past) ❶. Then, the backward pegging begins at the current date, with lower-level orders scheduled after higher-level orders (e.g., the semifinished material order scheduled after the finished material order) ❷. Finally, you can see that more gaps exist between operations of the same order on the right side ❸.

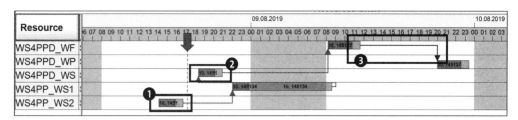

Figure 6.35 Stable Forward Scheduling Heuristic: Initial Scheduling State Example

Figure 6.36 shows the situation after the stable forward scheduling heuristic has been executed. On the left, you can see the heuristic has been executed by selecting the lowest level resource in the pegging structure. Then, the backlog has been resolved ❶, the order sequence has been corrected to resolve backward pegging of the orders ❷, and the gap between the operations of the same order is reduced ❸. However, the minimum interval between operations is respected.

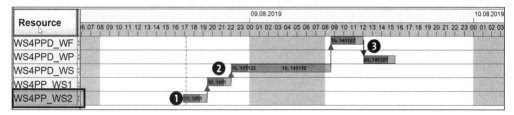

Figure 6.36 Stable Forward Scheduling Heuristic: After Heuristics Execution Example

Enhanced Backward Scheduling

The enhanced backward scheduling heuristic (SAP_DS_02) also finitely schedules the operations across the pegging structure. This heuristic is delivered with the standard algorithm /SAPAPO/SFW_HEUR_BW_EXT.

This heuristic schedules the operations in a backward direction. The current date's available capacity isn't considered as available by this heuristic, so during backward scheduling, the current date's operations may result in getting scheduled in the past. Therefore, it's important that after the enhanced backward scheduling heuristic, the stable forward heuristic is also executed.

The enhanced backward scheduling heuristic offers additional settings compared to the stable forward heuristics. The available heuristics settings are shown in Figure 6.37. If there is no available capacity on the resource, which is the current mode of the operation (activity) chosen in the **Mode Selection** setting, the alternative modes (if available for the operation) can be evaluated by the heuristic, and the mode with highest priority and available capacity for the desired date/time is selected.

The setup time (changeover) required by the operations on the resources can be reduced by choosing **Take Set-Up Sequences into Account** in the **Setup Sequence** field in the heuristic.

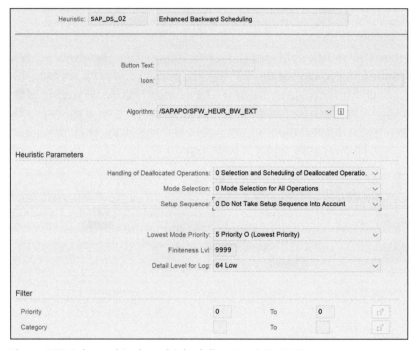

Figure 6.37 Enhanced Backward Scheduling Heuristic Settings

Additional filters are available to filter the order ATP categories and order priorities, so that only the important orders can be scheduled using this heuristic.

During manufacturing, there could be unplanned changes to the schedule due to scraps, machine breakdowns, or the last-minute need for a high-priority order to be executed. During such situations, a robust scheduling tool is required that can aid the production scheduler with rescheduling operations on resources that went to backlog, caused resource overloads, or violated the minimum interval requirements between the operations. In such cases, the enhanced backward scheduling and stable forward scheduling heuristics can be used to reschedule the orders (resource) impacted and propagate the scheduling change across the pegging network up to the finished material level. By doing so, this heuristic may violate delivery dates and PIR dates.

Create Planning/Fixing Intervals

The create planning/fixing intervals heuristics (SAP_DS_03) is provided to set, change, and delete the planning and fixing intervals on resources. This heuristic uses the standard algorithm /SAPAPO/HEUR_REL_FIXINT_MAINT. This heuristic takes the current date as a base and sets the planning and fixing intervals based on the heuristics settings.

Let's walk through the settings for both fixing and planning intervals, as follows:

- **Fixing interval**

  A fixing interval is created to lock the resource capacity for the defined duration and fix all the orders and operations that are scheduled within the fixing interval. This is to protect the capacity for the scheduled operations in the very short-term horizon and not allow any other operations to get scheduled in the fixing interval, which may disturb the existing schedule.

  Sequence-dependent setup activities can also be deactivated within the fixing interval. When there are setup activities that have setup groups, and the sequence of the operations are changed, the setup time required also changes based on the setup times defined for changeovers. Such setup activities are called sequence-dependent setup activities. Within the very short-term horizon, if operations are moved to handle shop floor uncertainties, redetermination of the setup times may lead to a major change in the schedule. When fixing intervals are created using the create planning/fixing intervals heuristic, it's possible to deactivate the sequence-dependent setup activities, meaning that when sequence-dependent activities are moved, the setup time isn't redetermined.

- **Planning interval**

  Planning interval is the duration within which the system can carry out scheduling. Outside the planning interval, the system considers the resource to be fixed, so it won't select or perform any scheduling actions for the objects outside the planning interval.

The heuristics settings provide the **Relative Interval Dates/Times** option for the heuristics execution (see Figure 6.38). This relative duration is used to calculate the planning or fixing interval from the current date.

The **Interval Type** options determine if the heuristics execution should create a planning or fixing interval. The **Function** options determine whether to replace an existing interval (**Replace Intervals**), add a new interval to an existing interval, create a new interval (**Add Interval**), or delete the intervals (**Delete All Intervals**). When a fixing interval is used, the options for deactivating the sequence-dependent setup activity are provided, and the operation can be fixed within the fixing interval. When the setup activities are deactivated, the start date of the fixing interval will be deactivated, and it will fix the resource from the past to the fixing interval end date.

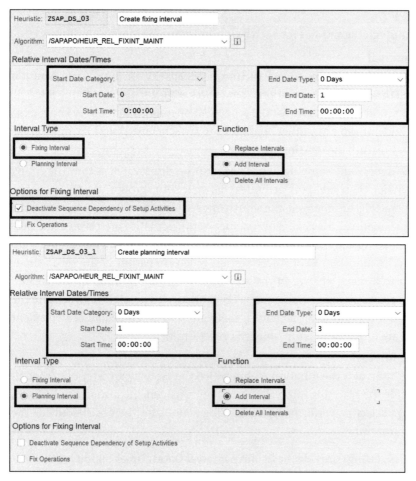

Figure 6.38 Create Planning/Fixing Intervals Heuristic Settings

Figure 6.39 shows a working example of the fixed and planned intervals when the heuristics are executed per the settings maintained in Figure 6.38. Note the current date ❶, and the resource is fixed from the past to one day in the future from the current date (until 00:00:00 time) ❷ in the fixing interval execution on the top portion. For the planning interval execution in the bottom portion, you can see that the fixing interval is applied from the past to one day in the future (from current date ❶) ❸, and fixing interval is also applied after three days ❹ from the end of the fixing interval at the start ❸. This results in the three days of planning interval ❹.

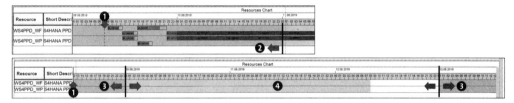

Figure 6.39 Working Model of the Create Fixing and Planning Interval Heuristic

6.3.6   Multiresource Scheduling Heuristic

The multiresource scheduling heuristic can be used in scenarios where alternative modes (resources) are available for manufacturing materials. Many of the detailed scheduling heuristics and scheduling functions offer switching modes (resources) if there are alternative modes available in the PDS and the primary mode doesn't have enough capacity.

Apart from switching alternative modes of the same PDS activity, with the multiresource scheduling heuristic, it's also possible to switch to resources that are alternative PDSs.

[Ex]

Example

The PDS for material A has an operation (resource R1) with one alternative mode (resource R2). In addition, there are two more PDSs available for the same material A, and the other two PDSs use two different resources (PDS2/resource R3, PDS3/resource R4) other than the original PDS. In case of a resource overload, the multiresource scheduling heuristic can schedule the operations on R2, R3, or R4, based on the mode priorities (alternative modes and alternative sources of supply are considered).

The multiresource scheduling heuristic is delivered with name SAP_MULT_SCH and algorithm /SAPAPO/HEU_MULTIRES_SCHED. This can be copied to another custom heuristic to adjust per the requirements. The settings are shown in Figure 6.40.

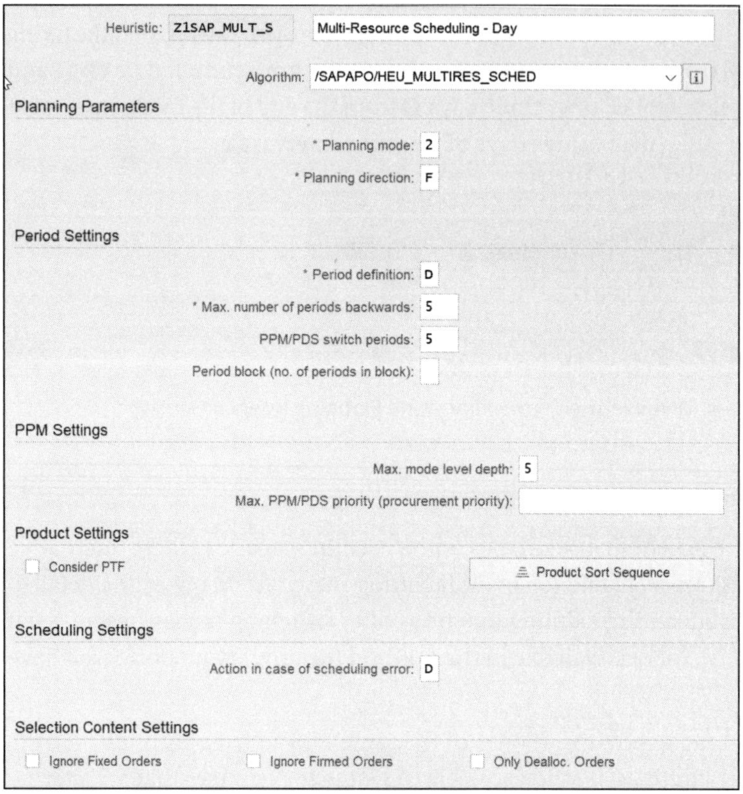

Figure 6.40 Multiresource Scheduling Heuristic Settings

The **Planning mode** can be bucket capacity-oriented (**1**) or time-continuous finite capacity-based scheduling (**2**). With the **Planning direction** of forward (**F**), the order start dates are considered for scheduling the order; with backward (**B**), the order end date is set, and then the order is backward scheduled.

The **Period definition** is a critical field for this heuristic with options of days (**D**) or weeks (**W**). The **Max. number of periods backwards** defines the number of days/weeks in the backward direction during which the system should perform finite scheduling. The **PPM/PDS switch periods** option refers to the number of days/weeks in which the system can schedule the impacted orders (due to resource overload) in the past before it tries to switch the PDS to schedule the orders on alternative resources. If all the modes of the current PDS of the order and the modes from the alternative PDS have the same priority, the alternative mode of the current PDS will be given the first priority before switching to alternative PDSs.

For longer horizons in which this heuristic is executed, the system might only schedule the high priority orders first without scheduling any other orders. To avoid this, the period block can be used. The planning period will be divided into a number of period blocks, and orders within the blocks are scheduled independently.

A working example of the multiresource scheduling heuristic is shown in Figure 6.41. In this example, the heuristic was executed from the DS planning board, but it can also be executed from the production planning run as a step. The heuristic settings from Figure 6.40 are used for executing this example.

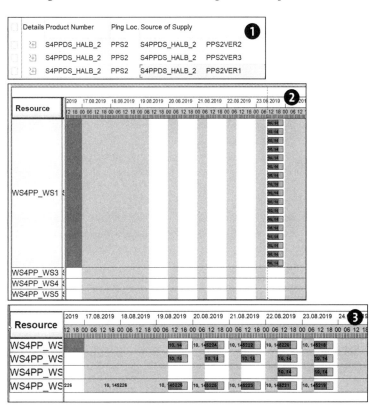

Figure 6.41 Multiresource Scheduling Heuristic Example

You can see in Figure 6.41 that there are multiple PDSs for the same material ❶, which have the following modes/resource:

- **PDS 1, mode 1**
  WS4PP_WS3_PPS2_001

- **PDS 2, mode 1**
  WS4PP_WS4_PPS2_001

- **PDS 3, mode 1**
  WS4PP_WS1_PPS2_001 (all the orders in the example uses this PDS/mode ❷)

- **PDS 3, mode 2**
  WS4PP_WS5_PPS2_001

Then, the current scheduling situation shows an overload on the WS1 resource ❷. After the heuristic is executed, you can see the overload is resolved ❸. The system scheduled the orders from the overload date (23.09.2019) until 19.08.2019 (five days from 23.09.2019) as the scheduling direction in this example is backward scheduling. After it finitely scheduled the orders on the original mode where the orders were placed before for the five days periods, then it scheduled the orders by switching the mode belonging to other PDSs of the same product and alternative modes of the PDSs.

> **Note**
>
> To get proper results from this heuristic, when using the period definition of **D**, the order length should be less than one day, and with weekly period definition, the order length should be less than a week. This heuristic is designed for process industries, but it can be also used for other scenarios, keeping this restriction in mind.

6.4   Triggering PP-DS Scheduling

The PP-DS detailed scheduling heuristics and functions can be executed as part of the production planning job and interactively from the DS planning board, the resource planning table, and the product planning table.

Apart from executing the heuristics in the background and in online mode to schedule the operations on the resources, another important aspect of detailed scheduling is to monitor the scheduling results from the scheduling tools and to adjust them to resolve any issues found even after the scheduling runs.

During the heuristics execution, depending on the strategy settings, there could be operations scheduled infinitely for dependent operation due to the error tolerance set in the strategy profile of the heuristics, or operations may be deallocated as part of the heuristics. Such exceptions can be displayed from the DS planning board, and the production scheduler needs to schedule those operations.

With embedded PP-DS, new SAP Fiori apps are available to monitor the resource utilization and change the shift schedule from the app itself to manage the resource capacity. In addition, it's possible to dispatch and deallocate operations on the resources and simulate the results before the changes are saved in the system. The DS planning board is also delivered as an SAP Fiori app in embedded PP-DS. This SAP Fiori planning board has limited functionality compared to the SAP GUI-based planning board. However, the app contains the functionalities required to execute and monitor basic scheduling.

We'll discuss each of these execution options and apps in the following sections.

6.4.1   Detailed Scheduling Planning Board

The DS planning board is one of the important tools production schedulers use to visualize the schedule and adjust it by dragging and dropping operations onto the required resources on the time line. Objects such as operations and orders are color-coded to make it easy for schedulers to identify different objects based on their status (e.g., scheduled operations vs. deallocated operations are displayed with different colors and patterns). Graphical representation of the scheduling situation and interactively simulating the resolution for the scheduling problems identified are the main objectives when using the DS planning board.

Multiple charts can be loaded onto the DS planning board to display the current scheduling satiation of the resources, the orders against the materials loaded on the DS planning board, stocks over time, and so on. These charts can be switched on and off per the requirements from the DS planning board profiles and can be interactively changed in the DS planning board transaction itself.

The settings and the constraints maintained in the strategy profile are the core driving the behavior of the interactive scheduling changes made on the DS planning board.

You can save the adjusted schedule into a simulation version, which later can be merged back into the active version by loading the simulation version onto the DS planning board and adopting it to the active version.

309

Planning Board Selection Screen

The DS planning board can be launched via Transaction /SAPAPO/CSPS0 or from the **SAP Easy Access** menu: **Logistics • Advanced Planning • Production Planning • Interactive Production Planning • Detailed Scheduling • Detailed Scheduling Planning Board – Variable View**. The selection screen of the DS planning board is displayed in Figure 6.42.

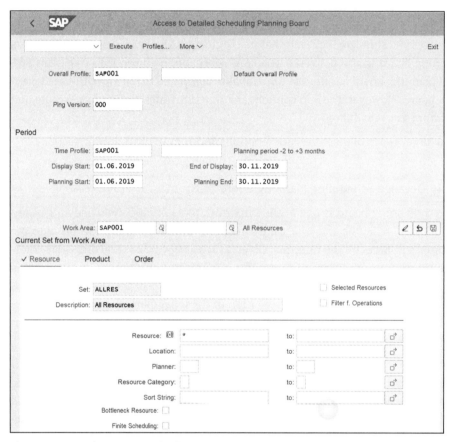

Figure 6.42 DS Planning Board Selection Screen

The various profiles used in the DS planning board, such as the DS strategy profile, heuristics profile, planning board profile, work area, and propagation range, are assigned to the overall profile. (We've covered the overall profile customization in Chapter 3, Section 3.6.1.) By assigning the **Overall Profile** to the DS planning board selection screen, all other relevant profiles are loaded per the customization.

The DS planning board can be used for active planning version 000 or for inactive planning versions. To use the DS planning board to work with the active planning version data, enter "000" in the **Plng Version** field.

The **Time Profile** assigned to the overall profile prefills the planning and display periods in the selection screen, which can be manually overwritten. The display period is the period for the duration used by the objects loaded onto the DS planning board. But making changes to the schedule either by manually rescheduling or using a function or heuristics within the DS planning board can only be performed for the **Planning Period** defined in the selection screen.

Work Area is like a selection variant where the selection criteria for the resources, products, and orders are already entered and saved. Therefore, you, as a production scheduler, can create your own work area with the resources and products you're responsible for scheduling. The selection criteria filled in by the work area also can be overwritten manually.

> **Tip**
>
> After changing the selection criteria for the resources, products, and orders, you can save it to a new work area by clicking the **Save** button to the right of the **Work Area** field on the selection screen.

In the **Resource** tab, set the **Selected Resources** checkbox to load only the resources you've entered explicitly in the selection criteria, manually or from the **Work Area** definition. If you don't set this indicator, the system will load additional resources derived as follows:

- The selected resources and corresponding operations on the resource are loaded.
- From the operations, the orders are loaded, and from the order, the system determines the other resources used by the order (operations).
- From the operations and orders, the system loads the products in the product chart, and the resources corresponding to other orders (operations) of the loaded products are also displayed in the resource chart.

You should select the **Selected Resources** checkbox to ensure that the volume of data loaded onto the DS planning board is predictable and doesn't lead to poor performance of loading and subsequent processing of the DS planning board.

The same is applicable for the selection of materials entered in the **Product** tab of the selection screen. Select the **Selected Products** checkbox to restrict the selection of products by the explicitly entered materials in the selection.

If the order/operation network display (pegging and order-internal relationship links) is activated in the DS planning board profile by not setting the checkbox in the **No Display** column for the **Network View: Operations** and **Network View: Orders** (**ChartNumbr 7** and **8**), as shown in Figure 6.43, the selected resource or selected product setting is ignored by the system, and the order network and corresponding resources and materials are loaded.

The DS planning board performance is impacted by the volume of data loaded and the number of charts loaded during start-up. To improve performance, use time segments in the time profile definition so that the data is loaded in segments as you work in the DS planning board and navigate through the resource time stream (scroll through the time scale). (Refer to Chapter 3, Section 3.6.2, for more information on time segments.) The reading of the SAP liveCache data for the display of the DS planning board can be improved by selecting the **Perf.Func.** checkbox. To select this checkbox, click on the **Profiles** option in the selection screen menu bar (refer to the top of Figure 6.42), and in the **Plng Board Profile** tab of the popup screen, select the **Perf.Func.** checkbox on the bottom-left part of the screen (see Figure 6.43).

You can hide the charts in the DS planning board by setting the **No Display** checkbox on the DS planning board profile, as shown in Figure 6.43.

After the right selection settings are made, click on the **Execute** button to load the planning board.

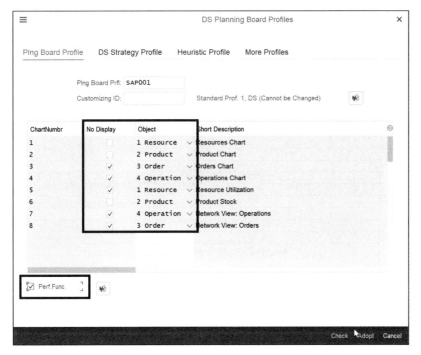

Figure 6.43 DS Planning Board Selection of Charts to Be Displayed, and Setting the Performance Function

Planning Board Navigation

The DS planning board, as shown in Figure 6.44, opens with the shuffler on the left side of the screen, which has the list of resources under the **Resource Pool** and a list of products under the **Product Pool**. You can display or hide resources and products from the corresponding charts by selecting the resource and clicking on the show or hide buttons in the shuffler ❶. The shuffler can be hidden by clicking on the **Display/Hide Shuffler** button on the menu bar ❷.

From the menu bar, you can navigate to the settings and perform actions line reschedule or deallocate selected operations. Manually performed scheduling changes within the DS planning board can be undone by using the **Undo Last Scheduling Function** button in the menu bar. You can navigate to the menu bar path **More** settings to manage all the settings for the display and function of the DS planning board, as shown in Figure 6.44.

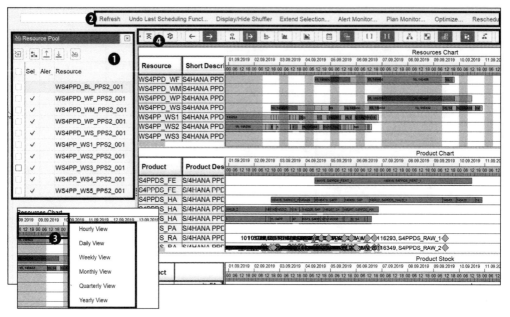

Figure 6.44 DS Planning Board: Navigation

Depending of the average duration of the orders, you can set the granularity for the timelines on the chart. If your orders are smaller (less than a day), you may set the time scale of days; for working with resources with bigger orders, the time scale can be set to weekly or monthly display. This can be changed from the menu bar settings, as well as by right-clicking (context menu) on the time bar on the individual charts, as shown in Figure 6.44 ❸. The toolbar ❹ can be customized, which is covered in Chapter 3, Section 3.6.4.

Further additional settings for the DS planning board display and functions can be accessed by clicking on the **More** button in the menu bar and clicking on the **Settings** option.

Context Menu

In the DS planning board, many of the available functions for the objects (resources, products, and operations/orders) are provided in the context menu (right-click on the objects to access these menus).

You can click on the context menu of **Resource** to expand the display, as shown in Figure 6.45, if there is more than one order scheduled at the same time on the resource via the **Expand Multiple Loading** option. You can also **Define Downtimes** on the resources and create/change/delete fixing intervals with the **Define Fixing Intervals** option.

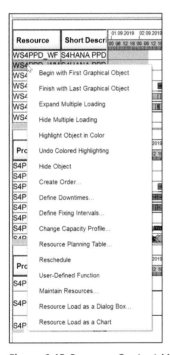

Figure 6.45 Resource Context Menu

On the product chart, the context menu provides options to navigate to production planning transactions such as the product or pegging overview of the product. You can load additional charts for displaying the product stock, and so on from the context menu.

The context menu of the orders and operation objects provides most of the possible actions for an order/operation.

Planning Board Features

The color and shape of the objects displayed in the DS planning board are configurable as covered in Chapter 3, Chapter 3.6.4. If you want to know what the object symbols represent, you can choose **More • Extras • Legend**. The legend lists the charts and individual graphical objects, including the object and status they represent.

To manually move orders in the product chart or the operations in the resource chart, you can click the operation/order, drag it to the desired position on the graphical representation of the resource capacity, and drop it in position. If the DS strategy allows the operation/order to be placed in the desired position, it will be placed there and scheduled according to the strategy profile (scheduling mode, direction, treatment of dependent operations, etc.).

To move multiple operations, as shown on the left side in Figure 6.46, you can press the ⌷Ctrl⌷ key, select all the required operations, and drag them while the ⌷Ctrl⌷ key is still pressed. Then release the dragged objects in the required position on the DS planning board. The current time stamp will be displayed on the bottom of the screen. In addition, you can drag a box around the objects by clicking to select multiple objects, as shown in the left side of Figure 6.46.

When there are alternative modes present for the activities (alternative modes from the same PDS), while selecting and dragging the operations manually, the system will highlight the resource rows belonging to alternative modes in green, as shown on the right side of Figure 6.46. This way, if there are capacity constraints in the primary mode, you can place the operation on one of the highlighted alternative modes. If there are alternative resources available from alternative PDSs, those aren't highlighted.

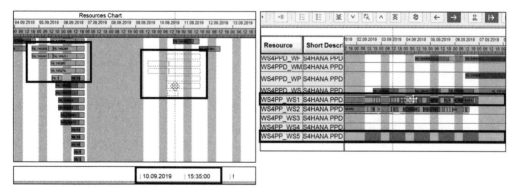

Figure 6.46 Moving Operations and Alternative Modes

The pegging relationships between orders and inter-order relationships can be displayed by choosing **More · Extras · Activity/Pegging Relationships · Show**. For individual objects, this can be done from the context menu of the object. In Figure 6.47, you can see the fixed pegging lines ❶, the dynamic pegging lines ❷, and the operation relationships lines ❸. By double-clicking on the pegging links, you can navigate to the pegging overview screen of the product view, where you can change the pegging relationships if necessary.

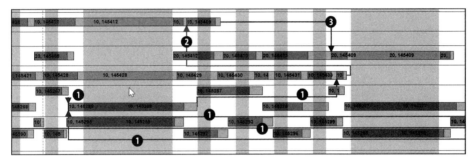

Figure 6.47 Display of Pegging and Operations Relationships

The alert monitor can be invoked by clicking on the **Alert Monitor** button in the menu bar or displaying the alerts by choosing **More · Extras · Alerts · Display**. This will highlight the objects in the DS planning board by making the object blink. In the same menu path, the **Hide** option can be used to stop the display of alerts in the chart objects. However, such graphics-intensive functions are performance intensive, and they can be switched on and off only on a need basis and not set as default for regular usage of the DS planning board.

Tip

To scroll on the time lines within the charts, you can use the `arrow` keys. If, after you've selected objects and started scrolling, you want to cancel the action and place the objects back in the original position, release the dragged objects on the time axis on top of the chart. This will cancel the drag action.

You can use the **Find** button on the menu bar to search for objects with order number, product, and so on. If you enter an order number and search, the system will highlight all the operations of the order present in the resource chart and the order in the product chart.

Execution of Functions

You can select one or multiple operations, orders, or resources to execute functions such as rescheduling (according to the set strategy) or deallocating the objects. To execute a heuristic on the selected objects, select the objects (e.g., relevant resources), and choose **More · Functions · Heuristics**, as shown in Figure 6.48. The heuristic you want to execute must be part of the heuristics profile you've assigned to the overall profile.

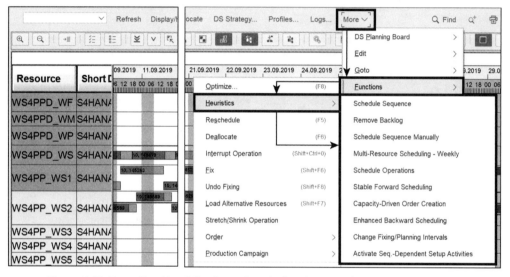

Figure 6.48 Executing Heuristics from the DS Planning Board

Unlike the interactive execution of production planning heuristics, most of the detailed scheduling heuristics don't have a dialog popup to change any heuristics settings already saved in the heuristics. Only with the schedule sequence manually heuristic (SAPOO3) is a new screen launched to list all the operations from the selected resources for this heuristic, as shown in Figure 6.49. Here, you can manually move the operations to the clipboard and sequence them manually (drag and drop between the **Clipboard** side and **Sequence to be planned** side). After you set the sequence for the operations, click on the **Schedule** button. The operations will be scheduled based on the strategy profile set in the heuristic.

Resource	Order	Priority	PeggedRq	PegReqOrNo	Reqmts Date	Reqmt Time	Loc	Product Number	Resour	Order	Priority	Pegged Rqmts	PegReqOrderNo.
WS4PPD_WP_PPS2_001	0000145409	0			10.09.2019	12:00:00	PPS2	S4PPDS_FERT_1	WS4	0000145414	0		
WS4PPD_WS_PPS2_001	0000145417	0	PPS2	0000145415	13.08.2019	22:05:01	PPS2	S4PPDS_HALB_1	WS4PP	0000145415	0		
WS4PP_WS1_PPS2_001	0000145255	0	PPS2	0000145418	09.09.2019	11:05:59	PPS2	S4PPDS_HALB_2	WS4PP	0000145414	0		
WS4PPD_WP_PPS2_001	0000145407	0			10.09.2019	12:00:00	PPS2	S4PPDS_FERT_1	WS4PP	0000145406	0		
WS4PP_WS1_PPS2_001	0000145256	0	PPS2	0000145419	10.09.2019	17:41:00	PPS2	S4PPDS_HALB_2	WS4PP	0000145415	0		
WS4PP_WS1_PPS2_001	0000145258	0	PPS2	0000145427	11.09.2019	21:46:01	PPS2	S4PPDS_HALB_2	WS4PP	0000145406	0		
WS4PP_WS1_PPS2_001	0000145263	0	PPS2	0000145428	19.09.2019	22:36:07	PPS2	S4PPDS_HALB_2	WS4PP	0000145411	0		
WS4PP_WS1_PPS2_001	0000145261	0	PPS2	0000145424	16.09.2019	08:56:04	PPS2	S4PPDS_HALB_2	WS4PP	0000145410	0		
WS4PPD_WS_PPS2_001	0000145427	0	PPS2	0000145414	12.08.2019	08:00:00	PPS2	S4PPDS_HALB_1	WS4PP	0000145252	0 PPS2		0000145416
WS4PP_WS1_PPS2_001	0000145259	0	PPS2	0000145421	18.09.2019	23:31:06	PPS2	S4PPDS_HALB_2	WS4PP	0000145412	0		
WS4PPD_WS_PPS2_001	0000145422	0	PPS2	0000145415	13.08.2019	22:05:01	PPS2	S4PPDS_HALB_1	WS4PP	0000145412	0		
WS4PPD_WS_PPS2_001	0000145424	0	PPS2	0000145415	13.08.2019	22:05:01	PPS2	S4PPDS_HALB_1	WS4PP	0000145416	0 PPS2		0000145415
WS4PP_WS1_PPS2_001	0000145264	0	PPS2	0000145425	17.09.2019	15:36:05	PPS2	S4PPDS_HALB_2	WS4PP	0000145426	0 PPS2		0000145415
WS4PPD_WS_PPS2_001	0000145420	0	PPS2	0000145415	13.08.2019	22:05:01	PPS2	S4PPDS_HALB_1	WS4PP	0000145418	0 PPS2		0000145415

Figure 6.49 Schedule Sequence Manually Heuristic

To check the logs of the actions performed in the DS planning board, you can click on the **Logs** button in the menu bar. This will display all the planning and scheduling logs generated from manual actions as well as the heuristics executions.

Simulation Session

All the schedule changes and the heuristics you executed in the DS planning board are always performed in a simulation session (sim session) by the system, until you adopt the changes to the active version while saving. When you navigate back from the DS planning board screen, the system prompts for you to **Adopt** the current scheduling data from the DS planning board into the active planning version or to **Save** the data to a simulation version, which can be worked on later before merging back to the active version, as shown in Figure 6.50.

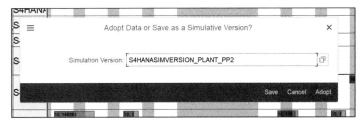

Figure 6.50 DS Planning Board: Option to Save the Data in a Simulation Version

[»]

> **Note**
>
> The simulation version saved from the DS planning board scheduling data shouldn't be confused with the inactive planning versions, which can be created by copying the active planning version 000. These are two different objects. The simulation version from the DS planning board only has the data loaded onto the planning board. Inactive planning versions (copy of 000) are created and maintained from the version copy report and Transaction /SAPAPO/MVM (Model Version Management).

When merging the simulation version data or the data from the DS planning board session (sim session) back with the active version, the merge will take place depending on the status of the objects. For example, if you've rescheduled an operation of a production order in the DS planning board, and the order has been confirmed in SAP S/4HANA in the meantime, then while merging the sim session (rescheduled operation) to the active version (operation confirmed), the status in the active version takes higher priority, and the rescheduling change from the DS planning board will be ignored during the merge. While working in the DS planning board, you can perform a refresh to load the current active version data onto the planning board; this overwrites any changes you've made so far in the DS planning board.

The simulation versions can be accessed from Transaction /SAPAPO/CDPSSO, as shown in Figure 6.51. The saved simulation sessions can be loaded onto the DS planning board (graphical processing ❶) or to the resource planning table (tabular processing ❷). In addition, from this transaction, the simulation version can be adopted to the active version ❸.

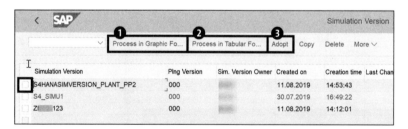

Figure 6.51 Accessing Simulation Versions

6.4.2   Production Scheduling Board

In embedded PP-DS, the Production Scheduling Board is delivered as a standard SAP Fiori app. This app can be used to perform order-scheduling functions such as schedule, deallocate, fix, interrupt, and so on. In addition, the heuristics assigned to the heuristics profile in the app customization can be executed from the app.

Activation of advanced planning (PP-DS) is mandatory for using the Production Scheduling Board app, and only the resources activated for advanced planning can be scheduled via the app.

This SAP Fiori app is delivered with the authorization business role SAP_BR_PRODN_ PLNR. After your user is assigned with a role, the Production Scheduling Board app appears under the **Advanced Planning** tab in the SAP Fiori launchpad, as shown in Figure 6.52.

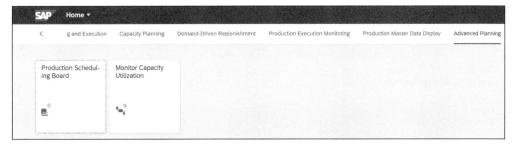

Figure 6.52 Production Scheduling Board App in the SAP Fiori Launchpad

The app works based on the area of responsibility (AOR), which is the resource planner and the plant. The settings and functions are defined in the application profile in Customizing.

To customize the application profile for the Production Scheduling Board app, follow the Customizing menu path: **SAP IMG Menu · Advanced Planning · Apps for Material Requirements Planning · General Settings · Define Application Profile**. In this customization, as shown in Figure 6.53, you create an application profile and assign the individual profiles, such as the heuristics profile, alert profile, strategy profile, and so on ❶. Then the application profile is assigned to the users in the customization node, **SAP IMG Menu · Advanced Planning · Apps for Material Requirements Planning · General Settings · Assign Application Profile to User** ❷. The time profile is assigned to the user from the Customizing menu path, **SAP IMG Menu · Advanced Planning · Apps for Material Requirements Planning · General Settings · Assign Time Profile to User** ❸.

After the business role is assigned to your user and the application profile, the time profile is assigned to your user, or an entry for all users (*) is maintained in the Customizing. At this point, you can launch the Production Scheduling Board app from the SAP Fiori launchpad.

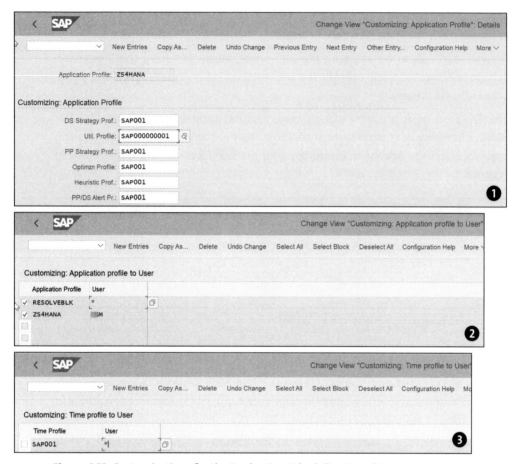

Figure 6.53 Customizations for the Production Scheduling Board App

When you launch this SAP Fiori app for the first time, the system will prompt you to set the AOR for the app (see Chapter 5, Section 5.6.4). It can be changed later in the app user settings.

In the app, you can add additional filters and set filter criteria by clicking on the **Filters** and the **Show Filter Bar** buttons accordingly. After setting the filter criteria, click on the **Go** button to load the resources on to the graphical board.

The operations are displayed in graphical format, as shown in Figure 6.54. For resources with operations in the time horizon, the resource node can be expanded to display the individual operations represented graphically on the scheduling board (e.g., expand the **Multiple Loading** option in the DS planning board). Only the find slot, insert operation, and infinite scheduling modes are available in the Product Scheduling Board app. The scheduling directions of forward and backward are supported.

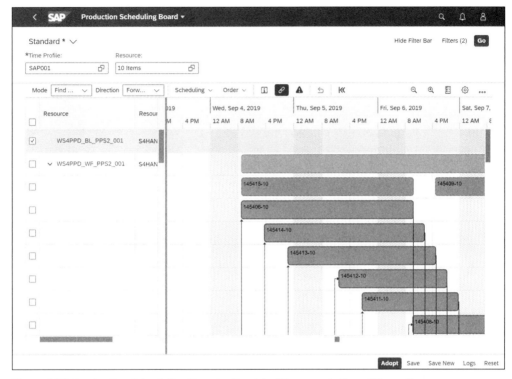

Figure 6.54 Production Scheduling Board – Graphical Representation of Operations

Scheduling functions such as schedule, deallocate, fixing, and so on are available by clicking on the **Scheduling** dropdown menu on the graphical area's toolbar (see Figure 6.55).

Order creation with reference to an existing operation is possible under the **Order** dropdown menu. The UI features are shown in Figure 6.55. You can also delete the order, change the order quantity, and change the source of supply of the order from the **Order** dropdown. The pegging and the inter-operation relationships can be displayed using the **Show Relationships** button ❶.

The time scale granularity (quarterly, monthly, weekly, daily) can be adjusted using the zoom in and zoom out buttons in the toolbar (the magnifying glass icons, ❷). You can also display alerts by clicking the **Alerts** button ❸, and display the legend (colors and shapes) of the graphical objects by clicking the **Legend** button ❹.

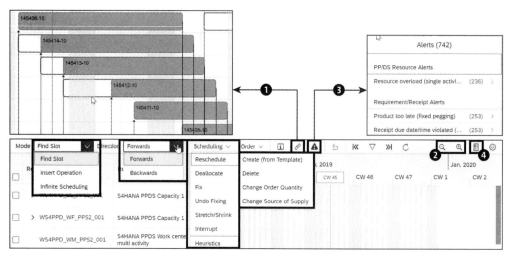

Figure 6.55 Toolbar in the SAP Fiori Production Scheduling Board App

To trigger a detailed scheduling heuristic, select the **Scheduling** dropdown, and navigate to the **Heuristics** option. All the heuristics assigned to the heuristics profile are available in the Production Scheduling Board app.

The operations can be dragged and dropped to the desired date and time. Multiple operations can be selected by pressing and holding the Ctrl key on the keyboard.

The **Operation Information** can be displayed by right-clicking the operation to open the context menu or by clicking on the information button on the toolbar. The overview, any components issues, alternative resources from the PDS alternative modes, order information, pegging, and the activity durations are displayed here, as shown in Figure 6.56. After you've displayed the information for an operation, the operation info side panel opens as well. Without closing this side panel, you can click on other operation to update the side panel with the currently selected operation's information. As the system fetches the information in real time for the alternative resources and pegging relationships, it could be performance intensive if you keep this side panel open at all times.

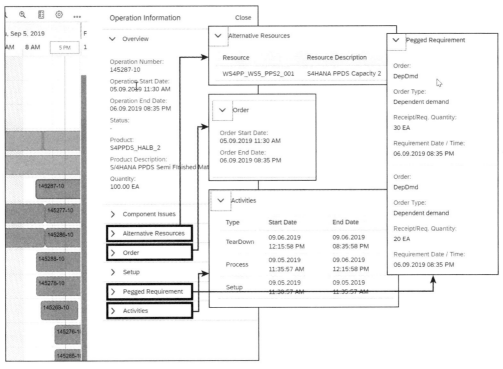

Figure 6.56 Operation Information in the Production Scheduling Board App

The data being changed in the Production Scheduling Board app by manual reschedulings and by heuristics is temporarily saved in sim sessions until you save and adopt the data into the active version. If you want to save the scheduling changes you've made, you can save the data in a simulation version by clicking the **Save** button, as shown in Figure 6.57. Later, you can continue to work on the same simulation version by adding a filter condition in the app for the simulation version and choosing the simulation version to load the data.

The simulation versions saved from the Production Scheduling Board app can only be accessed in the app. The simulation version saved from the app can't be processed from the SAP GUI transactions and the simulation versions created from the DS planning board can't be accessed from the Production Scheduling Board app.

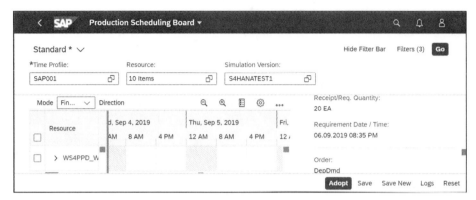

Figure 6.57 Working with Simulation Versions in the Production Scheduling Board App

6.4.3   Monitor Capacity Utilization App

Monitor Capacity Utilization is an SAP Fiori app to monitor the resource usage in an interactive graphical format to identify any resource overloads and take action to mitigate the scheduling issues by changing the operations or by updating the capacity of the resources.

This SAP Fiori app works based on the AOR assigned to the app just like the Production Scheduling Board app. If you have the AOR already assigned in the Production Scheduling Board app, the same will be considered for the Monitor Capacity Utilization app as well.

All the resources activated for advanced planning and within the AOR (plant and resource responsible) are displayed in a list with a graphical representation of the capacity utilization over the time horizon set in the filter criteria, as shown in Figure 6.58 (if you click a resource, you can see the utilization percentage per period ❶). You can add more filter criteria to narrow down the list of resources displayed as well ❷. Columns with details on the minimum and maximum loads on the resource for the period of analysis are listed, and the average utilization of the resource is also provided. The dates of first underload and first overload are also displayed as default columns. There are more than 30 columns available for you to manage and display in the settings of the app, which you can access via the gear button ❸.

You can also configure the chart display to a period other than the evaluation period by clicking on the chart settings on the app ❹. You can select the resources and launch other detailed scheduling tools such as the **Resource Planning Table** and the **Production Scheduling Board** tools ❺.

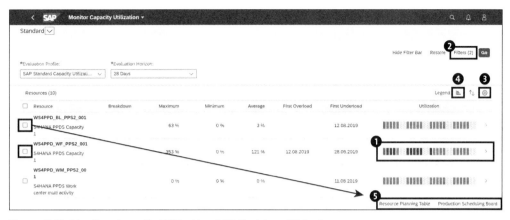

Figure 6.58 Monitor Capacity Utilization SAP Fiori App: UI Features

The **Evaluation Profile** is created in the Customizing of embedded PP-DS via menu
path: **SAP IMG Menu · Advanced Planning · Apps for Material Requirements Planning ·
General Settings · Define Evaluation Profile for Capacity Utilization**. The objects relevant for calculating the capacity utilization are defined here. Options are available to
include or exclude manufacturing orders (production and process orders), scheduled
operations on the resource, and deallocated operations on the resource, as shown in
Figure 6.59.

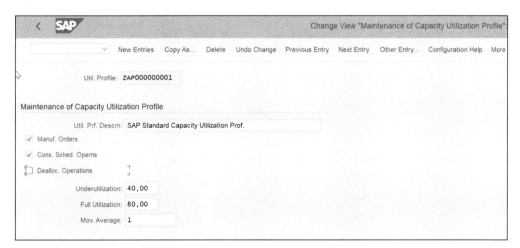

Figure 6.59 Customization of the Evaluation Profile for the Monitor Capacity
Utilization App

The definition for the percentage utilization to determine if the capacity is underutilized or overutilized is also made in this Customizing setting. The evaluation profile is then assigned to the user names under the Customizing menu path: **SAP IMG Menu · Advanced Planning · Apps for Material Requirements Planning · General Settings · Assign Evaluation Profile to User**.

To navigate to the detailed screen for the individual resources, click on the **Resource** row in the list (refer to Figure 6.58). This will open a new screen (see Figure 6.60) with a bar chart for the resource utilization and the shift details, along with the operations scheduled on the resource for the evaluation period. The capacity situation is displayed in a bar chart with colored legends displaying over-, under-, and normal utilization of the resource. The chart can be changed to analyze the capacity consumption by **Material**, **Activity**, and **Order Type**, as shown in Figure 6.60.

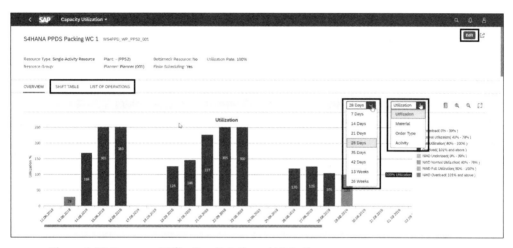

Figure 6.60 Resource Utilization Details and UI Options

In the detailed screen, you can change the resource availability data in **Edit** mode, as shown in Figure 6.61. On the **SHIFT TABLE**, you can change shift duration ❶, assign predefined shift definitions ❷, change the utilization rate of resources ❸, and add/delete an interval or create a downtime to manage the available capacity of the resource to resolve any scheduling issues ❹.

> **Note**
>
> Shift definitions can only be managed from the source (PP-DS resource master or Monitor Capacity Utilization app) to ensure data consistency. For this reason, only

the resources marked with external capacities (can be marked from the SAP APO resource view of the SAP S/4HANA work center master data) in the resource master data are allowed for editing the shift data in the SAP Fiori app.

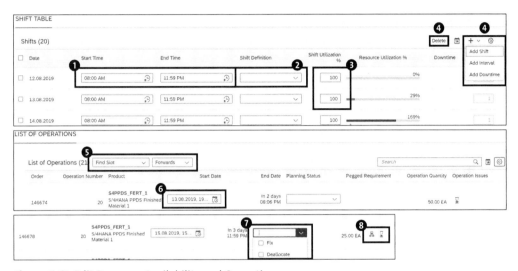

Figure 6.61 Edit Resource Availability and Operations

The operations scheduled on the app are also listed under **LIST OF OPERATIONS**, and you can change the scheduling mode/direction ❺, change the operation dates ❻, fix or deallocate the operations to manage the capacity ❼, and display pegging and component coverage issues ❽. You can simulate the shift and operation changes and save them after you achieve the desired capacity utilization results by clicking on the **Save** button.

6.5   PP-DS Optimizer

The PP-DS optimizer is an optional component of embedded PP-DS. The main purpose of the PP-DS optimizer is to create a mathematical model of the scheduling problems and resolve them by reducing the weighted objective functions associated with the scheduling problem, such as makespan (lead time) of the order, setup time, setup cost, delay cost, and mode cost. The PP-DS optimizer also respects the hard constraints provided and will attempt to respect the soft constraints. The result is a schedule that is optimized per the objective functions defined in the PP-DS optimizer profile.

The PP-DS optimizer can be executed from the detailed scheduling tools such as the DS planning board and product planning table. In addition, it's possible to schedule the PP-DS optimizer execution as a part of the background production planning run as a planning step.

The PP-DS optimizer engine is installed in one of the application servers of the SAP S/4HANA system or in a separate server. TCP/IP is set up between the SAP S/4HANA system and the PP-DS optimizer server. When the PP-DS optimizer is executed from the PP-DS tools, the data is collected from SAP liveCache and from the PP-DS application, and then the data is sent along with the PP-DS optimizer profile settings. The PP-DS optimizer creates the optimal plan by executing multiple iterations of the solution and sending the final solution back to embedded PP-DS.

The PP-DS optimizer settings are maintained in the PP-DS optimizer profile from the Customizing menu path, **SAP IMG Menu · Advanced Planning · Detailed Scheduling · Maintain Optimization Profiles**, or from the Customizing Transaction /SAPAPO/CDP-SC5. The list of optimization profiles is displayed in this transaction, as shown in Figure 6.62.

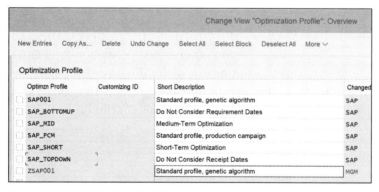

Figure 6.62 Optimization Profiles

Double-clicking on an optimization profile will take you to the screen with the optimization profile details, as shown in Figure 6.63.

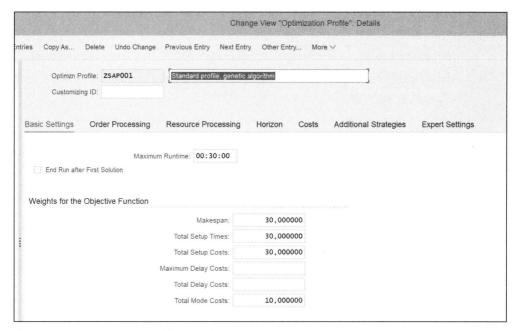

Figure 6.63 Optimization Profile: Details

We'll cover the important settings under the different tabs of the optimization profile in the following sections. The objective functions are the main drivers of the PP-DS optimizer functionality, so we'll cover the details of the objective functions before covering the critical settings on the different tabs.

6.5.1   Objective Functions

The PP-DS optimizer works based on the objective functions and the values defined against the objective functions, such as delay cost, mode cost, and so on. The objective functions are defined in the **Basic Settings** tab of the PP-DS optimizer profile.

The following objective functions are supported by the PP-DS optimizer as shown in Figure 6.64:

- **Makespan**
  Makespan is the total lead time of the order. The PP-DS optimizer reduces the makespan by reducing any gaps between the operations or by resequencing orders so that the orders aren't impacted by breaks in the resource. When a

weightage value is provided for the makespan, the value for the objective function is calculated as:

Weighted makespan = Weightage for makespan in profile × Makespan in seconds

The weighted makespans are calculated for all the orders in the optimization, and the total weighted makespan value is derived.

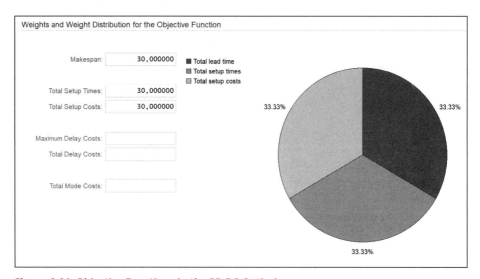

Figure 6.64 Objective Functions in the PP-DS Optimizer

- **Total Setup Times**

  When sequence-dependent setup activities are involved in scheduling, the detailed scheduling heuristics can't optimize the schedule by calculating the setup times in iterations in order to schedule the operations in the optimal sequence. In such scenarios, the **Total Setup Times** objective function can be set with a higher weightage value so that the PP-DS optimizer will reduce the total setup time required for all the operations within the optimization horizon by resequencing the operations. The weighted total setup time is calculated as:

  Weighted total setup time = Weightage for setup time in profile × Total setup times of all the operations in the optimization horizon

- **Total Setup Costs**

  Similar to the setup times, the relative setup costs are also defined in the setup matrix master data. Especially if the changeovers are based on multiple characteristics and generated setup matrices based on characteristics are used, the number of changeovers is high, and PP-DS optimizer can help reduce the setup costs.

Figure 6.65 shows an example of the generated setup matrix based on characteristics. The generated setup matrices based on characteristics can be accessed from Transaction /SAPAPO/CDPS_CHARMAT.

The time unit of measure maintained in the setup matrix is converted into equivalent time unit of measure of seconds for consideration by the PP-DS optimizer weighted objective value. The setup cost is a relative cost—not the actual cost—and no unit of measure or currency is maintained nor conversion applied when calculating the weighted setup cost totals.

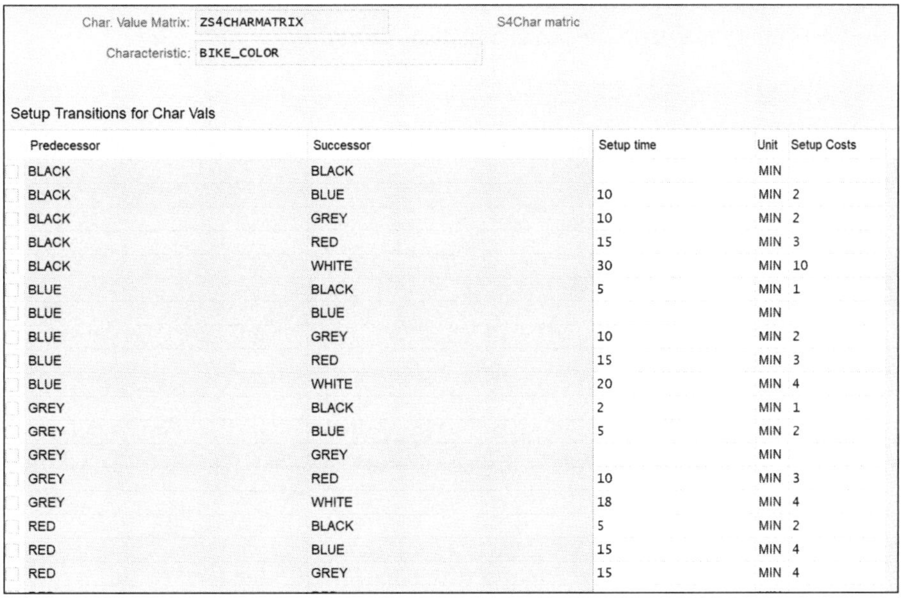

Char. Value Matrix: ZS4CHARMATRIX	S4Char matric			
Characteristic: BIKE_COLOR				

Setup Transitions for Char Vals

Predecessor	Successor	Setup time	Unit	Setup Costs
BLACK	BLACK		MIN	
BLACK	BLUE	10	MIN	2
BLACK	GREY	10	MIN	2
BLACK	RED	15	MIN	3
BLACK	WHITE	30	MIN	10
BLUE	BLACK	5	MIN	1
BLUE	BLUE		MIN	
BLUE	GREY	10	MIN	2
BLUE	RED	15	MIN	3
BLUE	WHITE	20	MIN	4
GREY	BLACK	2	MIN	1
GREY	BLUE	5	MIN	2
GREY	GREY		MIN	
GREY	RED	10	MIN	3
GREY	WHITE	18	MIN	4
RED	BLACK	5	MIN	2
RED	BLUE	15	MIN	4
RED	GREY	15	MIN	4

Figure 6.65 Generated Setup Matrix with Setup Times and Setup Costs

- **Maximum Delay Costs/Total Delay Costs**
  The maximum delay and total delay costs are calculated from the delay in seconds. The delay in delivering a requirement is derived by calculating the requirement date and the assigned receipt elements receipt date and then converting it into seconds. The requirement priority drives the delay costs; that is, the higher the priority (1 is higher), the higher is the delay cost. The list of **Delay Costs** up to a certain priority is defined in the **Costs** tab of the PP-DS optimizer profile, as shown in Figure 6.66. The delay costs are calculated as:

  Total delay cost = Total of ((Delay for the order in seconds) × (weightage maintained in the profile) × (delay cost for the priority of the order))

- **Total Mode Costs**

  When alternative modes are available to manufacture a material, the cost of using different modes can be reduced as an objective function using the PP-DS optimizer. In general, the higher the mode priority (A is the highest priority), the lesser is the mode cost. The mode cost is calculated as:

  Total mode cost = Fixed costs + (Variable costs × Duration of activity in seconds)

  The mode costs are also maintained in the **Costs** tab of the PP-DS optimizer profile, as shown in Figure 6.66. In Transaction /SAPAPO/CDPSC5, from the list of all PP-DS optimization profiles, double-click the profile you want to change, and navigate to the **Costs** tab to maintain the mode and delay costs.

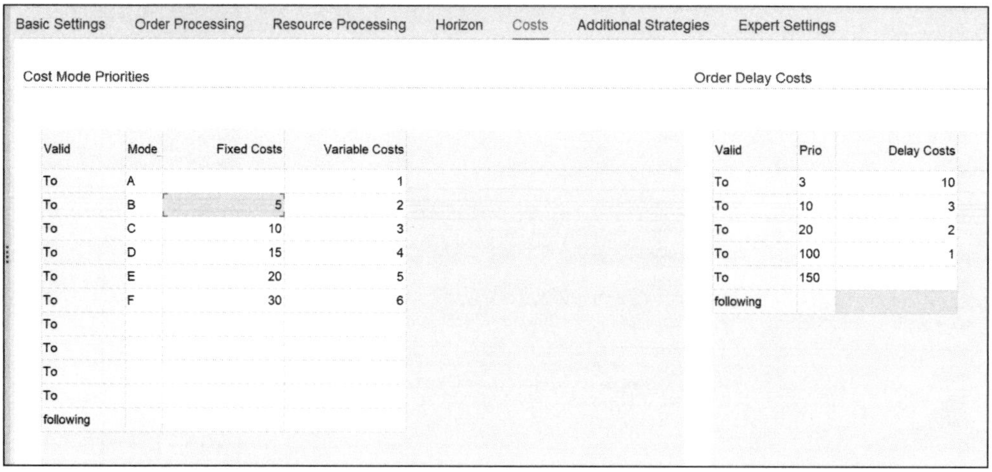

Basic Settings	Order Processing	Resource Processing	Horizon	Costs	Additional Strategies	Expert Settings

Cost Mode Priorities   Order Delay Costs

Valid	Mode	Fixed Costs	Variable Costs		Valid	Prio	Delay Costs
To	A		1		To	3	10
To	B	5	2		To	10	3
To	C	10	3		To	20	2
To	D	15	4		To	100	1
To	E	20	5		To	150	
To	F	30	6		following		
To							
To							
To							
To							
following							

Figure 6.66 Mode Costs and Order Priority Costs in the PP-DS Optimizer Profile

The constraints for the PP-DS optimizer can be configured within the optimization profile, which we'll discuss in the next section. However, certain constraints, such as resource availability (working times, utilization percentage), are hard constraints and can't be changed in the optimization profile.

6.5.2   Optimization Profile

We've covered the objective functions and cost definition in the optimization profile in the previous section. Now, we'll discuss some of the other important settings in the PP-DS optimizer profile.

Basic Settings

Let's start with the **Basic Settings** tab, as shown in Figure 6.67, which includes the following key settings:

- **Maximum Runtime**

  Depending on the volume of data involved and the complexity of the scheduling problems, the runtime for the optimization can vary. The PP-DS optimizer will keep iterating the solutions to further reduce the objective functions and to find the best possible solution. After a certain number of iterations, you may observe from the PP-DS optimizer logs that the runtime required to perform these iterations isn't worth the reduction in the objective function values. In this case, you can define a maximum runtime for the PP-DS optimizer, so that the PP-DS optimizer will end the iteration at the defined maximum runtime and will save the best solution it has found so far.

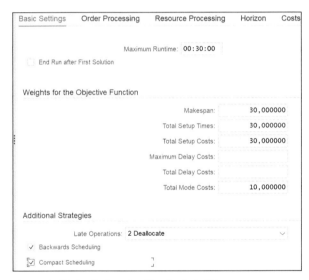

Figure 6.67 Optimizer Profile: Basic Settings

- **Backwards Scheduling**

  Backward scheduling is a follow-on step after the optimization to bring orders closer to the requirements. The PP-DS optimizer may schedule orders too early to reduce the objective functions defined; in those cases, backward scheduling can be executed by selecting the **Backwards Scheduling** checkbox under the **Additional Strategies** section so that the orders are scheduled closer to the requirement dates.

Executing backward scheduling may result in gaps between the operations, which can be avoided by selecting the **Compact Scheduling** checkbox under the **Additional Strategies** section of the **Basic Settings** tab.

Order Processing

In the **Order Processing** tab, shown in Figure 6.68, you define the options for the order categories that are relevant for the PP-DS optimizer run and settings based on the status of the orders and operations. The **Other Manufacturing Levels** settings determine whether the pegging relationships of the higher level and lower level orders in the pegging structure and their relationship to the order being optimized need to be considered as a secondary constraint by the PP-DS optimizer. If you select the **Ignore Upstream Orders** and/or **Do Not Consider Subsequent Orders** checkboxes, the schedule of the PP-DS optimizer may look optimized, but the material flow in terms of pegging relationships can be broken.

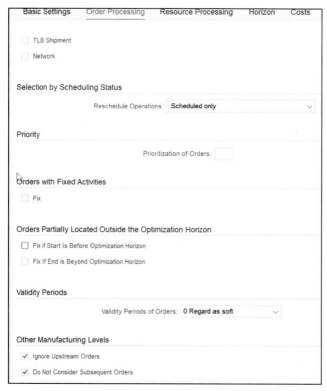

Figure 6.68 Optimizer Profile: Order Processing Settings

Resource Processing

In the **Resource Processing** tab of the PP-DS optimizer profile, as shown in Figure 6.69, the handling of capacities and scheduling relationship parameters and constraints are set for the PP-DS optimizer.

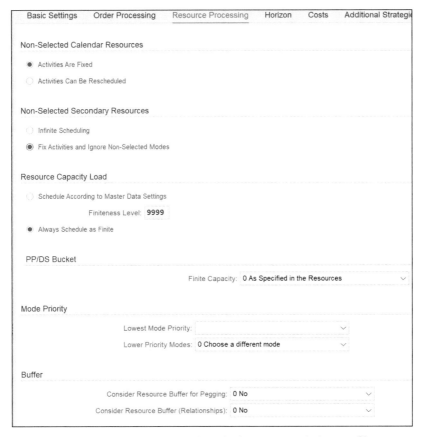

Figure 6.69 Resource Processing Settings in the PP-DS Optimizer Profile

When calendar resources are used, they are assigned to the location master data as inbound handling resources for scheduling goods receipt (GR) times of the orders. There is no capacity consumption with the usage of calendar resources, and these resources are only used for scheduling the GR activities. When there are orders in the optimization horizon with activities that use calendar resources, then how the PP-DS optimizer handles such activities is set under the **Non-Selected Calendar Resources** section of the **Resource Processing** tab. If the calendar resources are selected as part of the resource selection for optimization, these settings aren't relevant. When you select **Activities Are Fixed**, the system reschedules the product activity of the order, but the GR activity stays where it was before the optimization, thus impacting the overall duration of the order.

Resource Capacity Load settings control which resources are finitely scheduled during the optimization run. With the selection of **Always Schedule as Finite**, all the relevant resources being optimized will be scheduled finitely. The resource master data setting **Relevant for Finite Scheduling** isn't considered, and irrespective of the resource master data setting, the resource will be finitely scheduled by the PP-DS optimizer.

The **Lowest Mode Priority** setting, which the PP-DS optimizer can select from alternative modes, is defined under the **Mode Priority** section. The **Lower Priority Modes** setting directs the PP-DS optimizer behavior when there are activities with proprieties lower than the lowest mode priority allowed to be selected by the PP-DS optimizer. The system can choose a higher priority mode when you select **0 Choose a different mode** from the **Lower Priority Modes** dropdown.

Horizon

In the **Horizon** tab of the PP-DS optimizer profile, the **Start of the Optimization Horizon** and the **End of Optimization Horizon** are set. Options are available to set these dates relative to the current date. The relative dates work better when running the PP-DS optimizer as part of the production planning run as a batch job because there is no manual intervention required to change the dates for every job. The **Start of the Optimized Plan** is the date/time from which the system can start scheduling the optimized orders and operations on the resources.

During optimization, the operations that lie entirely within the optimization horizon are considered for rescheduling. The handling of the orders that lie partially within the optimization horizon is defined in the **Order Processing** tab under the **Orders Partially Located Outside the Optimization Horizon** section.

Note

The PP-DS optimizer in embedded PP-DS can't create new orders to fulfill any open demand. This is only possible in the PP-DS optimizer in the standalone PP-DS component of SAP APO.

Additional Strategies

The **Decomposition** setting in the **Additional Strategies** tab is used to split the scheduling problems into multiple smaller problems so that the PP-DS optimizer can efficiently solve smaller problems. Don't switch on the decomposition to just improve the performance of the optimization run because the quality of the planning results may be affected by switching on the decomposition.

Any increase in the makespan due to the backward scheduling can be controlled and avoided by selecting the **Do Not Increase Makespan** checkbox in the **Backwards Scheduling** section of the **Additional Strategies** tab. With this setting, the previously optimized makespans of the orders are protected from any change due to backward scheduling.

Expert Settings

The **Expert Settings** tab of the profile, as shown in Figure 6.70, has the settings related to logging the messages generated during the PP-DS optimizer run. The **Explain Result** option will write an explanation log on the changes the operations and orders have gone through during the optimization. The **Log Result** and **Log Interim Solution** will log the resulting objective function values and the value of the objective functions during the iterations performed by the PP-DS optimizer.

Figure 6.70 Expert Settings for Logging and Parallel Processing in the PP-DS Optimizer Profile

Parallel Processing is an important aspect of improving the PP-DS optimizer performance. But the sizing of the PP-DS optimizer server should be performed to handle such parallel processing workloads. The number of slots that can be used by the PP-DS optimizer is defined in the connection properties in Transaction RCC_CUST. The number of parallel processes defined in the **Max. No. of Parallel Processes** field should be less than the number of slots available for the PP-DS optimizer.

6.5.3   Execute and Monitor PP-DS Optimizer Runs

The PP-DS optimizer can be executed interactively from the DS planning board or from the product planning table. You can also run the PP-DS optimizer as a background job via the production planning run. In this section, we'll walk through each execution option.

PP-DS Optimizer in the Planning Run

After materials planning with MRP heuristics and, if required, aligning the receipt and requirement elements with a heuristic (e.g., top-down or bottom-up heuristics), the PP-DS optimizer can be executed to schedule the orders finitely on the critical resources and to optimize the schedule.

The optimization is available in the production planning run as a function, which isn't a heuristic. The heuristics are defined using an algorithm in the heuristics customization (Transaction /SAPAPO/CDPSC11), but the functions such as the optimization aren't listed in the heuristics list in the Customizing transaction; instead, they are listed as a function to be selected in the planning run transaction. The global parameters, such as the **Planning Version**, **Time Profile**, and **Propagation Range**, need to be set as shown in Figure 6.71. The optimization function takes only the resources as the object selection. The optimization can be one of the planning steps in the production planning run after the MRP steps (refer to Chapter 5, Section 5.5.1), or a separate variant can be created for the optimization through the planning run in Transaction /SAPAPO/CDPSB1 and can be scheduled as an independent job.

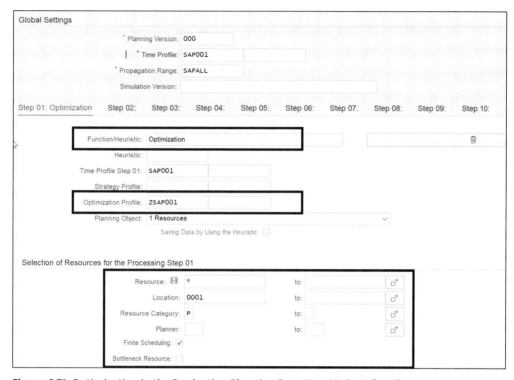

Figure 6.71 Optimization in the Production Planning Run: New Variant Creation

PP-DS Optimizer Execution from the DS Planning Board

From the DS planning board, the PP-DS optimizer can be executed for the resources selected as part of the DS planning board. The PP-DS optimizer profile settings can be changed interactively in the DS planning board before executing the optimization. As the PP-DS optimizer execution from the DS planning board is done in dialog/online mode, it's recommended to have a smaller value entered for the **Maximum Runtime** for the PP-DS optimizer in the settings to avoid any timeout situation.

Let's walk through the following steps to execute the PP-DS optimizer from the DS planning board:

1. Click on the **Optimize** button in the menu bar.

2. In the next screen, shown in Figure 6.72, set the **Date/Time** for the **Start of Horizon** and **End of Horizon** for optimization and the **Date/Time** for the **Start of Optimized Schedule**. Make sure the orders and operations you optimize are within

the optimization horizon. Operations outside the horizon are considered fixed for optimization. Click **Continue** to arrive at the optimization screen.

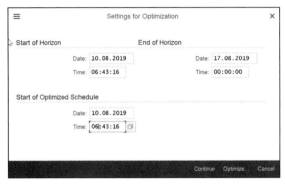

Figure 6.72 Horizon Settings for Optimization

3. Click on the **Settings** button (see Figure 6.73) on the optimization screen ❶ to navigate to the PP-DS optimizer profile settings ❷. After making any adjustments to the profile, click on **Copy** button ❸ to save the values for the current PP-DS optimizer run.

4. Click on the **Execute** button to start the PP-DS optimizer run ❹.

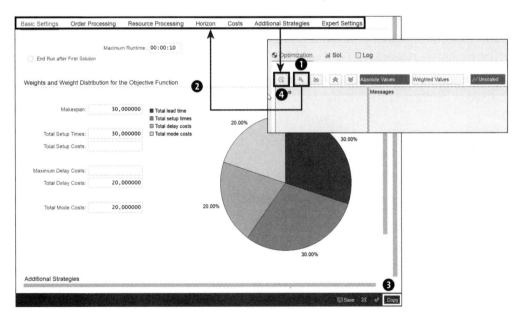

Figure 6.73 Accessing Optimizer Settings from the Interactive PP-DS Optimizer Execution

The list of resources selected for the optimization can be displayed from the PP-DS optimizer screen by clicking on the **Display Resource List** button.

The reduction in the objective values over time of the optimization is interactively shown in a graphical format. After the optimization is completed, the logs, results, and explanation logs are written if the PP-DS optimizer profile has the relevant settings in the **Expert Settings** tab. The messages generated during the PP-DS optimizer run with the statistical information about the resources and activities are displayed on the **Optimization** screen, as shown in Figure 6.74.

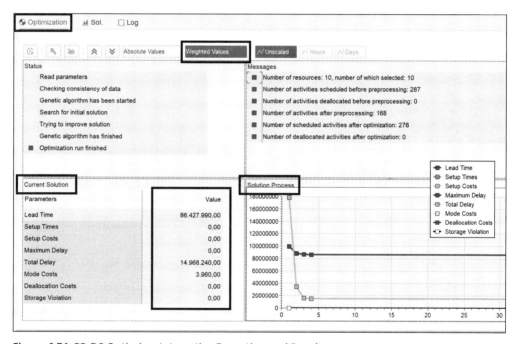

Figure 6.74 PP-DS Optimizer Interactive Execution and Results

The PP-DS optimizer finds an initial solution and then keeps iterating the solution to find better solutions. If the **End After First Solution** is set in the PP-DS optimizer profile settings (**Basic Settings** tab), the PP-DS optimizer will stop after the initial solution is found.

The **Absolute Values** button adjusts the solution process graph to show the total value of the objective function calculated. Switching the display to the **Weighted Values** shows the objective function parameter values by applying the weightage defined in the PP-DS optimizer profile. The current solution values are also displayed in the screen, as shown in Figure 6.74. The total lead time is reduced from 100000000 to 86427990, and the total delay is reduced from 180000000 to 14968240 in this example execution.

The PP-DS optimizer **Log** (see Figure 6.75) collects runtime (performance) information of the individual steps of the PP-DS optimizer run, including the reading of parameters for PP-DS optimizer, loading the data from SAP liveCache, executing the genetic algorithm in the PP-DS optimizer server, and writing the results back to SAP liveCache.

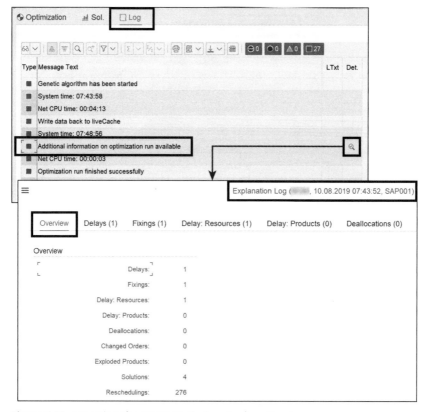

Figure 6.75 Accessing the PP-DS Optimizer Explanation Log

If the explanation log is set as **Active** in the profile, then an **Additional information on optimization run available** line is shown in the PP-DS optimizer log, and the explanation log can be displayed by clicking on the **Details** icon of the additional information log line. The explanation logs show any orders that are still scheduled with a delay because the PP-DS optimizer isn't able to find a solution to resolve this delay. The orders fixed for the PP-DS optimizer are shown in the **Explanation** log with the reason behind such **Fixings**, as shown in Figure 6.76.

Figure 6.76 Explanation Log: Fixings Detail

All the activities rescheduled by the PP-DS optimizer are listed in the **Reschedulings** tab of the explanation log. In addition, the interim solutions (the reduction in the objective functions) that the system calculated are shown in the **Solutions** tab of the explanation log, as shown in Figure 6.77.

Delay: Products (0)	Deallocations (0)	Changed Orders (0)	Exploded Products (0)	Solutions (4)

Interim Solutions

Time	Makespan	SetupTimes	Setup Cost	MaxDelCost	Tot.DelCst	Mode Costs	DeallCosts	StorCosts	St. Violn	Extrapol.
3	3.324.936,00	0,00	0,00	2.524.424,00	8.931.700,00	198,00	0,00	0,00	0,00	
4	2.940.034,00	0,00	0,00	984.816,00	1.733.228,00	198,00	0,00	0,00	0,00	
5	2.880.933,00	0,00	0,00	748.412,00	748.412,00	198,00	0,00	0,00	0,00	
5	2.898.933,00	0,00	0,00	820.412,00	820.412,00	198,00	0,00	0,00	0,00	

Figure 6.77 Explanation Log: List of Solutions Calculated

In the **Sol** (solution) tab of the PP-DS optimizer output (refer back to Figure 6.75), the end results of the objective functions are displayed in a bar chart.

Monitoring Background Optimizer Runs

When the PP-DS optimizer is scheduled as a background job from the production planning run, you can use Transaction /SAPAPO/OPT11 (RCCF [remote control and communication framework] Log Display) to monitor the PP-DS optimizer execution status and results. The same transaction can also be used to analyze the PP-DS optimizer runs executed interactively by users from the DS planning board, the product planning table, or any other applications.

The RCCF log display tool displays all the PP-DS optimizer executions for all the PP-DS optimizer executions, as shown in Figure 6.78. From the list of the PP-DS optimizer executions, you can click the clock icon under the **Mess. Log** column to display the application logs with the runtime distribution. Click the magnifying glass icon under the **Ext.Column** to open the explanation log for that execution, as shown in Figure 6.78.

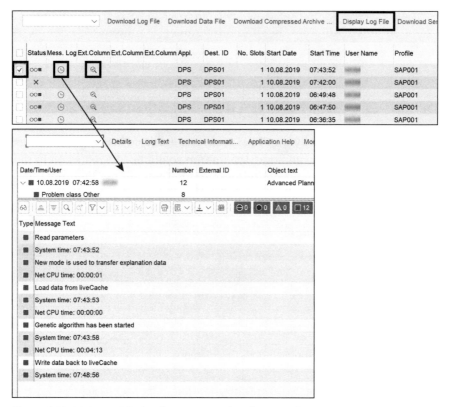

Figure 6.78 RCCF Log Display from Transaction /SAPAPO/OPT11

If you want to check the log file generated by the PP-DS optimizer engine, select the row from the list of executions, and click on the **Display Log File** button from the menu bar. The PP-DS optimizer log file has all the parameters and technical information of the PP-DS optimizer execution. For the most part, the PP-DS optimizer log file content can't be interpreted by the users or consultants.

If you want to terminate the PP-DS optimizer execution that is currently running in the system, you can use Transaction /SAPAPO/OPT_STOP (RCCF Active Session). This may be required if during interactive execution of the PP-DS optimizer, you observe that the objective functions aren't reduced after a point in time, and you want to save the solution as of that point and terminate the PP-DS optimizer run. To do a graceful termination, where the latest solution is saved and sessions are terminated by the PP-DS optimizer, you can use the **Stop Process** button, after selecting the current PP-DS optimizer session.

If you just want to end the PP-DS optimizer session abruptly without saving any solutions, click on the **End Process** button on the **RFCC: Active Session** screen, as shown in Figure 6.79.

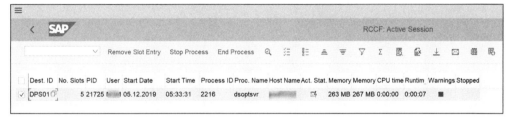

Figure 6.79 Optimizer Session Management

This transaction can be used to also monitor and terminate background PP-DS optimizer executions, if necessary.

6.6   Summary

In this chapter, we've covered the detailed scheduling functions and tools in embedded PP-DS. For scheduling in PP-DS, the strategy settings are very critical to ensure the schedule is set per the shop floor setup and requirements. We've covered in detail the functionality and working of various aspects of the strategy settings, including the scheduling modes, scheduling direction, cross-order relationships, and order-internal relationships.

The same strategy settings are also applied within many of the detailed scheduling heuristics. We've covered the basic detailed scheduling heuristics to perform functions such as sequencing, resolving backlogs, and scheduling deallocated operations. The multilevel scheduling framework heuristics including the stable forward scheduling heuristic, were also covered in detail in this chapter. The multiresource scheduling heuristic can be used to schedule operations on alternative modes, including modes from alternative sources of supply (PDSs).

The detailed scheduling heuristics can be executed via background jobs via the production planning run as well as in interactive mode. We've also covered the interactive detailed scheduling tools, such as the DS planning board, the Production Scheduling Board app from SAP Fiori, and the monitor capacity utilization SAP Fiori app.

The important settings, functionalities, and workings of the PP-DS optimizer and the monitoring of the PP-DS optimizer runs were also discussed in this chapter.

We've covered the monitoring of the production planning and detailed scheduling applications via the jobs and logs of those application executions. From the business process perspective, it's important to monitor the accuracy of planning and scheduling. The alert monitor tool is used for monitoring the accuracy of the plan and schedule, as well as to proactively monitor for any supply chain issues. We'll cover the alert monitor in the next chapter.

Chapter 7
The Alert Monitor

To identify planning and capacity issues in your embedded PP-DS system, you can use the alert monitor. In this chapter, we'll walk through the steps to set it up.

After the production planning and detailed scheduling heuristics are executed in background mode in regular frequencies—typically daily—not all planning and scheduling problems are completely solved by the various executed heuristics or by the PP-DS optimizer. In such cases, the planners and schedulers need to be notified to react to the specific planning and scheduling problems. These actions can be manual decisions to cancel or delay manufacturing orders, to add or reduce shifts and capacities to handle underutilization or overutilization of a resource, or to schedule production orders to meet specific customer orders that are delayed when the delay can't be resolved by the planning and scheduling heuristics.

For enterprise resource planning (ERP) systems such as SAP ERP, in classic material requirements planning (MRP), exceptions are generated during the MRP run that can be reviewed by the planners. However, these are static exceptions with little flexibility to customize the severity or scenarios for which the exceptions are raised.

Delivered standard in PP-DS for SAP S/4HANA (embedded PP-DS), the alert monitor is a powerful tool for identifying, monitoring, and managing exception situations in the planning and scheduling processes. The alert monitor is embedded into most of PP-DS applications and tools, so planners and schedulers always have visibility of the alerts when they are making any plan or schedule changes in the system. The alert monitor also has features to identify the alerts and send notifications to the users for alerts that require immediate action.

In this chapter, we'll cover the details of the alert monitor and the steps required to set up the alerts in the system.

7.1   Alert Profiles

The PP-DS alert monitor works based on alert profiles that are assigned to the overall profile of the PP-DS applications, such as the product view, production planning table, or the detailed scheduling (DS) planning board. In addition, the alert monitor itself can be used as a standalone tool to monitor alerts. When the alert monitor is called from the applications, the alerts relevant to the application are displayed. For example, when the alert monitor is called from the product view, the material-, location-, and order-related alerts are displayed; likewise, when the alert monitor is called from the DS planning board, it also show alerts related to resource capacities. PP-DS supports the following two types of alerts:

- **Dynamic alerts**
  Most of the alerts configured in PP-DS fall into this category. Dynamic alerts are generated at the time of the call to a planning or scheduling application or while determining the alerts from the alert monitor itself. Dynamic alerts aren't stored permanently and can't be set as completed or closed until the underlying planning or scheduling problem is addressed.

- **Database alerts**
  The use of database alerts in PP-DS is very limited. For example, when a material runs into an error or an exception during the production planning run, a database alert can be created and saved in the system for review and later deletion from the system.

In this section, we'll get started by activating the alert monitor and walking through how to set up alerts in the alert profile.

7.1.1   Activate and Access the Alert Monitor

PP-DS is delivered by default as an active application to be managed by the alert monitor. The activation and deactivation of the alert monitor for applications in the SAP S/4HANA system can be done from the Customizing menu path: **SAP IMG Menu • Advanced Planning • Alert Monitor • Activate/Deactivate Applications in Alert Monitor**. As shown in Figure 7.1, the **PP/DS** application is active as delivered. When advanced planning is activated in the SAP S/4HANA system, the alert monitor can be used in advanced planning, which is embedded PP-DS.

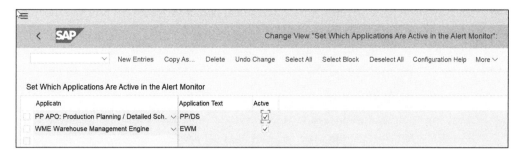

Figure 7.1 Activation of PP-DS for the Alert Monitor

The alert monitor can be accessed from Transaction /SAPAPO/AMON1 or the **SAP Easy Access** menu path: **Logistics · Advanced Planning · Monitoring · Alert Monitor · Alert Monitor**. The initial screen of the alert monitor transaction includes **Favorite Management**, which we'll discuss in Section 7.2.1. By clicking on the **Alert Profile** button, you can navigate to the alert profile maintenance screen, as shown in Figure 7.2.

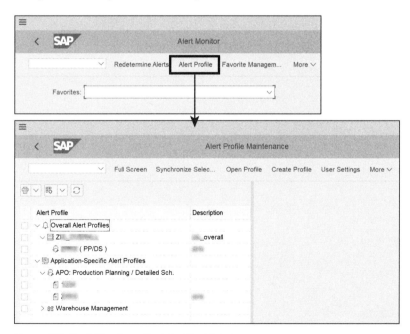

Figure 7.2 Alert Monitor: Alert Profile Maintenance

On the navigation tree on the left side of the screen, you'll see the overall alert profiles and the application-specific profiles. The individual application profiles, such as alert profiles for PP-DS, are created and then assigned to the overall profiles. The individual application profiles created in the alert monitor can be assigned to the application tool profiles, such as profiles for the DS planning board and order views in PP-DS.

7.1.2   Create Alert Profile

Let's start by creating the application profiles. Under **APO Application-Specific Alert Profiles · APO Production Planning/Detailed Scheduling**, right-click on the **PP/DS** folder or click on the **Create Profile** button at the top of the screen to create a new application alert profile, as shown in Figure 7.3.

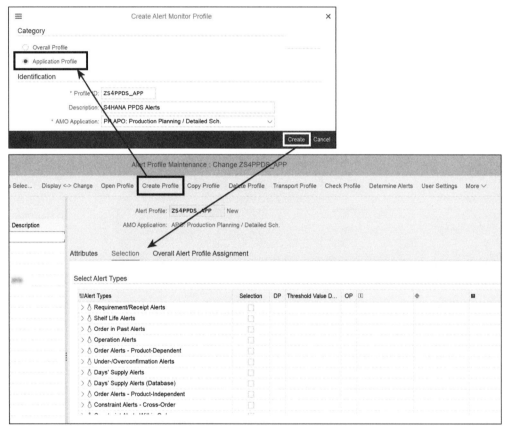

Figure 7.3 Creation of an Application Profile in the Alert Monitor

In the **Create Alert Monitor Profile** popup, select the **Application Profile** radio button, enter a **Profile ID** and **Description**, select PP-DS as the application, and click on the **Create** button. This will load the new profile in the right side of the screen with three tabs: **Attributes**, **Selection**, and **Overall Alert Profile Assignment**.

Select Alert Types

Click on the **Selection** tab, and you'll see the list of all available PP-DS alert types delivered in the embedded PP-DS standard system. Under each alert type, there are various alerts available for configuration. Expand the **Alert Types** folders (refer to Figure 7.3) to see the individual alerts under them. You can select all the individual alerts under any alert type by setting the **Selection** flag at the folder level or by setting the **Selection** flag at the individual alert type.

Depending on the alert selected, you define the threshold values for the alerts to be raised. You have the following options:

- **Information**
  Information alerts are considered the lowest-priority alerts to inform the user of a deviation from the plan or schedule. Users' reaction to an information alert is optional.

- **Warning**
  Warning alerts can be raised when the plan or schedule is about to cause a problem in the supply chain. User action is required to react to the warning alert.

- **Error**
  Error alerts can be raised when a violation of the plan or schedule is imminent or has already happened. These alerts must be addressed by the planners and schedulers immediately.

The default priority (**DP**) assigned to the alert is used by the system when there are no thresholds defined for the alert. For example, for the **Product too late** alert, if no threshold values are maintained for the information, warning, and error alerts, then the default priority assigned to the alert will be shown when there is any delay in covering a requirement element. The default priority of the alerts can be set for the alerts under the Customizing node: **SAP IMG Menu · Advanced Planning · Alert Monitor · Maintain Prioritization of Alert Types**. Click on the **New Entries** button, and using the value help ([F4]), you can select the alert item for which you want to set a default priority and set the **Priority** as **Information**, **Warning**, or **Error** (see upper-left area of Figure 7.4). The default priority will only be used when no threshold is defined or for

353

alerts that aren't relevant to threshold definitions (e.g., **Receipt with Violated Resource Network**). When there is no threshold defined for the alert—in Figure 7.4 for the **Product too late (dynamic pegging)** alert—the priority from Customizing (**3 Information**) is used in the alert profile, as shown in the upper screen in Figure 7.4.

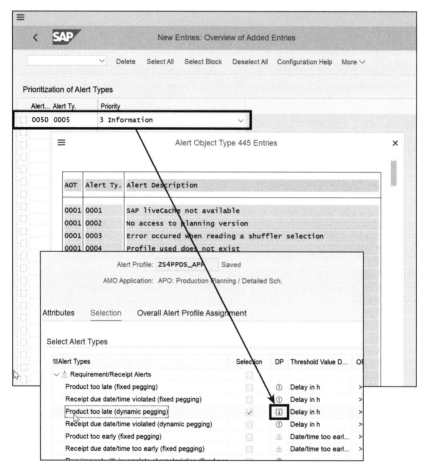

Figure 7.4 Customizing Setting for the Default Alert Priority

Set Up Alerts

Now, let's go through the steps to set up an alert in the alert profile. Let's use the **Requirement/Receipt Alerts** alert type. **Product too late (dynamic pegging)** is one of the alerts available under this alert type. You set the **Selection** flag at the alert level, as shown in Figure 7.5, and then click on the individual threshold buttons to set the values on the **Enter a Threshold Value** popup. If the delay for a requirement element exceeds the threshold set in the alert profile, the system will raise an alert accordingly. In the example shown in Figure 7.5, the system will create an information alert if the delay in hours (in covering the requirement element) is more than 24 hours, a warning if the delay is more than 48 hours, and an error if the delay is more than 72 hours.

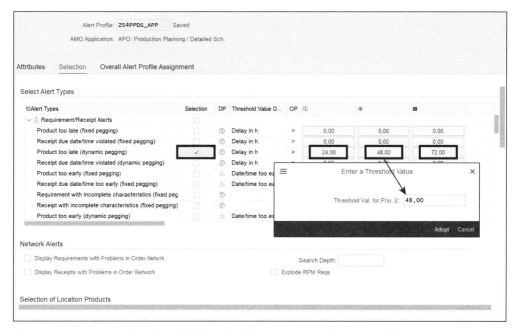

Figure 7.5 Setting Up Alert Thresholds in the Alert Monitor Application Profile

After the required alerts are selected and the thresholds are defined, the following settings can be maintained in the **Selection** tab of the alert profile, as shown in Figure 7.5 (accessed by scrolling down on the screen). (Certain settings are only relevant if a certain alert or alert type is selected. We'll cover some of the important settings that are valid for many of the alerts and alert types.)

- **Network Alerts**
  Network alerts are used to raise the alert at the higher level of the pegging hierarchy to notify the planner of an alert raised in a lower level of the hierarchy. For

example, a delay alert raised in the raw material coverage can be shown as a network alert of the sales order of the finished material. Select the **Display Requirements with Problems in Order Network** option to generate an alert when any of the pegged requirement elements raises an alert and/or the **Display Receipts with Problems in Order Network** to generate an alert when any of the pegged receipt elements raises an alert. The number of pegging levels the system needs to evaluate the alert for the lower levels is set in the **Search Depth** field. For example, if there are 10 levels of bills of materials (BOMs) and the corresponding pegging network created in PP-DS, and if the **Search Depth** is set to **3**, only the alerts raised within the top three levels are propagated to the top level as a network alert.

Note

As the network alerts are performance intensive, only use them for specific scenarios as required. Restrict the **Search Depth** to a minimum number so that the alerts aren't calculated for the entire pegging network of a product when accessing the product from tools such as the product view.

- **Selection of Location Products**

  Under this section, the selection of location products and available-to-promise (ATP) categories are defined that are relevant for calculating the alerts.

  The **Location Products** selection is only applicable in determining the alerts in the alert monitor. When the alert profile is used in another application, such as the product view or product overview, the product location selection from the alert profile isn't considered, and the selection entered in the application is considered.

  To define a set of location products for which the alerts needs to be calculated, click on the **Selection** icon next to the **Location Products** field, as shown in Figure 7.6. In the next screen for the **Selection Object**, enter the selection criteria. For example, for setting location selections, double-click on the **Location Name** field under the **Locations** node ❶. Enter the location to be selected in the **Value From – Value To** fields ❷. After the selection condition is maintained, it will be moved to the top of the list ❸, and further conditions can be maintained similarly. The checkmark in ❹ shows that this selection parameter (location name, in our example) has existing selection conditions, and the first value of the selection condition from the list of conditions ❸ is displayed in the **From** and **To** columns next to the checkbox ❹.

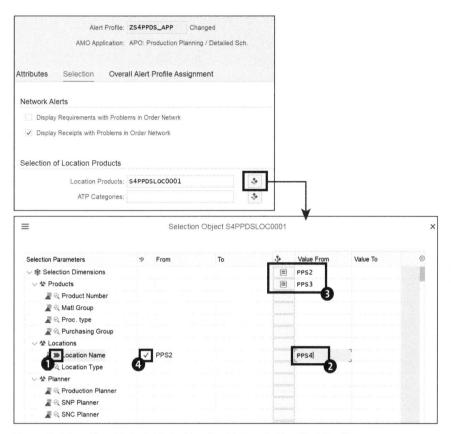

Figure 7.6 Location Material Selection Restriction in the Alert Profile

> **Tip**
>
> If multiple values are maintained for a selection (location or product), you'll see one value on the screen, and the selection parameter maintained (green checkmark) is set. Double-click on the row to see all the values maintained in the selection.

After entering the required selection conditions, click on the **Save Selection** button, and enter a name for the selection. The name of the selection is transferred back to the **Alert Profile** screen.

For the **ATP Categories**, similar selection conditions can be set to include or exclude certain receipt and requirement elements based on their ATP category.

The selection of the ATP category set in the alert profile will be applied irrespective of the PP-DS tool in which the alert profile is used.

- **Selection of Resources**
  Under **Selection of Resources**, you can maintain the restrictions for selection of resources considered for the alert types that are relevant to resources (e.g., average resource utilization).

After all the required settings are maintained, save the application profile in the alert monitor by clicking on the **Save** button. This application alert profile can be used in the PP-DS planning and scheduling tools.

In the **Attributes** tab of the alert profile, the basic attributes, such as the description of the alert profile, can be maintained. Other attributes are also displayed, such as the user who created and/or changed the alert profile and the creation and change time stamps.

After the alert profile is assigned to the overall profile as discussed in the next section, the **Overall Alert Profile Assignment** tab appears in the overall profiles to which the alert profile is assigned.

7.1.3   Create Overall Profile

To monitor the alerts from the alert monitor or to generate and send notifications to users for the PP-DS alerts, an overall alert profile must be created and assigned all the relevant application alert profiles and additional settings. You can create the overall alert profile, following the step to create an application alert profile (see Section 7.1.2), but select the **Overall Profile** option in the **Create Monitor Alert Profile** popup, as shown in Figure 7.7. In the overall profile, maintain the **Planning Version** that will be used to determine the alerts, and assign the **Alert Profile** that will be used to calculate the alerts.

The period for which the alerts should be generated when determining the alerts in the background or from the alert monitor is defined in the overall profile. To define a relative period from the current date, select the **Relative Time Interval** radio button. Then select the period type (**Months, Weeks, Days,** or **Hours**), and define the duration. The **Offset** fields can be used to move the current period by the offset defined. For example, if **Months** is selected as the period, "3" is entered as the duration, and "-3" is entered as the **Offset**, the alerts will be calculated for the past three months and the future three months.

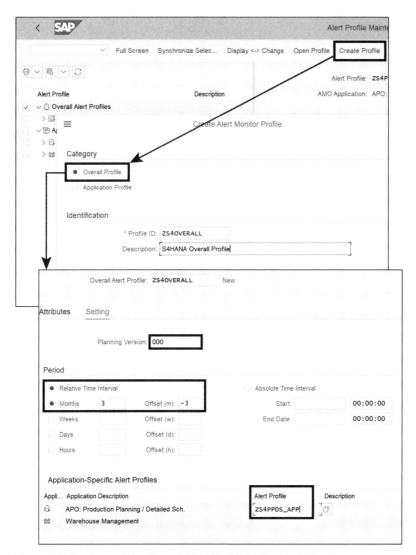

Figure 7.7 Creation of the Overall Alert Profile in the Alert Monitor

Note

The settings made in the overall alert profile are only used by the alert monitor when alerts are determined within the alert monitor. For other PP-DS applications (e.g., product view, DS planning board, etc.), the application-specific alert profiles are

359

selected, and the selection of planning version, materials, locations, resources, and time horizons are determined by the application to generate alerts based on the application-specific alert profile.

7.1.4   Transport Profiles

The overall profiles, alert profiles, and selection profiles created in the alert monitor can be transported to other systems in the system landscape. To do so, execute Transaction /SAPAPO/AMON1 to arrive at the **Alert Profile Maintenance** screen. You can generate transport requests using the **Transport Profile** button.

7.2   Alert Monitoring

You have a few different options when it comes to monitoring alerts using the alert monitor. In this section, we'll cover the monitoring of alerts from the alert monitor, alert generation in the background, and alert monitoring in PP-DS applications.

7.2.1   Monitor Alerts from the Alert Monitor

Overall alert profiles can be assigned to your user as favorites so that the alerts can be generated and monitored from the central alert monitoring (Transaction /SAPAPO/ AMON3).

The favorites are managed from the alert monitor Transaction /SAPAPO/AMON1. To manage the favorite overall alert profiles, launch Transaction /SAPAPO/AMON1, and click the **Favorite Management** button (see Figure 7.8 ❶). In the **Alert Monitor Administration** popup, the **Manage Favorites** tab is opened by default. Select the overall alert profile from the right side of the selection window (**Worklist of Overall Profiles**), and move it to the left side (**Favorites**) using the arrow button, as shown in Figure 7.8. Click the **Save and Exit** button when you're done.

After doing this, when you launch the alert monitor (Transaction /SAPAPO/AMON3), you can select the favorite from the drop-down menu ❷, and the system will determine and display all the alerts per the application profiles and the selection conditions maintained in the overall profile and the application profile.

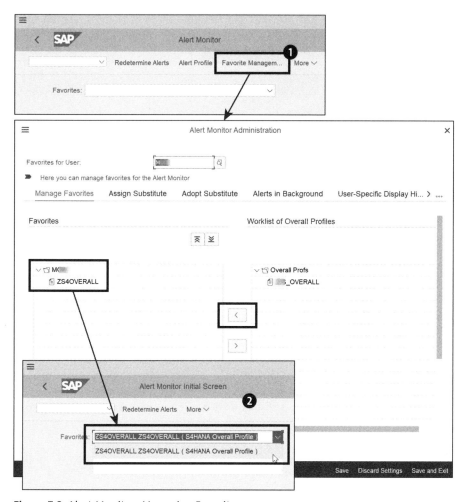

Figure 7.8 Alert Monitor: Managing Favorites

The alert monitor's display settings for the hierarchy in which the alerts are displayed can be customized from the user settings. From Transaction /SAPAPO/AMON3, choose **More · Alert Monitor · User-Specific Display Hierarchies**, as shown in Figure 7.9 ❶. Select and move the fields from the **Possible Nodes per Alert View** to the **User-Specific Display Hierarchies** pane ❷ in the order in which you want the alerts to be displayed. Click on the **Redetermine Alerts** button in the initial screen of the alert monitor ❸, and the determined alerts per the overall profile are arranged per the hierarchy set in this setting. The number of alerts per hierarchy node—in this example, **Location**, **Product Identifier**, and **Alert Type**—is displayed ❹. You can click on the number of alerts to navigate to the alert details ❺.

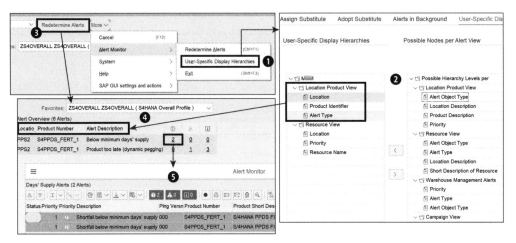

Figure 7.9 Alert Monitor Display Settings and Monitoring Alerts from the Alert Monitor

From the alert details shown in the **Alert Monitor** screen (see Figure 7.9), there are options to hide the alerts up to a certain duration. The alerts can be sent via email to email addresses. You can forward the alert to another user, and the forwarded alerts will be displayed in the receiving user's alert monitor. You can navigate to the product view transaction from the alert monitor to take actions on the alerts.

7.2.2   Generate Alerts in the Background

For alert profiles that are time intensive (with a lot of selection objects and many alert types activated in the alert profile), it's possible to generate the alerts in the background and display them to the users.

To set up the overall alert profiles for processing in the background, you use the alert monitor Transaction /SAPAPO/AMON1. As shown in Figure 7.10, click on the **User Settings** button, and navigate to the **Alerts in Background** tab ❶. In this screen, click the **New** button ❷, enter the **Ov. Alert Profile** ❸ for which the alerts are to be determined in the background, and click the **Save and Exit** button. Then in the bottom of the same screen shown in Figure 7.11, maintain the **Priority** for processing, **Start Date**, and **Start-Time**. Enter the **Repeat Intrvl** in which the background alerts are to be generated and the **FctryCalendar**, which is used to calculate the date and time of the frequency interval. If you want to trigger an email notification, enter an **E-Mail Address**. Click the **Save and Exit** button, and the list of alerts determined in the background will be sent via email to the recipient if an email address has been entered.

Figure 7.10 Alert Determination in the Background: Setup

Figure 7.11 Alert Determination in the Background: User-Specific Settings

After defining the settings for the background alert generation, you must schedule the background job with ABAP program /SAPAPO/READ_ALERTS_BATCH. The frequency of the schedule of this program should match the repeat interval maintained in the settings for the background alert generation. For example, if the frequency interval in the settings is defined as 4 hours, and the job /SAPAPO/READ_ALERTS_ BATCH is scheduled only every 8 hours, the alerts in the background will only be generated every 8 hours.

The job looks for all background overall alert profiles that are due to be redetermined per their repeat interval and then regenerates the alerts for all such profiles. In the program screen, you can either select **All Due Overall Profiles** or specific **Selected Overall Profiles**, which can be defined in the selection screen shown in Figure 7.12. If you select the **Ignore Due Dates** checkbox, irrespective of the repeat interval defined in the alert profile background settings, alerts will be generated for all profiles.

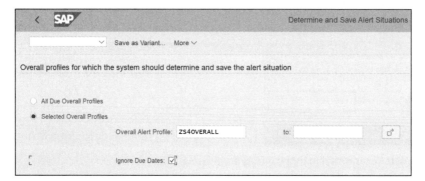

Figure 7.12 Alert Generation in the Background: Selection Options for the Batch Job

You can save the settings made in this screen as a variant by clicking on the **Save as Variant** button. Enter a **Variant Name** and a **Description** of the variant, and then save it by clicking on the **Save** button.

You can use the variant saved in the preceding step to schedule the background alert determination job with ABAP program /SAPAPO/READ_ALERTS_BATCH. After the background job determines the alerts, in the alert monitor transactions such as Transaction /SAPAPO/AMON1 or Transaction /SAPAPO/AMON3, there will be new options displayed on the screen next to the **Favorites** dropdown, which displays the list of all the profiles for which background generated alerts are available (see Figure 7.13). For one overall profile, only one set of determined alerts in the background is available at any point in time, and no historical data for the same profile is recorded. If another run of the alert determination is executed for the same overall profile, it will overwrite the results of the previous execution.

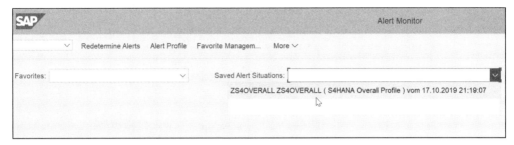

Figure 7.13 Monitoring Results of Background Alert Determination

7.2.3   Monitor Alerts from PP-DS Apps

All of the commonly used PP-DS applications support the alert monitor. The alert profile is assigned to the application profile of the corresponding application to generate the alerts.

Product View

In the product view (Transaction /SAPAPO/RRP3), the alert profile can be assigned from the initial screen of the transaction, as shown in Figure 7.14 by choosing **More · Settings · Alert Profile ❶**. Enter the **PP/DS Alert Pr.** name ❷, and click on the **Continue** button.

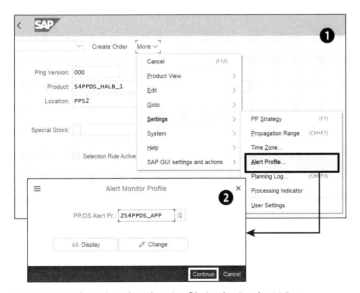

Figure 7.14 Changing the Alert Profile in the Product View

The alerts related to orders, dates, and quantities are displayed in the order views, that is, the product view, product overview, receipt, and requirement views. On the other hand, if there is an alert related to a resource capacity in which the product is manufactured, these alerts aren't displayed in the order views. The capacity-related alerts are only displayed in applications such as the DS planning board or the resource planning table.

As shown in Figure 7.15, the alerts will be in the same rows of the orders for which the alerts are raised in the product view. The **Quantity Alerts**, **Date/Time Alerts**, and **Network Alerts** columns will display the corresponding alerts. In addition, from the product view, you can navigate to the alert monitor window to take any alert-specific actions (send emails or forward alerts to another user). You can either click on the alert icon ❶ on the product view to see the details of the individual alerts ❷, or you can click on the **Alert Monitor** button on the menu bar to display all the alerts for the product location selected in the product view.

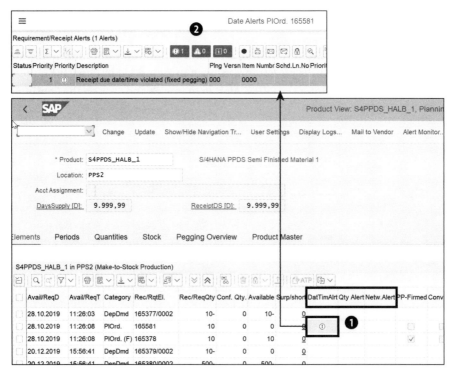

Figure 7.15 Alert Monitoring from the Product View

Product Overview

Product overview (Transaction /SAPAPO/POV1) is an excellent tool for material planners to monitor the alerts centrally for quantity, date/time, and order alerts. Like the product view, you can set the alert profile in the settings from the selection screen, as shown in Figure 7.16. You can define the selection criteria, such as duration (**Planning Horizon**) for the selection, **Location**, **Product**, **Planner** group, and so on. In addition, there is a filter (**Extended Selection**) available in the selection screen of the product overview to filter only the materials with alerts.

After the selection options are entered as shown in the upper-left area of Figure 7.16, click on the **Execute** button to see the results screen of the product overview. This screen lists all the materials with alerts and has columns displaying the highest priority alert available for the material in the corresponding row, as shown in the lower portion of Figure 7.16. In addition, the **Max. Alert** column displays the highest priority of all alerts available for that material.

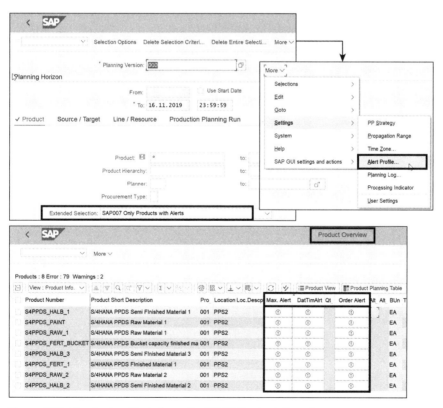

Figure 7.16 Monitoring Alerts from the PP-DS Product Overview

From the product overview, you can navigate to the product view by double-clicking on the **Product Number** in order to take actions to resolve the alerts.

Detailed Scheduling Planning Board

For monitoring alerts related to orders and capacities, you can use the alert monitor within the DS planning board (Transaction /SAPAPO/CDPS0).

In the DS planning board selection screen, click on the **Profiles** button and navigate to the **More Profiles** tab in the popup. Enter the PP-DS application alert profile that will be used in the DS planning board, and click the **OK** button or press [Enter]. After the DS planning board is loaded in the shuffler displayed on the left side of the screen, you can see the resource capacity related alerts highlighted in the resource pool, as shown in Figure 7.17. To view the details of the resource alerts and the order alerts, click on the **Alert Monitor** button in the menu bar. This will load the alert monitor in a separate window where you can take alert-specific actions. From the DS planning board, you can take actions to resolve capacity alerts by rescheduling orders to different dates, changing order quantities, and so on.

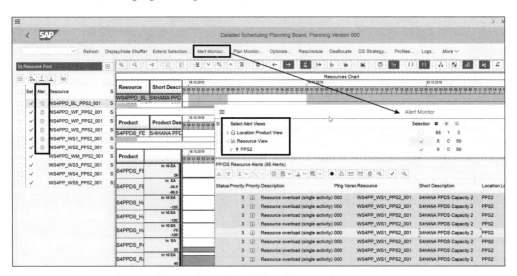

Figure 7.17 Alert Monitoring from the DS Planning Board

7.3   Summary

In this chapter, we covered the significance of the alert monitor in embedded PP-DS. We also discussed the steps to set up the alert profiles and the various options to monitor the alerts from the alert monitor, alert generation in the background, and alert monitoring from various PP-DS applications and tools.

So far in the previous chapters, we've covered all the major functionalities and features in embedded PP-DS. In the next chapter, we'll explore some special or advanced scenarios and functionalities that can be handled in embedded PP-DS.

7

Chapter 8
Advanced PP-DS Features

We've now walked through the standard features and functionalities available in your PP-DS for SAP S/4HANA system (embedded PP-DS). However, as you'll see in this chapter, some PP-DS features are designed for advanced scenarios or industry-specific requirements.

In this chapter, we'll provide the detailed steps required to deploy key PP-DS advanced features. These features use the functionalities covered in the previous chapters in addition to those discussed in this chapter. The most important advanced features—shelf-life planning, block planning, push production, and product interchangeability—will be covered in this chapter with step-by-step examples to set up these scenarios in the PP-DS system.

8.1 Planning with Shelf Life

One of the advanced feature in PP-DS that no other planning tool in any SAP system offers is shelf-life planning. Planning with shelf life is a very critical requirement for industries such as food, beverage, and pharma/life sciences.

Embedded PP-DS can consider the shelf-life date while planning and creating procurement proposals and in dynamic pegging. A receipt element in PP-DS that will expire on a certain date won't be considered for fulfilling a requirement element that is after the expiry date. In addition, if the minimum required shelf life is defined, the receipt element should have the defined minimum shelf life remaining to be considered for pegging to a requirement element.

The following PP-DS applications consider shelf life:

- **Heuristics**
  The planning of standard lots heuristic (Transaction /SAPAPO/HEU_PLAN_STAN-DARDLOTS) considers the shelf-life data defined while planning. The shelf-life data

restrictions can be violated if capacity or scheduling constraints are violated during the planning. But the alert monitor (discussed in Chapter 7) can be configured to raise an alert when the shelf-life conditions are violated.

- **Pegging**
  If shelf-life data is maintained in the product master, dynamic pegging will always consider this data while creating the pegging between the receipt and requirement elements.

- **PP-DS optimizer**
  The PP-DS optimizer considers the pegging relationship between the receipt and requirement elements that are created based on shelf life.

- **Detailed scheduling**
  The detailed scheduling (DS) strategies consider the shelf-life data in rescheduling activities and operations in order not to violate the dynamic pegging created between the receipt and requirement elements, which is created considering the shelf-life restrictions.

The steps to set up the shelf-life planning scenario in PP-DS are covered in the following sections.

8.1.1   Master Data

The master data for shelf-life planning is maintained in the material master for the SAP S/4HANA system. The required material-specific data is maintained in Transaction MM02 by navigating to the **Advanced Planning** view and the **Plant data / stor. 1** view (shown in Figure 8.1) of the material master.

Batches are commonly used to hold the shelf-life characteristics of the materials in SAP S/4HANA, and the same are transferred to embedded PP-DS along with the inventory data. The SAP S/4HANA applications, such as batch management, batch determination, and inventory management, use the shelf-life data defined in the **Plant data / stor. 1** view of the material master. The data defined here for the material is global for PP-DS and is location independent.

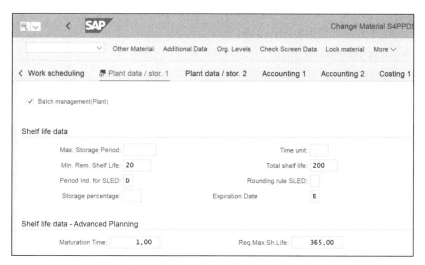

Figure 8.1 Defining Shelf-life Data in the Material Master

In the **Plant data / stor. 1** view under the **Shelf life data** section, you define the following data:

- **Min. Rem. Shelf Life**
  This is the minimum shelf life required for the product. In PP-DS, this value is considered during planning. When a receipt element doesn't have the minimum shelf life defined here, it can't be used to fulfill a receipt element.

- **Total shelf life**
  This is the value of the shelf life of the product. The expiry date of the receipt element is calculated by adding the total shelf-life duration to the date it's produced.

- **Expiration Date**
  Here you define how the shelf-life expiry is interpreted. **E** signifies the expiry date (date after which the product can't be used), and **B** signifies the best before date (date after which the product may not be usable).

Under the **Shelf life data – Advanced Planning** section in the **Plant data / stor. 1** view of the material master, you define the following values:

- **Maturation Time**
  This is the time required for the product to mature before it can be used or can be shipped out to a customer.

- **Req.Max.Sh.Life**

  The required maximum shelf life is the maximum allowed shelf life for a product that can be used for a requirement on the requirement date.

  The values defined here for a material that is relevant for advanced planning is made available to PP-DS immediately. When the total shelf life of a material is defined as more than zero, the material gets enabled for shelf-life planning in PP-DS.

The activation of the shelf-life planning and the values defined in the material master can be verified from the product master data in embedded PP-DS. As shown in Figure 8.2, from Transaction /SAPAPO/MAT1, under the **Properties** tab, the **Shelf Life** options relevant to PP-DS are displayed. This information can only be displayed from the PP-DS product master data, and the maintenance is done only from the SAP S/4HANA material master. These values are location independent.

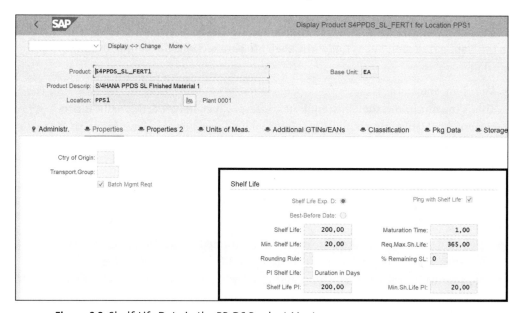

Figure 8.2 Shelf-Life Data in the PP-DS Product Master

It's also possible to maintain certain PP-DS location-specific shelf-life data in the **Advanced Planning** view of the material master. If location-specific shelf-life data is maintained in the material master, the same will be considered for planning. In the

Advanced Planning view of the material master (Transaction MM02) under the **Location Dependent Shelf-Life** section, you can select the **Shelf Life(Loc)** checkbox, and then define the total shelf life (**Loc. Shelf Life**), maturation time (**Loc. Matur.Time**), and **Min. Shelf Life/Max. Shelf Life** options, as shown in Figure 8.3.

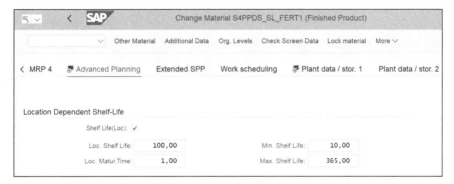

Figure 8.3 Location-Dependent PP-DS Shelf-Life Data in the Material Master

8.1.2 Integration of Batches with Shelf Life

In planning with shelf life, it's important to integrate the inventory data with the shelf-life information into PP-DS, so that they can be considered during planning. Specific prerequisites and steps are required to integrate the batches with classification (023 batch class) to PP-DS.

The advanced planning system's (PP-DS) configuration schema should be set to characteristics-dependent planning (CDP). The advanced planning configuration schema can be set or verified from the Customizing menu: **SAP IMG Menu • Advanced Planning • Basic Settings • Define Configuration Schema (CDP or Variant Configuration)**.

In SAP S/4HANA, when activating batch management, the batch level should be maintained at the material level so that the batch class type 023 can be assigned to the batches. The integration of batches with classification to PP-DS is only possible with the 023 class type. The batch level of SAP S/4HANA batch management can be set or verified from the Customizing menu, **SAP IMG Menu • Logistics – General • Batch Management • Specify Batch Level and Activate Status Management**, as shown in Figure 8.4. Select the **Batch unique at material level** option, and click the **Save** button.

Figure 8.4 Batch Management at the Material Level: Customizing

The creation of the batch class (class type 023) should follow these specifics in order
to integrate with the shelf-life data in embedded PP-DS (refer to Chapter 2, Section 2.6,
for details):

1. Create an organization area for the classification data to be used in creating the
   integration model and integrating the class to PP-DS.

2. Create a class of type 023 using Transaction CL02, and assign the organizational
   unit and the following characteristics in the **Char.** tab of the transaction (bottom
   part of Figure 8.5):

   - **LOBM_APO_SL_MAX (Max Shelf-Life/Shlf-Lfe in Sec)**
   - **LOBM_APO_SL_MIN (Min Shelf-Life/Maturity in Sec)**
   - **LOBM_APO_SL_UTC (Reference Time Stamp of Batch)**
   - **LOBM_VERAB (Availability Date)**
   - **LOBM_VFDAT (Expiration Date, Shelf Life)**
   - **LOBM_HSDAT (Date when Batch Was Produced)**

   Assignment of the **LOBM_APO_SL_MAX, LOBM_APO_SL_MIN**, and **LOBM_APO_
   SL_UTC** characteristics is mandatory because the mapping of the characteristics'
   values to PP-DS checks for these characteristics' names specifically. Without using
   these characteristics, the shelf-life data of the batches aren't integrated to PP-DS.

3. In the **Basic data** tab, assign the organizational area to the class in the **Organizational area** field.

4. In the **Char.** tab for the characteristics containing the characters **SL**, assign the
   organizational area in the **Org. Areas** column, as shown in Figure 8.5.

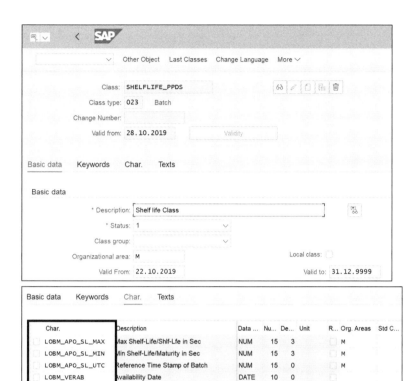

Figure 8.5 Prerequisite for Class and Characteristics

5. In SAP S/4HANA, only the **LOBM_VERAB (Availability Date)**, **LOBM_VFDAT (Expiration Date, Shelf Life)**, and **LOBM_HSDAT (Date when Batch Was Produced)** are calculated during the SAP S/4HANA material movement transactions, such as goods receipt postings. But the shelf-life characteristics are calculated in the background by the object dependencies assigned to these characteristics.

   In the standard SAP S/4HANA system, program RVBCOR08 is delivered to generate the object dependencies for these characteristics. Execute the report once in the system from Transaction SE38 or Transaction SA38.

6. After the program is executed, check the object dependencies to make sure they are created with the **Released** status. Go to the class, double-click on the characteristics, and choose **More · Extras · Object Dependencies · Assignments**, or click on the **Object Dependencies** button (the zig-zagging arrows) on the screen, as shown in Figure 8.6.

7. Check the status of the object dependency shown in Figure 8.6 by checking the value in the **S** column. In this example, the status is **1**, which means **Released**.

The object dependencies are assigned to the characteristics LOBM_VERAB, LOBM_VFDAT, and LOBM_HSDAT, which are used by the system to calculate the values for the other three characteristics, LOBM_APO_SL_MIN, LOBM_APO_SL_MAX, and LOBM_APO_SL_UTC, respectively.

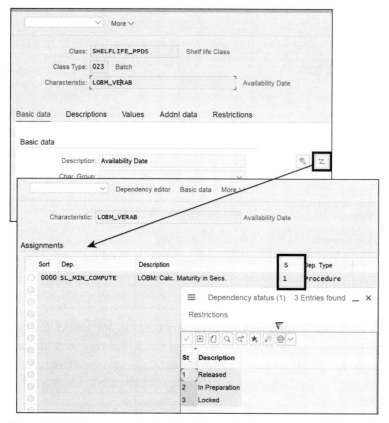

Figure 8.6 Object Dependencies for Characteristics Relevant to Shelf Life

8. Create an integration model for the organizational area assigned to the class, and activate the integration model (see Chapter 2, Section 2.1). This will create the class type 230 for use in PP-DS. You can verify that the class with class type 230 was created with the same class name in Transaction CL02.

9. Activate batch management for the material from Transaction MM02, navigate to the **Plant data / stor. 1** tab, and select the **Batch Management** checkbox.

10. Assign the batch class to the material in the material master by navigating to the **Classification** tab, entering class type "023" and the class name (in this example, "SHELFLIFE_PPDS") in the **Class** column, and activating advanced planning for the material.

After these steps are completed, when batches are created in SAP S/4HANA inventory management with shelf-life data entered, the batches are automatically transferred to PP-DS with the shelf-life information.

The batches are represented as versions in PP-DS, and the shelf-life details are displayed in the **Elements** tab of the product view (Transaction /SAPAPO/RRP3), as shown in the upper part of Figure 8.7.

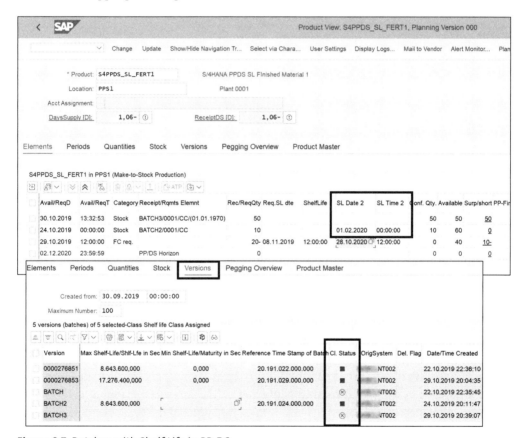

Figure 8.7 Batches with Shelf Life in PP-DS

The batches with quantities are displayed in the **Elements** tab of the product view, and the shelf-life expiry date is displayed in the **Sl.Date 2** column. If batches are created without the shelf-life classification data in SAP S/4HANA, those batches won't have any shelf life calculated in the PP-DS.

> **Note**
>
> In SAP S/4HANA, the shelf-life data maintained in the material master **Plant data / stor. 1** view is considered for calculating the shelf-life expiry for batches, and the same is transferred to PP-DS. The location-specific shelf-life data maintained in the **Advanced Planning** tab is only considered by PP-DS applications for objects created by PP-DS, such as planned orders, dependent demands, and so on.

In the **Versions** tab of the product view, all available batches for the material are displayed. As shown on the lower part of Figure 8.7, the green icon on the **Cl.Status** column indicates that the batch is classified correctly.

8.1.3   Pegging and Planning

While generating the dynamic pegging relationships for materials with shelf-life data, the system checks for the compatibility of the requirement element and the maturation time, as well as the shelf life of a receipt or stock element. Only compatible elements will participate in pegging relationships. The batch stocks without the correct classification for shelf-life data can only be assigned to requirement elements without any shelf-life requirement conditions.

When a receipt element such as a batch is available in PP-DS, the system considers its expiry date and the minimum shelf-life requirements to create dynamic pegging. For example, as shown in Figure 8.8, a forecast demand element is created with a requirement date of **31.01.2020**, and the system calculates the minimum shelf life required as **10.02.2020** by adding the **Min. Shelf Life** (10 days) to the requirement date (**31.01.2020**) ❶ and the required maximum shelf life as 30.02.2020 by adding the **Max. Shelf Life** (365 days) to the requirement date (**30.01.2021**) ❷. These dates are calculated from the location-specific shelf-life data maintained in the **Advanced Planning** view of the material master, as shown in Figure 8.9. Because none of the available receipts fulfill these shelf-life requirements from the demand elements, no dynamic pegging is established for this forecast.

If there is a receipt element with a shelf-life expiry date between **10.02.2020** and **30.01.2021**, then the forecast element will be pegged to that receipt element.

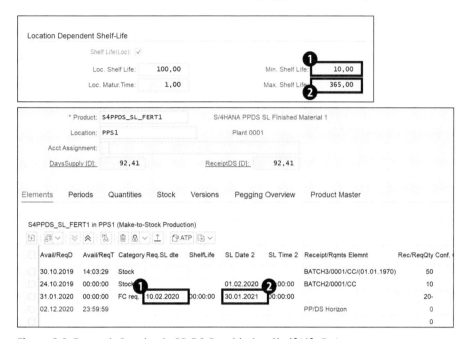

Figure 8.8 Dynamic Pegging in PP-DS Considering Shelf-Life Data

Figure 8.9 Pegging Considering Shelf Life: No Pegging without Suitable Elements

The planning of standard lots heuristic algorithm (/SAPAPO/HEU_PLAN_STAN-DARDLOTS; see Chapter 5, Section 5.3.1) in PP-DS supports planning of products with shelf-life requirements. In the standard system, heuristic planning of standard lots with shelf life (SAP_PP_SLO01) is delivered and can be assigned as the product heuristic for the relevant products, as shown in Figure 8.10. The **Plan with Shelf Life** setting in the **Planning of Std Lots with Shelf Life** heuristic screen, as shown in Figure 8.10, is required for the shelf life to be considered during planning using this heuristics.

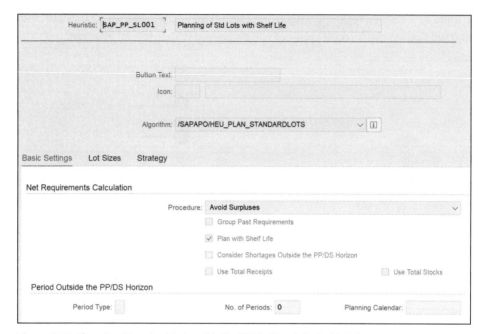

Figure 8.10 Planning Standard Lots with Shelf Life Heuristic in PP-DS

During net requirement calculation using the SAP_PP_SLOO1 heuristic, the compatibility of the receipt elements and requirement with respect to maturation time, minimum/maximum shelf life, and shelf-life expiry dates is considered. If there are fixed receipts without shelf-life compatibility for any of the requirement elements, excess receipts will result.

The following rules are applied to check for the compatibility of the stock or receipt element and the requirement elements:

- **Maturation time**
  The stock or receipt element must have completed the maturation time by the requirements date.

- **Minimum shelf life**
  The stock or receipt element must not expire at least before the required minimum shelf life of the requirements element.

- **Maximum shelf life**
  The stock or receipt element can have an expiry date at most until the required maximum shelf life of the requirements element.

8.2   Product Interchangeability

During the life of a product in product lifecycle management, there will changes required to the components of the materials. These changes could be due to a supplier stopping a specific component; due to safety, quality, or product improvement issues; or due to a regulatory mandate. These changes require components or products to be discontinued and substituted with a successor product or component.

In SAP S/4HANA, the discontinuation of a material and assigning a follow-up material can be done from the **MRP 4** view of the material master. However, this method has restrictions, such as the inability to create multilevel discontinuations (material B replaces material A, and then material C replaces material B) and that control for the use of existing stock for discontinued material may also require updating the discontinuation information in the bill of material (BOM) master data for material requirements planning (MRP) to consider the discontinuation. But SAP S/4HANA discontinuation supports certain functionalities such as parallel discontinuation, where a group of components can be replaced by another group of components with the discontinuation group assigned in the BOM master data. This isn't supported in PP-DS product interchangeability.

The interchangeability in PP-DS should only be considered for planning purposes during the transition period from the discontinued component to the replacement component. The existence of an interchangeability group won't eliminate the requirement to update the BOM master data, which is used by other areas, such as product costing, in SAP S/4HANA.

Embedded PP-DS supports the discontinuation and substitution via the product interchangeability functionality; detailed scheduling supports the discontinuation via the linear supersession chain where only one product in the chain is valid at any given point in time. The procurement planning (both in-house and external procurement) and order processing are supported in PP-DS interchangeability. It's also possible to use the use-up strategy in PP-DS product interchangeability to control whether the existing stock can be used to cover requirements until the stock completely depletes for the discontinued material or whether the discontinuation is in effect without consideration of the existing stock.

Following are some of the restrictions applicable to PP-DS product interchangeability:

- Embedded PP-DS only supports simple interchangeability (1:1). Configurable products can't participate in interchangeability.

- For integrating manufacturing orders with product substitutions, the interchangeability should not have multiple substitutions within one chain (e.g., product A – B – C).

- If shelf-life planning is in use, all the products in the interchangeability chain should have the same shelf-life conditions.

Now, let's go through the relevant master data to see how interchangeability works in the planning process.

8.2.1   Master Data

PP-DS product interchangeability works based on the following master data objects, which we'll discuss in this section:

- Interchangeability group (supersession chain)
- Assignment of the interchangeability group to the supply chain model
- Automatic generation and assignment of planning packages

Interchangeability Group

You create the interchangeability group of type supersession chain using Transaction /INCMD/UI or using the **SAP Easy Access** menu path: **Logistics · Advanced Planning · Master Data · Product and Location Interchangeability · Interchangeability Group**.

As shown in Figure 8.11, in the interchangeability transaction, the screen has four main sections:

- **Quick Search**
  This can be used for searching the existing interchangeability groups in the system; the search results are displayed at the bottom of the screen.

- **Header**
  The interchangeability group header has the **Group Type** (only supersession chain is supported in PP-DS), **Group** name, **Group Description**, and **Relevant for** fields. In the SAP S/4HANA 1909 system, advanced available-to-promise (aATP) and PP-DS aren't directly integrated, so select **1 Planning** in the **Relevant for** field. The **Status** is set to **In Process** when the group is created and saved without releasing the same. You can use the **Release** button on the menu bar to set the **Status** to **Released**.

Figure 8.11 Interchangeability Group in PP-DS

- **Location**

  In the **Location** tab, assign the locations for which the interchangeability group is relevant. The materials being maintained in the interchangeability group should be available in the locations defined in the **Location** tab of the header data.

- **Details**

  The **Details** section of the interchangeability transaction screen contains the details of the materials that are assigned as the preceding and succeeding materials in the interchangeability group and the attributes of the interchangeability relationship.

After the header data is entered, navigate to the **Location-Independent Attributes** section under **Details**, and click on the **Append Row** button (new document symbol icon) on the toolbar to add a new row. You can enter the details of the preceding and succeeding materials and the attributes in the row by clicking the number in the **Item No.** column and arriving at the **Basic Data** tab, as shown in Figure 8.12. You also can click the row in the **Attributes** tab, and the row will be expanded into a new screen, as shown in Figure 8.13.

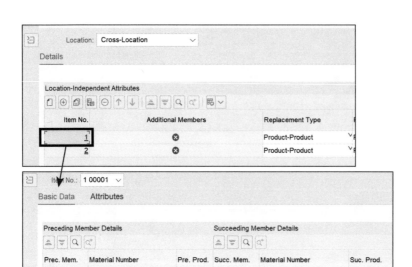

Figure 8.12 Maintenance of Interchangeability Group Details: Basic Data

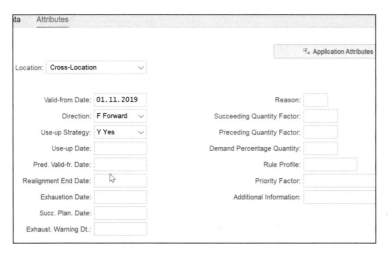

Figure 8.13 Maintenance of Interchangeability Group: Attributes

As shown in Figure 8.13, the group details can be maintained at a **Cross-Location** level or **Location-Specific** level in the **Location** dropdown. The cross-location details maintained are applicable for all locations assigned to the interchangeability header, and the products participate in interchangeability maintained in the details. If there is a requirement to maintain different values for specific plants, then select the location from the **Location** dropdown menu, and maintain the details. For example, material A is replaced by material B in plant 1, 2, and 3 from 01.Jan.2020. However, in plant 2, if the interchangeability is valid only from 01.Feb.2020, the same can be maintained as a location-specific **Valid-from Date** in the attributes.

PP-DS only supports linear supersession chains, which means that the chain can have only one preceding and succeeding material. Multiple interchangeability (nonlinear supersession chain) isn't supported in PP-DS, where a product has several successor products (1:N), or several products have one successor product (N:1). The materials participating in the supersession chain should follow these prerequisites:

- The materials in the supersession chain have to be different. Material A-B-A isn't supported.
- The supersession chain may not contain any assemblies.
- A material can only be contained in one supersession chain. When a material that is part of another interchangeability group is assigned to a supersession chain, the system will raise an error message.
- The base unit of measure must be the same for all materials in a supersession chain.
- A supersession chain may not contain any configurable products.
- The shelf-life data must be the same for all products in a supersession chain.

In the **Basic Data** tab (refer to Figure 8.12), enter the material to be discontinued in the **Material Number** field under **Preceding Member Details**, and enter the material that will replace the discontinued material in the **Material Number** field under **Succeeding Member Details**.

In the **Attributes** tab (refer to Figure 8.13), enter the date in the **Valid-from Date** from which the system should consider the interchangeability to switch the requirements of the discontinued material to the follow-up material. The interchangeability **Direction** field has two options:

- Full
  The preceding and succeeding materials can interchange each other.
- Forward
  The succeeding material will replace the preceding material from the valid-from date.

The value defined in the **Use-up Strategy** field is used to determine how the existing stock for the preceding material is treated. The options are as follows:

- **Yes**

  Use the existing stock first; only when the stock is depleted, switch over the demand for the preceding material to the succeeding material.

- **No**

  Irrespective of the existing stock for the preceding material, switch over the demand from the preceding material to the succeeding material on the valid-from date.

- **Restricted**

  With a restricted use-up strategy, a **Use-up Date** can be defined, and the existing stock of the preceding material is used up only until the use-up date.

The **Succeeding Quantity Factor** and **Preceding Quantity Factor** are used in scenarios where the replacement quantity factors between the preceding and succeeding material isn't equal. For example, material A replaces material B, but two quantities of material B are required to replace 1 quantity of material A. In this case, the **Preceding Quantity Factor** is defined as **1**, and the **Succeeding Quantity Factor** is defined as **2**.

Set the status of the interchangeability group to **Released** by clicking on the **Release** button in the menu bar of the screen, and click the **Save** button to save the interchangeability group data.

Assign the Interchangeability Group to a Model

For a released interchangeability group to be considered for planning, it must be assigned to the supply chain model. In embedded PP-DS, 000 is the active model. You can assign the group to the 000 model by executing Transaction /SAPAPO/INCMD_ MODEL or navigating to the transaction via the **SAP Easy Access** menu: **Logistics · Advanced Planning · Master Data · Product and Location Interchangeability · Assign Interchangeability Group to a Model**.

Enter the **Interchangeability Group** in the initial screen, and click on the **Execute** button, as shown in the upper-left screen of Figure 8.14. On the **Assignment of interchangeability group model** popup screen, all the available models defined in the system are listed. Select **Model Name 000**, and click on the **Assign Objects to Model** button (to the right of the green checkmark) to assign the interchangeability group to the model 000.

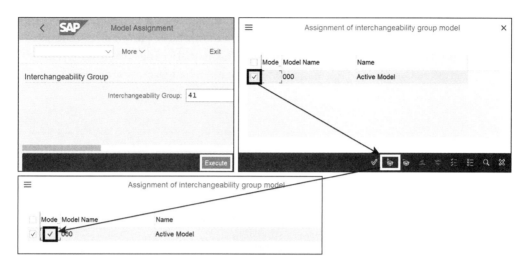

Figure 8.14 Assigning the Interchangeability Group to Model 000

Planning Packages

When materials are assigned to supersession chains, these materials must be planned together. When executing MRP in PP-DS or executing product heuristics, it's essential that all the materials in the chain are planned together to avoid any excess supply being created for the materials. When the interchangeability groups are assigned with a location in the interchangeability master data, the system automatically creates a planning package and assigns it to all the materials in the material master **Advanced Planning** view.

> **Note**
>
> Planning packages can also be used in regular planning scenarios if there is a requirement to plan certain materials together irrespective of their position in the BOMs (low-level codes). For interchangeability, a special planning package type 001 is delivered in the standard system.

For the automatic generation of the planning packages, several Customizing entries are delivered in standard embedded PP-DS.

The planning package type can be verified from the Customizing menu path: **SAP IMG Menu · Advanced Planning · MRP Planning Run · Maintain Planning Package Types**. As shown in Figure 8.15, the **Heuristic SAP_PP_I001** is assigned to **Package Type 001**. This heuristic calls the product heuristics assigned to the material in the material master for all the materials in the supersession chain in the correct order, and the product heuristics will decide which requirements are to be passed on to the successor product from the discontinued product. The heuristics will also consider settings such as the **Use-up Strategy** maintained in the interchangeability group master data.

Figure 8.15 Planning Package Type: Customizing

Setting the **Automat. Maintenance** checkbox in Customizing for the **001** package type enables the system to generate and update the material master with the planning package automatically.

In addition, the number range for the automatically generated planning packages must be maintained via the Customizing menu path: **SAP IMG Menu • Advanced planning • MRP Planning Run • Maintain Number Ranges for Automatically Generated Planning Packages**.

The planning packages that are automatically created by the system via the supersession chains can't be edited manually. When the materials are removed from the supersession chain, the materials are also removed from the planning package. The planning packages can be displayed from Transaction /SAPAPO/HEUR2 or from the **SAP Easy Access** menu path: **Logistics • Advanced Planning • Master Data • Product and Location Interchangeability • Define Planning Package**. As shown on the upper screen in Figure 8.16, the materials that are part of the supersession chain are listed in the product selection (**ProdSelection**) for the planning package. Note the **Plan. package** field at the top of the screen with the interchangeability group number as its description. In addition, in the material master, the planning package values are updated as shown in Figure 8.16 on the lower screen.

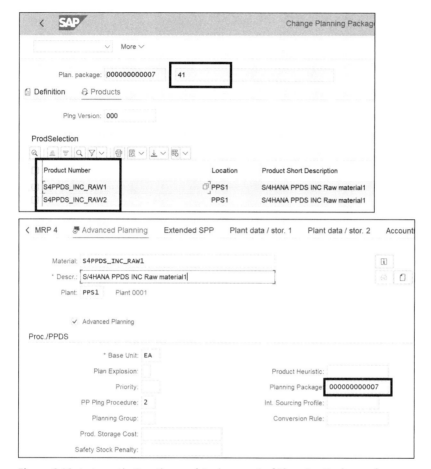

Figure 8.16 Automatic Creation and Assignment of Planning Packages for Interchangeability Group

8.2.2   Interchangeability in Planning Process

Materials involved in interchangeability can be planned via MRP runs in the production planning run, interactive planning by executing the product heuristics in the planning tools, or automatic planning triggered by the planning procedure definition.

In all these cases, the system considers the planning package and always executes supersession chain heuristic (SAP_PP_I001), which in turn will call the product heuristics assigned to the material master.

In the planning package created by the interchangeability group, the sequence of materials is also maintained according to the interchangeable direction (predecessor material first and successor material next). When MRP is executed for one material in the planning package, it automatically reads the package and executes planning for all the materials in the package according to the sequence of materials within the planning package.

In the PP-DS planning run, for the interchangeable products to the planned correctly, one prerequisite is that the MRP heuristics should have the setting to execute the product heuristics in the heuristics customization. In addition, while defining the planning steps in the production planning run, you must ensure that none of the interchangeable materials are part of a planning step that executed a procurement planning heuristic (e.g., planning of standard lots [SAP_PP_002]) other than MRP heuristics. By executing a procurement heuristics other than MRP heuristics, the planning package sequence of materials can't be ensured, and the planning results may be incorrect.

During the planning, the requirement of the predecessor product may need to be covered by the successor product based on the validity of the supersession chain and the use-up strategy maintained in the interchangeability group. In this case, the system will generate an order of type substitution order (**Subst.ord**) to transfer the demand from the predecessor (**RAW1**) to the successor material to cover the **DepDmd**, as shown in the **Elements** tab in Figure 8.17 ❶. The substitution order will have the predecessor material as an input (**RAW2** under **Requirements**) and the successor material as an output component (**RAW1** under **Receipts**) in the order ❷. The substitution orders can't be manually changed, and these are considered unfirmed orders for the purpose of planning, so that the planning run can adjust them per the demand and supply situation.

A pegging relationship is established between the original requirement element (in Figure 8.17, the **DepDmd**) and the substitution order. So during detailed scheduling activities, if the strategy profile is set to respect dynamic pegging, then the substitution orders can also be rescheduled along with the requirement element.

[»]

Note

MRP Live (Transaction MD01N) can't plan products with interchangeability, so a PP-DS planning run with MRP heuristics must be executed for such materials.

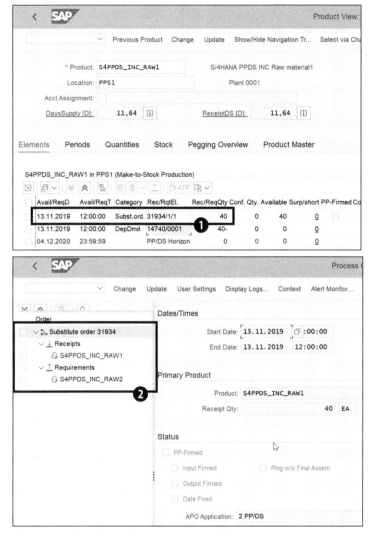

Figure 8.17 Planning with Interchangeability

Because the substitution orders aren't transferred to SAP S/4HANA, the demand and supply situation in transactions such as the stock requirements list (Transaction MD04) may state excess supply for the predecessor product and supply deficiency for the successor product. Therefore, it's essential that only PP-DS planning tools are used to monitor and plan these materials.

For in-house production orders with interchangeable components, it's mandatory that the planned orders are set with the conversion checkbox in embedded PP-DS so that the interchangeability is taken into account in the manufacturing order (production order or process order).

As shown in Figure 8.18, if there is an interchangeable component, the original component (predecessor) ❶ (RAW1 and RAW3) are listed in the production order (Transaction CO03) **Component Overview** screen with **0** quantity. The interchanged component (successor component) ❷ (RAW2 and RAW4) will be listed in the **Component Overview** screen with the original component requirement quantity of the corresponding predecessor materials, respectively.

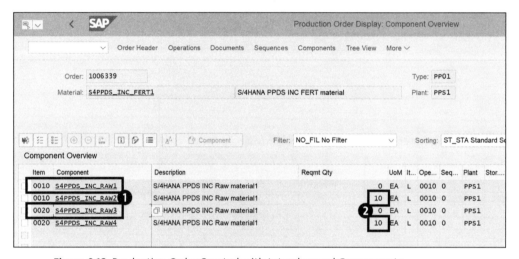

Figure 8.18 Production Order Created with Interchanged Components

8.3   Characteristics-Dependent Planning

As discussed in Chapter 2, Section 2.6, and Chapter 3, Section 3.2.4, embedded PP-DS supports variant configuration (VC) or characteristics-dependent planning (CDP). CDP can also be used in make-to-stock (MTS) scenarios. All the supply and demand elements, such as forecast elements, planned orders, production orders, and stocks/ batches, have their own classification (assignment of characteristics values), and PP-DS supports planning that considers these characteristics value assignments. When determining the net requirement calculation, the system checks the compatibility of the characteristics values and creates receipts if there are no matching receipt elements available to fulfill demand elements with specific characteristics values. In addition, the characteristics value compatibility is considered while creating pegging relationships.

Along with the material master classification, the classification master data—such as the object dependencies that are created in SAP S/4HANA to control the material and operation selections in BOMs and routings—can also be sent to the corresponding production data structure (PDS) master data in PP-DS.

Note

Conversion from VC to CDP or vice versa can be performed in embedded PP-DS using ABAP program /SAPAPO/CONFR_CFGREL_MAINTAIN. Caution should be exercised, however, when doing the conversion after master data and/or transaction data has already been created in the system because the conversion may lead to inconsistencies and/or data loss. The report performs a where-used list for finding the materials that will be impacted; if no inconsistencies are detected, it will complete the conversion. Adjustment of the materials to reassign the correct classification (classes of the correct type) must be done manually as a post step. In addition, the transaction data must be retransferred to PP-DS from SAP S/4HANA.

In the next sections, we'll cover how PP-DS planning and pegging processes consider the characteristics and also the steps to set up block planning.

8.3.1   Planning and Pegging

When embedded PP-DS is set with the CDP configuration schema, the system considers the characteristics value for the calculation of the net requirement for a product location to determine the deficit in supply quantity.

In the SAP S/4HANA material master, as shown in Figure 8.19 ❶, the material is assigned with **Class Type 300** (variant class). Upon integration (see Chapter 2, Section 2.6), this will create **Class type 400** (CDP classification) in PP-DS, as shown in Figure 8.19 ❷. The material is also set as a configurable material in the SAP S/4HANA material master (Transaction MM02) by setting the **Material is Configurable** checkbox under the **Client Specific Configuration** section in the **Basic Data 2** tab. The configuration relevance and classification of the material in PP-DS can be displayed from the PP-DS product master (Transaction /SAPAPO/MAT1) ❸.

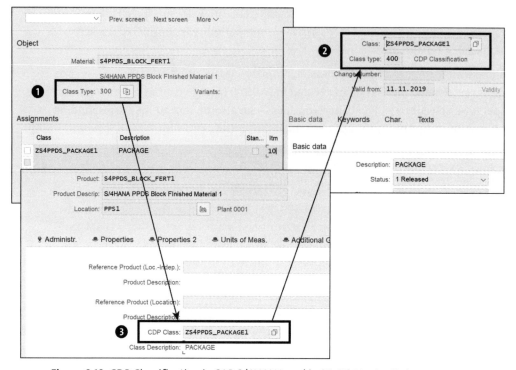

Figure 8.19 CDP Classification in SAP S/4HANA and in PP-DS Master Data

Heuristics such as the planning of standard lots heuristic can consider the characteristics value during planning. Any demand or supply element created for the CDP materials in PP-DS contains the classification (characteristics values), which is represented by a small triangle symbol in PP-DS transactions such as the product view, as shown in Figure 8.20. Clicking on the icon shows the characteristics values assigned to the demand element ❶ or the supply element ❷.

The pegging links dynamically generated by the system also consider the characteristics value, and no pegging link will be established between demand and supply elements that don't have the same characteristics values. As shown in Figure 8.21, in the **Pegging Overview** tab, although there are more supply elements present for this example material, no pegging is created because there is no supply element with the matching characteristics value of the demand elements. In our example, the supply elements have the characteristics value of 100 GM, and all the receipt elements have the characteristics value of 200 GM.

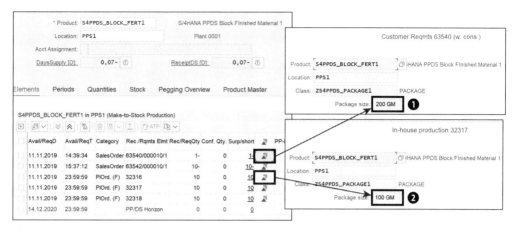

Figure 8.20 Pegging in a CDP Scenario Considering Characteristics Values

Figure 8.21 Pegging in CDP: No Pegging Created without Compatible Elements

With the previous demand and supply situation, if a planning heuristics such as the planning of standard lots is executed, it will create additional supply elements to fulfill the sales order demands. Like the shelf-life planning heuristic, this may result in excess supply being created for the material in question. But if the configuration (characteristics value – 200 GM packaging) is different for the customer order, and it can't be fulfilled with the receipt elements (planned orders – 100 GM packaging), the system will create additional supply elements to satisfy the sales order demand, as shown in Figure 8.22.

In our example, the receipt elements (sales orders) have the characteristics value of 200 GM, so the planning heuristic has created two receipt elements with the same characteristics value (**200 GM**), although there are other receipt elements present (the planned orders **32316**, **32317**, and **31318**) that don't have a matching characteristics value to fulfill the sales order demand elements.

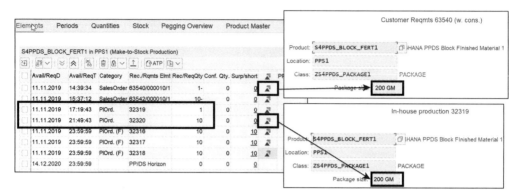

Figure 8.22 Planning Heuristics Considering Characteristics for Creating New Receipt Elements

Now, if you go to the **Pegging Overview** tab, you can see that the sales orders and planned orders that have the same characteristics values are pegged to each other, as shown in Figure 8.23.

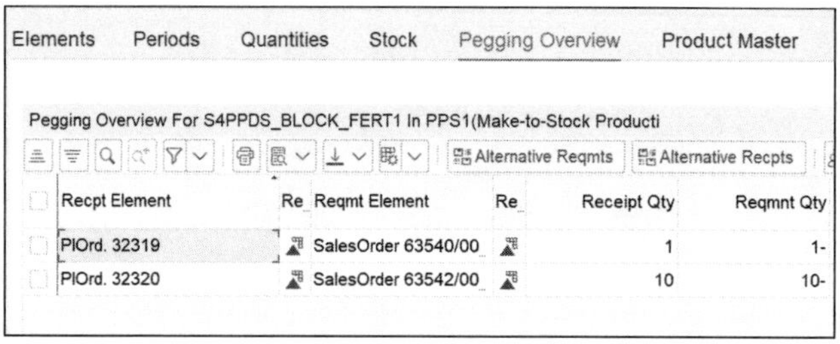

Figure 8.23 CDP: Pegging Considering Characteristics Values

8.3.2   Block Planning

One of the commonly used features of PP-DS in CDP is block planning. Block planning is the preassignment of capacities to produce materials belonging to certain characteristics. This is widely used in mill production (paper, metal, etc.).

In process-oriented manufacturing, when the manufacturing process for a product has started, it can't be interrupted or stopped due to the nature of manufacturing processes. In such cases, a preassigned capacity for the manufacturing resource is created via a campaign. This process is called *campaign planning*. A campaign is created for the resource in PP-DS, and a group of orders is assigned to the campaign. In addition, the setup and cleanup orders can be created at the start and end of the production campaign. The orders in the campaigns can be determined via the setup groups assigned to the operations of the orders, which in turn results in similar products and their orders being assigned to the campaign.

In discrete manufacturing, however, materials must be grouped based on the operation and resource in which the material is being produced. For example, a product may go through multiple operations, and if there is a bottleneck resource that requires considerable setup for switching the products, the schedule of that work center must be frozen to preassign its capacity to perform operations with certain characteristics. In PP-DS, this can be achieved via block planning. In block planning, blocks are created in the resources with specific characteristics, and operations with the same characteristics values will be scheduled in those blocks.

For campaign planning in process industries, the campaigns can also be integrated to SAP S/4HANA. However, in block planning, the blocks are only relevant in PP-DS, and only the schedule of the operation and the order are integrated back to SAP S/4HANA.

Master Data

The materials for which block planning is to be executed are assigned with class type 300 (variant class), which will generate class type 400 (CDP classification) in embedded PP-DS.

The blocks are created in the resource master data in PP-DS. You create the work center master data in SAP S/4HANA and activate the **Advanced Planning** checkbox in the **Basic Data** view of the work center master data (see Chapter 2, Section 2.4). This will integrate the work center into the resource master data on the PP-DS side. When resources are created in PP-DS, they are assigned to the 000 model and the 000 version, which are the active model and version in PP-DS. In addition, model-independent resource master data is generated.

Maintain Blocks

To create blocks for resources, the first step is to create the basic definition and reference cycle, which we'll discuss in this section. You can maintain blocks of the resource master data in PP-DS using the resource master Transaction /SAPAPO/RES01. The block basis definition is maintained at the model-independent resource. On the initial screen of the resource master data, select the **Model-Independent Selection** checkbox, as shown on the upper screen of Figure 8.24, and press ⌜Enter⌟. In the next screen, you'll see the resource master data that is assigned to the 000 version as well as the model-independent (no version assigned) resource data, as shown on the lower screen in Figure 8.24.

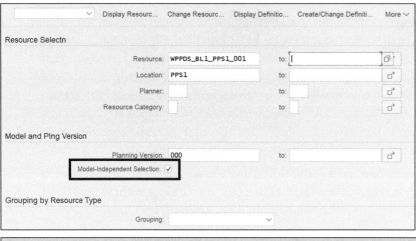

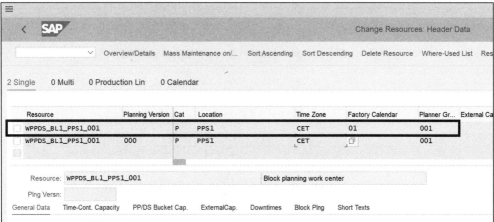

Figure 8.24 Model-Independent Resource Master Data

Now, in the model-independent resource master data, navigate to the **Block Plng** (block planning) tab, and assign the **CDP Class** (class type 400), in which the characteristics required to create the blocks are assigned (see upper area of Figure 8.25). Click on the **Create Blocks** button to launch the **Maintain Blocks** screen (see lower area of Figure 8.25).

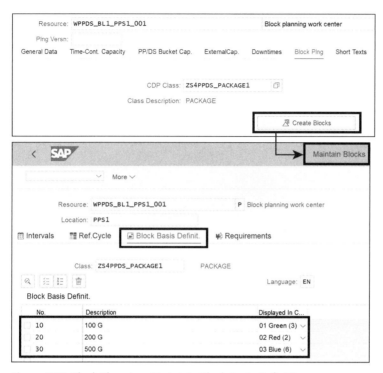

Figure 8.25 Block Planning: Maintain Block Basis Definition

In this screen, navigate to the **Block Basis Definit.** tab. List the block definitions by entering a number (**No.**) for the block and a **Description**; for example, in Figure 8.25, there are three block definitions maintained as **100 G**, **200 G**, and **500 G**. You also can set a color representation for these blocks in the **Displayed in C** column, which will be displayed in the DS planning board to visually differentiate one block from another.

You can assign the characteristics value associated with the block definition by selecting a block that is maintained and navigating to the **Requirements** tab, as shown in Figure 8.26. Assign a characteristics value for the defined block, and assign the characteristics values to all the blocks that are defined in the block basis definition, as shown in Figure 8.26. You can only assign values for the characteristics that are already defined in the classification master data, as shown in Figure 8.27.

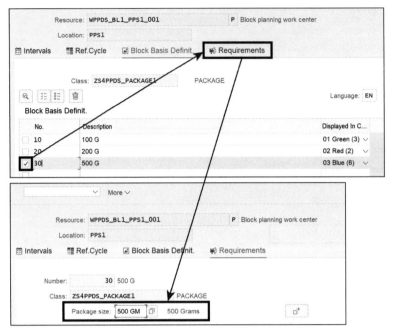

Figure 8.26 Assigning Characteristics Values to Defined Blocks

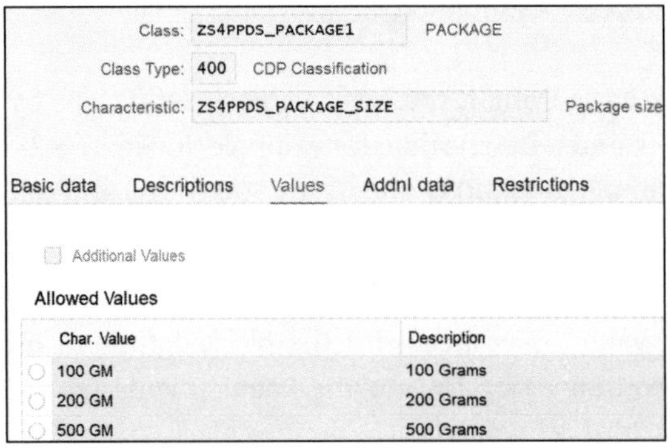

Figure 8.27 Example: Characteristics Values Defined in the Master Data

After the block basic definition is defined, the next step is to create reference cycles to define in what sequence the blocks are to be created on the resource capacity and the length (duration) of the individual blocks. Navigate to the **Ref.Cycle** tab (see Figure 8.28), and enter a **Sequence** number for the blocks to be created on the resource capacity. Enter the duration of the block in **Days (Length)**, **Time (Length)**, or

Equivalent **[s]** (seconds). If the blocks can be consumed by operations over its regular operating capacity, you can also define by what percentage overloads are allowed by maintaining the overload percentage in the **Rel. Overl** column. Then, in the **Number** column, enter the block number that was defined in the block basis definition, as shown in Figure 8.28. Click the **Save** button to save the block and reference cycle definition.

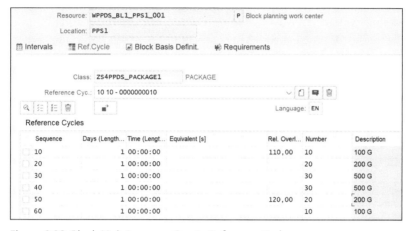

Figure 8.28 Block Maintenance: Create Reference Cycle

This completes the block master data maintenance.

Assign Block Intervals

The next step is to assign the block definition to the model-dependent resource master data. To do so, navigate to the resource master data by double-clicking on the resource assigned to the 000 version in the list of resources displayed in the **Change Resource: Header Data** screen (from Transaction /SAPAPO/RES01). Navigate to the **Block Planning** tab, and click on the **Maintain Blocks** button. In the **Maintain Blocks** screen, navigate to the **Intervals** tab, as shown on the left in Figure 8.29. You can add individual blocks (no reference to the reference cycle) by clicking on the **Insert Block** button ❶. In the **New Date (Valid To)** popup screen, fill in the **Preceding To (Date)** field and the time stamp in the **To (Time)** field, with the date and time until which you want the blocks to be generated on the resource. If the **Observe Productive Time** checkbox is selected, the blocks will be created by respecting the productive working times of the resource. Click on the **Execute** button to generate the corresponding block as shown in Figure 8.30 ❶.

You can insert the reference cycle by clicking on the **Insert Reference Cycle** button as shown in Figure 8.29 ❷. This will take you to the **Insert Reference Cycle as of** popup screen, where you can select the reference cycle from the **Reference Cycle** dropdown. Enter the date and time for which you want to insert the reference cycle in the **Preceding To (Date)** and the **To (Time)** fields, respectively. In the **Insert** field, enter the number of times you want to insert the reference cycle into the resource. If you select the **Overwrite, if Necessary** checkbox, the existing block definition on the resource will be overwritten by the reference cycle being inserted. Click on the **Execute** button, and you'll see that the blocks are inserted per the reference cycle definition, as shown in Figure 8.30 ❷.

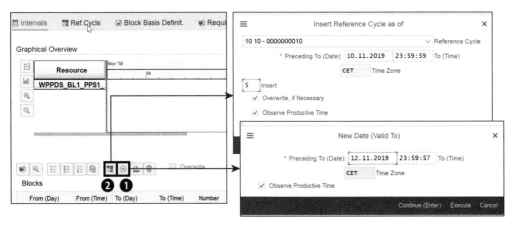

Figure 8.29 Block Planning: Maintain Block Intervals

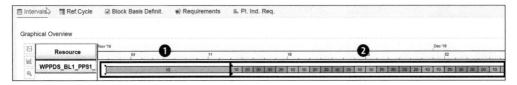

Figure 8.30 Block Planning: Display of Blocks in Block Maintenance

After the block intervals are maintained in the resource master, you can transfer the PDS master data from SAP S/4HANA to embedded PP-DS using Transaction /SAPAPO/CURTOADV_CREATE. If the resource assigned to the operation/activity of the PDS has block planning, the same is also assigned to the activity of the PDS, as shown in Figure 8.31. This enables the scheduling of the activities with characteristics on the blocks set with the same characteristics values.

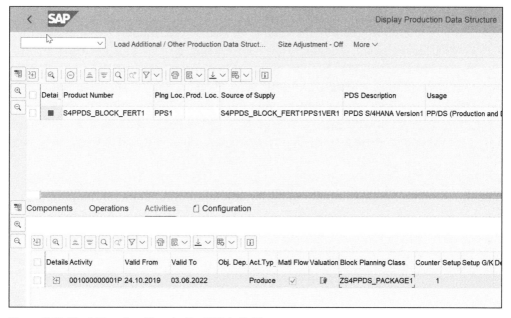

Figure 8.31 Block Planning Class in the PDS Activities

[+]

Tip

If the PDS master data is transferred before the resource classification is maintained for block planning, the PDS must be retransferred (absolute transfer) after the resource classification.

In SAP S/4HANA, object dependencies are defined to select the relevant components and operations depending on the classification of the receipt element being created. If there are object dependencies assigned to the BOM and routing master data, the same is transferred to the PDS in PP-DS. In PDS, the object dependencies can be evaluated at the operation level or at the activity level. The prerequisite for integrating the object dependency data is that the object dependency master data in SAP S/4HANA is assigned to the correct dependency groups.

The object dependency is only evaluated at the operation in PP-DS if you've assigned the dependency group SAPAPOOPR. The object dependency is only evaluated at the activity in PP-DS if you've assigned the dependency group SAPAPOACT.

Blocks in Planning and in Scheduling

When orders are created by planning heuristics or manually, the operations for which block planning-relevant resources are assigned will be scheduled on the corresponding block on the resource. In the strategy profile (refer to Chapter 6, Section 6.2.1), select **Take Into Account** in the **Block Planning** field, as shown in Figure 8.32. Blocks can also be set with fixing indicators; in this case, no new activities can be automatically scheduled in those blocks. To ignore the block fixings, choose **2 Take Into Account, Ignore Block Fixings** from the **Block Planning** field in the strategy profile.

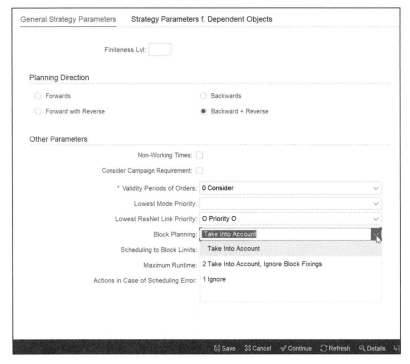

Figure 8.32 Block Planning: Strategy Profile Settings

The blocks can be displayed from the DS planning board (Transaction /SAPAPO/CDPS0; see Chapter 6, Section 6.4.1). Although the demand elements are on the same date/time, when the production planning heuristic is creating the receipt elements as mandated by the strategy profile, the blocks are considered, and orders are scheduled to place them on the correct blocks (with matching characteristics values).

In the DS planning board, the blocks are visually represented by the color set for the block definition in the master data. The orders are placed within the blocks as displayed in Figure 8.33. You can right-click on the graphical element of the blocks in the planning board to navigate to the block maintenance. From the block maintenance, the blocks can be created, changed, (extend/shrink duration), or deleted. In this example, you can see the characteristic value 100 GM ❶, 200 GM ❷, and 500 GM ❸ that we've used throughout this chapter.

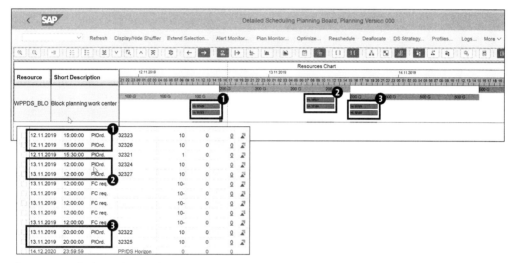

Figure 8.33 Blocks in the DS Planning Board and Assignment of Orders to the Blocks

From the DS planning board, the following heuristics are supported for the maintenance of blocks:

- **SAP_CDPBP_01 (reschedule blocks)**
  This heuristic can be used in situations where the block definitions or the schedule has changed, and the operations on the impacted blocks need to be rescheduled.

- **SAP_CDPBP_02 (adjust and reschedule block limits)**
  When there are overload or underload situations, the adjust and reschedule block limits heuristic can be executed to extend or to shrink the blocks and schedule the operations within these blocks accordingly.

- **SAP_CDPBP_03 (enhanced block maintenance)**
  This heuristics calls up the block maintenance screen for adjustment (creation, change) of the existing blocks on the resource.

8.4   Push Production

Push production is the process of creating a production plan to consume excess supply of a material. Push production is a purely manual process to create a production plan to consume materials with no requirements. The push production tool helps in making decisions to consume such products.

In a typical production planning scenario, the requirements of the lower-level materials in the BOM levels are determined by the demand of the materials in the higher levels of the BOM structure. Push production works in the opposite way by finding the higher-level materials that can be produced using the lower-level materials.

In industries such as dairy, food processing, and so on, raw materials are procured based on long-term contracts, and a slight reduction in the demand for certain finished products or a production scheduling problem such as machine breakdown to produce a specific product can result in an oversupply of raw materials. In addition, the shelf life of such raw materials plays a major role in determining if there is a push problem for a material. For products with excess coverage, a low shelf life is required to consume the material or to convert it into another material with a higher shelf life.

In this section, we'll cover the details on how to identify a push problem in the supply chain and how the push production tool can help in resolving the same.

8.4.1   Identify the Push Problem

The primary tool for identifying the push problem is the alert monitor (refer to Chapter 7). In the alert monitor, you activate the alert **Order creates surplus** under the **Order Alerts – Product Dependent** alert type. Enter the threshold for the **Variance in %** of the required versus excess receipts, as shown in Figure 8.34.

Planners can also monitor such materials from the product view (Transaction /SAPAPO/ RRP3) or from the product overview (Transaction /SAPAPO/POV1) to identify materials causing excess supply and trigger push production.

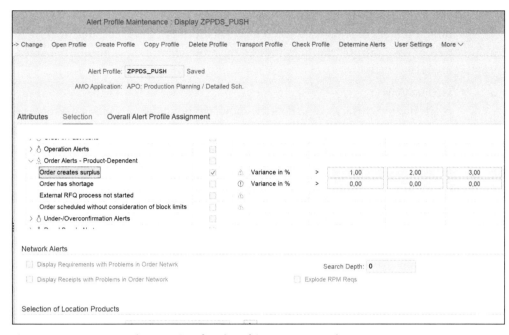

Figure 8.34 Setting Up Alert Monitor for Identifying Excess Supply

8.4.2   Launch the Push Production View

After the excess supply elements are identified for the products from the alert monitor or from the product overview, you can navigate to the product view (Transaction /SAPAPO/RRP3) and choose **More · Go To · Push Production**. The product view must be in edit mode (by clicking the **Change** button in the product view) to launch the push production.

This will launch a new **Push Production** screen, as shown in Figure 8.35. The push production tool has the following four panels in the screen:

- **Sources of Supply**
  In this panel, the system executes a where-used list for the material for which push production is being planned and lists all the PDSs that have the material as part of their components.
- **Surplus for Material**
  In this panel, all the supply elements (orders, stock elements) causing the excess stock for the material are listed.

- **Sources of Supply for Consuming Products**

  All the sources of supply are listed here. Quantities can be calculated by the system, or you can enter the quantities for the products that can consume the excess material.

- **Product View**

  At the bottom of the screen, this view shows the products for which a new order is being created to consume the excess supply of the material. In addition, the alerts are generated accordingly based on the new orders being created, which can help you determine how much additional supply you can create for the product without resulting in too much supply considering the shelf life or other demand elements of the product being produced.

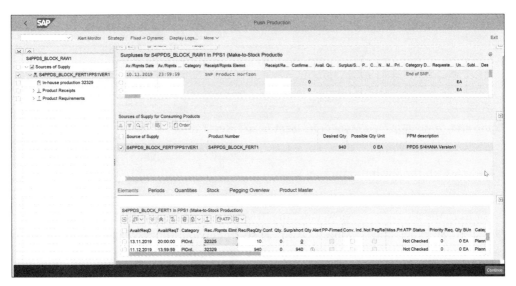

Figure 8.35 Push Production: User Interface

To consume the excess stock of the elements listed in the **Surplus for Material** panel, select the supply element, and then click on the **Adopt** button in the **Sources of Supply for Consuming Products** section. This will calculate the quantity of the product/PDSs that can consume the quantity of the selected excess supply element for the excess material.

Click on the **Create Order** button in **Sources of Supply for Consuming Products** to create a new planned order using the selected PDS, and it will load the product view, including the newly created planned order for the product. Although this is a manual process, it helps planners make decisions regarding consuming the excess supplies for critical materials in the production plan.

8.5 Summary

Embedded PP-DS offers many advanced features, including those covered in this chapter. Other industry-specific advanced features are also available in the PP-DS system that can be used by the specific industries. The features we covered in this chapter can be used across industries, although some of them have an industry flavor.

Following are some of the other advanced PP-DS industry-specific features:

- Container resource planning and scheduling is used by process industries such as chemicals and oil & gas.
- PP-DS repetitive manufacturing is used by automotive and automotive parts manufacturers or any industry with takt-based scheduling requirements where the products pass through the production line with a predefined time duration at every assembly or workstation, and components are consumed at the backflushing points.

We've covered the setup and working of the planning and scheduling features and also some of the advanced features offered by embedded PP-DS so far.

In the next chapter, we'll discuss some of the operations and administration tasks required to ensure the efficient use of embedded PP-DS.

Chapter 9

Administering PP-DS with SAP S/4HANA

In this chapter, we'll move on to the administration activities for PP-DS in SAP S/4HANA (embedded PP-DS). We'll provide best practices for maintaining an embedded PP-DS implementation, avoiding performance problems, and correcting data inconsistencies.

Embedded PP-DS is an integrated system where the PP-DS component resides within the SAP S/4HANA core at the application level. SAP liveCache, an in-memory database that contains the PP-DS application data objects and the application logic for processing the data, is also embedded in the same SAP HANA database, which is used by the SAP S/4HANA core system.

In SAP Advanced Planning and Optimization (SAP APO), the same core interface (CIF) technology is used to establish the communication between the enterprise resource planning (ERP) system (in this discussion, "ERP" refers to SAP ERP or SAP S/4HANA) and the SAP APO system. The trigger for communication is via integration models that determine the data objects to be sent and received from the ERP system or SAP APO. Even in the integrated embedded PP-DS system, the communications between the ERP system and embedded PP-DS are facilitated via a simplified CIF technology without an integration model for the transaction data. Planned orders, purchase requisitions, production orders, and purchase orders are updated simultaneously in PP-DS and the ERP system when the change/creation is triggered in PP-DS. But when the data is sent back from the ERP system to PP-DS, it still uses the queued remote function call (qRFC) communication (CIF queues). Therefore, the inherent technical challenges related to the qRFC communications are also applicable to the embedded PP-DS system to an extent.

SAP liveCache, which the embedded PP-DS system runs on, has its own database schema within the database. Therefore, it's still required to ensure the data consistency between the PP-DS data stored in the SAP HANA database and in SAP liveCache.

In this chapter, we'll cover the tools and methods to use for ensuring the smooth operation of the embedded PP-DS system, as well as discuss any troubleshooting tips and tricks where applicable.

9.1   Core Interface Queue Monitoring

For most of the master data objects required in embedded PP-DS, the transfer is executed via the activation of the **Advanced Planning** checkbox in the master data object or by executing ABAP programs to generate such data for PP-DS (see Chapter 2). In these cases, no CIF queues are generated, and integration models aren't required.

For transaction data objects, except for the following transfers, all other transfers use the CIF qRFC communication:

- Planned order and purchase requisitions from PP-DS to the ERP system
- Production orders, process orders, and purchase orders from PP-DS to the ERP system

The direction of the queues is determined by the configuration settings made in SAP S/4HANA and embedded PP-DS CIF settings. It's recommended to have inbound queue communication for both directions.

As shown in Figure 9.1, the queue directions are set in the following Customizing menu paths:

❶ In embedded PP-DS, **SAP IMG Menu · Advanced Planning Integration via Core Interface (CIF) · Integration · Basic Settings for Creating the System Landscape · Assign Logical System and Queue Type**.

❷ For SAP S/4HANA, **SAP IMG Menu · Integration with Other SAP Components · Advanced Planning and Optimization · Basic Settings for Setting Up the System Landscape · Set Target System and Queue Type**.

Because the queues are self-pointing (same logical system for SAP S/4HANA and embedded PP-DS), any queue failure can be monitored from the qRFC inbound monitor. The queue monitor can be launched from the **SAP Easy Access** menu, **Logistics · Advanced Planning · Administration · Integration · Monitor · Inbound Queue Monitoring**, or Transaction SMQ2.

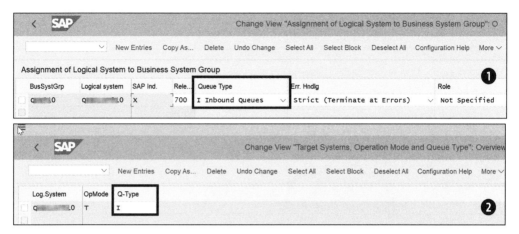

Figure 9.1 Setting the Queue Direction in Embedded PP-DS and SAP S/4HANA

The CIF queue name starts with the characters "CF". As shown in Figure 9.2, in Transaction SMQ2, you enter the **Queue Name** as "CF*", and ensure the correct **Client** is filled in. If you're filtering queues with a **Waiting** status, you can enter the value "X" in the **Waiting Queues Only** field ❶. Click **Execute**, and in the next screen, you'll see the list of CIF queues, including the number of queues in the list ❷ and the total number of RFCs ❸, as shown on the lower portion of Figure 9.2. One queue can contain multiple RFCs. For example, when a production order goods receipt is posted, the system must ensure that the production order update and the stock update should happen together successfully, so there will be two RFCs in the queue listed in the Transaction SMQ2 queue list. You can see this number in the **Entries** column ❹.

Following is the list of queue names for the commonly used objects for transfer between the ERP system and embedded PP-DS:

- **CFPLO***
  Planned orders, production orders, confirmations
- **CFPO***
  Purchase orders, purchase requisitions
- **CFSLS***
  Sales orders
- **CFSTK***
  Stock
- **CFRSV***
  Manual reservations

- **CFSDS***
  Scheduling agreement items

- **CFSHP***
  Shipments

- **CFFCC***
  Reduction of planned independent requirements (PIRs)

- **CFPIR***
  PIRs

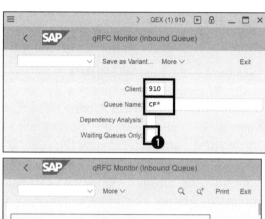

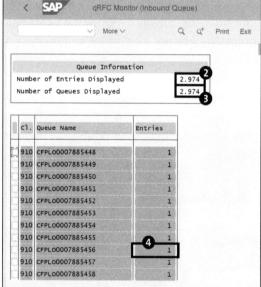

Figure 9.2 CIF: Inbound Queue Monitor

The * is replaced by the corresponding order number. For example, if a purchase req-uisition with ERP number 10000222 is being transferred from the ERP system to embedded PP-DS, the queue name will be CFPO10000222.

From the screen where the list of queues is displayed (refer to Figure 9.2), click on the **Change view** button or use the keyboard shortcut [F8] to display the queues with their statuses. In addition, you can double-click on a queue to see its details and sta-tus. The queues are processed according to the settings maintained in the inbound queue scheduler (Transaction SMQR).

You'll see the following common statuses for the CIF inbound queues, the various actions of which can be performed according to the status of the queues, as shown in Figure 9.3:

- READY

  The queue is ready for processing. This is usually a temporary status, and after the scheduler picks up and processes the queue, it will be removed from the list. But if the queues are locked manually, this may also cause the queues to be in **READY** sta-tus. The queues need to be unlocked for processing.

- RUNNING

  This is also a temporary status, indicating that the queue is currently being pro-cessed. If the **RUNNING** status stays for long that may indicate an issue, and the queue status needs to be reset. As some of the RFCs within the queue might have already successfully reset processes, the status may update the data again in embedded PP-DS.

- SYSFAIL

  This status indicates a serious error has occurred during the processing of the queue. This could be due to an application error or a runtime error generated during the queue processing. You can double-click on the error message to see the details regarding the reason for the failure. The **SYSFAIL** status queues aren't auto-matically reprocessed by the system. After the reason for the error is corrected, these queues can be reprocessed.

- WAITING

  The queue has dependency on other queues that weren't successfully processed. The dependent logical unit of work (LUW) is also listed in the queue details. After the dependent queues are processed, the waiting queues will also be processed.

- STOP

  An explicit lock or a generic queue lock on all CF* queues is set; for example, locks can be set for inbound CF* queue processing during a PP-DS planning run that is underway. Locks can be set using program RSTRFCI1 and unlocked using program RSTRFCI3.

- **RETRY**

  For temporary problems encountered during the processing of the queues, the **RETRY** status is set. The temporary problems usually are due to locking conflicts. In such cases, the system will automatically schedule a background program to reprocess these queues. In the background job monitor, you'll see jobs with job name qRFC* followed by the transaction ID (TID) displayed in the queue for processing these retry queues.

- **CPICERR**

  This status indicates a communication error or a network problem. The error details provide the technical information on the error.

- **NOEXEC**

  This status is set usually when the queues are recorded for troubleshooting the applications. In the CIF user settings (Transaction /SAPAPO/C4), if the **Debugging If the Value Is Set** field is set to **Debugging on, Recording of t/qRFCs (NO SEND)**, then the queues for such users will be set with the **NOEXEC** status.

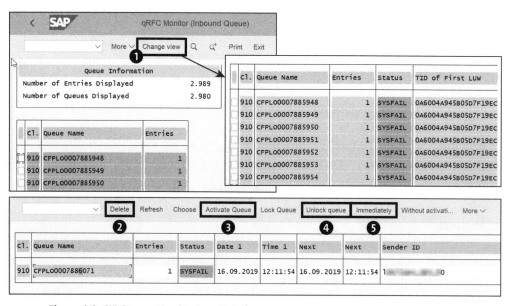

Figure 9.3 CIF Queue Monitoring: Details

Double-click on the queue to display the status and the details of the queue, or click on the **Change view** button to display the status of all the queues, as shown in Figure 9.3 ❶.

From the details of the queue, again double-click on the queue name to display all the LUWs within the queue. A failure of the first LUW processing can impact the whole queue. From there, you have the options to delete the queue ❷ or process the individual LUWs within the queue by clicking on the **Activate Queue** button ❸; if no error occurs, it will process the queue. You can also choose the **Unlock queue** option, which will immediately unlock the queue, removing the lock status and processing the queue if no error occurs ❹. Clicking the **Immediately** button will immediately set the **Lock** status for the queue ❺.

You can also display the content of the queue. For example, a queue for a planned order will have the header, component list, operation details, and so on. In the standard system, the display of the queue is in binary format without assigning a correct display program.

In the standard system, the display program /SAPAPO/CIF_QUEUE_EVENT2 is delivered for display of the CIF queues. In Transaction SMQE, choose **More • Edit • Register Display Program**. In the popup screen that appears, enter "CF*" as the **Queue Name** and "/SAPAPO/CIF_QUEUE_EVENT2" as the **Program Name**. Click on the **Continue** button to save the display program.

Click the queue name, and click the **Display LUW** button in the menu bar to display the queue contents, as shown in Figure 9.4.

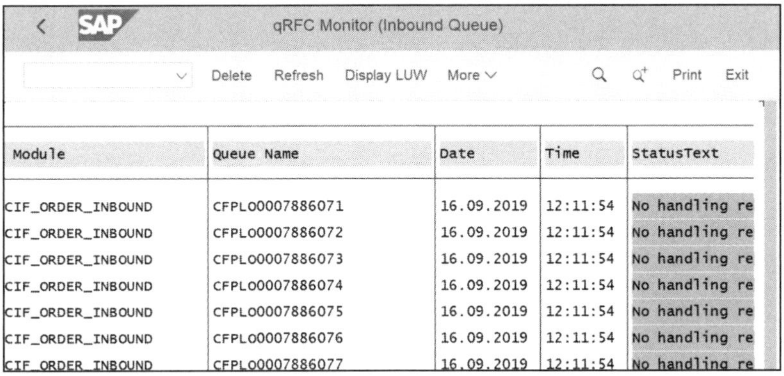

Module	Queue Name	Date	Time	StatusText
CIF_ORDER_INBOUND	CFPLO0007886071	16.09.2019	12:11:54	No handling re
CIF_ORDER_INBOUND	CFPLO0007886072	16.09.2019	12:11:54	No handling re
CIF_ORDER_INBOUND	CFPLO0007886073	16.09.2019	12:11:54	No handling re
CIF_ORDER_INBOUND	CFPLO0007886074	16.09.2019	12:11:54	No handling re
CIF_ORDER_INBOUND	CFPLO0007886075	16.09.2019	12:11:54	No handling re
CIF_ORDER_INBOUND	CFPLO0007886076	16.09.2019	12:11:54	No handling re
CIF_ORDER_INBOUND	CFPLO0007886077	16.09.2019	12:11:54	No handling re

Figure 9.4 Queue Monitor: Displaying the Queue Details

The queue details are displayed without the display programs ❶ and with the display programs ❷ in Figure 9.5. After the display program is registered, the data contained in the queue are displayed in a structured and readable format when displaying the queue details. This is helpful when the queue failures are due to data errors, and you want to understand what exact data is being sent from SAP S/4HANA to embedded PP-DS in a specific queue.

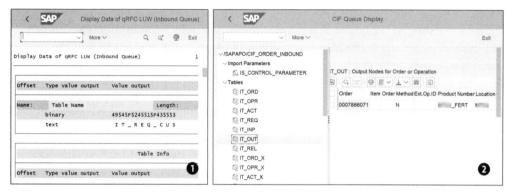

Figure 9.5 CIF: Display Queue Details and Contents

If the direction of the CIF queues are configured as outbound queues, Transaction SMQ1 can be used to monitor the outbound queues.

Tip

When automatic planning is used in a PP-DS planning procedure, during the planning run or when the automatic planning relevant events occurs in the system, an outbound queue with PP_PLANNING is created by the system, which will execute the planning for the impacted products. So, if you use automatic planning in planning procedures, the outbound queues must be monitored from Transaction SMQ1.

9.2   Core Interface Postprocessing

When queues are struck in the inbound queue due to errors or **WAITING** status, this may lead to other queues being struck due to dependencies on the queues. Eventually, this will lead to thousands of queues struck, and the communication between SAP S/4HANA and PP-DS will come to a halt. To avoid such situations, it's recommended to activate CIF postprocessing (CPP). With CPP, the queues that are to error out and stop in the inbound queue are transferred to the postprocessing queue, so that other queues are processed successfully if possible.

With the following exceptions, all queues that run into issues during processing are moved to postprocessing:

- When the queue processing generates a runtime error (short dumps)
- When the initial data transfer is processed for objects that require a model-based integration (purchasing master data, maintenance orders, etc.)
- When SAP liveCache isn't available
- When errors are triggered in enhancements (user exits, business add-ins [BAdIs]) in CIF

In all other circumstances, the faulty queue won't be listed in the inbound queue monitor, and a postprocessing record will be generated.

The activation of CPP in advanced planning is done from the Customizing menu path: **SAP IMG Menu · Advanced Planning · Integration via Core Interface (CIF) · Basic Settings for Data Transfer · CIF Error Handling · Activate CIF Error Handling**. You'll arrive at the screen shown in Figure 9.6. Select the **1 Post processing for Errors, No Splitting of LUWs** option in the **Err.Hndlg** column, and click the **Save** button to save the changes.

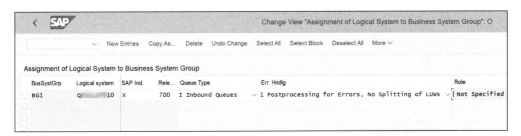

Figure 9.6 Activation of CPP for Queue Errors

The postprocessing records can be displayed and processed from Transaction /SAPAPO/ CPP, or you can follow the **SAP Easy Access** menu: **Logistics · Advanced Planning · Administration · Integration · CIF Error Handling · CIF Postprocessing**. You'll arrive at the screen shown in Figure 9.7.

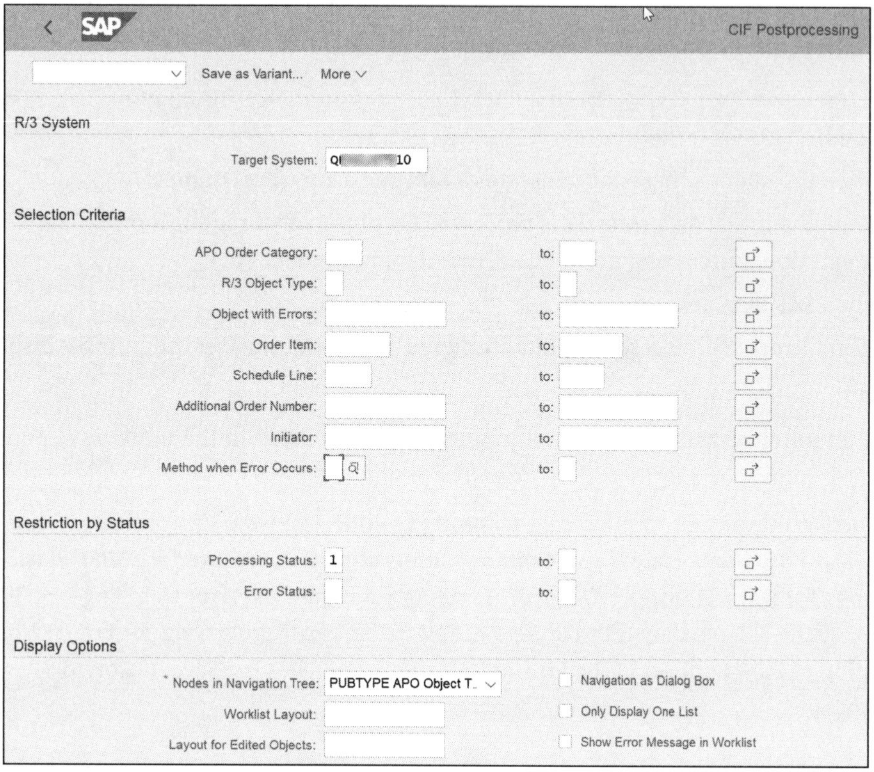

Figure 9.7 CPP: Selection Options

In this transaction, select the **Target System** (embedded PP-DS always has one logical system for CIF), and select other options as required. You can filter the records by the status of the postprocessing record and the error status of the records in the **Restriction by Status** section. The postprocessing status (**Processing Status**) indicates the status of the postprocessing after the record is created in CPP:

- **1 Still for Processing**
  The record is created, not processed yet, and needs to be retransferred.

- **2 Processed**
  The record has already been processed; no action is required.

- **3 Obsolete (Set Manually)**
  The user has set the record as obsolete from the postprocessing transaction. This can be revoked manually.

- **4 Obsolete (Set Automatically by System)**
  If the impacted transaction object is successfully transferred to PP-DS after the postprocessing record is created during an earlier attempt to transfer the same object, the system sets the CPP record as obsolete.

- **5 Retransfer Not Allowed**
  A retransfer of the data isn't allowed for this postprocessing record. These records are for informational purposes and can be set as obsolete after the record is analyzed.

The **Error Status** of the postprocessing records can have the following values:

- **No Errors**
  This object was successfully processed and didn't raised any errors. These records are still displayed in CPP because, when one qRFC within a queue (LUW) isn't processed in the CIF due to an error, all the objects in the same LUW queue are transferred to CPP.

- **Errors**
  The object was processed in the CIF and raised an error, so the postprocessing record is created.

- **Object Not Processed**
  This object is part of the same LUW queue but is placed after the qRFC that raised an error, so the system didn't attempt to process this (ignored). You won't know whether this object will be successfully processed in the CIF or will raise an error until you process the CPP record and transfer the data.

> **Tip**
> If you want to troubleshoot the CIF queues generated from the postprocessing, you can enter the OK code "DEBUG_ON" in the transaction search box at the top left of the CPP's initial screen. This will display additional options in the bottom of the screen to stop the queues for analysis.

Select the **Select Data from R/3** checkbox to also read and display any postprocessing records generated by SAP S/4HANA when processing inbound PP-DS data in SAP S/4HANA.

After you've entered the required selection options, click the **Execute** button to display the list of the postprocessing records. In the next screen, you'll see the list of CPP records organized by the direction of transfer (SAP S/4HANA to PP-DS or vice versa) and the type of object for which the record is created for (in-house manufacturing, external procurement, stocks, etc.).

[»]

> **Note**
>
> Though the transfer of data from PP-DS to SAP S/4HANA is synchronous, when any error occurs during the transfer, the postprocessing records are created for such records with queue name CIF_SYNCHRON_CALL in the postprocessing record.

As shown in Figure 9.8, the postprocessing screen has four panels in it. The left side of the screen is the navigation tree that lists the records; you can load the records for the object by double-clicking on the nodes. The worklist contains the individual records available for postprocessing. You can change the layout of the table by clicking on the **Choose Layout – Change Layout** button ❹ on the menu bar to add additional columns to display the status of the error or the status of the postprocessing and other informational columns available for selection. The **Objects Processed in this Session** panel lists the records you've selected from the worklist and processed. If the records are processed successfully, they will be marked with a green background. Any application log messages raised during the processing is displayed in the bottom panel of the screen.

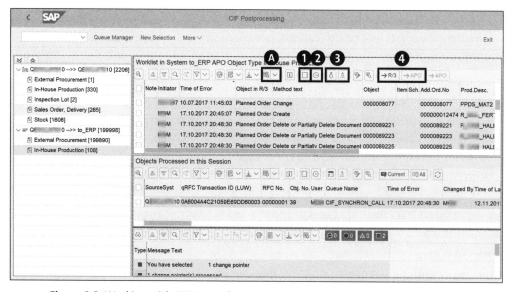

Figure 9.8 Working with CPP Records

From the worklist shown in Figure 9.8, you can select a record and choose an option from the menu bar:

❶ Display Application Log

The postprocessing records have the TID of the queue/LUW when the queue was processed. The **Display Application Log** option reads the application log of the listed TID and displays the log. For reading the application logs, the system uses the default user maintained in the RFC destination in the CIF settings. As the default user is usually created with a **System** user type, you may not see any logs or may encounter an error while reading the logs. In such cases, you can create another RFC connection and maintain a **Dialog** user type in the RFC settings. Assign this RFC destination in the application-specific RFC destinations in the SAP S/4HANA system and embedded PP-DS.

In SAP S/4HANA, use the Customizing menu path: **SAP IMG Menu · Integration with Other SAP Components · Advanced Planning and Optimization · Basic Settings for Setting Up the System Landscape · Assign RFC Destinations to Different Application Cases.** Click on the **New Entries** button to go to the screen shown in Figure 9.9 **❶**. Enter the **Logical system**, select **RL Display Application Log of Another system** in the **CIF applicatn** column, and then enter the **RFC Destination** with a dialog user assigned to it.

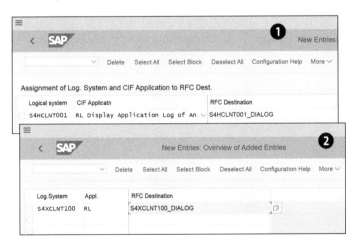

Figure 9.9 Assigning the RFC Destination for Log Display

In embedded PP-DS, go to the following menu path: **SAP IMG Menu · Advanced Planning · Integration via Core Interface (CIF) · Integration · Basic Settings for Creating the System Landscape · Assign RFC Destinations to Various Application**

Cases. Click the **New Entries** button to navigate to the screen shown in Figure 9.9 ❷. Enter the **Log.System**, select **RL** in the **Appl.** column, and enter the new **RFC Destination** with a dialog user assigned to it.

❷ **Display History**

This button in the menu bar of the CPP worklist shows all the actions performed on the postprocessing record selected. It lists the time stamp and user details of the postprocessing record creation, along with the history of any further actions, such as processing of the records performed.

❸ **Set/Reset Obsolete**

If you don't want to process a postprocessing record, you can mark them as obsolete using this option. Such records will be set with **Obsolete** (set manually) status. You can also revoke the manually set **Obsolete** indicator.

❹ **Send to R/3 or Send to APO**

These buttons will be activated by the system depending on the direction of the transfer.

Depending on the volume of the records created by postprocessing, the tables storing the postprocessing records may often grow larger. To address this, the older postprocessing records must be deleted by using Transaction /SAPAPO/CPPR or via the **SAP Easy Access** menu: **Logistics • Advanced Planning • Administration • Integration • CIF Error Handling • Reorganize CIF Postprocessing Records**. You may periodically schedule this transaction in the background to delete the old postprocessing records.

9.3   Core Interface Comparison and Reconciliation

Transaction data that is relevant for PP-DS is persisted in SAP S/4HANA and embedded PP-DS in database tables and in SAP liveCache in PP-DS. The data between SAP S/4HANA and embedded PP-DS may mismatch due to queue errors, incorrect processing of queues, inconsistencies raised within SAP S/4HANA that are propagated to PP-DS but have been already corrected in SAP S/4HANA, and other reasons. The inconsistencies could lead to incorrect quantities of orders, missing orders in the SAP S/4HANA system or in PP-DS, incorrect dates updated, and so on.

The data must be kept consistent between SAP S/4HANA and embedded PP-DS so that the planning results and alerts are correctly calculated in PP-DS. For this purpose, the CIF comparison and reconciliation (CCR) tool is delivered in the standard system. This tool reads the data in both SAP S/4HANA and embedded PP-DS and then performs comparison to identify any data mismatches. Then, the tool provides an option to the user to reconcile the date by sending it to PP-DS or SAP S/4HANA, depending on the object with inconsistency and the type of inconsistency.

To launch the CCR tool, you can use Transaction /SAPAPO/CCR or the **SAP Easy Access** menu: **Logistics Advanced Planning · Administration · Integration · CIF Comparison/ Reconciliation of Transaction Data · Execute Comparison/Reconciliation**.

The CCR tool has two tabs, as shown in Figure 9.10:

- **Load Results of Comparison**
  When the comparison is executed in background mode, the results can be retrieved for reconciliation from this tab.

- **Execute Comparison/Reconciliation**
  In this tab, you can maintain the selection of the data for comparison in interactive mode, and the results will be immediately displayed in the resulting screen.

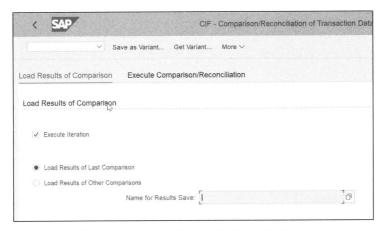

Figure 9.10 CIF Comparison and Reconciliation: Initial Screen

Before starting the CCR tool, ensure that the known sources for the inconsistencies are already corrected, such as the following:

- All CPP records are processed.

- CIF queues are monitored, and faulty queues are corrected and processed.

- If change pointers are collected in embedded PP-DS by setting the **Recording** column to **C Collect Changes** in Transaction /SAPAPO/C4, then process all the change pointers by executing Transaction /SAPAPO/C5.

427

Navigate to the **Execute Comparison/Reconciliation** tab, as shown in Figure 9.11, to start the comparison and reconciliation. In this screen, select the logical system in the **Partner System** field, and select the **Material (Product Name)** and **Plant (Location Name)** values. The **Model Name** is irrelevant in the embedded PP-DS system for many of the transaction data objects. Select also the transaction data object for which you want to execute the comparison in the **Documents To Be Checked** section.

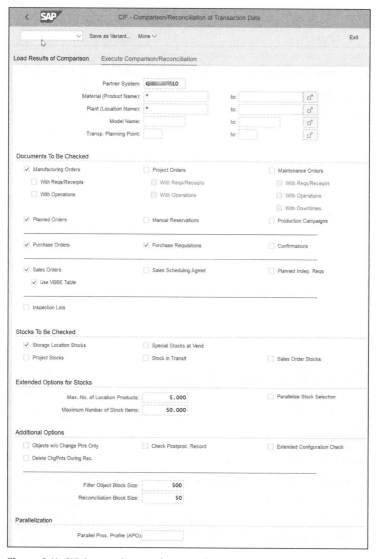

Figure 9.11 CIF Comparison and Reconciliation: Selection Screen and Settings

When the **Sales Orders** object is selected, select the **Use VBBE Table** checkbox to compare the current situation of table VBBE, which holds the requirements record, with PP-DS. To correct any inconsistencies within SAP S/4HANA between the sales document flow tables and table VBBE, you can execute program ATP_VBBE_CONSISTENCY.

When stocks are selected in the **Stocks to Be Checked** section, additional options to execute parallel selection and comparison are available in the **Extended Options for Stocks** section of the screen. The **Max. No. of Location Products** and **Maximum Number of Stock Items** fields limit the number of product locations selected for the comparison of stock values. As the system memory requirements are high for the stock comparison, these options are provided to control the number of stock elements being compared.

When **Parallelize Stock Selection** is selected, the system uses the parallel processing destination maintained in the **Parallel Proc. Profile (APO)** field under the **Parallelization** section of the screen. With this setting, the set number of parallel processes in embedded PP-DS is triggered to select the stock objects, and the same number of parallel processes are triggered in SAP S/4HANA to read SAP S/4HANA stock objects. The comparison is then executed within the parallel processes.

> **Note**
>
> As SAP S/4HANA and PP-DS use the same set of application servers of the SAP S/4HANA system, setting parallel processing for stocks leads to consumption of twice the number of dialog work processes in the system. Therefore, configure the parallelization profiles so that the number of work processes in the system doesn't become depleted with the parallel processing of stock CCR comparison.

The parallel processing profiles in SAP S/4HANA and PP-DS are created in Customizing, which determines the server group, number of parallel processes, and block size that can be used by CCR. The parallel processing profile in PP-DS is created from the Customizing menu path: **SAP IMG Menu • Advanced Planning • Integration via Core Interface (CIF) • Basic Settings for Data Transfer • CIF Comparison/Match for Transaction Data • Maintain Parallel Processing Profiles**. Click the **New Entries** button here and you'll reach the screen shown in Figure 9.12. Here, enter a name for the **Paral. Proc. Profile** and a **Description**. Enter the number of parallel processes the system can use to process the data in the **Parallel Processes** field, and enter the **Logical system** and the **Server Group** names. In the **Block Size** field, enter the number of objects you want to process in one parallel process. Higher block sizes require high system memory to process the data.

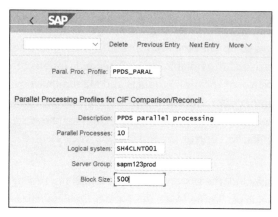

Figure 9.12 Maintain a Parallel Processing Profile for CCR

The **Background Processing** section of the screen (not shown) is used when CCR is executed in background mode for comparison of the selected data objects. Set the **Save Results** checkbox, and enter a **Name for Save** with an identifiable name that can be later loaded into the **Load Results for Comparison** tab of CCR.

Note

The CCR in background mode can only compare the consistency of the selected data objects. The reconciliation must be performed interactively as it requires the user to decide on the course of action to be taken, such as to send the record to the SAP S/4HANA system or to PP-DS or to delete the object from either of the sides.

After the selections are made in the CCR **Execute Comparison/Reconciliation** tab, click the **Execute** button. In the resulting screen, the compared objects and the results of the comparison are displayed, as shown in Figure 9.13. The **Results** panel on the left side of the screen lists the results of the comparison. Under the results, double-click on the **Documents** icon to display the summary of the comparison results. The summary lists all the object types along with the **Total** number of orders that were processed for that object, the number of records with **Error**, and the disaggregation of the errors such as orders **Not in APO** (PP-DS), orders **not in R/3** (SAP S/4HANA), and **Contents** (the dates and/or quantities aren't matching). The **ChgPointer** column shows the number of change pointers in the system that aren't processed yet. The number of change pointers isn't counted toward the number of errors.

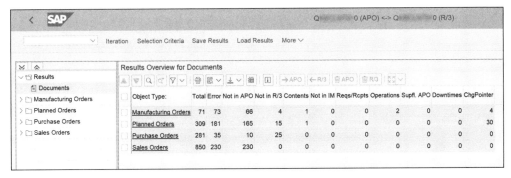

Figure 9.13 Results of CCR Comparison

You can click on the **Object Type**, such as **Manufacturing Orders**, **Planned Orders**, and so on, to display the list of orders that have errors in the comparison results summary. On the **Results** panel, you can expand the folder structures for the individual objects. Navigate to the **Manufacturing Orders** folder to access the details screen shown in Figure 9.14. This screen further classifies the errors according to error categories such as **Missing in SAP APO**, **Missing in R/3 Without Exten**, and so on ❶.

In the details list, an error code shows the details for the error. For example, for a mismatch in contents, the error code details will include the quantity and/or dates of the order in SAP S/4HANA as well as in embedded PP-DS. The error code is set according to the inconsistency identified by the comparison. For example, a production order missing in PP-DS will have error code 152, and a production order missing in PP-DS that was converted from a planned order which was integrated into PP-DS will have error code 167.

[«]

Note

The CCR compares the current persisted data in SAP S/4HANA and embedded PP-DS. It doesn't consider any changes to the data made via CIF enhancements during the creation of the data. If you have CIF enhancements that change the data in either the SAP S/4HANA system or PP-DS during the original transfer of the data, the same logic also must be coded in the CCR BAdIs to take this into account. The BAdI /SAPAPO/CIF_DELTA3 can be used for this purpose.

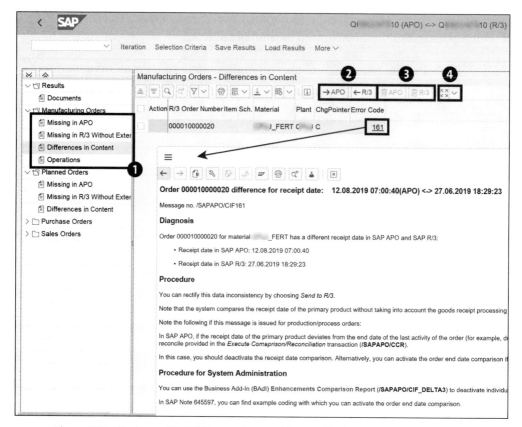

Figure 9.14 Working with CIF Comparison and Reconciliation

Depending on the error code, the system activates the **Send to SAP APO** (PP-DS) or **Send to R/3** (SAP S/4HANA) icons ❷ in the icon bar. In addition, the option to delete the order from either the SAP S/4HANA system or PP-DS is also activated for the corresponding error situations ❸. The action of sending to R/3 or sending to SAP APO will create CIF queues that will be processed to rectify the inconsistent data. If there are change pointers present, those can be processed by clicking on the **Process Change Pointers** icon ❹.

After you've taken necessary action to reconcile the data between SAP S/4HANA and PP-DS, you can start an **Iteration** of the results to confirm that the inconsistencies you've corrected are processes and the inconsistency is resolved. If the number of inconsistent objects isn't reduced by the number of orders for which you've triggered the reconciliation, then monitor the CIF queues or the CPP records to identify the reason for the processing failure.

You can also save the results of the comparison by clicking the **Save Results** button in the menu bar. The saved results can be later loaded for reconciliation from the **Load Results of Comparison** tab in the initial screen of the CCR transaction.

> **Note**
>
> The CCR comparison can be executed in background mode, but in the standard system, the reconciliation must be performed manually in interactive mode as this involves manual decision-making.

9.4   Core Interface Application Log Management

When data is transferred from the SAP S/4HANA system to PP-DS and vice versa through CIF, application logs are created in the system. It's essential to create the right level of logs so that any problems can be analyzed, and the root causes can be identified and addressed. Depending on the volume of data being transferred between the two components (ERP system and PP-DS) of the SAP S/4HANA system, CIF alone generates a large amount of log data that needs to be deleted periodically for optimal operation of the system.

In SAP S/4HANA, the CIF logs can be activated from the Customizing menu path: **SAP IMG Menu · Integration with Other SAP Components · Advanced Planning and Optimization · Basic Settings for the Data Transfer · Set User Parameters**. Click the **New Entries** button, and you'll reach the screen shown in Figure 9.15 ❶. Here, enter the **User Name** for which the logging level is to be changed, enter "Q" in the **RFC Mode**, set the required logging level in the **Logging** column, set the **Debug** column as blank, and click on the **Save** button. You can set the **Logging** level for the users here to the following levels:

- **No logging**
  No logs are written to the application log.

- **Normal**
  Basic information is logged in the application log, such as the number of records and product/locations, and so on.

- **Detailed**

  The content of the CIF transfer is logged per the settings made in the customization of the detailed log under the Customizing menu path: **SAP IMG Menu · Integration with Other SAP Components · Advanced Planning and Optimization · Basic Settings for the Data Transfer · Configure Application Log**.

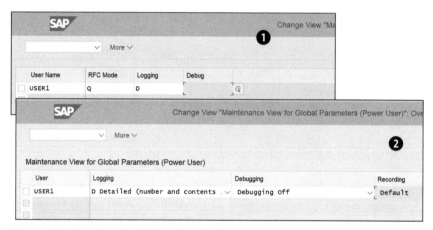

Figure 9.15 Changing the CIF Logging Level

The application log for CIF in embedded PP-DS is activated from the Customizing menu path: **SAP IMG Menu · Advanced Planning · Integration via Core Interface (CIF) · Basic Settings for Data Transfer · Set User Parameters**. Click the **New Entries** button, and you'll reach the lower screen shown in Figure 9.15 ❷. Here, enter the user name for which the logging level is to be changed in the **User** column, set the required logging level in the **Logging** column, set the **Debugging** column as **Debugging off**, select **Default** in the **Recording** column, and click the **Save** button.

The application logs can be displayed from Transaction SLG1 by entering the object value as "CIF*" to read the application logs created by CIF. If you want to search the application log with a specific search term, such as an order number or material number, you can use Transaction CFG3 or Transaction /SAPAPO/C7 and enter the search term in the **Character String 1** and **Character String 2** fields in the selection screen.

You can delete the old CIF application logs from Transaction /SAPAPO/C6 with the "CIF*" value for the log object. You can also schedule a background job with program /SAPAPO/RDELLOG to delete the CIF application logs in the background.

9.5   SAP liveCache Housekeeping and Reconciliation

SAP liveCache is a special SAP in-memory and object-oriented database. In the embedded PP-DS system, SAP liveCache is an integral part of the SAP HANA database. SAP liveCache holds PP-DS application data and database procedures that provide the application logic (for creating orders, scheduling orders, etc.). Certain master data and transaction data are persisted in SAP liveCache as well as in the SAP HANA database tables. In this section, we'll go through key housekeeping and reconciliation activities available for SAP liveCache, as well as some key transactions.

9.5.1   Housekeeping

For the efficient operation of SAP liveCache, you must perform certain housekeeping activities daily. You can monitor the status of these housekeeping jobs from Transaction /SAPAPO/OM13 or from the **SAP Easy Access** menu: **Logistics • Advanced Planning • Administration • LiveCache/LCA Routines • Tools • Analyze LiveCache and LCA Objects**.

In the transaction, the **Versions** tab provides the technical information about SAP liveCache such as the version details. The **Checks** tab, as shown in Figure 9.16, provides the status of SAP liveCache with respect to the details of the SAP liveCache connections to the application, any active traces running currently, and the simulation versions saved in the system.

As shown in Figure 9.16, under the **Programs Scheduled Periodically** section, the mandatory SAP liveCache housekeeping jobs are listed along with the statuses of these jobs. A red light is displayed if there is no job scheduled in the system for these reports. These background jobs must be scheduled in all clients of an SAP S/4HANA system where SAP liveCache is active.

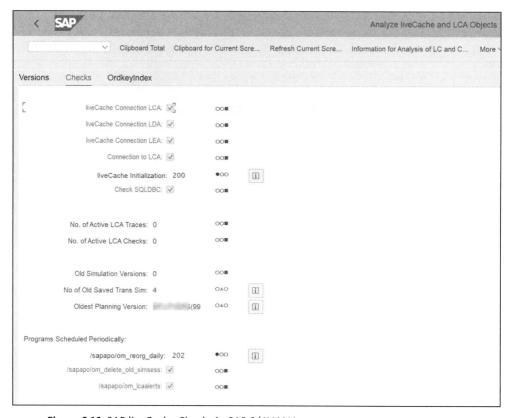

Figure 9.16 SAP liveCache Checks in SAP S/4HANA

Let's walk through each of the mandatory jobs:

- **/sapapo/om_reorg_daily**
  This report is recommended to be executed once a day during periods when SAP liveCache is operating (not, e.g., stopped during a data backup) and when the system usually has a light workload (e.g., at night). This report performs the following activities in SAP liveCache:
  - Old log files and lock entries are deleted.
  - Stopped transactional simulations that are older than eight hours are deleted.
  - The trace file numbers of the SAP liveCache application routines are checked.
  - Forecast orders are deleted, and initial zero stock is reorganized.
  - Flagged models and planning versions are deleted.
  - Housekeeping checks are performed and logged.

The results of the individual steps of the job are logged (Transaction /SAPAPO/OM11).

- **/sapapo/om_delete_old_simsess**
  When PP-DS transactions are executed in interactive mode using planning and scheduling tools or during background mode, the system always creates a simulation session (sim session) to perform the changes to the data for planning and scheduling. At the end of the planning job or when you save the data from interactive tools, the data from the simulation session is merged to the active version. Simulation sessions that aren't deleted at the end of the transaction continue to consume memory in SAP liveCache and can cause errors. This program is recommended to be scheduled for the clients connected to SAP liveCache every 30 minutes. The following tasks are performed by this program:

  - Unnecessary transactional simulations are flagged for deletion.
  - Unnecessary transactional simulations that are flagged for deletion are deleted. Obsolete transactional simulations are selected or deleted.
  - Unnecessary locks are deleted from the lock server.

- **/sapapo/om_lcaalerts**
  This program is recommended to be scheduled once every day in all the clients of the SAP S/4HANA system that are connected to SAP liveCache. This program determines the alerts and displays them in the Transaction /SAPAPO/OM13 checks. In addition, the alerts can be monitored from the DBA cockpit using Transaction DBACOCKPIT.

9.5.2   Data Reconciliation

In the embedded PP-DS system, certain master data and transaction data are persisted in the SAP HANA database and also in SAP liveCache within the SAP HANA database. The consistency of the data between the two is ensured. However, due to programming errors or system issues, it's possible that the data in SAP liveCache isn't in sync with the data in the database tables. Such inconsistencies can be detected and corrected from the data reconciliation tool, which can be started from Transaction /SAPAPO/OM17 or from the **SAP Easy Access** menu: **Logistics · Advanced Planning · Administration · Live-Cache/LCA Routines · Tools · LiveCache Consistency Check**.

This comparison and reconciliation should be executed during quiet periods, when there aren't many activities (data updates) being performed in PP-DS.

The initial screen of the tool includes the option to select the objects that can be compared and reconciled, as shown in Figure 9.17. Select all the relevant objects per your usage of PP-DS. Depending on the objects you select for the consistency check, additional fields may be populated to set additional selection criteria or to influence the consistency check functionality.

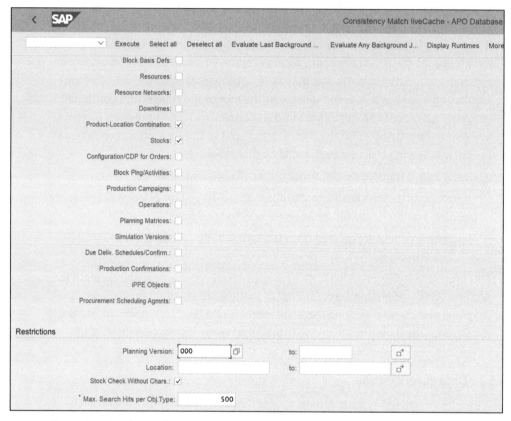

Figure 9.17 SAP liveCache: PP-DS Database Consistency Check

Set the **Max. Search Hits per Obj.Type** field to a higher value depending on the number of individual inconsistent records within the object type are to be checked. For example, if you set the value of 100, as soon as the number of inconsistent records reaches 100 for the selected object, the system stops the check for that object and starts the check for the next object in the selection.

You can click the **Execute** button to execute the check online in interactive mode This will take you to the **Results of the Consistency Check** screen, as shown in Figure 9.18. The **Result Overview** tab displays the summary of the check performed and the results of the check. The list is organized by the object type and the error type detected by the consistency check. Depending on the number of objects you've selected and for which an inconsistency was detected, additional tabs are loaded in the screen. As shown in Figure 9.18, these additional tabs have the detailed results of the consistency check.

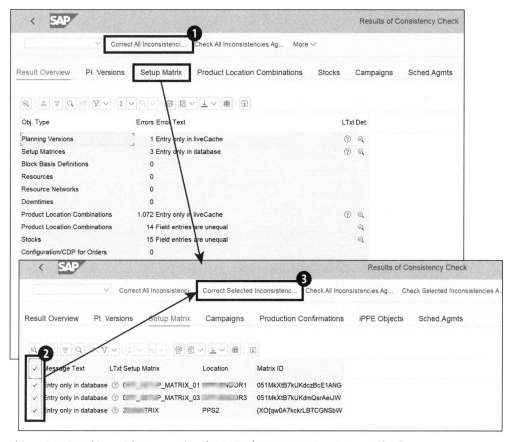

Figure 9.18 Working with Transaction /SAPAPO/OM17OM17 Consistency Check

You can correct all the inconsistencies detected by clicking on the **Correct All Inconsistencies** button in the menu bar ❶. You also can navigate to the individual object by clicking the corresponding tabs (in our example, the **Setup Matrix** tab) and then selecting the records you want to correct ❷. Finally, click on the **Correct Selected Inconsistencies** button ❸ to correct the inconsistent data.

As shown in Figure 9.19, from the **Result Overview** tab, if you click on the **Correct All Inconsistencies** ❶ button, the system opens a popup for you to select the objects to be corrected. When you select the objects and click on the **OK ❷** button, another popup appears with the option to process the correction in background mode **❸**. Click **Yes** to trigger a background job for the correction of the inconsistencies.

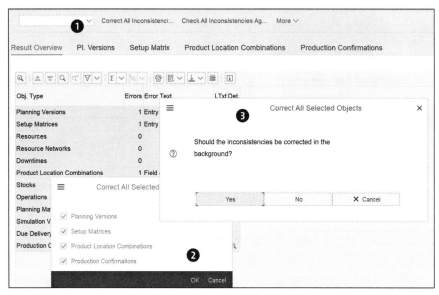

Figure 9.19 Option to Correct the Inconsistencies in the Background

To correct a huge number of inconsistencies, it's recommended to execute the correction in background mode to avoid timeout errors. In interactive mode, after the correction is completed, you can also trigger an iteration of the check by clicking on the **Check All Inconsistencies Again** button.

From the tabs for the individual objects, you can select the records you want to correct and trigger a selective correction using the **Correct Selected Inconsistencies** button shown previously in Figure 9.18 **❸**.

If the same inconsistency for the same objects occurs repeatedly after correction, it may be the result of an underlying application or programming issue. This will require detailed analysis to identify the root cause. You may execute this consistency check on a weekly basis.

[+]

Tip

You can also schedule the consistency check to be executed in a background job via ABAP program /SAPAPO/OM_SYNC_LC_DB and a selection variant you've saved in the initial screen of Transaction /SAPAPO/OM17. In background mode, only the consistency check is executed, and the results are saved. You can load the results of the background job checks by clicking on **Evaluate Last Background**. Alternatively, you can select from a list of background job results by clicking on **Evaluate Any Background Job** from the initial screen of Transaction /SAPAPO/OM17.

9.5.3   Overview of SAP liveCache Transactions

Multiple transactions specific to SAP liveCache are delivered in the embedded PP-DS system and are useful for analyzing SAP liveCache issues. In the standard system, a cockpit transaction is delivered that collects all the SAP liveCache transactions and reports. Activities such as activating traces, analyzing the SAP liveCache logs, and displaying the contents of SAP liveCache are just a few of the transactions that can be executed from the cockpit. Caution must be exercised in providing authorization to the SAP liveCache transactions as some of these transactions can impact the performance and functioning of SAP liveCache.

You can launch the overview of SAP liveCache transactions using Transaction /SAPAPO/OM00. As shown in Figure 9.20, the transactions and reports are listed in the screen, and you can double-click on any of the transactions to execute them directly.

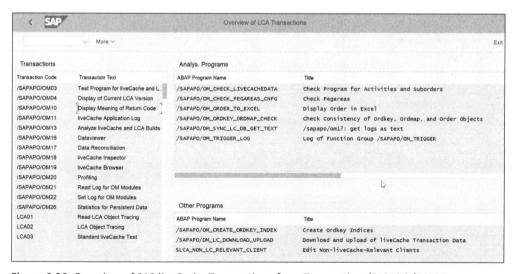

Figure 9.20 Overview of SAP liveCache Transactions from Transaction /SAPAPO/OM00

9.6   Administration of PP-DS Master Data

Critical PP-DS master data objects, such as the products, locations, and PDSs, must be correct at all times in PP-DS to ensure the correctness of the planning and scheduling results. Two other important and basic PP-DS master data objects that require maintenance with respect to SAP liveCache are the pegging areas and resources, which we'll cover the details of in this section.

9.6.1   Pegging Areas

When materials are activated for advanced planning, pegging areas are created in embedded PP-DS. The pegging area is identified by the PEGIDs in the database tables, and the same is created in SAP liveCache as well. In make-to-stock (MTS) scenarios, the pegging areas represent the material location combination, and in make-to-order (MTO) scenarios, the pegging area is created as the combination of the material, location, and sales orders.

When materials are discontinued or when the sales orders are closed, the pegging areas are still present in the SAP liveCache. In high data volume scenarios, these unnecessary and/or inconsistent pegging areas can be deleted, which helps the overall performance of the planning jobs. The inconsistent and unnecessary pegging areas can be detected and corrected by ABAP program /SAPAPO/DM_PEGKEY_ REORG, which can be executed in the embedded PP-DS system using Transaction SE38 or Transaction SA38.

As shown in Figure 9.21, the selection screen has multiple checks for detecting the unnecessary and inconsistent pegging areas. You can select the required checks ❶ and enter other selection conditions such as planning version, product number, and location. You can execute the report in test mode by selecting the **Execute in Test Mode** checkbox. In test mode, the results of the consistency check are displayed, but no change will be saved in the system. Without the test mode, the system executes the consistency checks and corrects the pegging areas by deleting the inconsistent pegging areas ❷.

[+]
> **Tip**
>
> Pegging areas are automatically created by the system while advanced planning is activated. If advanced planning is activated and you get an error for nonexistent pegging areas, you can execute Transaction /SAPAPO/RRP_NETCH with the **Create Pegging Areas** checkbox selected to create any missing pegging areas in PP-DS.

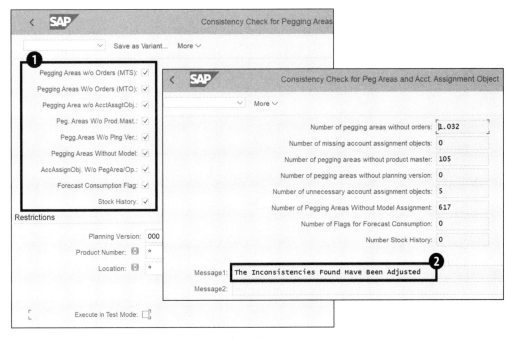

Figure 9.21 Pegging Areas Consistency Check and Correction

9.6.2   Resources

When advanced planning is activated for resource master data in SAP S/4HANA, the resources are integrated into PP-DS. In PP-DS, the resource time stream, which represents the available capacity of the resource and the schedule of the resource based on the shift definitions, is created in SAP liveCache.

The resource time stream is created in SAP liveCache for a limited horizon, which is defined in the CIF settings in Transaction CFC9. From the date of the resource creation in PP-DS, the time stream is extended to the number of days in the past and future based on the values defined in **Days in Past** and **Days in the Future** defined in Transaction CFC9, as shown in Figure 9.22. For example, if the resource is created and activated for advanced planning on January 1, 2010, with a 30 days past and 120 days future in Transaction CFC9, the resource time stream will be created from December 2, 2018, to May 1, 2019. The past and future values from Transaction CFC9 are copied to the PP-DS resource master, as shown in Figure 9.22, when the resources are integrated to PP-DS.

If the resource master data (e.g., downtimes) is changed in PP-DS or the resource master data is changed in SAP S/4HANA, the time stream will be adjusted relative to the change date.

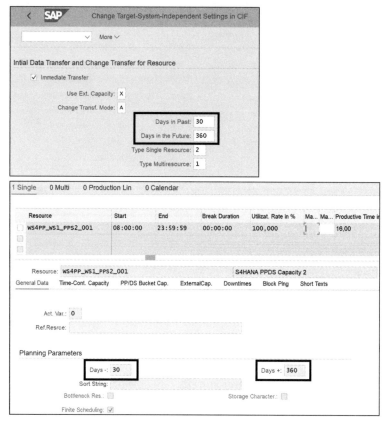

Figure 9.22 Resource Time Stream Length Settings

When orders are created for products that have resources in their PDSs and when the resource time stream isn't created for the order date, the system raises an error message, and no orders can be created. Therefore, the length of the time stream must be set with a long enough duration for planning runs to create orders in PP-DS. As days pass by, the time streams aren't automatically extended related to the current date and stay static for the duration when it was created.

To re-create the resource time stream in SAP liveCache with respect to the current date, execute ABAP program /SAPAPO/CRES_CAPACITY_LENGTHEN; you'll arrive at the screen on the top left of Figure 9.23. This will adjust the time stream so that the time streams older than the **Days-** are deleted, and the time stream is generated up to the **Days+** date in SAP liveCache. You can schedule this report daily in the background. You have the options to select the **Planning Version**, **Resource**, and **Location** in the selection screen of this program ❶. In addition, you can improve the performance of the program/job by setting the number of parallel tasks in the **NUMTASKS** field.

The resource time stream can be displayed from Transaction /SAPAPO/RES02, and any inconsistencies in the resource time stream in SAP liveCache can also be monitored and corrected. You'll arrive at the selection screen shown at the top right of Figure 9.23 ❷, where you enter the resource names in the **Resource** field, enter "000" in the **Planning Version**, select the **Check Existence in LC** radio button, and click the **Execute** button. You'll arrive at the results screen shown at the bottom of Figure 9.23, where the **Status in LC** column shows whether the resource time stream is correctly saved in SAP liveCache. If the status isn't green, you can select such lines and click on the **liveCache** button to save the resource to SAP liveCache again ❸.

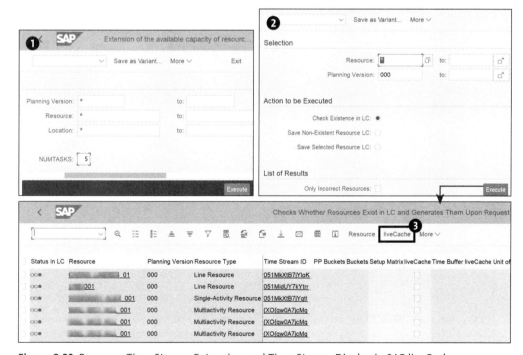

Figure 9.23 Resource Time Stream Extension and Time Stream Display in SAP liveCache

9.7   Summary

In this chapter, we covered the administration of the PP-DS system with respect to the CIF and SAP liveCache in detail. The monitoring and reconciliation of the inconsistencies between SAP S/4HANA and embedded PP-DS, monitoring and processing postprocessing records, and monitoring and correcting the inconsistencies between the SAP HANA database and the SAP liveCache application data are more application driven than technical troubleshooting. Therefore, it's helpful for the power users/ super users in PP-DS to be trained in these tools and be able to execute these tasks. Other technical monitoring of the system, such as monitoring the SAP liveCache status and application log management, belongs to the technical operation of the SAP S/4HANA system.

In the next and final chapter, we'll cover the options to migrate to the embedded PP-DS system.

Chapter 10
Migration to Embedded PP-DS

Now that you've walked through how PP-DS in SAP S/4HANA (embedded PP-DS) works, it's time to take a look at your tools and options to get it up and running, whether you're setting up a new implementation or migrating from SAP Advanced Planning and Optimization (SAP APO).

SAP S/4HANA is the latest enterprise resource planning (ERP) offering from SAP, and it provides a great level of simplification and modernization compared to the other ERP systems. If you're already running an SAP ERP system, it's possible to convert the SAP ERP system into an SAP S/4HANA system. Often, the conversion to SAP S/4HANA from SAP ERP is an opportunity for companies to simplify their business processes, and the complexity they've built over the years into their SAP ERP system.

Production planning and detailed scheduling (PP-DS) was originally a component of SAP APO. With PP-DS in SAP S/4HANA, PP-DS is part of the core system, which means no add-ons or switch framework business functions need to be installed or activated in the SAP S/4HANA system to use it. It's controlled by the Customizing settings we've covered in previous chapters.

The SAP APO system functionalities are partially succeeded by two SAP products, SAP S/4HANA and SAP Integrated Business Planning for Supply Chain (SAP IBP), as shown in Figure 10.1:

- SAP APO demand planning capabilities are partially available in SAP IBP for demand.

- SAP APO supply network planning capabilities are partially available in SAP IBP for response and supply.

- The PP-DS component of SAP APO capabilities are partially included in SAP S/4HANA manufacturing (embedded PP-DS).

- SAP APO global available-to-promise (GATP) capabilities are partially available in advanced ATP (aATP) in SAP S/4HANA.

SAP IBP is a cloud-only offering, and embedded PP-DS is available in the on-premise version of SAP S/4HANA from the 1610 release onward. SAP S/4HANA Cloud (as of the latest version 1911) offers production planning and scheduling features but not the advanced planning (PP-DS) capabilities.

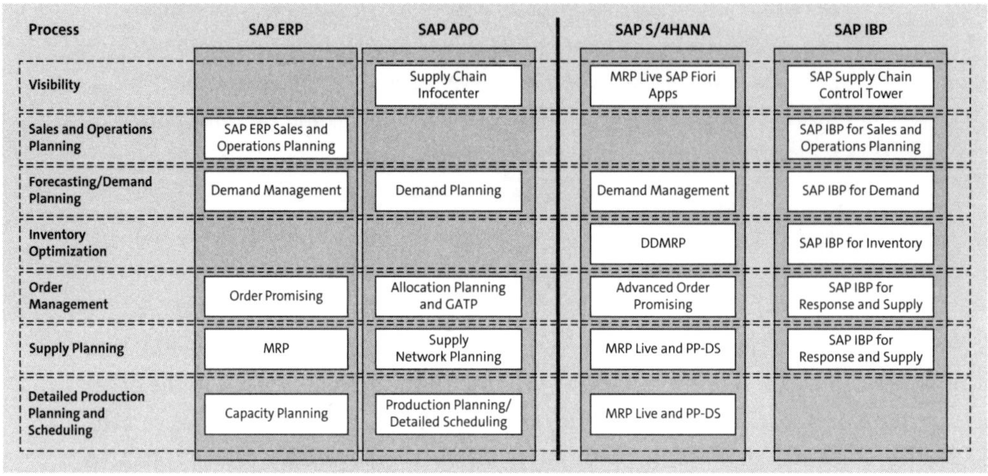

Process	SAP ERP	SAP APO	SAP S/4HANA	SAP IBP
Visibility		Supply Chain Infocenter	MRP Live SAP Fiori Apps	SAP Supply Chain Control Tower
Sales and Operations Planning	SAP ERP Sales and Operations Planning			SAP IBP for Sales and Operations Planning
Forecasting/Demand Planning	Demand Management	Demand Planning	Demand Management	SAP IBP for Demand
Inventory Optimization			DDMRP	SAP IBP for Inventory
Order Management	Order Promising	Allocation Planning and GATP	Advanced Order Promising	SAP IBP for Response and Supply
Supply Planning	MRP	Supply Network Planning	MRP Live and PP-DS	SAP IBP for Response and Supply
Detailed Production Planning and Scheduling	Capacity Planning	Production Planning/ Detailed Scheduling	MRP Live and PP-DS	

Figure 10.1 Transformation of SAP APO Features into SAP S/4HANA and SAP IBP

Due to the simplifications and architecture changes in embedded PP-DS, there are no automated tools delivered to migrate from the PP-DS component of SAP APO to embedded PP-DS. In this chapter, we'll cover the various migration approaches (new implementation, system conversion, or landscape transformation) and what options are available to migrate specific data from PP-DS into the embedded PP-DS system.

10.1   New Implementation

The new implementation approach is also generally referred to as a greenfield implementation. If you're running a non-SAP legacy ERP system or using an SAP ERP system, and you choose not to carry forward the business processes and custom-developed objects into the new SAP S/4HANA system, the new implementation or greenfield approach can be considered, as shown in the top row of Figure 10.2.

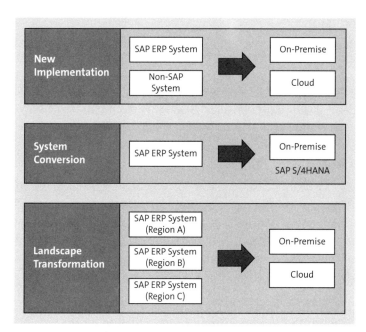

Figure 10.2 SAP S/4HANA Transition Scenarios

You would follow the SAP Activate and/or the SAP Model Company approach to define and realize the business solution in the SAP S/4HANA system. From a technical perspective, a new installation of SAP S/4HANA is performed. You can migrate the data from the legacy systems or from an SAP ERP system into the new SAP S/4HANA system. This is applicable for master data and historical transaction data objects that you want to carry forward to the SAP S/4HANA system. The standard data migration tools, such as the SAP S/4HANA migration cockpit, can be used to migrate the data.

For PP-DS, in the new implementation scenario, as the business processes are redefined, the processes and scenarios you currently follow in the PP-DS component of SAP APO may not be relevant anymore, and you can define and configure the PP-DS processes in the SAP S/4HANA system per the newly defined business processes.

For certain PP-DS master data objects, specifically the product master, the data maintained within the PP-DS component of SAP APO and not generated from the SAP ERP system, such as product heuristics or planning procedure fields, can be extracted from the SAP APO product master tables and combined with the master data migration using the standard data migration tools.

10.2   System Conversion

The system conversion approach is applicable when you want to technically convert the existing SAP ERP system to an SAP S/4HANA system (see the middle row in Figure 10.2). This transition approach is also called a brownfield approach. Many mandatory changes are required in the business process and data due to the simplification items that are made mandatory in the SAP S/4HANA system. For example, you must convert your vendor and customer master data in SAP ERP into business partners before converting to SAP S/4HANA.

The technical conversion is performed based on the Software Update Manager (SUM) tool, and if the SAP ERP system is running on a non-SAP HANA database, the SUM tools with the Database Migration Option (DMO) are used to complete the conversion of the SAP ERP system into an SAP S/4HANA system. The conversion of the SAP ERP system into an SAP S/4HANA system has multiple steps, as shown in Figure 10.3:

1. **System requirements**
   The source SAP ERP system, the operating system, and the database should have the minimum required versions to be supported for the conversion.

2. **Maintenance planner**
   The maintenance planner tool runs checks such as for the compatibility of the source SAP ERP system with respect to the add-ons installed, for switch framework business functions, and so on. If there are incompatible add-ons or business functions identified, the conversion will be stopped.

3. **Simplification item checks**
   The simplification items check is performed to ensure that all the prerequisites mandated by the simplification items are already taken care of in the source system (e.g., customer and vendor to business partner).

4. **Custom code analysis**
   The custom code checks have to be executed in the source SAP ERP system to identify the impact of the custom code with respect to the simplification items, such as functionalities that aren't available in SAP S/4HANA anymore, data structure changes, and so on.

5. **Conversion**
   The actual conversion is executed via the SUM, and, if applicable, the database conversion is performed along with the SAP S/4HANA conversion via the DMO.

6. **Post-conversion**
   After the technical conversion, mandatory application-specific post-conversion

activities need to be performed. In addition, any adjustments to the custom code for adoption of the SAP S/4HANA simplification and database table structure changes need to be implemented.

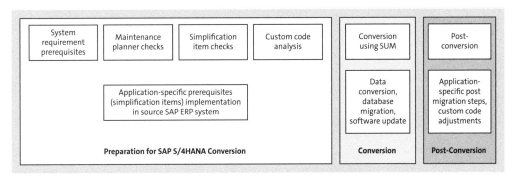

Figure 10.3 Overview of Steps: Conversion of SAP ERP to SAP S/4HANA

In the system conversion scenario, if you already use the PP-DS component of SAP APO and want to bring in embedded PP-DS, it can be a post activity after the conversion. You have to manually bring in the custom code objects from SAP APO to the SAP S/4HANA system, such as custom heuristics, business add-ins (BAdIs) or user exit implementations, and so on. As there are simplification items applicable in embedded PP-DS, you may have to adjust the existing custom code objects in the embedded PP-DS system.

After the custom code is adopted from the PP-DS component of SAP APO to embedded PP-DS, you can manually make the configuration in the SAP S/4HANA system with reference to the PP-DS component of SAP APO system. Then, you can maintain the data specific to PP-DS using tools such as the migration cockpit or mass data maintenance within the SAP S/4HANA system, especially for material master and resource master data. You also can generate other master data objects, such as the production data structures (PDSs) and external procurement relationships within the SAP S/4HANA system (see Chapter 2).

For the transaction data that is already in SAP S/4HANA, after setting up the configuration and master data, you can use the PP-DS delta transfer ABAP program /SAPAPO/PPDS_DELTA_ORD_TRANS to transfer the transaction data into embedded PP-DS.

As shown in Figure 10.4, the conversion process ❶ converts the SAP ERP system into the SAP S/4HANA system. Then, you set up the embedded PP-DS system by following the steps described in Chapter 3. After PP-DS is set up in the SAP S/4HANA system, you manually implement ❷ other configurations and customizations, such as any custom heuristics, enhancements, and so on, in embedded PP-DS. Extract the master data settings that are specific to PP-DS, such as product heuristics, planning procedures, and so on, from the PP-DS component of SAP APO and update the master data in embedded PP-DS and the relevant master data in SAP S/4HANA using tools such as mass maintenance or data services ❸. After the master data is updated in SAP S/4HANA, the master data along with the transaction data can be integrated ❹ into embedded PP-DS, as explained in Chapter 2 and Chapter 4.

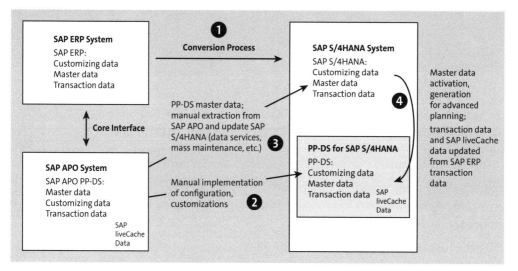

Figure 10.4 Option to Adopt the PP-DS Component of SAP APO to Embedded PP-DS

> **Note**
>
> In any of the transition scenarios, if you already operate the PP-DS component of SAP APO and are transitioning into embedded PP-DS, it's expected that the data (materials/locations) that you're planning in embedded PP-DS is only planned in embedded PP-DS, and the same data isn't to be planned in demand planning or supply network planning in SAP APO. Or, you have parallel activities to implement SAP IBP for demand planning and response and supply, and embedded PP-DS is the production planning and scheduling system for all products/locations.

Side-by-side operation of SAP APO demand planning and supply network planning is supported with SAP S/4HANA, but the materials/locations planned in embedded PP-DS can't be integrated into SAP APO demand planning and supply network planning in the standard supported architecture.

10.3   Landscape Transformation

If your SAP landscape is a complex one with multiple SAP ERP systems and other legacy systems, and you want to simplify the landscape by consolidating the multiple SAP ERP systems into one SAP S/4HANA system, then the SAP Landscape Transformation options can be considered for the migration to SAP S/4HANA (see the bottom row in Figure 10.2).

The landscape transformation process uses the Data Management and Landscape Transformation (DMLT) tools. This conversion approach can be specific to a certain use case. For example, for a new install of an SAP S/4HANA system with the Customizing data maintained and using DMLT tools, the application data (master data and transaction data) can be converted and loaded into the SAP S/4HANA system.

In addition, by using this selective data transfer approach, it's possible to selectively convert the data into the SAP S/4HANA system. For example, this approach can be used if you want to merge or split company codes and create the SAP S/4HANA system.

For embedded PP-DS, the landscape transformation approach also provides tools such as preconfigured transformation content for SAP S/4HANA, object-based transformation, and transformation engines to migrate the data from the PP-DS component of SAP APO into the embedded PP-DS system.

The prerequisites for using the SAP Landscape Transformation methodology to migrate data from the PP-DS component of SAP APO to embedded PP-DS are as follows:

- Installation and upgrade of the SAP HANA integrated SAP liveCache
- Upgrade of the PP-DS optimizer to the required version (if the PP-DS optimizer is used)
- Manual transfer of all custom objects (enhancements such as BAdIs and user exits, extensions, and custom code)

The master data, client-specific Customizing data, transaction data, and SAP live-Cache data can be migrated to the embedded PP-DS system using the SAP Landscape Transformation approach. Transformation rules for adopting the data into the embedded PP-DS data structures, filtering out any unrequired data, or selectively transferring data are also possible.

As shown in Figure 10.5, SAP Landscape Transformation supports the migration of data from SAP source systems such as SAP ERP and SAP APO, as well as non-SAP legacy systems. The data sourced from the source systems is transformed to meet the requirements of the target environment using various tools with SAP Landscape Transformation, such as the preconfigured transformation content for SAP S/4HANA. The data is also validated and then sent to the target environment, such as the SAP S/4HANA system.

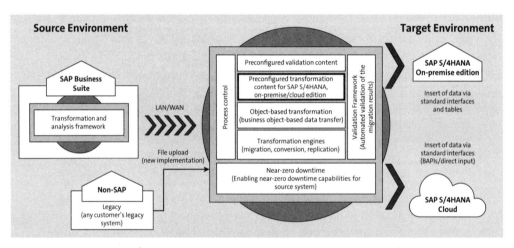

Figure 10.5 SAP S/4HANA Data Migration Using SAP Landscape Transformation

Such a migration may be only required in the following scenarios:

- You have complex scenarios configured in the PP-DS component of SAP APO, such as integrated product and process engineering (iPPE), data maintained only in SAP APO for automotive processes, or complex characteristics-based setup matrices maintained in SAP APO.

- Manually moving this complex data such as the iPPE and characteristics matrix, and so on to embedded PP-DS isn't an option.

- You want to reduce the downtime of the migration from the PP-DS component of SAP APO to embedded PP-DS and have business continuity in terms of bringing in the PP-DS component of SAP APO transaction data such as the scheduled orders and orders with their SAP APO–specific status (output firmed, date firmed, etc.).

In other scenarios, the embedded PP-DS data is generated from SAP S/4HANA data, and the transaction data can be sent from SAP S/4HANA to embedded PP-DS using the delta transfer report discussed in the previous section.

10.4   Summary

In this chapter, we've provided an overview of the approaches available to migrate from an SAP ERP system to the SAP S/4HANA system. You've seen how PP-DS data from SAP APO can be transitioned into embedded PP-DS in the different migration approaches.

Irrespective of the transition approach followed for the SAP S/4HANA conversion, the PP-DS component of SAP APO to embedded PP-DS data migration can be a manual/semi-manual approach as explained in the SAP S/4HANA greenfield and brownfield scenarios, or the SAP Landscape Transformation tools can be used for complex PP-DS component of SAP APO implementations to reduce the manual effort in bringing the application and SAP liveCache data into the SAP S/4HANA system.

10

Appendix A
SAP Notes

The following table lists the release information notes and high priority correction notes for SAP S/4HANA 1909 that are relevant for production planning and detailed scheduling in SAP S/4HANA.

SAP Note	Description
2841107	Release Information Note: Production Planning and Detailed Scheduling for SAP S/4HANA 1909
2825650	Restrictions and Implementation Recommendations for Production Planning and Detailed Scheduling for SAP S/4HANA 1909
2666947	Restrictions and Implementation Recommendations for Production Planning and Detailed Scheduling for SAP S/4HANA 1809
2752467	Documentation Correction for Production Planning and Detailed Scheduling (PP-DS) Versions 1610 to 1809 (Including All FPSs)
2841072	Simplification List: Production Planning and Detailed Scheduling for SAP S/4HANA 1909
2074788	Patch Strategy for SAP HANA – Integrated liveCaches
2074843	Version Matrix for SAP HANA – Integrated liveCaches
2037585	Upgrade of SAP HANA – integrated liveCaches
1686826	Installation Help for Installing SAP SCM Optimizers
2467135	Compatibility of SCM Optimizer 13.0 with SAP Product Versions
712066	Restrictions of the Production Planning and Detailed Scheduling (PP-DS) Optimizer
1577112	SCM Optimizer: Sizing Information
2456834	Transition Guide for SAP APO

SAP Note	Description
2861401	INT-PDS: Production Version Locked for Automatic Sourcing Locks Corresponding PDS
2861080	Storage Location for PDS Output Not Derived from Material Master
2860113	Subcontracting – PDS Contains Components That Are Not Relevant in PP-DS
2857498	Rapidly Growing Database Tables: /SAPAPO/CURTOWUL, /SAPAPO/CURTORUL, and /SAPAPO/CULLINDX
2856363	Syntax Error in SAPLMMRPFIX
2847572	PDS-EXP: Subcontracting Phantom Assemblies Not Found
2838982	Dynamic Where Clause When Creating Contract or Inforecord Integration Model
2838525	Incorrect Storage Location Determination in PDS
2835095	/SAPAPO/RRP3: Planning of Standard Lots with Shelf Life Heuristic Generates Unwanted Surplus
2830063	PDS-EXP: PDS Explosion Slow around Program /SAPAPO/SAPLDM_PEGAREA
2823033	/SAPAPO/OM17 Does Not Create Missing Resources
2819866	Key Completion of PR - S4 Line Number Is Not Updated on PPDS Side
2819291	Short Dump GETWA_NOT_ASSIGNED in SCM Inbound
2818814	Alternative Sequence and Validity
2818511	Duplicate /SAPAPO/POSMAPN Records after Conversion of an Unchecked Delivery
2816294	Planned Orders Created MRP Area with Stock Transfer Special Procurement Type
2814895	PDS-DEL: Performance
2810812	INT-PPS: Confirmation for Combined Order Is Not Flowing to Embedded PP-DS
2806334	Faulty Delivery Date Because Non-Zero GR Activity
2799574	Filtering Alerts Based on ATP Categories
2791762	Cross-System Stock Transfer Using PO and SO Requirements Duplicity (2)

SAP Note	Description
2788693	Third-Party Provision – Delivery Address Vendor Is Not Converted from/to Business Partner
2787659	/SAPAPO/PPT1: When Creating a New Order in PPT the Order Jumps to the Previous Bucket
2785891	/SAPAPO/RPT: Setup Duration Displayed Incorrectly When Rescheduling the Order
2785284	Cross-System Stock Transfer Using PO and SO: CIF Queue in RETRY
2784126	Performance Issue with FM /SAPAPO/TR_TRQTA_GET While Accessing View /SAPAPO/V_TRQTA
2780405	ROC Reduction Causing BOP Failure
2774372	/SAPAPO/RRP3: End Date of the Horizon Is Incorrectly Calculated in SAP_PP_004 When Number of Periods is "999"
2749207	Consider Goods Receipt Processing Time Flag with Wrong Value
2736101	Wrong/Missing CDP Values in PP-DS Transactions
2735412	S4 – Wrong Scheduling of Orders with More Lines
2642218	Input Components Missing after Planned Order Updated in SAP ERP
2862343	/SAPAPO/RLCDELETE Delete Transaction Data ABAP Dump
2861080	Storage Location for PDS Output Not Derived from Material Master
2860022	Report: PDS without /SAPAPO/CURTOWUL
2860630	MRP Live Log Shows Error "Object is locked at present"
2543746	Handling Resource Isn't Determined in CIF
2852604	Product-Dependent Rates Can Only Be Maintained Planning Version Independently
2771824	Location Inconsistency in Table /SAPAPO/LOCMAP
2745533	Runtime Error MOVE_CAST_ERROR in FUNC /SAPAPO/EOGL_PDS_EXPL_LC
2736101	Wrong/Missing CDP Values in PP/DS Transactions
1989677	Invalid ATINN/CHAR_NAME Combinations in Database Table /SAPAPO/TMC01CC

SAP Note	Description
2832880	INT-PPS: Order Start Date Changes Repeatedly
2825804	PDS-EXP: Characteristic-Based Setup Matrix Is Not Used
2671330	Heuristic for the Determination of Low-Level Code (Use Low-Level Codes from R/3) Terminates with Error CX_SY_OPEN_SQL_DB
2636404	Use Material Variant Components as CDP-Relevant Input in PP-DS
2475301	Limits When Working with Alternative Modes
2848865	PP-DS on S4; /SAPAPO/CPP: Block Formation Not Considered, in Case of Error All Objects Are Not Updated at S4
2839006	Alternate SOS Is Not Picked Up While Creating Order through Product Heuristic Run
2827266	Error 665 in Delta Report for Plant Maintenance Orders
2819915	PP-DS S4: Long Runtime for Order Comparison Due to No Parallelization for Order Selection at S4
2819866	Key Completion of PR - S4 Line Number Is Not Updated on PP-DS Side
2819121	Subcontracting Reservation Not Transported to S4

Appendix B
The Author

Mahesh Babu MG works as a services architecture expert in SAP Digital Business Services, Center of Expertise (SAP DBS CoE). He currently leads the Manufacturing and Product Lifecycle Management team in the SAP DBS CoE. He has more than 14 years of professional experience in SAP ERP, SAP APO, and SAP S/4HANA products across various industries with a focus on production planning, production planning and detailed scheduling, and the core interface. He started his career with Tata Consultancy Services as a production planning consultant and worked in implementing, rolling out, and supporting SAP logistics and production planning and control. As a principal consultant at SAP Labs India, he handled product support for multiple SAP APO components before moving to his current role at SAP America, Inc. He holds a degree in chemical engineering from Coimbatore Institute of Technology, Anna University (India).

Index

- Implement production planning for discrete, process, and repetitive manufacturing with SAP S/4HANA

- Configure and run MRP, batch management, capacity planning, and more

- Analyze your data with standard analytics and SAP Fiori apps

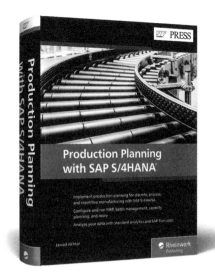

Jawad Akhtar

Production Planning with SAP S/4HANA

Allocate your materials, personnel, and machinery with SAP S/4HANA! This comprehensive guide will show you how to configure production planning in SAP S/4HANA for discrete, process, and repetitive manufacturing. Next, you'll learn to run those processes using step-by-step instructions. Master production workflows, like batch management, S&OP, demand management, PP-DS, and MRP. With industry examples throughout, this guide is your one-stop shop for PP with SAP S/4HANA!

1,010 pages, pub. 03/2019
E-Book: $79.99 | **Print:** $89.95 | **Bundle:** $99.99

www.sap-press.com/4821

- Implement QM with SAP S/4HANA for planning, inspections, and notifications

- Integrate QM processes across your supply chain

- Master batch management, stability studies, quality issue management, FMEA, and more

Jawad Akhtar

Quality Management with SAP S/4HANA

Keep your product standards high with this comprehensive guide to quality management in SAP S/4HANA! You'll learn how to make QM an integral part of your existing supply chain by connecting to materials management, production planning, warehouse management, and other logistics processes. Step-by-step instructions will show you how to both configure and use key QM processes like batch management and audits. Implement quality plans, inspections, and notifications in SAP S/4HANA to be confident in your product's quality!

950 pages, pub. 11/2019

E-Book: $79.99 | **Print:** $89.95 | **Bundle:** $99.99

www.sap-press.com/4924

- Configure SAP S/4HANA for your materials management requirements

- Maintain critical material and business partner records

- Walk through MRP, inventory management, purchasing, and quotation management

Jawad Akhtar, Martin Murray

Materials Management with SAP S/4HANA

Business Processes and Configuration

Materials management has transitioned to SAP S/4HANA—let us help you do the same! Whether your focus is on materials planning, procurement, or inventory, this guide will teach you to configure and manage your critical processes in SAP S/4HANA. Start by creating your organizational structure and defining business partners and material master data. Then get step-by-step instructions for defining the processes you need, from creating purchase orders and receiving goods to running MRP and using batch management. The new MM is here!

946 pages, pub. 10/2018
E-Book: $79.99 | **Print:** $89.95 | **Bundle:** $99.99

www.sap-press.com/4711

- Configure and run inventory management in SAP S/4HANA

- Plan, execute, and optimize goods receipt, stock transfers, and more using SAP Fiori applications

- Analyze your inventory, from KPI monitoring to custom queries

Bernd Roedel, Johannes Esser

Inventory Management with SAP S/4HANA

Jump-start your inventory operations in SAP S/4HANA! Review basic inventory practices and consult step-by-step instructions to configure SAP S/4HANA for your organization's requirements. Then put the system to work! Run the SAP Fiori applications that guide your core inventory workflows: inventory planning, goods receipt, core inventory, production planning, and inventory analysis. This hands-on guide to inventory has the details you need!

494 pages, pub. 09/2019
E-Book: $79.99 | **Print:** $89.95 | **Bundle:** $99.99

www.sap-press.com/4892

Interested in reading more?

Please visit our website for all new book
and e-book releases from SAP PRESS.

www.sap-press.com